Mr. Chips 101 Plans

Plus hundreds
of different ways
to become a
Do-It-Yourself Expert

Published by: DECO PLANS INC.
and: BLAIR ADVERTISING INC.

2

PUBLISHERS
DECO-PLANS INC.
BLAIR ADVERTISING INC.

EDITOR
Jean-Paul St-Michel

ASSISTANT TO THE EDITOR
Lise Keir

CONTRIBUTING EDITOR
Harold R. Fues

PRODUCTION
Pierre St-Michel

ART PRODUCTION
Maurice A. Corbeil
Michel Lafortune

PUBLIC RELATIONS
Monique Germain

TECHNICAL CONSULTANT
William H. Keir, P. Eng.

PROJECT PHOTOGRAPHS BY:
Raymond Poitras
Wayne Jackson
Ronald Handfield

VALUABLE ASSISTANCE WAS PROVIDED BY:
Black & Decker Mfg. Co. Limited
Canada Sand Papers Limited
Council of Forest Industries of British Columbia
Cyanamid of Canada Limited
Lepages Limited
Sico Paint Inc.
St. Regis Paper Co.

CREDITS

Pages 53, 64, 73 and 74, taken from Popular Mechanics magazine, ©Copyright 1974, The Hearst Corporation.

Pages 7, 71 and 72, taken from Popular Mechanics magazine, ©Copyright 1973, The Hearst Corporation.

Pages 40, 51, 58, 67 and 68, taken from POPULAR MECHANICS MASTER SHOP GUIDE. ©Copyright 1969, The Hearst Corporation.

Pages 77, 78, 79 and 80, taken from GOOD HOUSEKEEPING GUIDE TO FIXING THINGS AROUND THE HOUSE, ©Copyright 1974, The Hearst Corporation.

Pages 35, 36, 37, 38, 39, 41, 42, 43, 44, 45, 46, 47, 48, 49, 50, 55, 56, 57, 69, 70, 75, 76, 83, 84, 85, 87, 88, 89, 95, 96, 97, 98, 99, 100, 101, 102, 103, 104, 105, 106, 107 and 108 taken from POPULAR MECHANICS DO-IT-YOURSELF ENCYCLOPEDIA, ©Copyright 1968, The Hearst Corporation.

ISBN 0-910990-70-0

Editorial offices located at 2366 East, Marie-Victorin, Longueuil, P.Q., Canada J4G 1B5.

Printed in Canada — single copy price $9.95

Contents

Foreword

A fascinating world of creativity awaits the do-it-yourselfer who has the will and determination to see things through.

Equipped with just a few basic tools, some plans and, of course, the necessary materials, anyone can participate in this "on-the-job" training program which allows amateurs without formal training to compete successfully with professionals who have years of experience.

Much of this has come about because the ever increasing interest in do-it-yourself activities has led manufacturers to devise tools and materials which anyone can use, with "trade secrets" and techniques becoming as available to the amateur as they are to the tradesman.

In our book, "Mr. Chips 101 Plans", we've tried to put it all together for you. Interesting projects which are fun to build and a pleasure to own. Plus information on the type of tools and materials you'll need to build these projects.

And, should you ever get stuck with a project — just watch Mr. Chips on your TV screen. It could be that he'll be demonstrating a way to solve your problem on his very next TV program.

But now — to work!

Sincerely,
The publishers

PART I

Your home workshop

Whether you're into do-it-yourself projects as a hobby or as a money saving activity, you'll need a place where you can put it all together.

Because of the noise, fumes and dust involved, most housewives would prefer it if their husbands moved the workshop out of the house, into the garage or the garden shed. But, it's cold out there! Worse, if you're an apartment dweller, without the luxury of this dilema, the question of where to put your workshop takes on even greater significance.

Yet, as much as we all admire a well laid out and roomy workshop as we see it pictured here — your workshop needn't be as elaborate to be functional. The following pages will show you how.

When you're into more than just the occasional household repair or basic do-it-yourself project, you'll not only need more space, you'll also need a lot more tools. And it is the storing and displaying of these tools which in no small measure determines the space you'll need.

For it is impossible to work quickly and efficiently if at every point and turn you are hampered by a frustrating search for the appropriate tool.

Expert do-it-yourselfers have long ago learned that they can do better work if they break up their work area into different work stations. That way, they can bring the work to the tools as the work progresses in stages.

First, there is the power tool area, where all the sawing, cutting, shaping, drilling and sanding of the individual pieces takes place.

Then, there is the assembly area, where hand tools are used for nailing, screwing, fastening or gluing individual pieces together.

And last but not least, there is the finishing area, where the assembled project takes on color and individuality, and becomes an object of pride and accomplishment.

So, a lot of thought and effort needs to go into the lay-out of a truly efficient home workshop. The correct flow of work is just as important as is proper lighting and ventilation.

Therefore, before you begin designing your workshop, imagine a fairly complicated project being built there.

Sketch out how you would handle the job and "what" you would do "where". Only after you've had a few dry runs at an imagined project like this, should you freeze the final design of your home workshop.

To aid you in your plans and to see how other do-it-yourselfers have designed their home workshop, the pictures accompanying this text will give you an indication of the kind of fingertip tool-control you should strive for.

When thinking of building a home workshop and space is at a premium, the one thing you cannot do without is a workbench. For household repairs and do-it-yourself projects can be enjoyed only when there is a convenient and efficient place to do them.

Your workbench should then have ample space, enough strength to stand steady hammering, planing, sawing or chiseling — and it should be equipped with a vise, some clamps and a drawer or shelves for storing your tools.

The simplest workbench is the sawhorse workbench. Two sawhorses, some clamps and presto—you're in business! The beauty of this set-up is that it is easy to assemble, easy to store and you can take this workbench to where the work is to be done.

Variations of this basic sawhorse bench have shallow tool trays fitted between the leg supports of the sawhorse, or have a piece of perforated hardboard fastened to one side of the sawhorse which then becomes a built-in tool panel for countless small tools attached with clips.

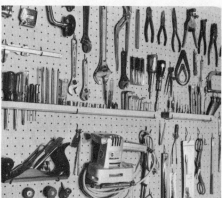

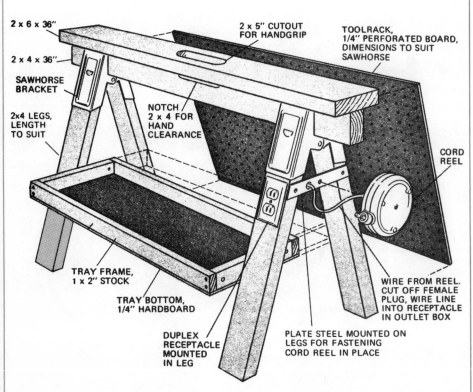

2 x 6 x 36"

2 x 4 x 36"

SAWHORSE BRACKET

2 x 4 LEGS, LENGTH TO SUIT

NOTCH 2 x 4 FOR HAND CLEARANCE

2 x 5" CUTOUT FOR HANDGRIP

TOOLRACK, 1/4" PERFORATED BOARD, DIMENSIONS TO SUIT SAWHORSE

CORD REEL

TRAY FRAME, 1 x 2" STOCK

TRAY BOTTOM, 1/4" HARDBOARD

DUPLEX RECEPTACLE MOUNTED IN LEG

PLATE STEEL MOUNTED ON LEGS FOR FASTENING CORD REEL IN PLACE

WIRE FROM REEL. CUT OFF FEMALE PLUG, WIRE LINE INTO RECEPTACLE IN OUTLET BOX

Tool Cabinet — Workbench

Every workshop needs a small workbench. This easy to build version can't be beat for rigidity because it is braced in all directions with plywood. A cabinetmaker's vise can be mounted on either front corner of the solid double-thickness plywood work surface. The tool cabinet, with hooks and shelves for convenient tool storage, mounts on the wall behind the bench. Over-all size approximately 60" x 24" x 68" high.

Where space is really tight, just one sawhorse, with a 2" x 6" x 36" work surface nailed to the top, will do.

Apartment dwellers, by necessity, need to look for a different set-up and many have found the backs of closet doors the only practical solution to their workshop requirements.

Folding, perforated hardboard panels, framed for depth and joined by piano hinges, make a handy tool cabinet to hang on closet doors. A collapsible board of one inch plywood, complete with folding legs, attached below the tool cabinet, rounds out this hide-a-way workshop.

The whole set-up should not take up more than 5" in depth when folded and attached to the back of a closet door. Just be sure that the closet door has sufficient strength to hold the attached workshop.

If space is still at a premium, but there is at least a 1½' x 5' basement corner available to you, a somewhat more permanent and more comfortable set-up is the one pictured here.

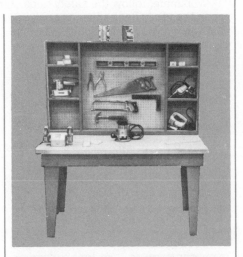

As you can see, it combines both a workbench and a tool cabinet into a unified work station where everything is within easy reach. A more elaborate set-up would feature the same workbench completely enclosed, with shelves and doors, a multiple electric outlet strip along the front and fluorescent lighting mounted over the work station.

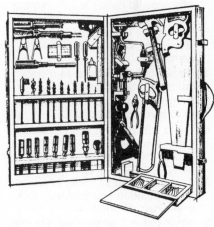

Folding Tool Box

No more hunting for little-used tools. This lightweight two or three compartment folding tool box keeps all your tools at hand; where you need them, when you need them. Designed for use by either carpenter or the home handyman, the tool box is organized so that every item is clearly visible and easy to reach.

For those do-it-yourselfers who'd rather spend their time building projects than worbenches, there are commercially available alternatives which feature every convenience you could possibly think of.

The All Purpose Workmate, shown here, has a set of folding legs to take it from workbench height to saw horse height in seconds. The workbench top itself is split and becomes a giant vise, by means of individually adjustable handles, to hold pieces of material up to $4\frac{1}{8}$" in width.

Vise holes, drilled into the bench top, hold swivel pegs, allowing you to extend the vise capacity to a 10" parallel or 24" diagonal grip.

The Workmate is completely portable, and in collapsed position, fits into the trunk of a car or can be hung from a garage wall.

Your new Workmate is a quality piece of equipment that has been carefully designed and manufactured to provide years of dependable service.

Safety Rules:

1. Do not load with more than 350 lbs.
2. Do not apply an unbalanced load which could cause the Workmate to tip.
3. Do not use lower platform as a step when Workmate is in workbench position.
4. Do not use Workmate as a stepladder or standing platform.
5. Do not store Workmate outdoors or in damp condition.
6. Avoid applying excessive force when clamping in only the lower half of the vise jaws or when using the swivel pegs.
7. Be sure that table locks in sawhorse position and that legs lock in workbench position.
8. When using a power tool with the Workmate, follow the safety rules in the tool's instruction manual.
9. Wear safety glasses when using power tools.
10. See below for correct method of securing power tools in Workmate. Never mount power tools directly in vise; pressure may damage tools.
11. An even pressure of jaws on work piece is essential. Tighten both jaw handles uniformly.

Maintenance Tips:

1. Pivot screws are of low friction design. No lubrication is necessary.
2. If binding of vise jaw occurs, cleaning or lubrication of slider and vise screw may be required.
3. Pivot screws should be checked for tightness.

How to Store your Workmate:

1. Store swivel pegs upside down in table top until next application.
2. Fold in all four extension legs and clamp in locked mode.
3. Place one foot on platform.
4. Using thumbs simultaneously pull both retainer latches toward you.
5. Pull unit straight up until latch releases.
6. Close unit and clamp in locked mode.
7. You can now store your workmate conveniently in minimum space.

PART II

Hand tools

Although power tools have taken much of the drudgery out of repetitive work, hand tools are still needed to start and finish most do-it-yourself projects.

To prove the point, just walk into any hardware store or home center, and immediately you'll be impressed by massive displays of hundreds upon hundreds of different types of hand tools — all beckoning to be bought.

Yet, in order to work on the projects listed in this book, only a few basic hand tools are required. Some of them you probably already own, picked up here and there over the years when you needed to do quick repairs around the house. Others you'll still have to buy.

When buying hand tools, however, resist the temptation to buy low-priced tools. It really is no fun working with tools that could break at the wrong moment, can't keep a keen edge or require more pressure or effort than necessary. Not only is it economical in the long term to invest in quality tools but poor tools usually result in poor workmanship and could discourage you from seeing things through. Even a man with experience cannot do a good job without having good quality tools.

The basic tools you have, or will need, should include a claw hammer, a crosscut saw, a few good screwdrivers, some pliers and wrenches, a hand drill, one or two chisels and gouges, a plane, some clamps, a vise and an oilstone. A ruler and a carpenter's square will round out your basic tool kit.

In time, as you become more expert in your hobby of home carpentry, you'll no doubt require more sophisticated tools.

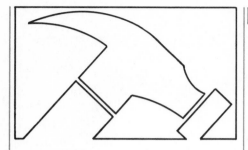

Hammers

The hammer is one of the oldest tools known to man and one of the most often used. There are generally three types namely, common hammers, soft hammers and sledges. Each has its special uses. The curved claw hammer is the most common type and is useful for all types of carpentry and repair work around the house. It is the kind of hammer you will need for our projects.

Claw hammers range in weight from 7 to 28 ounces, and measure from 11 to 14 inches in length. A 10 to 16 ounce hammer, preferably bell faced (slightly convex), is probably your best choice enabling you to do most carpentry work efficiently. Make sure the head is made of drop-forged steel as cast iron heads can be dangerous — they may chip or break. Check hammer handle often for tight fit into hammer head socket. A loose fit is extremely dangerous as the head may fly off and cause serious injury.

Other types of hammers you may consider buying are tack hammers and mallets. Tack hammers are used for very light work only, such as upholstering, have cast iron heads, are from 9 to 12 inches long and have head weights from 4 to 7 ounces. Mallet heads are made of either wood, rubber or plastic, have various sizes of hammering faces and are used mainly to drive chisels or shape metal without marring.

When nailing let the weight of the hammer head do most of the work, your part of the operation is to guide it to the nail head. To facilitate this it is important to hold the hammer at the end of the handle, thus taking advantage of leverage of the handle. With a little practice driving or removing nails can become very easy and accurate.

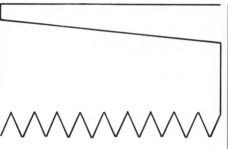

Saws

There is a variety of saw types to choose from, each type serving very specific purposes. For most of the projects listed in this book, the crosscut saw is your best choice.

Crosscut saws are designed to cut across the gain of the wood. You can easily tell a crosscut saw by examining its teeth which are shaped like tiny knife points. These saws are designed to be used at a 45 degree angle to the work. The number of teeth per inch is usually expressed as points per inch commonly ranging from 7 to 12 points; 7 or 8 point blades are quite satisfactory for general work. The number of points per inch is usually stamped on the blade. Blade lengths vary from 20 to 28 inches, a 26 inch blade being quite adequate to handle most home projects.

Before cutting, be sure to measure and mark accurately. The mark line should be highly visible and the cut should always be on the "outside" or waste portion of the cut. It is best to start your cut by gently drawing the saw upward a few times, establishing the "guiding cut" before proceeding with the cutting proper; pressure should be only applied on the downstroke.

Other saws to consider are the back-saw, the keyhole saw, and the coping saw. The backsaw is a small crosscut saw with a reinforced back for precise sawing when doing cabinet work or when using mitre boxes. Their length varies from 10 to 20 inches, with 10 to 14 teeth to the inch. Keyhole saws have narrow, tapered blades to fit into narrow spaces. The coping saw uses different blades varying in thickness from a thread-like wire to 1/8 inch width, and is used for interior cut-outs.

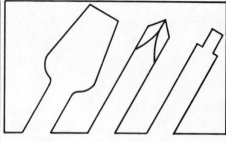

Screwdrivers

Almost everyone has a screwdriver, but more often than not it is usually of the wrong kind or wrong size to be used in ambitious do-it-yourself projects. For screwdrivers must be matched to screw size and type in order to do an effective job. And that means a careful selection of quality tools best suited to your needs.

Slotted screws are most common, but some screws are cross-slotted, requiring a screwdriver with a Phillips head. Then, of course, screws vary in size and length, requiring screw-drivers of differing blade lengths and differing tip sizes. There are, therefore, such an infinite variety of screwdrivers on the market — ranging from the 3 inch "stubbie" all the way to an 18 inch "mechanic's special" — that the selection of a practical, basic set of screwdrivers becomes quite difficult. Your basic set should, however, include at least the following: one No. 1 with a 1/8 inch blade, one No. 2 with a 1/4 inch blade, one No. 3 with a 5/16 inch blade, one No. 4 with a 3/8 inch blade, at least two sizes of Phillips screwdrivers, and some "stubbies" for tight quarter turning.

Other types of screwdrivers you may wish to consider are the Z-shaped offset screwdriver, the spiral rachet screwdriver and screwdriver bits. The Z-shaped offset screwdriver, with rachet or non-rachet handle, comes in extremely handy when driving screws into difficult to reach places. The spiral ratchet screwdriver, which turns under pressure, is a real effort saver. Screwdriver bits are used with an ordinary brace for driving or removing very large screws, the brace gives more leverage and driving power than a standard screwdriver.

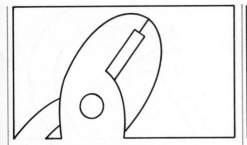

Pliers

Although you think more of metal and electrical work when thinking of pliers, your basic carpentry tool kit should not be without them. They'll come in mighty handy for holding parts in position, pulling bent nails, and for 101 other uses.

The most practical, general purpose plier is the so-called slip joint plier. It's adjustable joint makes it possible to open the jaws to different widths — usually three. The inside of the jaws are "milled" to provide better gripping. Your best investment is a slip joint plier made of forged alloy or carbon steel, with cutting edges, and between 6 to 8 inches long.

Not to be forgotten is a pair of carpenter pincers. They'll come in handy when removing old nails, or prying out loose old boards.

Wrenches

Wrenches are used for tightening and loosening nuts, for bolt assembly when putting together patio furniture, and for gripping and holding pipes and rods. Most of them are designed to be used in the assembly of metal parts and plumbing work. They are also useful as general purpose tools.

The most versatile type of wrenches to own are the monkey wrench, the straight adjustable wrench or the single end adjustable wrench. Their usefulness is derived from the fact that the jaw opening can be adjusted to grip a great variety of different nut and bolt sizes.

Open ended wrenches are non-adjustable and in order to work with a variety of bolt and nut sizes you need a set which fits the most common size types.

Your best bet is to own a set of open ended wrenches for ease of handling, and an adjustable wrench for the less common sizes of bolts and nuts you'll come across from time to time.

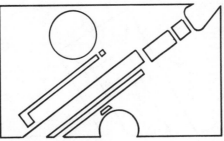

Hand drills

Hand drills are crank-operated hand tools. Each turn of the crank drives a meshed system of wheel gear and pinion, which in turn drives the drill chuck at least three revolutions for each turn of the crank.

This speeds up the work and allows you to drill comfortably in wood, metal and plastic.

Before starting to drill in wood, use an awl to help start the hole. This will keep your drill from wandering and breaking. Since it is important to drill straight, take a few sightings with a try square before going too far.

To avoid splitting the wood when drilling through, stop when just the tip of the bit appears on the opposite side. Back out slowly, then drill into the small exit hole from the other side.

Bit braces

The bit brace can drill larger holes than the hand drill. Some bit braces feature a ratchet which transforms back and forth handle movements into clockwise or counterclockwise turning motions. This enables you to drill holes or drive screws even in cramped spaces.

There are many bits available for both the hand drill and the bit brace. The most common bits for woodwork are called augur bits and can be used for boring holes up to an inch in diameter. For even larger size holes the expansive bit can be used to cut holes up to 3 inches diameter. Another helpful type of bit is the countersink bit which enlarges and tapers the end of a hole already drilled. This comes in handy when screw heads need to be flush with the surface of the material they've been worked into.

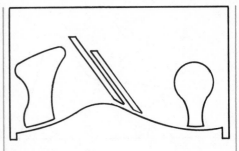

Planes

After the measuring and sawing is done, working with wood still requires a plane of some sort to shape the work to final size and to smooth off rough edges.

The plane accomplishes this by holding a "chisel" or metal blade in a metal base which can be held with both hands, allowing you to work rapidly, shaving off thin layers of wood with each stroke.

As with all tools, there are different types of planes available, all varying in shape, size and weight — depending on the use intended. The most widely used planes are the jack plane, the fore plane, the jointer plane, the smoothing plane and the block plane. The first three planes are used for rough work and initial smoothing, which is followed up by the use of a smoothing or block plane for finish work.

Before beginning to plane, be sure the work is securely clamped. Make certain the work is positioned in such a way that you can plane with the grain. Whenever possible you should plane diagonally from corner to corner.

A try square will come in very handy when checking the planed surface. Pencil mark all high spots yet to be planed away.

When planing ends of boards, doors, etc., be sure your plane blade is adjusted for a thin or medium cut. The work definitely needs to be secured and you must work from the corner towards the center as the danger of breaking off corners is too great when planing from the center to the corner.

The type of work shown in this book can be most efficiently tackled by a junior jack plane, about 11½ inches long, which is adequate for both rough cutting and smoothing work.

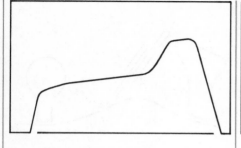

Special planes

The spokeshave is probably the most often used special purpose plane as it will smooth or chamfer either a convex or concave edge, the type of edges most applicable to furniture work. Looking like a large safety razor with handles on either end, the spokeshave is either pushed or pulled along the work, always making sure it cuts with the grain.

The hand router is very useful when cleaning out and smoothing squared grooves, such as have been either chiseled out first, or removed with a number of rough saw cuts. This type of work is often encountered when fitting shelves or sliding cabinet doors into recessed grooves.

The rabbet plane, on the other hand, cuts a recessed step along the edge, rather than into the surface of a board, making this tool indispensable for cabinet and drawer work. Looking very much like a plane, it is somewhat shorter, and most often stubnosed for working close into corners.

Since planes are used for shaping work down to size, the drawknife is often considered a special purpose plane. Its cutting edge is roughly 10 to 12 inches wide. Supported by two handles, and working somewhat like a large spokeshave, the drawknife is drawn toward the user, roughcutting large pieces prior to planing.

Surform tools and cabinet scrapers round out your collection of special purpose planes. Cabinet scrapers are mainly used to remove small bumps left by a plane, or for removing paint. Surform tools look very much like files and are used to trim down rough edges, and to shape and form wood, plastic or metal. Some are flat, some are cylindrical in appearance, but all have replaceable blades which feature many tiny cutting teeth that work like individual planes.

Chisels

Wood chisels should not be used for smoothing or forming work easier done by a plane. Their main purpose is the removal of chips or small sections of wood too difficult to remove by other means.

There are three different types of wood chisels: the butt chisel, the pocket chisel and the mill chisel. These chisels vary in length from 7 to 16 inches and in blade width from 1/8" to 2".

Wood chisels feature tapered steel blades; one side flat and the other bevelled to form a sharp cutting edge, with plastic or wooden handles fitted over the tang of the blade.

Hand pressure is sufficient when working in soft wood. It is also more accurate. However, for cuts in hard wood the driving force of a mallet or hammer may be needed to force the chisel into the wood. When working in hardwood, hold the chisel in one hand, bevel edge down, and strike the end of the handle lightly with a mallet or hammer held in your other hand.

When chiseling soft or hard wood, always work with the grain from the edge toward the thicker end as the cutting end cannot be controlled when chiseling against the grain. Always chisel toward the waste wood, and begin in such a way that, if splitting occurs, the split is in the waste wood and not in the work you are trying to finish.

Gouges

Gouges are also chisels, the most important difference being that their blades are hollow and are mainly used for cutting grooves or for paring edges.

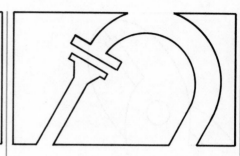

Clamps

Clamps and vises are needed for final assembly. The most popular clamp type used when gluing is the C-clamp, available in sizes from 1 to 8 inches, with the maximum jaw opening determining clamp size. It's handy, portable and easy to use, as the jaw opening is quickly varied by means of an adjustable bolt which goes through one end of the clamp's jaw.

Adjustable hand screws are a bit more versatile in that they operate with two steel clamping screws through crosswise pivots in their jaws, so that the jaws can be set to any required angle. Jaw openings vary from 3 to 10 inches.

Bar and pipe-bar clamps are used when gluing large pieces of work. The pipe-bar clamp consists of nothing more than a fixed jaw attached to a large piece of pipe with another, adjustable jaw sliding along the pipe, toward the work. More elaborate versions feature a sliding jaw driven along a threaded section of the pipe by means of a crank handle.

Spring clamps come in handy when holding together small pieces, when working with fast setting glue, or when high clamping pressure is not needed. Jaw openings vary from 7/8" to 8 inches and many spring clamps feature plastic covered jaws to protect the finished surface of the work from marring.

Vises

Vises hold the work as well and are designated as either bench vises or woodworking vises. The bench vise is bolted to the top of the workbench. The woodworking vise is mounted on the edge of the bench, jaws flush with the top of the bench. Both vises can exert powerful pressure on the work.

12

PART III

Power Tools

Power tools are one of the most important reasons why do-it-yourself projects have become so popular. By letting you work fast and accurately, they take much of the drudgery out of your work. You can zip through some fairly ambitious projects in just a week-end, instead of tying up valuable time hand sawing or hand sanding some little job that seems to take forever to finish.

Rather than give you a detailed description of each type of power tool available, we have concentrated on the power tools you'll need when working on the 101 projects listed in this book. This does not mean, however that you must own all of these tools in order to complete most of the jobs.

Since all power tools come complete with detailed instructions on proper use and maintenance, we have omitted this aspect in our discussions. This does not imply, however, that achieving and maintaining good alignment, proper maintenance and safety precautions are not important. On the contrary, we would suggest you select a safe place in your workshop where you file all instruction manuals for your power tools, and that you refer to them from time to time in order to refresh your memory on what to do to obtain maximum safety and performance.

Double Insulation

Not all home power outlets feature three-pronged receptacles for proper grounding of power tools. To overcome this problem, select power tools which are of double insulated construction. These products incorporate built-in protection against electric shock hazards while eliminating the need for grounding. they are equipped with convenient two-prong plugs which can be safely used with all standard receptacles.

Safety

Read the safety instructions which are provided with your power tools. Always use safety glasses with power tools.

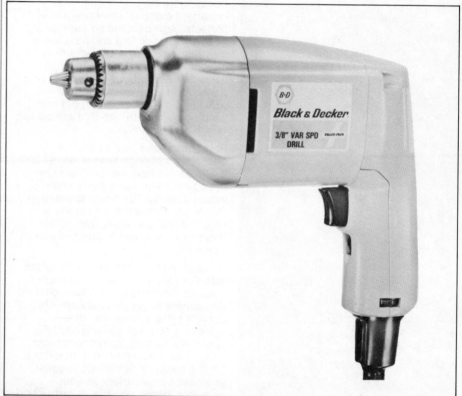

Portable electric drills

Portable Electric Drills

A portable electric drill is the first "must-have" item on any home handyman's shopping list. This low-cost power tool is so versatile, and can be adapted to so many more different uses than just straight drilling, that owning one is almost a necessity. Listed below are the various drill types, their functions and features.

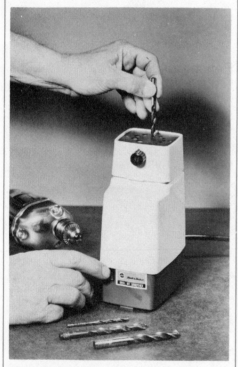

Size and Type of Drill

All drill sizes are specified in terms of the maximum shank diameter of a drill bit the drill chuck can hold. The most common drill sizes are $\frac{1}{4}$ inch, $\frac{3}{8}$ inch and $\frac{1}{2}$ inch, with drill speed decreasing as drill size increases. The $\frac{1}{4}$ inch drill is the most popular drill with home handymen because its high speed drilling capability is ideal for work with most woods and compositions, yet can be used for odd, intermittent light drilling in masonry or metals. Its high speed can also be used to great advantage with

sanding, polishing or buffing accessories, usually offered as part of a drill kit.

Greater Versatility

The $\frac{3}{8}$ and $\frac{1}{2}$ inch drills offer greater versatility in that they are capable of drilling larger hole diameters and because of their lower speeds and greater torque can be used for prolonged drilling in either metal or concrete. Larger drill sizes are usually reserved for heavy, industrial usage and are of little interest to the average do-it-yourselfer.

Speed Requirements

Because speed requirements can vary when drilling different types of material, two speed or variable speed drills have a decided advantage over single speed drills in that they eliminate the need to own several single-speed drills. Some drills offer the additional advantage of reversing action. This comes in quite handy when backing off screws or removing jammed drill bits.

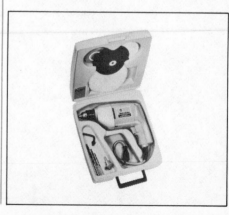

How to use your Drill

Drill bits have a tendency to wander once you start, especially on metal. To overcome this problem it's best to center-punch the exact spot you want to drill. Then drill from a dead start. Do not turn the drill on before the bit is in position.

This procedure is not necessary with a variable speed drill which can be started at a very slow speed to establish the hole.

Avoid Excessive Pressure

Use just enough pressure to keep drilling. Excessive pressure will overload or stall the motor. Never change direction of pressure — you will break the bit or distort the dimensions of the hole.

The break-out side of a hole will usually splinter unless you take precautions to avoid this. Either ease up on the feed pressure when you're about to break through, or clamp a piece of scrap wood on the break-out side.

When drilling into small pieces of wood or metal, be sure they are clamped down securely because the twisting force of the drill could send them flying. It is always a good idea to drill a small hole first when making larger holes, as the larger bit will then have an easier time. Drilling in metal or hardwood goes smoother if you put a few drops of oil on the drill bit first.

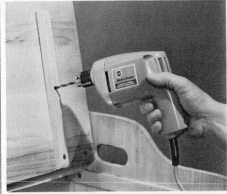

Cordless Drill

If dangling cords annoy you, or you need to work too far away from a convenient outlet, consider investing in a cordless drill. There are a variety of models which are compactly designed and easy to handle. Complete with battery and charger, they can be recharged to full capacity within 16 hours. So, if you need a low-speed (800 RPM) drill around the cottage, the backyard, or wherever you lack electricity, you'll find a cordless drill a handy investment.

Circular Saw

The portable circular saw has found its way into many home workshops. Use it for fast, on-the-job trimming of sheathing, roof and floor boards, paneling, and a host of other sawing requirements. All that is needed to go from one job to the next is a quick change of blades: a combination blade for all purpose wood cutting, another specifically designed for plywood, a planer blade for smooth cutting, one for ripping and friction cutting, or abrasive blades for cutting through metal or masonry.

Circular saw

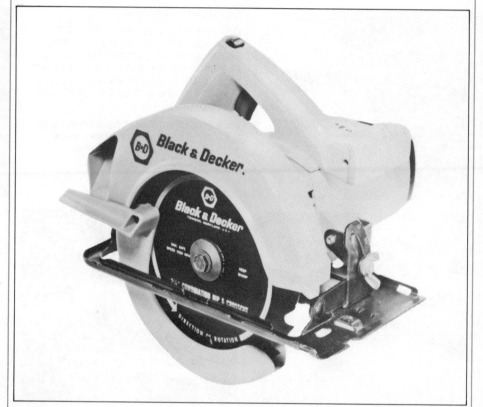

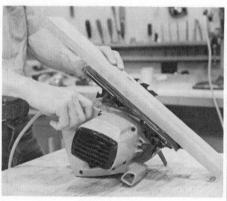

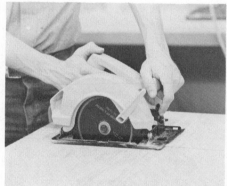

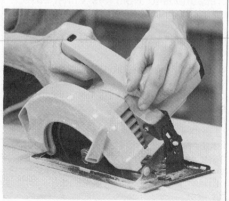

Size and Type of Saw

Circular saws come in a wide range of types and models for home or construction use. The first saw you choose should be able to cut a 2 x 4 at 45° angle, and a saw with a blade diameter of 7 inches or more is your best choice. Heavy work or consistent use over extended periods of time require the purchase of "Professional" models.

Additional Features

Other features to look for are tilting shoes with graduated scales showing the precise angle for bevel or angle cuts, automatic spring-actuated blade guard that retracts when blade enters the work, depth and angle adjustments, plus auxiliary knob handles on certain models which afford additional control.

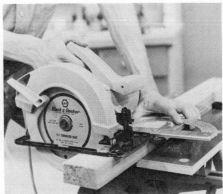

How to Use your Circular Saw

Before you use your new saw, make several cuts on scrap wood to get familiar with the various adjustments. It's a good idea, too, to do this every time you adjust the saw for different types of cuts in order to avoid disappointments. Always use the correct blade for the job and be sure it is properly sharpened.

Sawing in wood that is wet or green can cause binding because the kerf,

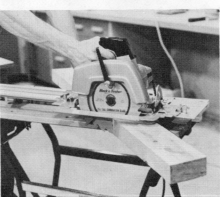

the cut left by the saw, has a tendency to close in again after the blade has passed. Should this be the case, use a thin piece of scrap wood to keep the kerf open behind the blade.

The rotation of the blade, as viewed from the open side, is counter-clockwise, meaning the cutting action is "up". So, for best work, place the good face of the work "down". When replacing a blade, replace it with the blade arrow pointing in the right direction. Also, waxing the bottom of the saw from time to time will help it glide smoothly over the work.

Choosing a Blade

For most of the projects listed in this book, a combination crosscut and rip blade will do a good job of cutting hardwood, softwood, plywood and hardboard.

Safety

When working with portable circular power saws, be sure the work is firmly supported and will not move when sawing. Always start your saw before it enters the work and move it straight along the cutting line.

Guiding pressure should be just enough to keep the blade cutting. Veering or forcing the blade can cause jamming, stalling, even motor damage. It will also increase the possibility of kickback.

Always make sure that the power cord is well out of the way, your left hand is nowhere near the blade, and that your right hand has got a firm grip on the saw.

Sabre saw

Jig Saw (or Sabre Saw)

The second most important power tool to own is the versatile jig saw (or sabre saw). Although not as fast-cutting as the portable circular saw, it does an excellent job for general purpose sawing when used with the proper blades. It will crossout a 2 x 4, cut curves or scroll work in plywood, metal, composition or plastic. And because it is so compact and light-weight, you can use it for making cut-outs, even in finished walls or ceilings, when adding electrical outlets or fixtures, or for making openings for pipes and basins in bathrooms or kitchen tops. You do not even need to pre-drill these cut-outs as the sabre saw will make its own starting hole.

When selecting your jig saw, first determine its future use. Professional models are always advisable if the saw is to be intended for heavy-duty sawing or continuous use. Another important consideration are two-speed switches, variable speed switches and tilting shoe models. Single-speed saws are fine for light woodwork, but multiple-speed saws are much more versatile and are much smoother and easier to guide at lower speeds. Tilting shoes are necessary when making bevel cuts.

Safety Precautions

While the jig saw is lightweight and easy to use, it is nevertheless a power tool that needs to be treated with respect. Never use the wrong blade or wrong speed for the job. Keep blades sharp at all times. Keep children and visitors at a safe distance from your work. Have your work properly secured and, when sawing, never reach under or behind the material being cut. Watch that power cord. And don't overreach.

18

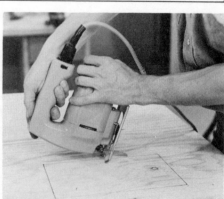

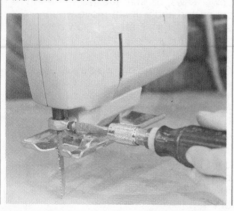

Be sure that the jig saw you buy is of the double-insulated kind if your workshop is not wired to accept three-pronged power tools.

Since the blade cuts on the "up" stroke, the good side of the material is always placed face down. For smoother cuts, it's always advisable to select a blade with more teeth per inch and to use a transparent, self-adhesive tape over the cut line to minimize feathering and splintering on the up stroke of the blade. This is especially called for when working with plywood.

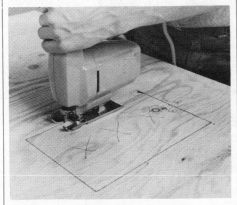

Always keep a firm grip on the tool to prevent vibration. Feed pressure, regardless of tool speed or blade being used, should be just enough to keep the blade cutting. Plan your cuts before your start so as to minimize any backtracking.

Special Features

One of the jig saw's main attractions is its ability to penetrate material without needing a starting hole. To achieve this, rest the saw on the front edge of the baseplate and tilt it so that the blade is clear of the surface of the material to be cut. Then start the saw and slowly tilt the tool back to make blade-to-work contact. The blade will first start to cut a groove, then slowly penetrate the material until the saw sits firmly on the baseplate and you can finish the job in the regular manner. The saw can also be used for cutting circles or arcs simply by using its edge guide, which doubles as a circle-cutting guide on many jig saw models. The edge guide may have a hole through which a nail can be used as the centre point, or it may feature a special built-in point that screws into place.

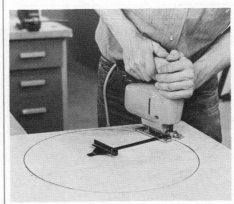

Blade Selection

When buying jig saw blades always buy the best. There are many specialty blades available, but the following three do most of the work:

Alternate-set blades, or general purpose blades, are used mainly for rough cutting. A good rule of thumb is to use blades with six teeth per inch on wood more than one inch thick, and blades with 10 teeth per inch in material less than one inch thick.

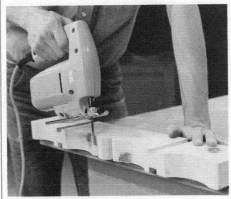

Taper-ground blades have back edges ground thinner than set blades which makes for more beautiful finish cuts in hardwood, although the blades are more difficult to turn.

Wave-set metal cutting blades look like backsaw blades, although much thicker. These blades require the use of cutting oils when sawing metal in order to prolong their cutting life.

Jig saw accessories are sanding sticks for wood and files for metal. Both are good for smoothing internal edges usually too difficult to get at with other tools.

ECONOMY BLADES FIT MOST POPULAR JIG SAWS, SABRE SAW BRANDS WITH ¼" SHANK

FOR CUTTING WOOD, PLYWOOD, MASONITE, PLASTICS ETC.

METAL CUTTING

Shop Around

Considering the versatility of the jig saw, it will pay you to shop around before settling on a model just right for you. This is one tool you'll use often.

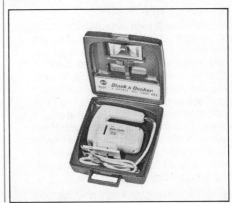

Router

Router

When you add a router to your power tool inventory, you've crossed over from amateur to amateur expert. For with just a moderate amount of skill, and plenty of imagination, you can now produce artistry in wood.

A router lets you plane edges, cut multi-curved moldings, produce relief panels, rabbet and dovetail for professional joints, trim plastic laminate, mortise doors, make signs or cut delicate grooves for professional inlay work. In short, a router adds the professional touch to your projects.

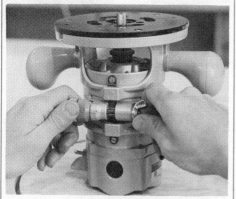

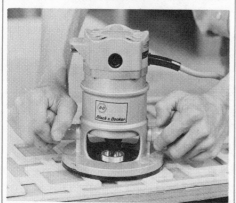

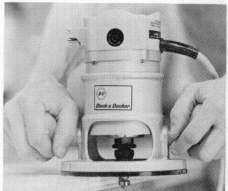

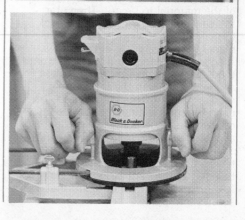

How to use your Router

As with any power tool, let the router come up to speed before contacting the wood. Feed from left to right, being neither too fast or too slow. Your ears will soon tell you whether you are pushing things by working too fast or cutting too deep. You'll also find that softwoods cut more easily than hardwoods and you'll have to make allowances for that. Repeated shallow passes make for a better job, and it's best to cut with the grain of the wood wherever possible.

Besides cutting grooves and dadoes

which are needed in shelving and furniture work, most routers are used for decorative edging to give completed projects that professional touch. Even circular cuts can be made with a router, and they add beauty to any cabinet door or drawer front.

Other router accessories are: straight and circular guide, power plane, hinge mortising template kit, dovetail kit, circle cutting attachment, and veneer trimming guide.

Repetitive, artistic designs can be achieved by means of home made

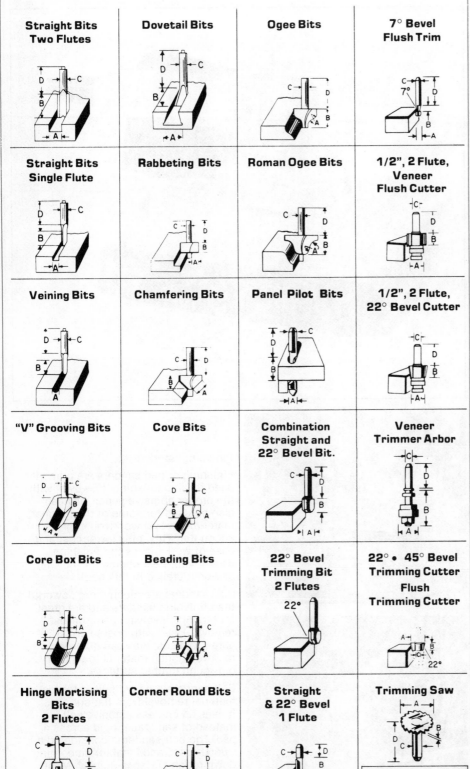

Straight Bits Two Flutes	Dovetail Bits	Ogee Bits	7° Bevel Flush Trim
Straight Bits Single Flute	Rabbeting Bits	Roman Ogee Bits	1/2", 2 Flute, Veneer Flush Cutter
Veining Bits	Chamfering Bits	Panel Pilot Bits	1/2", 2 Flute, 22° Bevel Cutter
"V" Grooving Bits	Cove Bits	Combination Straight and 22° Bevel Bit.	Veneer Trimmer Arbor
Core Box Bits	Beading Bits	22° Bevel Trimming Bit 2 Flutes	22° • 45° Bevel Trimming Cutter Flush Trimming Cutter
Hinge Mortising Bits 2 Flutes	Corner Round Bits	Straight & 22° Bevel 1 Flute	Trimming Saw

A	B	C	D
Cut. Dia.	Depth of Cut	Shank Lgth.	Overall Lgth.

21

or store bought templates, assuring not only accuracy of repetition but also faster work.

Router Size and Type

The main difference between various models and types of routers is in the power rating of their motors and in their bearing construction. The greater the workload, the greater the horsepower needed and the heavier the bearing required. A low-powered router, however, can do most of the jobs a high-powered router can do, if the user proceeds in stages, i.e. deep cuts are made by progressively deeper cuts until the desired depth of the cut has been accomplished.

Safety

Although the router is a fairly simple tool to operate, never become careless. The high RPM's, plus the power of the motor, create considerable torque necessitating a firm grip on the router even before you turn the switch on. You should also remember that the router shaft and bit turn at a very high speed and cut extremely fast. So, be sure the bit is always tightly locked in the chuck and that your fingers are nowhere near it.

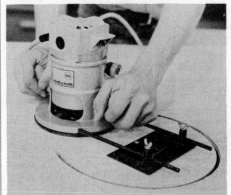

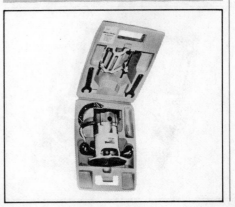

Dual Action Finishing Sander

Time-consuming hand sanding is a thing of the past, now that power sanders do the job quicker, easier and with much more professional results. Whether you need to prepare a wall surface for painting, or need to remove rust or paint from a car, outdoor furniture or boat hull, you'll never want to be without a power sander once you've used one.

Dual action finishing sander

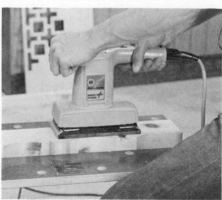

Types of Sanders

There are various types of sanders to choose from: finishing sanders, dual action sanders featuring both orbital and straight-line sanding, disc sanders and belt sanders. Dust collection attachments can be fitted to belt sanders and certain finishing sanders.

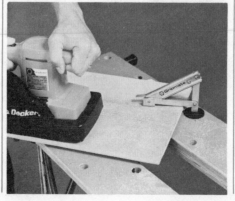

Finishing Sanders

Finishing or pad sanders are primarily used for fine finishing. However, with the proper abrasive paper they can also be used for some of the rougher, material-removal work you might encounter. This, plus lower cost and ease of work makes the finishing sander your best choice for the kind of work detailed in this book.

Disc sanders are much more powerful than finishing sanders and are great for big jobs involving paint or rust removal. Used with coarse grit abrasive discs, they can quickly remove enough material to smooth out rough lumber surfaces.

Belt sanders are best suited for fast material removal from flat surfaces. It uses an endless abrasive belt instead of sandpaper held across a pad. The belt sander is considered a "workhorse" and ideal for smoothing down rough surfaces quickly. Most belt sanders can be equipped with a dust collector bag assembly. This is a very worthwhile feature to consider.

Belt sanders derive their name from an endless abrasive belt which is driven over two drums. Popular sizes are 3" and 4" which indicate the width of the belt to be used and, in most cases, designate the contact area between the abrasive and the work.

Since the belt sander removes material rather swiftly, it is always a good idea to let the sander come up to speed before contacting the work. When up to speed, be sure the full platen area rests solidly on the work and that you keep moving the tool constantly. Tilting the tool, or staying in one place too long, may cause gouges and depressions which will be difficult to remove.

When working with small, individual pieces, be sure they are securely clamped as the fast belt motion of the sander could make them fly backward and create an accident.

Never use abrasive paper which is coarser than need be. The resultant deep scratches may be hard to remove. As a general rule, work your way through progressively finer grits and follow up with a finishing sander using super-fine paper for best results.

How they Work

Finishing sanders are usually driven, in a small, orbital motion, covering a sanding surface of about 3⅝" x 9" (⅓ sheet) or 4½ x 11" (½ sheet) inches wide at a speed of up to 10,000 orbits per minute. With dual action sanders this orbital motion can be changed to straight line motion for a "hand sanded" finish on wood, metal or plastic.

Since the weight of the tool provides enough pressure for most of the work you'll encounter, you need only hold and guide the sander, making sure it is kept in constant motion in order to avoid gouging the material you work on.

A recommended technique when sanding is to work with the grain of the wood, using short, overlapping strokes, from 5% to 15%, especially when you have switched from orbital to straight-line sanding. A special sheepskin pad is a valuable accessory for polishing or waxing jobs.

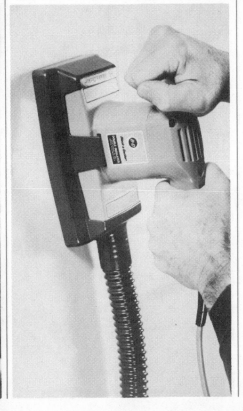

Radial arm saw

Radial Arm Saw

The radial arm saw is the most versatile stationary power tool the ambitious do-it-yourselfer can own. With the proper attachments it can be turned into a shaper, jointer, surfacer, sander, router, or a jig saw as well.

What makes the radial arm saw so different from a bench saw, and so useful, is the fact that the saw cuts from above; the motor and saw blade are attached to an overhead arm which can be turned and locked at any angle.

The arm is held by a post at the rear of a stationary work table. An elevating handle permits the raising or lowering of this post, thereby allowing the depth of cut to be adjusted at will. The motor of the saw moves along the overhead arm, allowing the blade to be rotated to any angle in either a horizontal or vertical plane.

This overhead versatility makes for more accurate cuts, less operator fatigue and, with the proper attachments, gives you a veritable power tool station to handle most of your power tool needs.

24

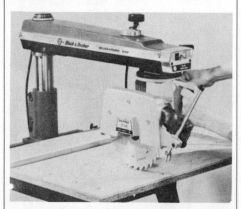

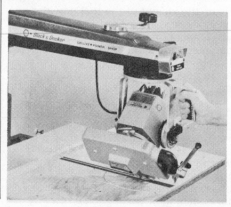

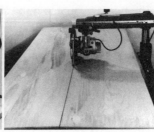

CROSSCUTS to any length
with consistent accuracy.

BEVEL CUTS those
precision corner joints.

RIP CUTS from thin strips
to the center of 4' x 8' panels.

TILT ARBOR SHAPER. 50%
more shapes per cutter set-up.

DRUM SANDER. Makes
finishing intricate curves easy.

SABER SAW. Intricate
curve work fast and easy.

JOINTER. Puts straight
edges on wood.

DADO. Cuts grooves along
visible layout marks.

HORIZONTAL DRILL. Bores
accurately at any angle.

COMPOUND CUTS for picture
framing & shadow boxes.

SURFACER: Sizes and
smooths rough stock fast.

DISC SANDER. Makes
all types of surfacing easy.

How to Operate the Saw

Just like the portable power saw, the radial arm saw will accept a variety of cutting blades to handle almost any type of job such as cutting plywood, hardwood, softwood, etc. When cross-cutting, the work is securely put into place and the operator moves the saw across the work. When used for ripping, the saw is locked into place and the material is fed to the saw.

Before starting any sawing job, the blade should be set in such a way that it just breaks through the bottom face of the work as it will otherwise cut deeply into the saw table. The blade should be well above the table before you switch on the saw. Then use the elevating handle to lower the running blade to the working level.

Be sure the work is firmly held against the guiding fence of the saw table when making crosscuts, and that the saw is guided through the work in a continuous, steady motion. Make sure your supporting hand is well clear of the cutting area and that you do not force the cut and jam the blade. When you've finished the cut, return the saw to its starting position.

When using the saw for rip cutting, set the blade to run parallel with the guiding fence. Be sure you feed the work from the opposite side to the kick-back assembly on the blade guard. Support the overhang of an extra long piece of lumber so that it keeps level with the table.

The saw table should be cleared of sawdust to avoid build-up against the guiding fence, but it should never be cleared while the blade is running.

When using the saw for any other purpose than straight sawing — such as mitering, angle cutting or decorative grooving — the radial arm can be swung to any desired angle, the saw tilted to whatever position necessary, and soon you're on your way to use this tool in 101 different ways

Safety

As with any power tool, observe basic safety rules when using the radial arm saw. Of special importance to you is the use of safety goggles or safety glasses, proper grounding, work that is securely in place, and the fact that your work supporting hand should never be near the running blade.

Accessories and special cuts

Unfortunately it is beyond the scope of this book to describe, in detail, the extreme versatility of this machine and the considerable number of accessories which are available to enable the user to turn out a great variety of top quality work.

Accessories which are available for this type of machine include:

- A Dado head for cutting grooves, rabbets, mortises, tenons, dadoes, etc. in a single pass.
- A Shaper-Jointer for straight and irregular shaping, tongue and groove cutting, planing, jointing and chamfer cutting.
- A Sabre saw for cutting all types of intricate scrollwork and irregular shapes in plastic, wood and light metal.

Conversion to a router, a disc, belt or drum sander and even a lathe are all possible with readily available accessories.

The following illustrations will give a few examples of what can be achieved with this type of saw.

The Shaper-Jointer

The shaper-jointer can be used for cutting all common shapes of mouldings such as is shown in figures 1 and 2. Cutting a glue-joint as shown in figure 3 is also a very useful operation which can be done with this accessory.

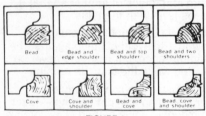

FIGURE 1

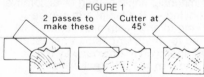

FIGURE 2

Other designs can be made by positioning the cutters as you desire.

Glue-Joint Knives

These cutters are used the same way as, and sometimes in place of the Jointing Knives.

One advantage is a longer glue line.

The boards you use must be flat and the cutters adjusted so the center of the knives is in the center of the boards.

The male and female are both the same except one is upside down. (See Figure 3)

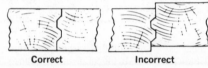

Correct   **Incorrect**

FIGURE 3

Remember, never shape or mould without a guard.

The Sanding Disc.

The sanding disc is 8" in diameter and has a slight bevel on its edge to make surface sanding a little easier.

The paper can be adhered to the disc in one of four practical ways.

- Self-adhering paper—easy to use.
- Disc Stick—a tacky substance, very widely used. Safe as long as you don't get the disc too hot. The paper will fly off when the disc-stick melts. It is very reasonable in price. Quick and easy to use.
- Special rubber cement (glop by Carborundum).

Only use Cabinet-Back Paper (heavy). Do not use Finishing Paper (too thin).

The fine wood dust from the sander is explosive when it is about 70% dust and 30% air. Do not smoke or work near open flame with the sanding disc.

The dust from most woods when inhaled will cause chocking. Wear a dust-mask or a surgical mask while sanding.

Drum Sander

This sander is designed to sand inside curves; however, it is very good for sanding any edge: inside, straight or outside.

It can be used for straight edge sanding in the same manner that the Jointer is used except we do not use a Jointer Fence.

It can be used for surface sanding on lumber up to 3" wide or on lumber up to 6" wide if you turn the lumber around and take a second pass.

Special Cuts

Kerfing or Bending Wood

If you rip a piece of wood thin enough it will bend quite easily.

Wet this piece and it will bend even more easily and have less tendency to crack.

By cutting a slit cross-grain and leaving a thin piece of wood on the bottom you can bend the wood at this cut until the slit or kerf is closed at the top. (See Figure 4).

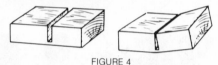

FIGURE 4

By cutting several slits, one alongside the other, the piece will appear to bend. (See Figure 5).

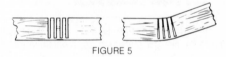

FIGURE 5

You can determine the number of slits it takes to bend the lumber 90° by measuring the angle of the first bend and dividing this angle into 90°. An easier method is by trial and error on a piece of scrap of the same thickness.

Once you determine the number of cuts you will always get a bend of 90° regardless of the distance between the cuts. The wider the cuts are spaced, the bigger the arc. (See Figure 6).

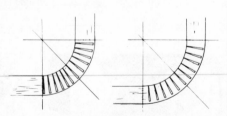

FIGURE 6

Wear Safety Glasses

Be sure the stone, brush of buffer is rated to revolve at 3400 rpm without flying apart.

When grinding or sharpening iron or steel watch out for sparks. They can start fires.

Bench grinder

Bench Grinder

Sharp and clean tools are necessary for quality work and shop safety. A bench grinder goes a long way in taking the drudgery out of sharpening your tools and helps you in getting maximum, safe use from them. When using a bench grinder, however, be sure that you wear goggles and that the eye shields and spark arrestors are in place. It makes no sense to sharpen tools for safer work, only to get hurt in the process of sharpening them.

Types of Bench Grinders

Bench grinders are basically double-shaft motors which mount a grinding wheel on each shaft and provide covers, guards, eye shields, etc., for operator protection. There are different types of grinding wheels for different types of materials, but most grinders come usually equipped with one coarse and one medium grit wheel.

Grinding Wheels

Grinding wheels supplied with the bench grinder have been matched to its motor speed, so it pays to check the RPM ratings of new grinding wheels before you mount them. Also, check all wheels for cracks, even new ones, and this is usually done by putting the wheel on a rod and tapping its side. If you don't get a clear, ringing sound, discard the wheel.

Always let the grinder come up to full speed before applying the work. Run the work on the coarse wheel first and then switch over to the finer grit wheel. Allow the work to cool off between passes to prevent damage to the work from overheating, use light feed pressure only and dip the work in water frequently.

The bench grinder can be used to clean and polish, using wire-brush or fibre-brush wheels. For high polish operations, cloth buffing wheels with appropriate buffing compounds will do a fast, first class job.

Shop vacuum cleaner and cordless system

Shop Vacuum Cleaner

A clean workshop is a safer workshop, and a much more pleasent place to work. Invest in a shop vacuum cleaner, and use it after every drilling or sawing job. Control the dirt and dust before it gets a chance to settle on your work, and on your clothes.

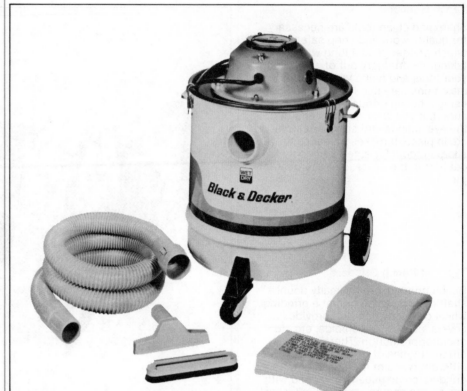

Cordless System

A handy addition to round out your power tool selection is the cordless power system as illustrated, consisting of an interchangeable, rechargeable power pack and various tool heads. The power pack will drive a cordless ¼" drill at moderate (750 RPM) drilling speeds, light a cordless sealed-beam emergency lantern, power a small cordless vacuum cleaner, 1 Qt. sprayer, grass shear, or shrub trimmer. The initial purchase includes a 16-hour battery charger to recharge the handle.

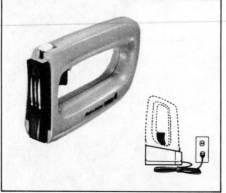

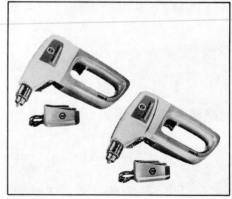

PART IV

Shop Guide

Although our book is more project than theory oriented, you'll find that this Shop Guide will come in quite handy.

Sub-divided into 4 main headings: Useful Mathematics, Accessories, Basic Carpentry and Wood Finishing; the Shop Guide contains a wealth of practical know-how information it would take years to acquire.

Refer to it whenever in doubt as to what hinge to use, which screw to choose, how to apply a certain finish, or whatever problems you encounter when working on any of our projects.

Also, we recommend that you study the section on Basic Carpentry if you've never worked with wood before. It is easy to understand, well illustrated, and will make your mastery of the subject that much easier.

29

Useful Mathematics

A knowledge of basic mathematics and terms is a prerequisite for understanding some of the geometry which is useful when measuring and marking work. A compass, a protractor and a set square are the only drawing instruments you really need. An understanding of the following terms will also be helpful.

30

The **diameter** of a circle is the length of any straight line which passes through the centre of the circle and terminates on the circumference.

The **radius** is the distance from the centre of the circle to the circumference.

The **circumference** of a circle is the distance around the outside of the circle and is equal to 3.1416 times the diameter.

The following are a few practical examples which will be found to be of value to the do-it-yourselfer.

Drawing a Line at 90 Degrees

Set the point of the compass at point A on the base line, mark off a small arc on either side of this point at B and C. Now after increasing the compass setting to span from B to C use these points as the compass pivot points and mark off arcs at D and E as shown. A line joining the points where the arcs intersect will be at 90 degrees to the base line.

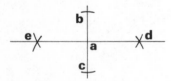

Dividing any Angle in Two

Place the point of the compass at A and draw an arc intersecting the lines enclosing the angle at points B and C. Then using B and C as the centres, mark two arcs intersecting at point D. Line AD then bisects the angle.

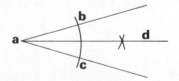

Finding the Centre of a Circle Using a Compass

First draw a line AB through any part of the circle. Then using the points A and B as centres, strike arcs intercepting at points C and G. Join these two points and extend the line to cut the circumference at points D and E. The centre of the circle can then be found by determining the halfway point F between D and E.

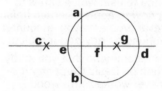

To Divide 90 Degrees into 30 Degrees Angles

With A as the centre point draw an arc to intercept the horizontal and vertical lines at C and B respectively. Using the same radius and point C as the centre draw an arc across the first arc at point D. Repeat this operation using point B as the centre and intercepting the first arc at point E. Lines joining A to E and A to D will then divide the 90 degree angle into 30 degree angles.

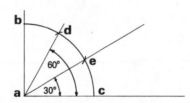

To Divide a Line into a Number of Equal Parts

In order to divide line AB into an equal number of parts, draw line AC at any angle and divide it into the required number of easily measured parts. Join the last point D to point B and then proceed to draw parallel lines to it from each of the marks on line AC.

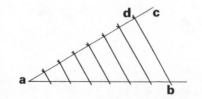

To Draw an Elipse

To draw an elipse of known external dimensions, first draw lines AB and CD at 90 degrees to each other and intercepting at point G. Then using point C as the centre and with a radius equal to AG draw arcs through line AB at points E and F. Drive fine nails or thumb tacks at E, F and C and tie a taut loop of string around these three points. Replace the pin at C with a pencil and, keeping the string taut, proceed to draw the elipse.

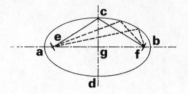

To Determine Areas and Volumes

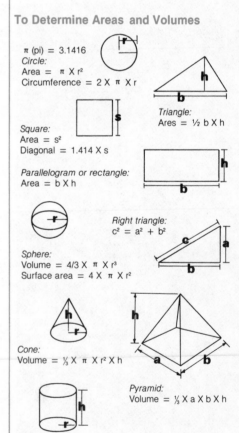

π (pi) = 3.1416
Circle:
Area = π X r²
Circumference = 2 X π X r

Square:
Area = s²
Diagonal = 1.414 X s

Parallelogram or rectangle:
Area = b X h

Sphere:
Volume = 4/3 X π X r³
Surface area = 4 X π X r²

Cone:
Volume = ⅓ X π X r² X h

Cylinder:
Volume = π X r² X h

Triangle:
Ares = ½ b X h

Right triangle:
c² = a² + b²

Pyramid:
Volume = ⅓ X a X b X h

Rectangular solid:
Volume = h X a X b
Surface area = (2 X a X b) + (2 X b X h) + (2 X a X h)

How to measure

Linear dimensions, for example, lengths, widths, thicknesses, diameters, etc., and angular measurements, comprise the greater part of the measuring done in the home workshop. Although there is a great variety of measuring instruments, we will deal here with the basic rule, calipers, combination square, protractor and T-bevel.

The rule:

By far the most important measuring tool for woodworking is the rule. For general work the folding wood rule and the steel tape are indispensible for all but very accurate work requiring the use of a finely divided steel rule.

The degree of accuracy to which work may be produced when measurements are made by a rule depends on the quality of the rule and on the skill of the user.

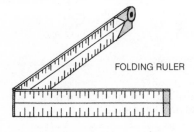

FOLDING RULER

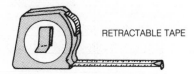

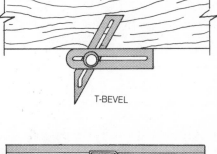

RETRACTABLE TAPE

An important factor is that of possessing a good rule and getting used to its markings. The most useful and convenient markings are inches on one face of the rule and metric units on the other.

When using a rule, the eye which is observing the reading should be, as near as possible, opposite to the mark being read. This avoids what is called "parallax" and the reader may demonstrate for himself the errors which parallax may cause if he reads the large hand of a clock when it is vertical, by looking at it, not from the front, but from a very acute side angle.

Calipers

To measure the diameter of a circular part, or to measure the thickness of material where accuracy is necessary will require the use of calipers.

When working with calipers they should be adjusted by tapping one leg (if stiff joint type are used) or by adjusting the screw, until, when the work is straddled by the legs, it is just possible to feel the contact between the calipers and the work. The contact should not be too heavy, otherwise, the legs may be slightly sprung and a false reading obtained.

When a nice feel has been obtained the size should be read on a rule by resting the end of one leg on the end of the rule and taking the reading at the other end, as shown.

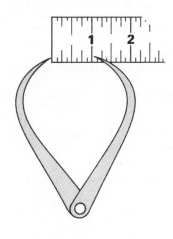

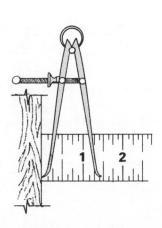

The Combination Square, Protractor and T-Bevel

The combination square may be used for measuring or drawing lines at 90 degrees and 45 degrees but is also a very useful tool for checking flatness of surfaces in any position. Most of these instruments are also fitted with one or two spirit level vials. Yet another use to which this tool can be put is as a marking gauge to draw a pencil mark lengthwise on a wood surface. This can be done by adjusting the blade to the required width and sliding it along the edge of the wood with a pencil held at the end of the blade.

The T-bevel is used for transferring an angular measurement from say a protractor or other source to a piece of wood to be marked, by placing the stock of the T-bevel against the edge of the work, with the blade flat along the surface.

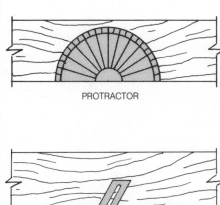

PROTRACTOR

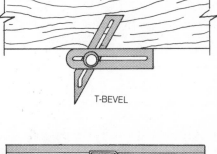

T-BEVEL

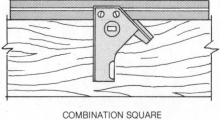

COMBINATION SQUARE

Metric system

Metric System

The "S.I." format of the Metric System of measurement is now in the process of being adopted in Canada and the United States to varying degrees. Whether we are being dragged, kicking and screaming, into the Metric age or whether we welcome it as a long overdue revision to our antiquated system, it is here to stay.

The Système International d'Unités (International System of Units), is the modern form of the original French metric system, and is being adopted for two basic reasons: simplicity and universality. Simplicity because it is based on tens and multiples thereof, and universality because 95% of the world's population is now using, or is in the process of converting to, the metric system.

The measurements throughout this book are based on the Imperial and U.S. system of measures using inches, pounds, and gallons, etc., because we believe that at the present time it is the system with which the great majority of our readers are familiar. However in order to ensure that, when necessary, there is enough information available to use the metric system, we are including in this section sufficient description of the S.I. system to allow conversion of measurements of length, volume, mass (weight) and temperature.

First of all we must familiarize ourselves with a few prefixes which are used to describe multiples of, or divisions of, the basic S.I. units, these are:

Prefix	Meaning	Symbol
mega	one million times	M
kilo	one thousand times	k
hecto	one hundred times	h
deca	ten times	da
deci	one tenth	d
centi	one hundredth	c
milli	one thousanth	m
micro	one millionth	µ

A few examples of this are:

1 centimetre (cm) = 1/100 metre (m)
1000 grams (g) = kilogram (kg)
1 litre (l) = 1000 millilitres (ml)

The Following are Useful Tables for Quick Conversion:

Length

The basic unit for measuring length is the metre and the most common multiples of this are the millimetre, centimetre and kilometre.

Conversion to Metric and Back:

To convert	to	multiply by (approximate)	multiply by (exact)
inches	millimetres	25	25.4
feet	centimetres	30	30.48
yards	metres	0.9	0.9144
miles	kilometres	1.6	1.6093
millimetres	inches	0.04	0.0393
centimetres	inches	0.4	0.3937
metres	yards	1.1	1.094
kilometres	miles	0.6	0.621

Simple Conversion Table of Length

Inches	1	2	3	4	5	6	7	8	9	10
Centimetres	2.54	5.08	7.62	10.16	12.70	15.24	17.78	20.32	22.86	25.40
Feet	1	2	3	4	5	6	7	8	9	10
Metres	0.3	0.6	0.9	1.2	1.5	1.8	2.1	2.4	2.7	3.0
Miles	1	2	3	4	5	6	7	8	9	10
Kilometres	1.6	3.2	4.8	6.4	8.0	9.7	11.3	12.9	14.5	16.1

Temperature

While the basic metric unit of temperature is the degree Kelvin, the unit choosen for everyday use is the degree Celcius. Although the scale is identical to the one previously known as Centigrade, the name was changed to avoid confusion with a French angular measure of the same name.

Simple Conversion Table of Temperature

To convert	to	
fahrenheit	degrees celcius	C = 5/9 (F-32)
degrees celcius	fahrenheit	F = 9/5 C + 32

Conversion of Fahrenheit to Celcius and Back:

Degrees Fahrenheit	Degrees Celsius
400	204.4‡
212	100.0
200	93.3
100	37.8
90	32.2
80	26.7
70	21.1†
60	15.6
50	10.0
40	4.4
32*	0*
30	−1.1
20	−6.7
10	−12.2
0	−17.8

*(Water Freezes)   †(Room Temperature)   ‡(Hot Oven)

Mass (weight)

The gram is the basic metric unit of mass and the most common forms for everyday use is the gram, the kilogram and the megagram (usually called the metric ton or tonne).

Be careful of the confusion which may arise with this last unit when using the word "tonne", as it is sometimes used in Canadian French meaning a ton of 2000 pounds.

Conversion to Metric and Back:

To convert	to	multiply by (approximate)	multiply by (exact)
ounces	grams	28	28.35
pounds	kilograms	0.45	0.4536
short tons	metric tons	0.9	0.907
grams	ounces	0.035	0.0353
kilograms	pounds	2.2	2.2046
metric tons	short tons	1.1	1.1023

Simple Conversion Table of Weight

Ounces (av.)	1	2	3	4	5	6	7	8	9	10
Grams	28.3	56.7	85.0	113.4	141.7	170.1	198.4	226.8	255.1	283.5
Pounds	1	2	3	4	5	6	7	8	9	10
Kilograms	0.45	0.91	1.36	1.81	2.27	2.72	3.18	3.63	4.08	4.54

Liquid Volume

The basic metric unit for liquid volume is the litre and for most practical purposes for the do-it-yourselfer the units we should familiarize ourselves with are limited to the millilitre and the litre.

Imperial and U.S. Liquid Volume to Metric and Back:

To convert	to	Imperial Measure		U.S. Measure	
		multiply by (approximate)	multiply by (exact)	multiply by (approximate)	multiply by (exact)
ounces (fl.)	millilitres	28	28.41	29	29.57
pints	litres	0.6	0.5682	0.5	0.4731
quarts	litres	1.1	1.1365	0.95	0.9463
gallons	litres	4.5	4.5459	3.75	3.785
millilitres	ounces (fl.)	0.035	0.0352	0.03	0.0338
litres	pints	1.76	1.7598	2.1	2.1134
litres	quarts	0.9	0.8799	1	1.0567
litres	gallons	0.2	0.2199	0.25	0.2641

Simple Conversion Table of Volume — Imperial Measure

Ounces (fl.)	1	2	3	4	5	6	7	8	9	10
Millilitres	28.4	56.8	85.2	113.7	142.1	170.5	198.9	227.3	255.7	284.1
Ounces (fl.)	11	12	13	14	15	16	17	18	19	20
Millilitres	312.5	341.0	369.4	397.8	426.2	454.6	483.0	511.4	539.8	568.3
Pints	1	2	3	4	5	6	7	8	9	10
Litres	0.57	1.14	1.70	2.27	2.84	3.41	3.98	4.55	5.11	5.68
Gallons	1	2	3	4	5	6	7	8	9	10
Litres	4.5	9.1	13.6	18.2	22.7	27.3	31.8	36.4	40.9	45.5

U.S. Measure

Ounces (fl.)	1	2	3	4	5	6	7	8	9	10
Millilitres	29.57	59.14	88.7	118.3	147.8	177.4	207	236.5	266.1	295.7
Ounces (fl.)	11	12	13	14	15	16	17	18	19	20
Millilitres	325.3	354.8	384.4	414	443.5	473.1	502.7	532.2	561.8	591.4
Pints	1	2	3	4	5	6	7	8	9	10
Litres	0.47	0.94	1.42	1.89	2.36	2.84	3.31	3.78	4.26	4.73
Gallons	1	2	3	4	5	6	7	8	9	10
Litres	3.78	7.57	11.4	15.1	18.9	22.7	26.5	30.3	34.1	37.8

With a little practice we will soon be able to "think metric" and it won't be long before you remember your favourite film star's measurements as 900 — 550 — 900 instead of 36 — 22 — 36.

2
Accessories

Most tools would be of little use to the do-it-yourselfer without an ample stock of accessories and supplies to finish the job; i.e. screws, nails, hinges, etc. Although at first glance a nail is a nail, using the correct one for the job at hand requires experience or at least good "book-knowledge" of what is called for.

On the following pages, therefore, we have listed a detailed cross-section of helpful information on the type of supplies and accessories you'll need to finish most of the projects listed in this book.

Please refer to this information from time to time as it will definitely aid you in achieving professional results.

34

Drive the right nail

NAIL	PURPOSE	TYPE OF POINT	TYPE OF HEAD	SPECIAL FEATURES	*STANDARD SIZES
BOX 8d 2½'' grooved	General construction, carpentry	Diamond	Large flat	Available with grooved shank	3d (14½), 4d & 5d (14), 6d & 7d (12½), 8d (11½), 10d (10½), 16d (10), 20d* *(9)
BRICK SIDING ¾''	Installation of brick siding	Diamond	Checkered flat	Galvanized and painted to match siding. Available in red, black, buff	¾'' (13), ⅞'' (13), 1'' (13), 1¼'' (13), 1½'' (13), 1¾'' (13), 2'' (12½), 2½'' (11½)
CASING 8d	Fine finish work	Diamond	Deep countersunk		4d (14), 6d (12½), 8d (11½), 10d (10½), 16d (10)
COMMON 6d 2½'' grooved	General construction, carpentry	Diamond	Flat	Available with grooved shank	2d (15), 3d (14), 4d & 5d (12½), 6d & 7d (11½), 8d & 9d (10¼), 10d & 12d (9), 16d (8), 20d (16), 30d (5), 40d (4), 50d (3), 60d (2)
CONCRETE AND MASONRY 1¾'' 2½'' fluted	Fastening into concrete, masonry	Diamond	Flat or square	Some with fluted shanks	Available in fractional lengths of ½'' to 3'' and in various gauge sizes.
FLOORING 8d hardwood 2½'' hardwood, grooved	Floor construction	Diamond or blunt	Deep countersunk	Available in grooved shank to eliminate squeaks. These have flat countersunk heads and blunt points. Sizes: 6d, 7d, 8d—All 11½ ga.	Standard flooring nail: 8d (10). Hardwood flooring nail: 8d (11½)
WALLBOARD 4d 1½'' grooved	Installing gypsum wallboard	Diamond	Flat	Smooth or grooved shank. Available also with coating for extra holding power	Smooth shank: 4d (14), 5d (13½), 6d (13). Grooved shank: 1¼'', 1⅜'', 1½''—all 12½ ga.
DUAL-HEAD 6d	Temporary lumber construction	Diamond	Dual		6d (11½), 8d (10¼), 10d (9), 16d (8), 20d (6)
FINISHING 8d	General construction, carpentry	Diamond	Brad		3d (15½), 4d (15), 6d (13), 8d (12½), 10d (11½)
INSULATION BUILDING BOARD 1¾''	Installing insulation board	Needle	Flat	Available in barbed shank with diamond point	1¼'' and 1¾'' (17), 2'' (11)
ROOFING 1'' Smooth 1'' Barbed	Roofing installation	Diamond	Large flat or umbrella	Available with grooved or barbed shanks and coated	Fractionally from ⅞'' to 2'', usually in 11 ga.
FIBERBOARD 1⅛''	Fast nailing of soft materials	Needle	Flat	Available bright, galvanized or cadmium-plated	1'', 1⅛'', 1¼'', 1⅜'', 1½'', 1⅝'', 1¾''—all 17 ga.
UNDERLAY 1¼''	Installing floor underlayment	Diamond	Flat	Available with grooved shank	1¼'' (14)
WOOD SHINGLE 3½d	Installing shingles	Diamond	Flat	Available with grooved or barbed shank	3d (13), 3½d (12½), 4d (12)

*Figures in parentheses are gauge numbers

Nails might well be called universal fasteners. There are few common materials, other than rocks and some metals, you can't drive a nail into. There are even nails that can be driven into masonry.

Nowadays nails are of many types, sizes and shapes and are designed for specific purposes. That's why it's important to know which one to use where. Because of the many new building materials in sheet form that have been developed for builders and do-it-yourselfers, special nails have been made available. When you buy any of these materials for quick construction of a built-in, garage addition, an outbuilding for storage, or perhaps a patio roof, you'll need one of the special nails for the job. As an example, suppose you're roofing a patio with those colorful fiberglass panels. Obviously just any nail won't do. There's a nail specified for the purpose and no other should be used. It has a special head which keeps out water, sealing the hole tightly when it's driven home properly. And it's designed to hold, in any weather short of tornado-force winds.

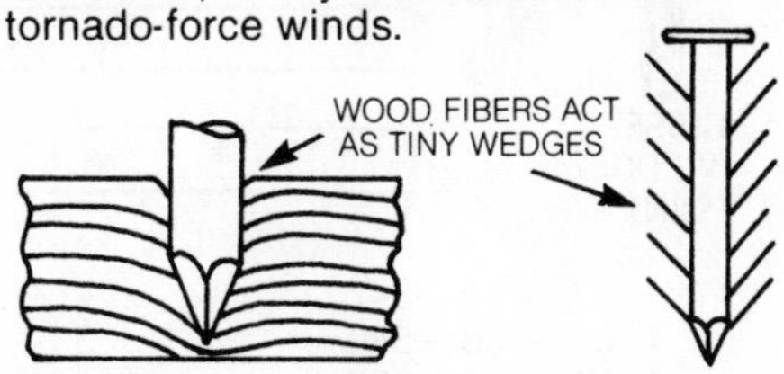

What makes it hold so tenaciously? A look at the sketch on this page, tells why. As the nail is driven, the point breaks some of the tiny fibers in the wood and forces them downward. The point also wedges others apart as it is driven in. It is these severed and wedged fibers that offer such resistance to withdrawal of the nail. They grip the body of the nail tightly and they seldom relax their hold.

Carpenters and others who use nails as fasteners pretty generally follow a simple rule: at least two-thirds of the length of the nail should be in the holding piece when the nail is driven home.

Nails designated as "common" come in 6 to 20d sizes. "d" being the symbol for penny. The 20d is about the largest size that can be driven handily with an ordinary hammer.

The accompanying charts and details show most of the nails now commonly available.

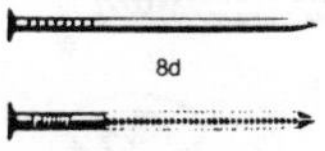

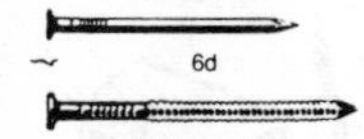

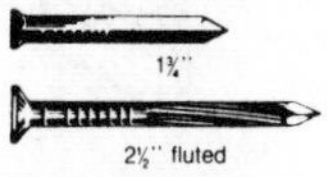

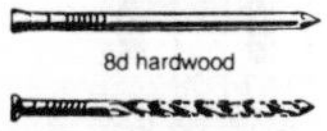

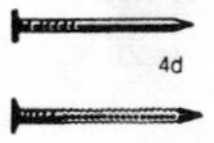

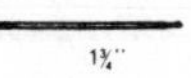

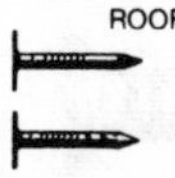

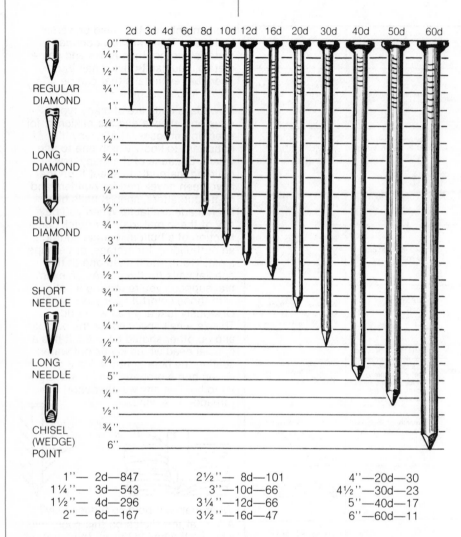

TYPES OF NAIL

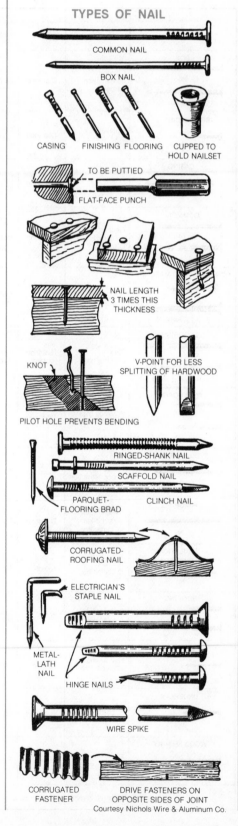

COMMON NAIL

BOX NAIL

CASING FINISHING FLOORING CUPPED TO HOLD NAILSET

TO BE PUTTIED

FLAT-FACE PUNCH

NAIL LENGTH 3 TIMES THIS THICKNESS

KNOT

V-POINT FOR LESS SPLITTING OF HARDWOOD

PILOT HOLE PREVENTS BENDING

RINGED-SHANK NAIL

SCAFFOLD NAIL

PARQUET-FLOORING BRAD   CLINCH NAIL

CORRUGATED-ROOFING NAIL

ELECTRICIAN'S STAPLE NAIL

METAL-LATH NAIL

HINGE NAILS

WIRE SPIKE

CORRUGATED FASTENER

DRIVE FASTENERS ON OPPOSITE SIDES OF JOINT

Courtesy Nichols Wire & Aluminum Co.

REGULAR DIAMOND

LONG DIAMOND

BLUNT DIAMOND

SHORT NEEDLE

LONG NEEDLE

CHISEL (WEDGE) POINT

1'' — 2d — 847	2½'' — 8d — 101	4'' — 20d — 30
1¼'' — 3d — 543	3'' — 10d — 66	4½'' — 30d — 23
1½'' — 4d — 296	3¼'' — 12d — 66	5'' — 40d — 17
2'' — 6d — 167	3½'' — 16d — 47	6'' — 60d — 11

There's only one nail type and size that is *the* best for a particular job.

For general carpentry and construction, choose one of the general-purpose nails — common, box, casing and finishing nails.

All nails of a particular size are the same length, but diameters vary from one type to another. Box nails, for example, are smaller in diameter than common nails, so they are a good choice to use in a job where the wood may split.

Finishing nails have brad-type heads for use where countersinking is not important; casing nails have heads designed for counter-sinking.

You can order nails either by size or length, but size is the more common way to order. Above is the approxi-mate number of common nails you receive per pound.

Special-purpose nails may appear confusing because they have such a variety of heads and points. Drywall (wallboard) nails, for example, have long "diamond" points so they'll penetrate the drywall cleanly and easily. Dual-head nails give you an extra piggyback head for easy removal when tearing apart concrete forms.

You also have your choice of materials from which nails are made. Common materials include steel, aluminium, copper and brass. To fasten a particular metal, use a nail of the same material. For example, use aluminum nails to secure aluminum gutters to aluminum siding. This reduces the corrosive action that occurs when different metals are placed in contact with each other.

Choose the right screw

WOOD SCREWS

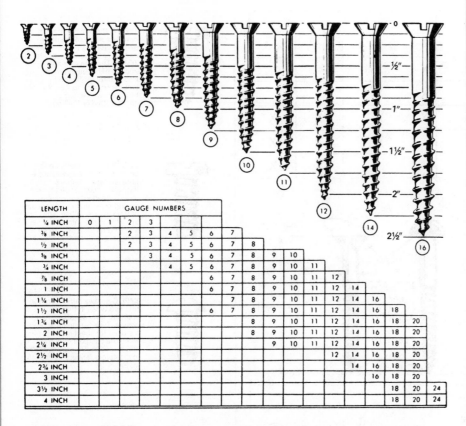

LENGTH	GAUGE NUMBERS																	
	0	1	2	3	4	5	6	7	8	9	10	11	12	14	16	18	20	24
¼ INCH	0	1	2	3														
⅜ INCH			2	3	4	5	6	7										
½ INCH			2	3	4	5	6	7	8									
⅝ INCH				3	4	5	6	7	8	9	10							
¾ INCH					4	5	6	7	8	9	10	11						
⅞ INCH							6	7	8	9	10	11	12					
1 INCH							6	7	8	9	10	11	12	14				
1¼ INCH								7	8	9	10	11	12	14	16			
1½ INCH							6	7	8	9	10	11	12	14	16	18		
1¾ INCH									8	9	10	11	12	14	16	18	20	
2 INCH									8	9	10	11	12	14	16	18	20	
2¼ INCH										9	10	11	12	14	16	18	20	
2½ INCH													12	14	16	18	20	
2¾ INCH														14	16	18	20	
3 INCH															16	18	20	
3½ INCH																18	20	24
4 INCH																18	20	24

WHEN YOU BUY SCREWS, SPECIFY (1) LENGTH, (2) GAUGE NUMBER, (3) TYPE OF HEAD — FLAT, ROUND OR OVAL, (4) MATERIAL — STEEL, BRASS, BRONZE, ETC., (5) FINISH — BRIGHT STEEL BLUED CADMIUM NICKEL OR CHROMIUM PLATED.

The sizes go up with the numbers and only the average sizes in common use are shown.

Slots in screwheads are of three common types: those slotted all the way across the head; another in which a stopped slot is milled into the head; and a third having the head recessed or cross-slotted to take the tip of the special Phillips screwdriver.

Lengths of common screws usually are in inches and even fractions of an inch as 1, 1¼, 1½ and so on. Those having a length of less than 1 in. also come in eighths as ⅜ in., ⅝ in. and so on.

When turning in screws it's important to use a screwdriver of the correct size. If the blade tip is too small it may twist out of the slot; if too large it may slip out of the slot or damage the wood when you seat a flathead screw. When seating a flathead screw, select a blade having a width slightly less than the full width of the slot in the screwhead. The blade should fit the slot snugly with a minimum of side play. Otherwise it may slip out when you apply torque, and damage the wood, the slot or both.

The size of the screw hole also is important. The wood must be counterbored and countersunk if you're using flathead screws. The first portion of the counterbore must be just large enough (see the table) to take the shank, and the second portion should be of a diameter and depth to take the threaded section, the diameter being measured at the bottom of the threads. In softwoods and end grain, the depth of the counterbore is stopped a little short of the full length of the screw. In hardwoods the counterbore should normally be the full length.

Ideally, the length of the screw used should be such that the full thread is turned into the stationary piece of the assembly, with the shank in the piece being attached. Put another way, the length of the smaller hole should equal the thickness of the stationary piece, and the larger should equal the depth of the piece being joined to it. Of course this ratio isn't always possible, but the common rule is to approach it as nearly as possible in any joinery which is to be made with screws. This position of the screw in the parts being joined normally gives the maximum holding power.

A wood screw has far greater holding power that a nail in either hard or softwood. A project joined with nails only can be racked out of shape or the joinery pried apart by judicious use of hammer claws or a pry-bar. But not so with screws; you have to back them out one by one with a screwdriver in order to disassemble the joints without damage.

A screw cuts its own threads in wood when turned into a counterbore of the proper size. As the screw is driven, the raised threads force the wood fibers apart, and the advance of the threads draws the parts being joined tightly together when the screwhead is finally seated. Once seated, a screw won't shake loose and it won't let go.

Most wood screws are made of steel, but screws also are available in brass, bronze and aluminum. Steel screws also come plated with brass, zinc, cadmium and chromium to resist rust and make them more attractive to the eye when used in exposed locations.

Screws with flat heads are perhaps the most commonly used, but wood screws also are available in all ordinary sizes with oval, round, fillister and square heads, the latter supplied as lagscrews and as special screws for attaching ornamental hinges and latches. On some of these the heads are not only square, but they also are slotted so that they may be installed with a screwdriver. On lagscrews you have to use a wrench, as the head is square but not slotted.

Sizes (the shank diameters) are designated by numbers. Only sizes (numbers) 2 through 16 are detailed.

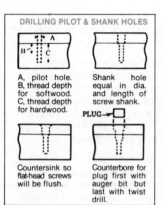

DRILLING PILOT & SHANK HOLES

A, pilot hole.
B, thread depth for softwood.
C, thread depth for hardwood.

Shank hole equal in dia. and length of screw shank.

PLUG

Countersink so flat-head screws will be flush.

Counterbore for plug first with auger bit but last with twist drill.

Lengths	Diameters				
	¼	⅜, ⁷⁄₁₆, ½	⅝, ¾	⅞, 1	
1	X	X			
1½	X	X	X		
2, 2½, etc., to 10	X	X	X	X	
11 & 12		X	X	X	
13 to 16			X	X	

Table title: LAG SCREWS — LENGTHS AND DIAMETERS (in inches)

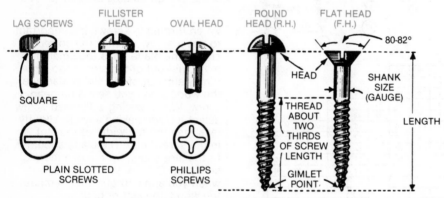

LAG SCREWS — SQUARE

FILLISTER HEAD

OVAL HEAD

ROUND HEAD (R.H.)

FLAT HEAD (F.H.) — 80-82°

HEAD

SHANK SIZE (GAUGE)

LENGTH

THREAD ABOUT TWO THIRDS OF SCREW LENGTH

GIMLET POINT

PLAIN SLOTTED SCREWS

PHILLIPS SCREWS

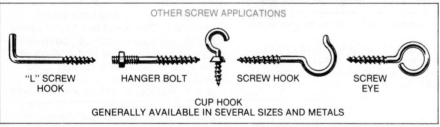

OTHER SCREW APPLICATIONS

"L" SCREW HOOK

HANGER BOLT

SCREW HOOK

SCREW EYE

CUP HOOK

GENERALLY AVAILABLE IN SEVERAL SIZES AND METALS

Head choice is an important item in selecting the right screw for the job.

Two factors are important:
1. The shape of the head.
2. The style of head. (slot configuration).

Shown above are the common head shapes. Lag screws, used in heavy construction where great holding power is required, usually have a *square head* (although some lag screws are made with hexagonal heads). In either case, the lag screw can be driven with a wrench, providing much more leverage than a screwdriver.

Fillister heads have a shoulder (see above), which elevates the slot above the work surface. This minimizes the possibility of marring the wood with the screwdriver, and gives the driven screw a better appearance.

Oval heads must be countersunk into the surface, but the rounded top permits a deeper slot.

Round heads are one of the two most common types. These heads protrude more than other types, except fillister, but offer good slot depth and holding power.

Flat heads don't protrude above the surface. They can either be driven flush or slightly countersunk and concealed with wood putty or plugs.

The most common slot configurations include plain slotted screws; and Phillips screws, with a cross-shaped slot that permits maximum driving pressure.

SHEET-METAL SCREWS

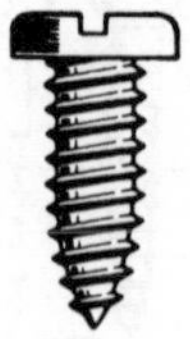

TYPE A sheet-metal screws have coarse threads and are used for joining pieces of sheet metal of gauges from .015 to .050 in. They are available in diameters ranging from Nos. 4 through 14 and in lengths from ¼ to 2 in. You can buy them with either style head, slotted or Phillips.

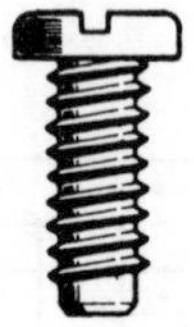

TYPE B sheet-metal screws can be used for the same applications as Type A screws, but they are recommended for the more rugged jobs involving joining sheet metal with gauges of from .050 to .200 in. They are available in the same diameters and lengths as Type A in both Phillips and slotted.

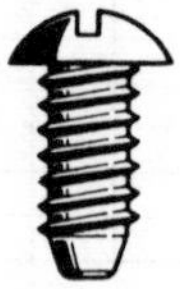

TYPE C screws differ from the first two types in that they have standard threads rather than coarse. Type C tapping screws are used for sheet-metal joining when the gauges range from .030 to .100 in. They are available in diameters ranging from 3/16 in. to 1¼ in.

TYPE F sheet-metal screws are used primarily for joining metals ranging in thickness from .050 in. all the way up to ½ in. They are sold in diameters from No. 2 to ¼ in. and in lengths from 1/8 in. to ¾ in. Like the three above types, you can get Type F screws with either Phillips or slotted heads.

TYPE U screws actually seem more like nails than screws. Their heads are not slotted because they're installed with a hammer rather than with a screwdriver. Type U screws are used with heavier-gauge metals —.050 in. to ½ in.— and are made in lengths from 1/8 in. through ¾ in. One common use is attaching metal nameplates to sheet metal.

TYPE 21 sheet-metal screws are commonly used for fastening other materials to metal — fabrics, cardboard and leather, for instance. Like the Type U screws, they have plain heads and are installed with a hammer. This type of screw is available in three lengths: 11/32, 7/16 and 1/2 in.

38

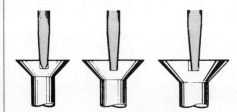

Selecting the right screwdriver is extremely important, as shown in the drawing above. The blade should be as near the length of the slot as possible. It should also be thick enough to fill the slot completely, yet thin enough to reach to the bottom. A worn blade, such as the one on the left, not only is difficult to use, but is likely to damage the slot. So is a blade that's too thin, as shown on the right. The middle view shows a blade that's just right for proper fit.

Most homeowners are concerned with only two general types of screws — wood screws and sheet-metal screws.

wood screws

Always use wood screws:

When you require maximum holding power, such as hanging a door.

When there's a chance you'll have to take the work apart some day. It's easier to back out a screw than pull a nail.

When there's a chance you'll mar the piece of work while installing the fastener. You're safer driving a screw into a piece of work than hammering a nail.

When you plan to leave the fastener exposed. Most screws, especially those selected for appearance, are more decorative than nails.

If your job doesn't fall into one of these categories, use nails instead of screws. They're cheaper and easier to install.

screw sizes

Although you can get screws as long as 6 in. on special order, commonly available lengths range from ¼ in. to 4 in. *Below* 1 in., lengths are available in increments of ⅛ in.; *from 1 in. to 3 in.* length goes up in ¼-in. steps; *above 3 in.* this increases to ½-in. intervals.

Screw diameters are expressed in arbitrary numbers. Don't let this throw you. The numbers don't represent real measurements on any common scale. Your hardware store probably carries diameters ranging from No. 2 (.086 in.) to No. 18 (.294 in.). When in doubt, refer to the chart below, which shows the diameter's actual size, with the proper gauge number beneath. Note, of course, that several different lengths are available in the same gauge number.

As for type of metal, steel and brass screws are the most common. Use steel for heavy work, brass for light ornamental work. Use plated or aluminum screws where there's a chance of corrosion.

sheet-metal screws

Sheet-metal screws (also called tapping screws or self-threading screws) are used to fasten pieces of metal together, or to attach objects to metal. They have sharp threads that cut their own grooves. (For a chart on such screws, see page 38).

DRILLING LEAD HOLES

SCREW SIZE	DRILL SIZE (No. and Diameter)	
No. and Diameter	HARDWOODS	SOFTWOODS
0 (.060")	70 (1/32")	
1 (.073")	66 (1/32")	71 (1/32")
2 (.086")	56 (3/64")	65 (1/32")
3 (.099")	54 (1/16")	58 (3/64")
4 (.112")	52 (1/16")	55 (3/64")
5 (.125")	49 (5/64")	53 (1/16")
6 (.138")	47 (5/64")	52 (1/16")
7 (.151")	44 (3/32")	51 (1/16")
8 (.164")	40 (3/32")	48 (5/64")
9 (.177")	37 (7/64")	45 (5/64")
10 (.190")	33 (7/64")	43 (3/32")
12 (.216")	30 (1/8")	38 (7/64")
14 (.242")	25 (9/64")	32 (7/64")
16 (.268")	18 (5/32")	29 (9/64")
18 (.294")	13 (3/16")	26 (9/64")
20 (.320")	4 (13/64")	19 (11/64")
24 (.372")	1 (7/32")	15 (3/16")

NOTE: Lead holes aren't usually required for Nos. 0 and 1 screws. For sizes smaller than No. 6, lead holes can be eliminated in softwoods, except near the edges and ends of boards.

39

Gauge Numbers	0	1	2	3	4	5	6	7	8	9	10	11	12	14	16	18	20	24
Actual Cross Section of Screws	•	•	●	●	●	●	●	●	●	●	●	●	●	●	●	●	●	●
Basic Decimal Diameter	.060	.073	.086	.099	.112	.125	.138	.151	.164	.177	.190	.203	.216	.242	.268	.294	.320	.372
Fractional Dia. Nearest 64th	1/16 —	5/64 —	5/64 +	3/32 —	7/64 +	1/8 —	9/64 —	5/32 —	5/32 +	11/64 +	3/16 +	13/64 —	7/32 —	15/64 +	17/64 +	19/64 —	21/64 —	3/8
Drill Number	52	47	42	37	32	30	27	22	18	14	10	4	2	D	I	N	P	V
Pilot or Anchor-Hole Sizes — Hardwood — Slotted Screws	70	66	56	54	52	49	47	44	40	37	33	31	30	25	18	13	4	1
Hardwood Phillips Screws			70	66	56	54	52	49	47	44	40	37	33	31	30	25	18	13
Softwood Slotted Screws	75	71	65	58	55	53	52	51	48	45	43	40	38	32	29	26	19	15
Softwood Phillips Screws			75	71	65	58	55	53	52	51	48	45	43	40	38	32	29	26
Threads Per Inch	32	28	26	24	22	20	18	16	15	14	13	12	11	10	9	8	8	7
Maximum Head Diameter	.119	.146	.172	.199	.225	.252	.279	.305	.332	.358	.385	.411	.438	.491	.544	.597	.650	.756

Drill sizes for body clearance holes are given in either numbered or lettered drill sizes. Dimensions are given in decimal or fractional parts of inches. In general, pilot holes should be about 90 percent of screw-core size for hardwood, 70 percent for softwood. In end grain and also in softwoods, such as pine, it frequently is unnecessary to drill a pilot hole. There are nearly 300 standard wood screws of various sizes, lengths and types. Regular screws have gimlet points; cone and diamond points are special. Length is measured from the threaded tip to the largest bearing surface of the head. Body diameters — gauge sizes — increase in steps of .013 in. Tolerance from specified sizes ranges from .004 in. plus, to .007 in. minus. A 10 percent variation of threads per inch is permitted. Head dimensions of wood screws are identical to those of machine screws of the same size and type.

How to set a screw

COUNTERSINK

SHANK HOLE

PILOT HOLE

COMBINED DRILL AND COUNTERSINK

SCREW-MATE

TWIST DRILL

LEAD HOLE BIT

COUNTERSINK

SCREW

SPADE BIT

FORSTNER BIT

COUNTERBORE

PLUG CUTTING BIT

After selecting the right screw size and type for the job with the help of the chart on page 37, the next step is the preparation of the wood to ensure that the finished job is not marred by poorly fitted screws.

Except for very small screws, drilling pilot holes is a must, as not only is it less tiring to drive screwnails with these pilot holes but it ensures that the wood will not split and that the screw will be sunk in to the desired depth to allow the head of the screw to be covered where required.

The simplest method of drilling pilot holes is to use a combination bit where the hole is to be countersunk or a "Screw-mate" where the hole is to be counterbored. If, however, it is felt that the additional investment for these special drills is not justified, then the use of twist drills is quite satisfactory.

With the help of the table on page 39 select the appropriate drills for the pilot hole, the shank clearance hole and the countersink or counterbore.

After clamping the two pieces of wood together drill the pilot hole to the full depth of the screw when working with hardwood. In softwood and end grain the depth of the pilot hole should be a little shorter. The second operation is the drilling of the shank clearance hole to about ⅓ the length of the screw and finally, where the screw head is to fit flush with the wood surface, the hole is countersunk.

In order to assist in drilling the holes to a specified depth, wrap a piece of adhesive tape around the drill at a point equal to the desired depth of the hole.

If the screw head is to be sunk well into the wood, then the counterbored hole should, of course, be drilled before the pilot hole, using a spade bit or a forstner bit.

Where the surface finish is to be painted, then the screw head in a counterbored hole can be covered with putty, however, where the surface is to be varnished, the screw head can be covered with a wooden plug fitted and glued into the counter-bored hole. A plug cutting bit is used to remove a plug from a piece of matching wood. The plug, if well fitted, planed down and finished, will be virtually unnoticeable.

Useful tips

When drilling lead holes in softwoods, such as pine or spruce, make them only half as deep as the threaded portion of the screw. If you're working with hardwoods — oak, maple or birch, for example — drill the lead hole as deep as the full length of the screw.

Many craftsmen apply soap to the threads to make a screw easier to drive. DON'T do this. It isn't a good practice because, through a chemical reaction, the soap eventually turns to a form of glue and actually cements the screw into the hole. It also causes the screw to corrode. Later, if it becomes necessary, you may have trouble backing out the screw. You're better off using paraffin, graphite or beeswax on the threads. They work just as well as soap and involve less risk.

A screw that's frozen in place often can be freed by heating it with the tip of a soldering iron.

After you've backed out a screw, the hole that remains is slightly larger than that cut by the threads originally. Before you replace the screw, fill the hole with wood putty or use a plastic plug to provide a firm grip. Or use a larger screw when reassembling the work.

There are two ways of removing a screw that has broken off in the hole. If you know the size of the screw, you can drill dead center into the screw with a drill that's the same size. This will clear the hole, but it's somewhat risky because you have to drill straight absolutely in order not to mess up the core threads. If you don't know the size of the screw, and thus can't choose the right drill to remove it this way, try using a drill that's smaller than the diameter of the broken screw. Just drill a small hole in the end of the broken screw and then use a screw extractor. If you don't have a screw extractor, tap a square-end nail into the hole, and use the nail like an Allen wrench to back out the stub.

Setting a screw into end grain reduces its holding power by 40 percent.

Choose
the right bolt

MACHINE SCREWS

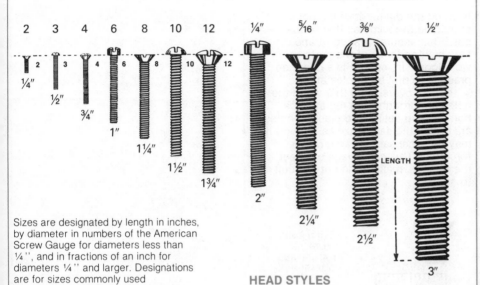

LENGTH

Sizes are designated by length in inches, by diameter in numbers of the American Screw Gauge for diameters less than ¼", and in fractions of an inch for diameters ¼" and larger. Designations are for sizes commonly used

HEAD STYLES

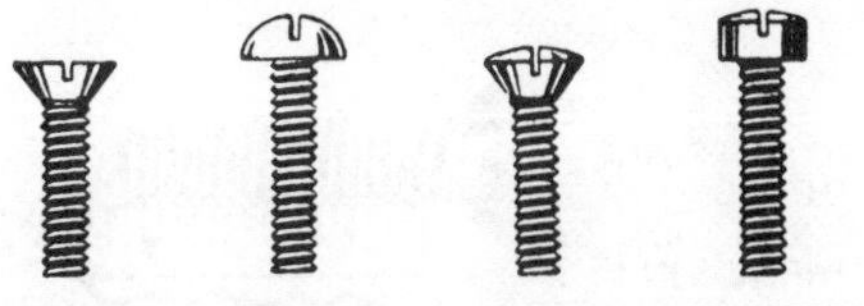

FLAT   ROUND   OVAL   FILLISTER

Machine screws—the commercial term for screws to be driven in drilled and tapped holes—are used for assembly of metal parts. Machine screws are regularly made in mild steel and brass, with four types of head—flat, round, oval and fillister. Furnished plain and also with commonly used platings and degrees of finish—nickel, brass, copper, cadmium, electrogalvanized, Parkerized and zinc-plated.

tap size		drill size no.	drill diameter in inches
diameter	threads per in.		
2	56	51	.0670
3	48	5⁄64"	.0781
4	40	43	.0890
6	32	36	.1065
8	32	29	.1360
10	24	25	.1495
12	24	17	.1730
¼"	20	8	.1990
5⁄16"	18	F	.2570
3⁄8"	16	5⁄16"	.3125
½"	13	27⁄64"	.4219

When the job calls for use of a bolt rather than a screw or other type of fastener, the homeowner must decide what type and size of bolt is best adapted to the purpose.

If the parts to be joined are of metal, then a machine bolt with either a square or hex head usually is best.

If the head bears on metal, then no washer will be required under the head in average work. But if the parts are subject to vibration, shear or shake, use a lock washer under the nut.

On the other hand if the parts are of wood, or if the part against which the head must bear is of wood, then it is generally best to use a carriage bolt. The head of the latter is relatively larger in proportion to the body diameter and is crowned in a manner similar to that of an oval-headed screw. The body has square shoulders just below the head. When it is tapped into a hole, the squared portion of the head prevents the bolt from turning when you tighten or loosen the nut. When the nut is turned down on wood, always use a flat washer under it to prevent crushing or other defacement of the material.

Machine screws differ from machine bolts in that they usually are threaded the full body length and the heads are available in a range of shapes, or types, commonly known as flat, round, oval and fillister, also in the socket (Allen) and Phillips types. The flat and oval heads are much the same as those of ordinary wood-screw heads of the same types, the heads being shaped to seat in countersunk holes in the same manner as flat-head wood screws. But round and fillisterhead machine screws are designed to seat directly on a flat surface or onto a lock washer. All machine-screw heads are slotted so that they may be driven with an ordinary screw driver, excepting those with Allen and Phillips heads, the former to be driven with an Allen wrench and the latter with a Phillips driver.

Machine screws are designed mainly for assembly of metal parts, where they usually are driven into tapped holes rather than being drawn tight with nuts. They are widely used in the assembly of small machines,

BOLT SIZE diameter of thread and width of square	CARRIAGE-BOLT DIMENSIONS (in inches)					
	AMERICAN STANDARD CARRIAGE BOLTS, ROUND HEAD, SQUARE NECK					
	diameter of head	height of head	bolt length and shorter	depth of square	bolt length and longer	depth of square
No. 10 (3⁄16")	7⁄16	3⁄32	1⅛	⅛	1¼	7⁄32
¼	9⁄16	⅛	1¼	5⁄32	1⅜	¼
5⁄16	11⁄16	5⁄32	1¼	3⁄16	1⅜	9⁄32
⅜	13⁄16	3⁄16	1½	7⁄32	1⅝	5⁄16
7⁄16	15⁄16	7⁄32	1½	¼	1⅝	11⁄32
½	1 1⁄16	¼	1⅝	9⁄32	2	⅜
9⁄16	1 3⁄16	9⁄32	1⅝	5⁄16	2	13⁄32
⅝	1 5⁄16	5⁄16	1⅝	11⁄32	2	7⁄16
¾	1 9⁄16	⅜	1⅝	13⁄32	2	½
⅞	1 13⁄16	7⁄16	1⅝	15⁄32	2	9⁄16
1	2 1⁄16	½	1⅝	17⁄32	2	⅝

household appliances, models and experimental apparatus, instruments and in units having parts that must be easily assembled and disassembled in use, or for substitution or replacement. Machine screws come in a wide range of sizes from 0-80 up, are threaded both coarse and fine, and lengths and diameters are held to close dimensions.

42

Stove Bolts

"Stove" bolts acquired the name a long time ago and it stuck, even though their use has diversified widely from the purpose for which they were originally designed, that of fasteners in the assembly of stoves. Now they are perhaps among the most widely used fasteners where it is necessary to hold parts together with small bolts. They have slotted heads, like common wood screws, which come either flat or round. They are available in diameters from $\frac{5}{32}$ to $\frac{1}{2}$ in. and in lengths from $\frac{3}{8}$ to 6 in. Stove bolts are not precision-made, being manufactured by upsetting and swaging processes, and the threads generally are rolled rather than die-cut. On the shorter lengths the threads are rolled the full body length. On longer bolts threads may vary from 1 to 2 in. in length. Nuts furnished with stove bolts are ordinarily square, but, any nut tapped with a coarse thread may be used.

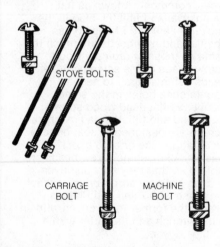

STOVE BOLTS

CARRIAGE BOLT   MACHINE BOLT

Stove bolts usually are carried in stock in standard sizes. Intermediate or extra-length bolts are often available on special order if not stocked. Machine and carriage bolts are ordinarily made with full-diameter shanks. The standard sizes generally are available at any well-stocked hardware store

Hole Size

In wood the diameter of the hole should be the same as that of the bolt. This assures a snug fit and offsets any tendency of the parts to work loose. In metal it is a common practice to drill bolt holes about $\frac{1}{64}$ to $\frac{1}{32}$ in. oversize so that when the holes are brought into register the bolt will slip easily into place. If holes are drilled the same size as the bolt it may be necessary to tap it rather forcefully. This can swage or upset the threads, making the nut difficult to start.

TO DETERMINE DIAMETER, MEASURE AND COMPARE WITH CHART

TO DETERMINE THREAD, COUNT THE THREADS IN 1"

Above, methods of determining diameter of body and number of threads per inch with ruler

Length of Bolt

Length of the bolt ordinarily should be such that all the threads of the nut engage—with perhaps two or three threads over—when the nut is drawn tight. Of course, you may not always have at hand a bolt, or bolts, that meet this ideal specification. But don't use a bolt of any size that's a thread or two short of full engagement with the nut when the latter is tightened. It might loosen or strip and let you down at some critical time later on. Better to use a bolt that's too long, cutting the excess off the threaded end if clearance is a problem. If you do have occasion to reduce the length of a bolt by cutting off a portion of the threaded end, cut it as nearly square as possible freehand. Then file the end smooth and bevel, or "break" it slightly with a file so that the nut will "take" the threads easily. Avoid use of bolts with damaged threads.

WASHERS

Outside Dia.	Size of Hole	Thickness Wire Gauge	Size of Bolt
$\frac{9}{16}$"	$\frac{1}{4}$"	No. 18	$\frac{3}{16}$"
$\frac{3}{4}$"	$\frac{5}{16}$"	No. 16	$\frac{1}{4}$"
$\frac{7}{8}$"	$\frac{3}{8}$"	No. 16	$\frac{5}{16}$"
1"	$\frac{7}{16}$"	No. 14	$\frac{3}{8}$"
$1\frac{1}{4}$"	$\frac{1}{2}$"	No. 14	$\frac{7}{16}$"
$1\frac{3}{8}$"	$\frac{9}{16}$"	No. 12	$\frac{1}{2}$"
$1\frac{1}{2}$"	$\frac{5}{8}$"	No. 12	$\frac{9}{16}$"
$1\frac{3}{4}$"	$\frac{11}{16}$"	No. 10	$\frac{5}{8}$"
2"	$\frac{13}{16}$"	No. 9	$\frac{3}{4}$"
$2\frac{1}{4}$"	$\frac{15}{16}$"	No. 8	$\frac{7}{8}$"
$2\frac{1}{2}$"	$1\frac{1}{16}$"	No. 8	1"
$2\frac{3}{4}$"	$1\frac{1}{4}$"	No. 8	$1\frac{1}{8}$"
3"	$1\frac{3}{8}$"	No. 8	$1\frac{1}{4}$"
$3\frac{1}{4}$"	$1\frac{1}{2}$"	No. 7	$1\frac{3}{8}$"
$3\frac{1}{2}$"	$1\frac{5}{8}$"	No. 7	$1\frac{1}{2}$"
$3\frac{3}{4}$"	$1\frac{3}{4}$"	No. 7	$1\frac{5}{8}$"
4"	$1\frac{7}{8}$"	No. 7	$1\frac{3}{4}$"
$4\frac{1}{4}$"	2"	No. 7	$1\frac{7}{8}$"
$4\frac{1}{2}$"	$2\frac{1}{8}$"	No. 7	2"
$4\frac{3}{4}$"	$2\frac{3}{8}$"	No. 5	$2\frac{1}{4}$"
5"	$2\frac{5}{8}$"	No. 4	$2\frac{1}{2}$"
$5\frac{1}{4}$"	$2\frac{7}{8}$"	No. 3	$2\frac{3}{4}$"
$5\frac{1}{2}$"	$3\frac{1}{8}$"	No. 2	3"

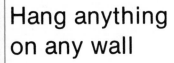

Hang anything on any wall

More and more, the walls of our homes are being put to work. Today we hang dozens of things from walls — and new fasteners have been developed for specific jobs.

Yet many homeowners aren't even familiar with the old standbys, such as toggle and "Molly" bolts. A comprehensive "selector chart" is needed on all wall fasteners, old and new, and on the next three pages you'll find just that.

In most homes, there will be hollow walls above grade and a poured or block wall in the basement. In hollow walls you want a fastener that passes through the plaster or drywall face (or the wall of cinder block or hollow tile) and spreads out to anchor against the back. In solid walls, you want a fastener that holds by expanding against the sides of the hole you sink it into, whether in concrete, brick or stone.

Two additional considerations determine your choice of fastener: the weight of the fixture you're hanging, and the type of load it presents. A *light* load is under 10 lbs., (picture frames, pin-up lamps, metal soap dishes) while a load of 25 lbs. or more is *heavy*. A *shear* load is one which exerts a straight-down pull (such close-to-the-wall items as mirrors or wall clocks) while *combination* loads exert an outward pull as well (shelves, cabinets), and require stronger anchorage. *Dead* loads, where the pull is constant, need less anchorage than *shock* loads which must withstand sudden impact or increased weight, and *vibration*

loads (such as air conditioners) call for special treatment — usually a fastener that can be retightened.

We've listed those "Load in Concrete" figures only to provide a comparison between types of fasteners, as quoted by the manufacturers, these figures represent test loads in "first-quality" concrete — not safe working loads. The latter are usually calculated at one-fourth test load. When in doubt, use more fasteners or a heavier-duty type. Overfastening can't hurt.

Except for a couple of driven types listed, fasteners must be set into a drilled hole. A carbide-tipped masonry bit in an electric drill (particularly a variable-speed type) makes fast work of this in plaster, ceramic tile, brick and concrete. Large-diameter masonry anchors, however, call for hand-hammering with a star drill.

To select the right length hollow-wall fastener, you must know the thickness of the surface wall. You can determine this by drilling a small trial hole at the mounting location and inserting a crochet hook or sturdy wire with a hook bent at one end. Catch the hook against the back of the wall and jamb your thumb against the face of the wall. Back the hook out and measure between its lip and your tumbnail. This is the thickness the fastener must penetrate before its anchoring device can function. Where the fastener must pass through the mounting plate you must add that thickness, too.

"All-Purpose" Fasteners

	PLASTIC ANCHOR	NYLON EXPANSION (NYCAM)	NYLON DRIVE ANCHOR	NEOPRENE SLEEVE (WELL-NUT)
		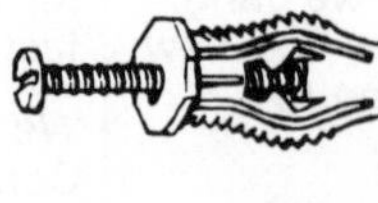	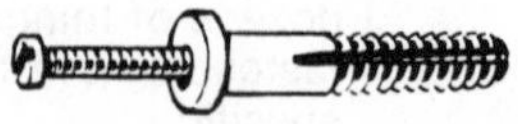	
SIZE RANGE AND LOAD CAPACITY	Screw* Size / Anchor No. & Length / Holding Power 4, 6, 8 / No. 1, $\frac{7}{8}$'' / 650 10, 12 / No. 2, 1'' / 850 14, 16 / No. 3, 1$\frac{1}{2}$'' / 1075 *Although most brands come in three sizes, the recommended screw ranges differ. Where screws are not packaged with the anchors, use size recommended on package. Jordan offers a 2$\frac{1}{2}$'' length for $\frac{3}{8}$'' lag screws.	One size (about 1'' long, requiring a $\frac{3}{8}$'' hole) serves all applications, comes with 1$\frac{1}{8}$'' self-tapping screw. Shear load tests: 280 lbs. in cement block, 50 in $\frac{3}{8}$'' plasterboard.	Dia. / Lengths $\frac{1}{4}$'' / $\frac{3}{4}$, 1, 1$\frac{1}{2}$'' $\frac{3}{16}$'' / 1, 1$\frac{1}{2}$'' Both Tap-It (U.S. Expansion Bolt) and Jif-Eze (Jordan) come in choice of head style (round, flat, mushroom) and not all lengths avbl. in all head styles. Shear tests: 800 lbs. in solid wall, 365 in hollow.	One standard size: shank dia. is $\frac{1}{4}$''; length $\frac{15}{16}$. Load in concrete: 370; in brick: 440; in cinder block: 470. Over a dozen other dia.-length combinations avbl. on special order (without screws).
INSTALLATION PROCEDURES	Except for larger sizes, anchors are molded in strips; break one off and force into hole of size recommended on card; insert screw through fixture and drive into anchor.	Drill hole at least 1$\frac{1}{2}$'' deep, pinch anchor between fingers and tap in place with hammer. Insert screw through fixture and tighten.	Insert fastener through fixture's mounting hole and push into wall hole. Tap nail until its head seats against fastener's.	Drill hole same diameter as neoprene shank (in solid wall, drill just deeper than length of screw); push Well-Nut in, up to flange, hold fixture against it while tightening screw through mounting hole. Shank bulges as nut draws up, forms rivethead against back of hollow wall or pressure fit in solid wall.
	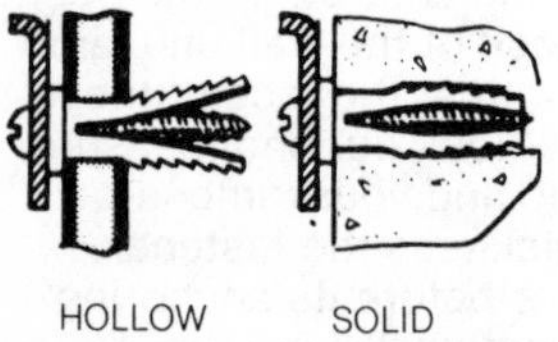 HOLLOW SOLID	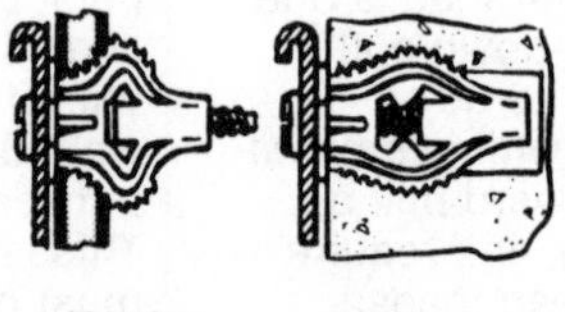 HOLLOW SOLID	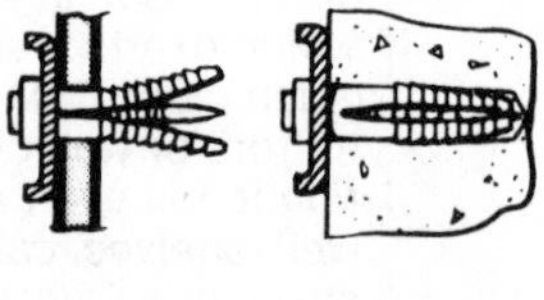 HOLLOW SOLID	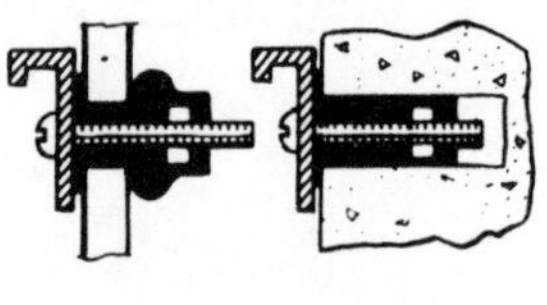 HOLLOW SOLID
RECOMMENDED USES	Mounting any item normally held with wood screws — large pictures, mirrors, shelf brackets, drapery hardware, kitchen and bath accessories, awnings, mailboxes, Peg-Board hang-up panels... on concrete, tile, brick and hollow plaster walls.	Mounting any item such as drapery hardware, brackets and fixtures to any type wall: plaster, drywall, brick, marble, concrete, cinder block, stone, or even wood.	Drapery hardware, shelf brackets, mirrors, pipe straps, outlet boxes — anything with mounting hole that will pass anchor — to plaster, brick, stone, tile, concrete, composition or hardboard.	Coat hooks, drapery hardware, shelf brackets, bathroom fixtures, electrical equipment, auto accessories and trim, hi-fi speakers on dry wall, tile, glass, marble, masonry, plaster, metal, or wood.
ADVANTAGES OVER OTHER TYPE	Since anchor is rustproof, it's fine for bathroom fixtures, outdoor installations. Small hole means little wall damage. Strips keep supply handy for quick use. Screw can be removed and reinserted.	One type and size of fastener for all light hanging needs. Very thin lip lets you mount flush to wall, 1-pc. nylon construction.	Average installation time: 12 seconds, compared with 25 for the simplest wood-screw anchor. Comes with nail ready for tapping.	Ideal for mounting hi-fi speakers, window fans, other installations where vibration should be dampened. Creates watertight seal, will plug leaks: insulating quality in electrical installations. Neoprene stays flexible so fastener is removable, reusable.
DISADVANTAGES	Hole size is critical — anchor must fit snug, and is only as good as the wall material. For light shear load only. Won't hold against much horizontal pull, especially in crumbly masonry.	Fairly large hole required; not satisfactory in hollow wall more than $\frac{3}{8}$'' thick, so won't expand behind most plaster walls.	Fixture can't be removed without withdrawing entire anchor, as well. Mounting hole in fixture must be at least $\frac{3}{16}$'' in dia. White nylon head shows around nail. More expensive than plain plastic anchor.	Standard size not suitable to all situations (hollow walls can only be $\frac{3}{8}$ to $\frac{9}{16}$'' thick). Over-tightening ruins fastener.

Masonry Wall Fasteners

| FIBER ANCHOR (LEAD CORE) | LEAD SCREW ANCHOR | LAG SCREW SHIELD | NAIL ANCHORS |

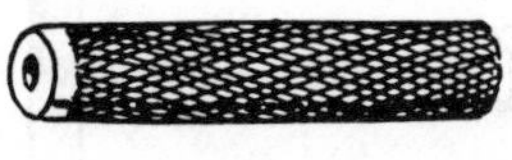

SIZE RANGE AND LOAD CAPACITY

Fiber Anchor (Lead Core)

Screw Size	Anchor Lengths	Load in Concrete
5-6	⅝, ¾, 1	550
7-8	⅝, ¾, 1, 1¼, 1½, 2	885
9-10	¾, 1, 1¼, 1½, 2	1150
11 12	¾, 1, 1¼, 1½, 2	1525
14	1, 1¼, 1½, 2	1590
16	1, 1½, 2	2150
20	1, 1½, 2	2830
22	2	3500

Lead Screw Anchor

Screw Size	Anchor Lengths	Load in Concrete
6-8	¾, 1, 1½	to 400
10-12-14	1, 1½	to 900
16-18	1, 1½	to 3000
20-22-24	1¾ or 2	1600 up

Lag Screw Shield

Screw Size	Shield Lengths	Load in Concrete
¼	1, 1½	450, 600
5/16	1¼, 1¾	800, 1200
⅜	1¾, 2½	1200, 2000
7/16	2¼ only	1650
½	2, 3	2000, 3000
⅝	2 or 2½, * 3½	2500, 3500
¾	2 or 2½, 3½ or 3¾ *	3000, 4000

*Long Standard Sizes differ with brands

Nail Anchors

Shield Dia. (Inches)	Shield Length (Inches)	Working Load (Pounds)
3/16	⅞	375
	1¼	110
¼	1	200
	1¼	240
	1½	325
5/16	1¼	300
	1¾	350
	2¼	375
	2¾	375
⅜	2	450
	3¼	485
½	2¼	525
	3½	625

INSTALLATION PROCEDURES

Fiber Anchor: Use drill, plug and screw of same size. Clean hole of loose particles. Insert plug just below surface, drive screw through fixture into lead core. Only threaded section should enter plug, so use proper length plug, recess in deeper hole if necessary.

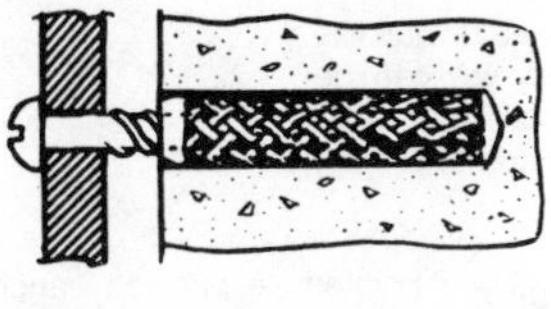

Lead Screw Anchor: Screw length = thickness of mounting plate + length of anchor + ¼". Drill hole ¼" deeper than anchor, set it flush with wall surface, drive screw through fixture.

Lag Screw Shield: Drill hole same size as outside dia. of shield. Set in shield flush with or slightly below surface, insert screw through fixture and into shield, which expands as screw enters.

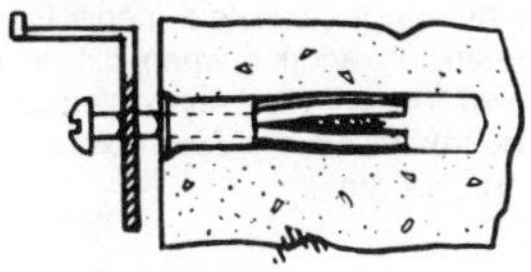

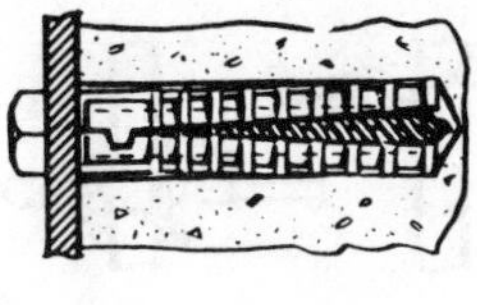

Nail Anchors: Drill hole same dia. as shield, insert anchor through fixture's mounting hole and into wall. When flange is seated firm against fixture, drive nail home with a couple blows.

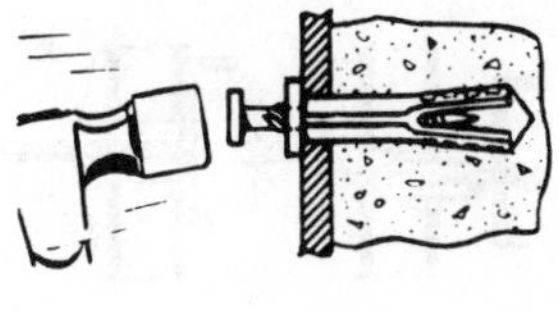

RECOMMENDED USES

Fiber Anchor: Mounting any item you'd normally attach with wood, sheet metal or lag screws (for latter, there are larger sizes than listed)—outlet and fuse boxes, mirrors, bathroom fixtures, fireplace tools, awnings, etc.

Lead Screw Anchor: Mounting any item you'd normally attach with wood, sheet metal or lag screws (for latter, there are larger sizes than listed)—outlet and fuse boxes, mirrors, bathroom fixtures, fireplace tools, awnings, etc.

Lag Screw Shield: Mounting any item too heavy for plain screws — especially to a brick wall where hole can be drilled into mortar joint without marring brick.

Nail Anchors: Light, dead loads: furring strips, pipe, metal window frames, downspouts, outlet boxes — to concrete block, brick, mortar, stone.

ADVANTAGES OVER OTHER TYPE

Fiber Anchor: Easy, inexpensive, versatile. Screw may be removed and replaced without affecting anchorage. Once screw is in, plug grips wall firmly.

Lead Screw Anchor: Flared end prevents loss of fixture through drilled hole in concrete block, etc. also makes it easier to start screw.

Lag Screw Shield: Heavy ribs assure powerful gripping action. Choice of long or short for each screw dia. lets you minimize drilling in hard masonry, or use long size for more strength in weak masonry and brick.

Nail Anchors: Fast — small hole means quicker drilling — and economical. Choose aluminum type for outdoor jobs, spiral nail type for vibrating loads.

DISADVANTAGES

Fiber Anchor: Hole size is more critical than with most fasteners. Holding power depends on strength of wall material: poor in crumbly concrete, plaster.

Lead Screw Anchor: Size for size, less holding power than fiber anchor; hole in wall must be exact fit.

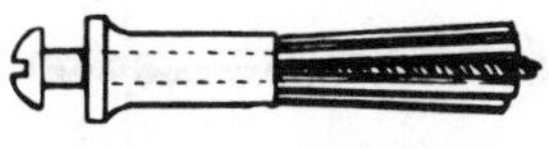

Lag Screw Shield: Requires fairly large masonry bit, greater installation time since screw must be driven with wrench.

Nail Anchors: Limited holding power; fixture can't be removed once nail is set. Mounting hole must be large enough to pass shield. Except for one type with spiral nail, poor resistance to vibration or jarring.

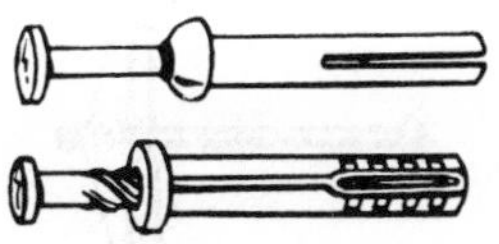

For Hollow Walls Only

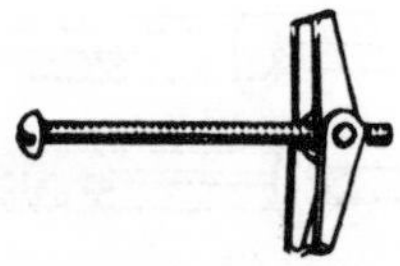

TOGGLE BOLT	EXPANSION BOLT

SIZE RANGE AND LOAD CAPACITY

Bolt Length	Diam.	Load (lbs.)
2, 3, 4''	⅛''	200
2,3,4,5,6''	³⁄₁₆''	450
3,4,5,6''	¼''	925
3,4,5,6''	⁵⁄₁₆''	1150
3,4,5,6''	⅜''	1500
4,6,8''	½''	1800

*Some makes have 2½, 3½ & 4½''
as well.

Size*	Overall Length	For Wall Thickness	Load
XS	¾-⅞''	0 to ¼''	200
MS	1-1½''	¹⁄₁₆ to ½''	to
S	1½''-2¼''	⅛'' to ¾''	500
L	2-2¾''	⅝'' to 1¼''	Difs
XL	2½''-3½''	1¼'' to 1¾''	with
			make

*There is no industry standard so
these are compromise listings. Some
brands have each length in several
diameters.

INSTALLATION PROCEDURES

Insert bolt through fixture and spin the toggle head on several turns. Fold wings and push them through proper size hole in wall. Tighten bolt to draw wings snug against back of wall.

Insert unit in drilled hole, tap to embed cap teeth in wall surface, turn screw to draw split sleeve into "spider" against back of wall; remove screw and reinsert after passing through mounting hole of fixture.

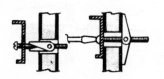
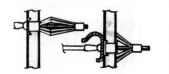

RECOMMENDED USES

Large hanging cabinets, heavy-duty shelf standards, wall radiators or vent fans, bathroom grip bars.

Mirrors, wall cabinets, lamps and clocks, adjustable shelf brackets, window cornices, shades and blinds, coat hooks.

ADVANTAGES OVER OTHER TYPE

Simple, immediate-action installation, great strength for combination loads. Alignment of mounting holes with wall holes isn't critical.

Requires smaller hole than toggle, centers bolt precisely. Remains in place for reuse if fixture is removed. Bolt is easily inserted through fixture *after* positioning on wall.

DISADVANTAGES

Requires large insert hole to pass wings, so bolt "floats", does not position fixture precisely. Mounting plate must be big enough to hide hole. If fixture is removed, wings drop off, are lost in wall (See Variations). Installation awkward where fixture requires several bolts, since all must be inserted through fixture before positioning.

Slower installation (unless special tool is used). Less strength, since smaller bolt and thinner anchor metal is involved. Mounting holes must exactly align with fastener—tricky where several are involved.

Variations and Improvements

TOGGLE BOLTS

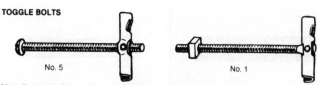

No. 5   No. 1

Not all standard types have spring-loaded wings. Gravity types shown above have "tumble" heads, pivoted off-center, creating strong, one-piece bearing bar. No. 5 is otherwise identical to a spring-wing, but type No. 1 has head riveted directly to stud.

Recent innovations in toggle design include spring-wing with teeth (left) that bite into back of wall to keep nut positioned so bolt can be removed and replaced. Simplified tumbler, below, is lowest-price toggle, with S-head in constant tension so bolt never loosens up.

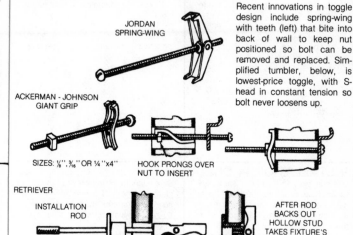

JORDAN SPRING-WING

ACKERMAN - JOHNSON GIANT GRIP

SIZES: ⅛'', ³⁄₁₆'' OR ¼''x4''

HOOK PRONGS OVER NUT TO INSERT

RETRIEVER

INSTALLATION ROD

T-NUT TURNS ONTO STUD

SIZES ¼'', ⁵⁄₁₆'' OR ⅜'' DIA. TO 4'' LENGTH

AFTER ROD BACKS OUT HOLLOW STUD TAKES FIXTURE'S MOUNTING BOLT

As name implies, here's a toggle that stays locked in wall like an expansion anchor when fixture is removed, yet can be retrieved for reuse by reinserting installation rod. Rod makes long bolt unnecessary. Also comes with longer stud to project from wall for nut.

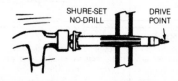

SHURE-SET NO-DRILL   DRIVE POINT

Pointed expansion anchor eliminates drilling step. Just drive it through wall till flange teeth embed, then turn screw to expand sleeve as with standard type. Ideal for softboard, other drywall.

New addition to plastic anchor line has ⅜-in.-thick flange for mounting perforated storage panels. When shoulder seats against wall, flange automatically — without separate spacers — creates proper clearance for insertion of hanging hooks.

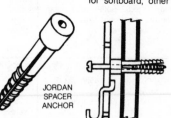

JORDAN SPACER ANCHOR

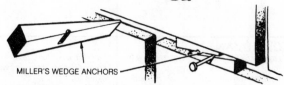

MILLER'S WEDGE ANCHORS

For any laid masonry with recessed mortar lines. Two (or more) lead tapers are wedged between bricks or stones, nail driven into best edge-notch for positioning fixture. No damage to masonry, and anchors can be removed without a trace by withdrawing nail.

Cabinet hardware

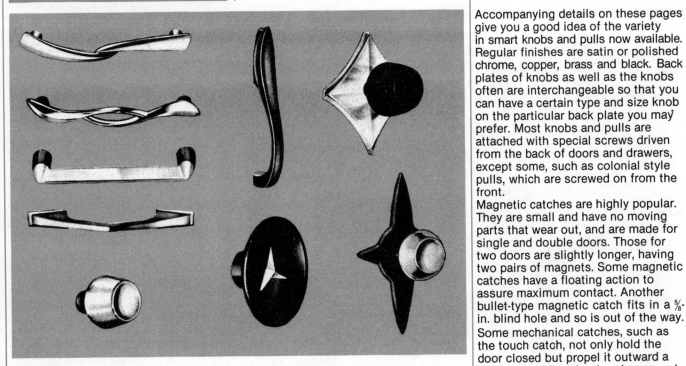

Accompanying details on these pages give you a good idea of the variety in smart knobs and pulls now available. Regular finishes are satin or polished chrome, copper, brass and black. Back plates of knobs as well as the knobs often are interchangeable so that you can have a certain type and size knob on the particular back plate you may prefer. Most knobs and pulls are attached with special screws driven from the back of doors and drawers, except some, such as colonial style pulls, which are screwed on from the front.

Magnetic catches are highly popular. They are small and have no moving parts that wear out, and are made for single and double doors. Those for two doors are slightly longer, having two pairs of magnets. Some magnetic catches have a floating action to assure maximum contact. Another bullet-type magnetic catch fits in a $\frac{5}{8}$-in. blind hole and so is out of the way.

Some mechanical catches, such as the touch catch, not only hold the door closed but propel it outward a few inches when the door is pressed lightly. This is an advantage on flush cabinet doors having no pulls or knobs, nor recessed finger holds. There also is a combined pull-and-spring-action catch which is reversible for right or left-hand doors, The catch releases by finger pressure on the upper end of the pull. The polyethylene friction catch with a ball-head wood screw for silent action comes at low cost and is quite efficient for small doors. Noise-less catches have a spring-cushioned rubber roller which cradles in the strike and prevents the door from striking against the frame. Another smooth-operating, silent catch is similar but has two rubber rollers that move with a floating finger action to grip and release the strike. There's also a cabinet door closer which closes small doors automatically.

Exposed hinges should match other door hardware in color and design, especially the colonial-style hinges. Some of these have a separately attached strap. Many hinges are made to fit various types of doors — overlapping doors, overlapping-rabbeted doors, and flush doors.

Most cabinet hinges are reversed to fit either right or left-hand doors. Non-reversible hinges are purchased for right or left-hand doors as for example the various types of partially

SEMI-CONCEALED HINGES

 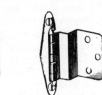  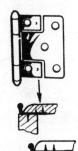

OVERLAPPING DOOR	OVERLAPPING DOOR WITH OFFSET	FLUSH DOOR	OVERLAPPING DOOR

SURFACE HINGES

SEPARATE STRAP

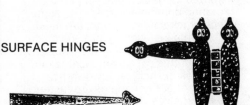

TWO-TONE IN BRASS, BLACK AND COPPER

IN CHROMIUM BRONZE AND COPPER

IN BLACK AND COPPER

OFFSET

FLUSH

ALUMINUM SLIDING-DOOR PANEL TRACK

48

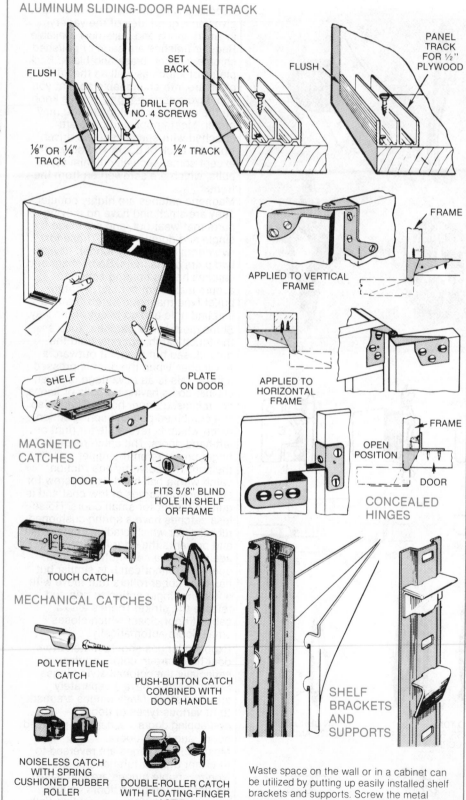

FLUSH

SET BACK

FLUSH

PANEL TRACK FOR ½" PLYWOOD

DRILL FOR NO. 4 SCREWS

⅛" OR ¼" TRACK

½" TRACK

FRAME

APPLIED TO VERTICAL FRAME

SHELF

PLATE ON DOOR

APPLIED TO HORIZONTAL FRAME

MAGNETIC CATCHES

DOOR

FITS 5/8" BLIND HOLE IN SHELF OR FRAME

FRAME

OPEN POSITION

DOOR

CONCEALED HINGES

TOUCH CATCH

MECHANICAL CATCHES

POLYETHYLENE CATCH

PUSH-BUTTON CATCH COMBINED WITH DOOR HANDLE

SHELF BRACKETS AND SUPPORTS

NOISELESS CATCH WITH SPRING CUSHIONED RUBBER ROLLER

DOUBLE-ROLLER CATCH WITH FLOATING-FINGER ACTION

Waste space on the wall or in a cabinet can be utilized by putting up easily installed shelf brackets and supports. Screw the metal strips to the wall and snap brackets in place.

or wholly concealed hinges. Some are made for attachment to the top and bottom corners of doors. A shallow mortise in the door edges produces maximum concealment.

Sliding cabinet doors of glass or of other material require tracks to hold them in position and to permit by-passing with sufficient clearance. For lightweight doors you can use wood, plastic or metal tracks, as shown, but for heavier doors tracks with rollers or ball bearings are best.

Heavily loaded drawers that are difficult to open and close can be transformed into easy-sliding, fingertip-control drawers by using specially designed guides and rollers now available. Some guides have plain rollers and others have ball-bearing rollers. One design is such that when drawers are released when still open a few inches they will close automatically. Guides on drawers are either installed at the sides or underneath, and require a specified clearance between drawer and framing. One type consists of a single guide installed centrally under a drawer, and two rollers installed on the frame. Another type carries the drawer entirely on rollers. All these units have variously styled mountings to suit different drawer installations.

One good way to utilize waste space is to install adjustable shelves, using adjustable brackets and supports.

As a substitute for permanent shelves in corner base cabinets, where stored articles are usually hard to reach, you can install rotating shelves, or concealed lazy susans. There are three methods of installation. Where the corner is accessible through a single door set at an angle, circular-metal shelves carried on brackets on a rotating column are used. The same type brackets and column are used where the installation must be made in cabinets that corner at a 90-deg. angle. In this case a segment is cut out of each shelf, and two vertical doors set at right angles are fastened to the shelves. The doors fit flush with the cabinet front when the susan is closed and move inside the cabinet as the shelves turn. In the first arrangement it is also possible to rotate the shelves on small individual rollers which are mounted on blocks screwed to the frame. Regular shelves can be arranged to slide outward from other base cabinets, by using easily installed metal-shelf slides.

Choose the right hinge

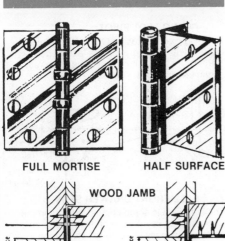

FULL MORTISE　　　**HALF SURFACE**

WOOD JAMB

Clearance

FULL MORTISE　　　**HALF SURFACE**

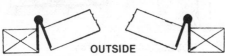

OUTSIDE

Notice that on doors opening out, the left-hand door takes a left-hand hinge and the right a right-hand hinge. On doors opening in, the hand is reversed

LEFT HAND　　　**RIGHT HAND**

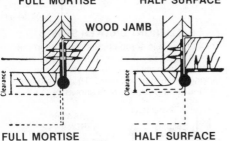

Pins also come in a variety of ornamental heads, or caps. Such hinges are commonly used on the finest cabinet work. There are various other cap styles for practical applications as in the sketches below

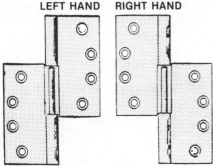

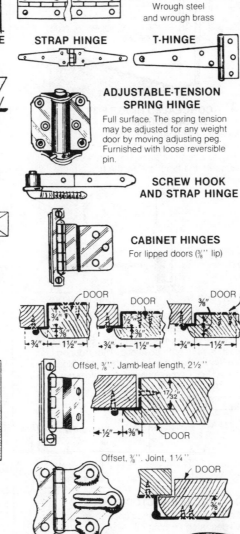

DOUBLE-ACTING FLOOR HINGE

Ball bearing. Holds the door open at 95 deg. For 1¼'' to 1¾'' doors. Beveled edge. Reversible side.

CONTINUOUS HINGE
Wrough steel and wrough brass

STRAP HINGE　　　**T-HINGE**

ADJUSTABLE-TENSION SPRING HINGE

Full surface. The spring tension may be adjusted for any weight door by moving adjusting peg. Furnished with loose reversible pin.

SCREW HOOK AND STRAP HINGE

CABINET HINGES
For lipped doors (⅜'' lip)

DOOR　DOOR　⅜''　DOOR
¾''　½''　¾''　⅜''
¾'' · 1½''　¾'' · 1½''　¾'' · 1½''

Offset, ⅜''. Jamb-leaf length, 2½''

17/32''

½''　⅜''　DOOR

Offset, ⅜''. Joint, 1¼''

DOOR
⅜''

Basically a hinge is a simple item consisting of two metal leaves and a pivot pin. It's commonly known as a butt hinge. One of the leaves ordinarily is attached to a fixed member such as a door jamb or the back of a box or chest; the other leaf is attached to the member that is to swing outward or upward from an opening, or pivot from the bottom or top of an opening.

Hinges of the common types are available with fixed and loose pins and in a wide range of pin styles and leaf shapes. Some are made as reproductions of old types such as the rattail, butterfly and those originally hand-forged at the fire. The latter are finished in attractive simulations of hand-hammered iron. Others are of advanced contemporary design adapting them to use with modern fixtures and furnishings.

Selecting the hinge for the job it is to do is important if it is to give satisfactory service. There are seven points to consider:

1. The type of hinge required.
2. The type of metal required or desired.
3. The finish desired.
4. The hinge weight and bearing structure.
5. The size of the hinge required.
6. The pin style desired.
7. The "hand" of the hinge.

This list is not as imposing as it may appear. In general, common door hinges are of four types: the full-mortise, half mortise, half surface and full surface. Again, in general, you have a choice of three groups of hinge weights and bearing structures; regular weight with plain bearing; extra heavy with plain bearing; and regular weight with ball bearings—that's right, ball bearings.

In cabinet hinges you can just about write your own ticket. You can buy a hinge to swing almost anything you're of a mind to hang—lipped doors, flush doors, slab or overlay doors, with hinges either concealed, visible or partly visible.

Hinges commonly come in five metals: steel, stainless steel, brass, bronze and aluminum. The latter four are rustproof and corrosion-resistant. Hinges of ordinary steel, a ferrous metal, are not corrosion-resistant or rustproof but have greatest strength

49

Nine hinges you should know about

1 SELF-BALANCING LID HINGE
Dual-purpose unit is spring loaded to support the lid at various angles and prevent its slamming shut. It permits full use of the cabinet interior and eliminates the need for conventional hinging. Exterior mounting needs no mortise. If light lid requires only one support, use companion hinge, without a spring

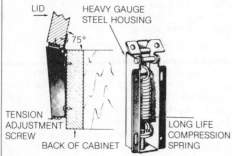

LID
HEAVY GAUGE STEEL HOUSING
75°
TENSION ADJUSTMENT SCREW
LONG LIFE COMPRESSION SPRING
BACK OF CABINET

50

and wearability. Hinges of steel should be protected with paint if exposed to weathering. Common cabinet and door hinges are also supplied plated.
There are also special-purpose hinges, such as two-way door and panel hinges, spring-actuated hinges that close the door when you release it, and hinges that hold the door open until released. It's a common practice (and generally recommended) that all outside doors of 1¾-in. thickness be hung on three hinges rather than a pair.

Of course it's important that the pins of the three hinges be in precise alignment. Most hardware dealers will give you a simple template with which you mark the location of the hinge leaves on both the door and jamb. You also punch-mark the location of the screws with the same template. There also are special tools available for marking and locating hinge mortises and screw holes on both door and jamb.

But as a do-it-yourselfer you rely on the simple template and careful workmanship. Good fitting calls for neatly cut mortises in both door and jamb. That means you work with a razor-sharp chisel and a light hand on the hammer; and you take special care to locate screw holes exactly on center. Hinges (except exterior steel ones) should not be painted, and they should be lubricated occasionally. Lift the pin slightly and run a single drop of light oil around it. Then tap it lightly back in place.

2 RISING-PIN HINGE
Got a problem where a door opens over a thick carpet, a loose runner or a warped floor? Don't trim it off or leave a gap—just hang it on spiral-barrel hinges that lift the door as it opens

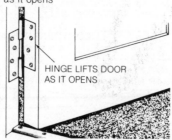

HINGE LIFTS DOOR AS IT OPENS

3 CONCEALED HINGE FOR LAY-ON DOORS
Ideal for chipboard or plywood doors, this hinge is fully hidden when closed, opens 90 deg. to a positive stop. The notch can be plugged and taped below the box after installation

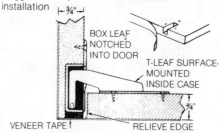

¾"
BOX LEAF NOTCHED INTO DOOR
T-LEAF SURFACE-MOUNTED INSIDE CASE
¾"
VENEER TAPE
RELIEVE EDGE

4 FLUSH JOINT FOR DROP-LEAF HINGE
Invisible hinge offers easy mortising and a flush joint in both positions. The dropped leaf sits under the edge of the table and hides its own edge. Comes only as in photo, so a pair is formed with two as shown

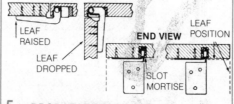

LEAF RAISED
END VIEW
LEAF POSITION
LEAF DROPPED
SLOT MORTISE

5 DROP-LEAF STOP PIVOT
Combination hinge and support provides sure 90-deg. stop for light fall flaps, consists of two separate parts that fit together during mounting. Long leaf is recessed in edge of flap; other is screwed to inside face of side. Stud on the first strikes shoulder on second

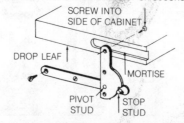

SCREW INTO SIDE OF CABINET
DROP LEAF
MORTISE
PIVOT STUD
STOP STUD

6 RISING-SLOT PIVOT
Climbing pivot spares you having to relieve edge of leaf for clearance. As leaf drops, slanted slot forces it up, but brings it to rest in alignment with fixed shelf

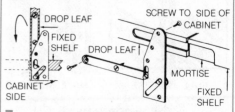

DROP LEAF
SCREW TO SIDE OF CABINET
FIXED SHELF
DROP LEAF
CABINET SIDE
MORTISE
FIXED SHELF

7 FALL-FRONT DRAWER STAY
Trick drawers in some chests slide out in the conventional way, then drop their fronts for shelf-type access to contents. Here's the locking hinge-stay you need. Thumb release lets the front pivot down as shown

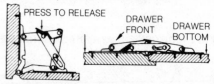

PRESS TO RELEASE
DRAWER FRONT
DRAWER BOTTOM

8 DOUBLE-ARM BAR STAY
This shouldn't really be called a hinge, since the flaps must be hinged separately. Bracket opens both front and top flaps of the bar cabinet at once while lifting the shelf forward for easy access. Only top bar of bracket is anchored to the cabinet; the bar that parallels it is at an angle to accept the shelf

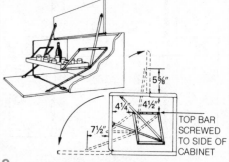

5⅝"
4¼" 4½"
7½"
TOP BAR SCREWED TO SIDE OF CABINET

9 LAZY-TONG FLAP HINGE
Insoluble problem: hanging a flap so it tucks flush under the table edge yet rises snug against that edge, using an invisible hinge that needs no mortising. It's solved with a pair of these plus a pull-out support of wood or metal

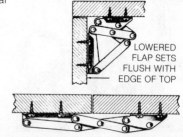

LOWERED FLAP SETS FLUSH WITH EDGE OF TOP

The right drill sizes

Of all the common tools, twist drills are most difficult to specify because they are sized in three different ways:

Some sizes are expressed in *numbers,* some in *letters,* and some in *fractions* (representing fractions of an inch). To add to the problem, the three categories are mixed together.

However, the sizing chart at the right should unscramble this for you. It shows, from top to bottom of succeeding columns, the twist drill sizes from the smallest to the largest, with their corresponding decimal equivalents. Unless you're a machinist, you won't be using all of these sizes, and if you're an average homeowner you probably can get along with those listed by fractions. However, the number and letter sizes *are* available if you want to do really precision work.

And that's the kind of work you must do if you plan on tapping (threading a hole) into metal. The chart at the lower right shows you the twist drill to use to drill the hole in preparation for tapping.

As a general guide, the larger the twist drill, the slower you should operate it.

DECIMAL EQUIVALENTS
of fraction, wire gauge and letter size drills

Drill Size	Decimal	Drill Size	Decimal	Drill Size	Decimal	Drill Size	Decimal	Drill Size	Decimal	Drill Size	Decimal
80	.0135	54	.0550	30	.1285	6	.2040	21/64	.3281	5/8	.6250
79	.0145	53	.0595	29	.1360	5	.2055	Q	.3320	41/64	.6406
1/64	.0156	1/16	.0625	28	.1405	4	.2090	R	.3390	21/32	.6562
78	.0160	52	.0635	9/64	.1406	3	.2130	11/32	.3438	43/64	.6719
77	.0180	51	.0670	27	.1440	7/32	.2188	S	.3480	11/16	.6875
76	.0200	50	.0700	26	.1470	2	.2210	T	.3580	45/64	.7031
75	.0210	49	.0730	25	.1495	1	.2280	23/64	.3594	23/32	.7188
74	.0225	48	.0760	24	.1520	A	.2340	U	.3680	47/64	.7344
73	.0240	5/64	.0781	23	.1540	15/64	.2344	3/8	.3750	3/4	.7500
72	.0250	47	.0785	5/32	.1562	B	.2380	V	.3770	49/64	.7656
71	.0260	46	.0810	22	.1570	C	.2420	W	.3860	25/32	.7812
70	.0280	45	.0820	21	.1590	D	.2460	25/64	.3906	51/64	.7969
69	.0292	44	.0860	20	.1610	1/4	.2500	X	.3970	13/16	.8125
68	.0310	43	.0890	19	.1660	E	.2500	Y	.4040	53/64	.8281
1/32	.0312	42	.0935	18	.1695	F	.2570	13/32	.4062	27/32	.8438
67	.0320	3/32	.0938	11/64	.1719	G	.2610	Z	.4130	55/64	.8594
66	.0330	41	.0960	17	.1730	17/64	.2656	27/64	.4219	7/8	.8750
65	.0350	40	.0980	16	.1770	H	.2660	7/16	.4375	57/64	.8906
64	.0360	39	.0995	15	.1800	I	.2720	29/64	.4531	29/32	.9062
63	.0370	38	.1015	14	.1820	J	.2770	15/32	.4688	59/64	.9219
62	.0380	37	.1040	13	.1850	K	.2810	31/64	.4844	15/16	.9375
61	.0390	36	.1065	3/16	.1875	9/32	.2812	1/2	.5000	61/64	.9531
60	.0400	7/64	.1094	12	.1890	L	.2900	33/64	.5156	31/32	.9688
59	.0410	35	.1100	11	.1910	M	.2950	17/32	.5312	63/64	.9844
58	.0420	34	.1110	10	.1935	19/64	.2969	35/64	.5469	1	1.000
57	.0430	33	.1130	9	.1960	N	.3020	9/16	.5625		
56	.0465	32	.1160	8	.1990	5/16	.3125	37/64	.5781		
3/64	.0469	31	.1200	7	.2010	O	.3160	19/32	.5938		
55	.0520	1/8	.1250	13/64	.2031	P	.3230	39/64	.6094		

Twist drills, for general use, should be sharpened at an angle of 59° as shown

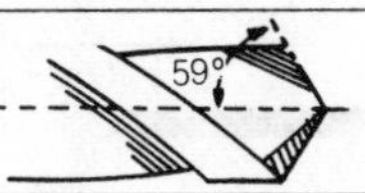

Wood-Boring Bits

Size Inches	Length Inches
3/8-in.	6½-in.
1/2-in.	6½-in.
5/8-in.	6½-in.
3/4-in.	6½-in.
7/8-in.	6½-in.
1-in.	6½-in.
1⅛-in.	6½-in.
1¼-in.	6½-in.

Masonry Drills

Size Inches	Shank Inches	Length Inches
3/16-in.	3/16-in.	4-in.
1/4-in.	1/4-in.	4-in.
1/4-in.	1/4-in.	6-in.
5/16-in.	1/4-in.	6-in.
3/8-in.	1/4-in.	6-in.
1/2-in.	1/4-in.	6-in.
1/2-in.	3/8-in.	6-in.
5/8-in.	1/2-in.	6-in.
3/4-in.	1/2-in.	6-in.

Wood or Metal Drills

Diameter Inches	Length Inches
1/16-in.	1⅞-in.
5/64-in.	2-in.
3/32-in.	2¼-in.
7/64-in.	2¼-in.
1/8-in.	2¾-in.
9/64-in.	2¾-in.
5/32-in.	3-in.
11/64-in.	3¼-in.
3/16-in.	3½-in.
13/64-in.	3⅜-in.
7/32-in.	3¾-in.
15/64-in.	3⅞-in.
1/4-in.	4-in.
9/32-in.	4½-in.
5/16-in.	4¼-in.
21/64-in.	4½-in.
11/32-in.	4½-in.
3/8-in.	5-in.
25/64-in.	5¼-in.
13/32-in.	5⅛-in.
27/64-in.	5⅝-in.
7/16-in.	5½-in.
29/64-in.	5⅝-in.
31/64-in.	5⅝-in.
1/2-in.	6-in.

TAP DRILL SIZES
based on approximately 75% full thread
National coarse and fine threads

Thread	Drill	Thread	Drill
0-80	3/64	7/16-14	U
1-64	No. 53	7/16-20	25/64
1-72	No. 53	1/2-12	27/64
2-56	No. 50	1/2-13	27/64
2-64	No. 50	1/2-20	29/64
3-48	No. 47	9/16-12	31/64
3-56	No. 45	9/16-18	33/64
4-40	No. 43	5/8-11	17/32
4-48	No. 42	5/8-18	37/64
5-40	No. 38	3/4-10	21/32
5-44	No. 37	3/4-16	11/16
6-32	No. 36	7/8-9	49/64
6-40	No. 33	7/8-14	13/16
8-32	No. 29	1-8	7/8
8-36	No. 29	1-12	59/64
10-24	No. 25	1-14	59/64
10-32	No. 21	1⅛-7	63/64
12-24	No. 16	1⅛-12	1 3/64
12-28	No. 14	1¼-7	1 7/64
1/4-20	No. 7	1¼-12	1 11/64
1/4-28	No. 3	1⅜-6	1 7/32
5/16-18	F	1⅜-12	1 19/64
5/16-24	I	1½-6	1 11/32
3/8-16	5/16	1½-12	1 27/64
3/8-24	Q	1¾-5	1 9/16

Taper pipe

Thread	Drill
1/8-27	R
1/4-18	7/16
3/8-18	37/64
1/2-14	23/32
3/4-14	59/64
1-11½	1 5/32
1¼-11½	1 1/2
1½-11½	1 47/64
2-11½	2 7/32
2½-8	2 5/8
3-8	3 1/4
3½-8	3 3/4
4-8	4 1/4

Straight pipe

Thread	Drill
1/8-27	S
1/4-18	29/64
3/8-18	19/32
1/2-14	47/64
3/4-14	15/16
1-11½	1 3/16
1¼-11½	1 33/64
1½-11½	1 3/4
2-11½	2 7/32
2½-8	2 21/32
3-8	3 9/32
3½-8	3 25/32
4-8	4 9/32

The right jig saw blade

	Blade Type	Description of Blade and Use	Type of Cut	Speed of Cut	Blade Length	Teeth per Inch
ECONOMY BLADES		BLADES FIT MOST POPULAR JIG SAWS, SABRE SAW BRANDS WITH ¼" SHANK				
	Wood Cutting Coarse	Cuts soft woods 3/4" & thicker. Canted shank provides built-in blade relief, thus helping to clear the saw dust and cool the blade. Blade material: High carbon steel.	Rough	Fastest	3"	7
	Hollow Ground	For cutting plywood up to 1" thick. Hollow ground for very smooth finish. Blade material: Heat treated high carbon steel. Straight shank.	Fine	Medium	3"	10
FOR CUTTING WOOD, PLYWOOD, MASONITE, PLASTICS, ETC.						
	Flush Cutting	Hard or soft wood over 1/4" thick. Blade material: High carbon steel. Set teeth for fast cutting.	Rough	Fast	3"	7
	Double Cutting	Most wood and fiber materials. Tooth design allows for cutting in both directions with equal speed. Blade material: High carbon steel.	Rough	Fast	3"	7
	Double Cutting	Cuts most wood and fiber materials. Tooth design allows for cutting in both directions with equal speed and quality of cut. Blade material: High carbon steel.	Medium	Medium	3"	10
	Knife Blade	For cutting leather, rubber, composition tile, cardboard, etc. Blade material: High carbon steel. Straight shank.	Smooth	Fast	3"	Knife Edge
	Scroll Cut	For cutting wood, plastic and plywood 1/4" to 1" thick. Set teeth and thin construction allows this blade to make intricate cuts and circles with radii as small as 1/8". Blade construction: High carbon steel. Straight shank.	Smooth	Medium	2-1/2"	10
	Fleam Ground	For cutting green or wet woods 1/4" to 2-1/2" thick. Fleam ground provides shredding type cutting action which is most effective in sawing hard, green or wet materials. Blade material: High carbon steel. Provides longest cutting life possible. Straight shank.	Smooth	Medium	4"	10
	Hollow Ground	For cutting plywood and finish materials 3/4" and thicker where fine finish is desirable. Hollow ground for very smooth finish on all wood products. Blade material: High carbon steel. Provides the longest life woodcutting blade possible. Straight shank.	Smooth	Medium	4"	6
	Fleam Ground	For cutting green or wet woods 3/8" to 2-1/2" thick. Fleam ground provides shredding type cutting action which is most effective in sawing hard, green or wet materials. Blade material: High carbon steel. Provides longest cutting life possible. Straight shank.	Coarse	Fast	4"	6
	Wood Cutting Coarse	Cuts most plastics and wood up to 4" thick. Special tooth design with extra large gullets provide extra chip clearance for fast cutting in thicker materials. Blade material: High carbon steel.	Rough	Fast	6"	4
	Wood Cutting Medium	Makes fairly smooth cuts in wood up to 4" thick. Extra thick back provides greater resistance to breaking during intricate scroll-type cutting. Blade material: High carbon steel.	Medium	Medium	6"	7
	Wood Cutting Fine	Cuts soft woods under 3/4" thick. Canted shank provides built-in blade relief, thus helping to clear the saw dust and cool the blade. Blade material: High carbon steel. More teeth per inch allows for finer quality of cut.	Medium	Medium	3"	10
	Hollow Ground	For cutting plywood 3/4" thick and under. Hollow ground for very smooth finish. Blade material: Heat treated high carbon steel. Straight shank for square cuts to work surface.	Smooth	Medium Fast	3"	7
	Skip Tooth	Cuts most plastics and plywood. Special tooth design with extra large gullets provide extra chip clearance necessary for cutting plywood and plastic. Blade material: High carbon steel.	Rough	Fast	3"	5
	Wood Cutting Hollow Ground	Hard woods under 3/4" thick. Hollow grinding provides no tooth projection beyond body of blade, thus imparting an absolutely smooth finish. Canted shank for blade clearance. Blade material: Heat treated high carbon steel.	Smooth	Medium	3"	7
METAL CUTTING						
	Metal Cutting	For cutting ferrous (iron) metals 1/4" to 3/8" thick and nonferrous (aluminum, copper, etc.) 1/8" to 1/4" thick. Blade material: M-2 high speed steel. Heat treated to spring temper hardness. Capable of cutting ferrous and nonferrous metals alike. Straight shank.	Medium	Medium	3"	14
	Metal Cutting	For cutting hard ferrous (iron) metals 1/64" to 3/32" thick. Blade material: M-2 high speed steel. Heat treated to full hardness spring temper. Capable of cutting all hard ferrous materials. Straight shank.	Very Fine	Slow	3"	32
	Metal Cutting	For cutting ferrous (iron) metals 1/8" to 1/4" thick and nonferrous metals 1/16" to 1/8" thick. Blade material: M-2 high speed steel. Heat treated to spring temper hardness, capable of cutting ferrous and nonferrous metals. Straight shank.	Smooth	Medium	3"	18
	Metal Cutting	For cutting ferrous (iron) metals 1/16" to 3/16" thick. Blade material: M-2 high speed steel. Heat treated to full hardness spring temper. Capable of cutting hard ferrous material. Straight shank.	Fine	Slow	3"	24

The right saw blade

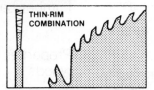

For ripping all hardwoods and softwoods. Has heavy hub, is taper-ground for extra clearance.

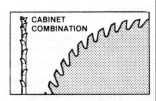

Finest combination blade for fine trim and finish work. Use it to rip, crosscut, miter.

CABINET COMBINATION

Cabinetmaker's combination blade cuts in any direction through either hardwoods or softwoods.

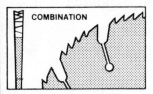

Cabinetmaker's blade. Produces free, smooth and accurate cuts in any direction in hardwoods.

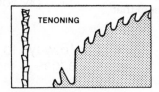

All-purpose blade, wide-kerfed for cutting tenons, splines in all hardwoods and softwoods.

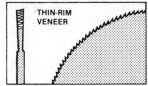

For satin-smooth finish cuts in either plywood or thin veneers without splintering.

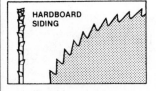

Best blade for cutting tempered hardboard (Masonite) underlayment, siding, perforated board.

METAL CUTTING

Intended for aluminum, brass, bronze, zinc and lead. A truly professional blade.

NAIL CUTTING

For rough-cutting (rip and crosscut) through all woods that have an occasional nail.

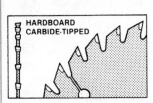

Excellent for wood, but can be used when cutting hardboard siding. Its 32 teeth cut fast, straight.

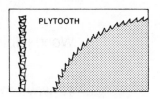

Fine-tooth, smooth-cutting blade for plywood, composition board, soft board and the like.

For light-gauge sheet steel, roofing, guttering and downspouts, up to $\frac{1}{16}$-in. thickness.

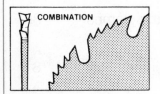

Good for ripping , crosscutting, mitering on all hardwoods and softwoods. Comes taper-ground.

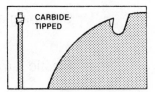

Carbide-tipped combination blade for long cutting life: ideal for abrasive materials.

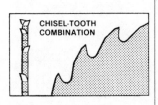

All-purpose, fast-cutting blade for all woods. An excellent contractor's framing blade.

When one type of saw blade is used to cut all kinds of material, it's almost like using one size nail to build a house. Only when a plywood blade is used to cut plywood, or a hardboard blade is used to cut hardboard, for example, can you turn out the best work and get the most from your bench saw or portable power saw.

That's why a selection of blades having a wide range of tooth patterns is available, each designed to cut a specific material in the best, fastest and smoothest way.

For general-purpose cutting, both with and across grain, a flat combination blade is your best bet, but, again, it won't match the extra-smooth cut you get with a hollow-ground planer blade. Thus it's important to keep several types of saw blades on hand so you can switch from one to the other, whatever your cutting requirements.

53

3
Basic carpentry

The following pages provide a good review of basic carpentry techniques. Starting with the basic box, we take you right up to making drawers, shelves and wood joints.

Please study the material thoroughly. The information provided is vital to building most of the projects listed in this book. Even if you've previously worked with wood, you may find that some of the hints and techniques illustrated here will aid you greatly. Once you've mastered them, complicated projects will seem that much easier.

Lumber basics

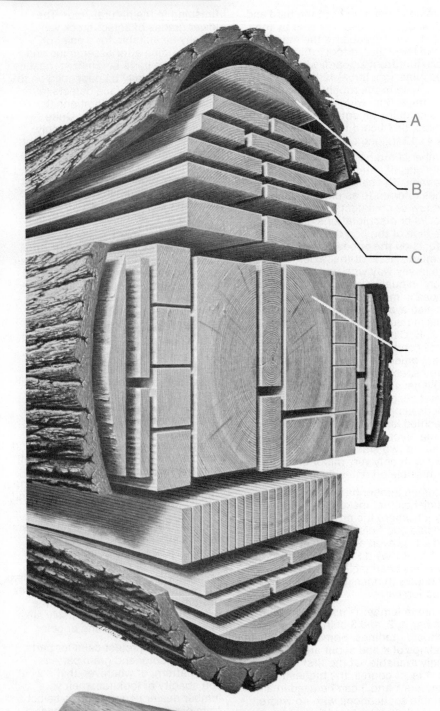

If you live in an average home of wood construction it contains from 1000 to 3000 pieces of lumber in many of the common classified forms. If it's an older structure the chances are it was built of both hard and softwood lumber, the former cut from broad-leaved (deciduous) trees and the latter from the conifers (evergreens).

Hardwood lumber in the structure will likely be in the form of interior trim, floors, doors, stairways, built-in cabinets and moldings in various forms and applications. Softwoods, from the conifers, will be in the framing, sheathing, roof deck, siding, sash frames, exterior trim and also the shingles if the roof is of wood.

How the Log is Used

A. **Debarking the log** is essential to its full utilization because bark cannot be used for papermaking, and therefore any piece dropped in the chipper has to be free of bark. But the bark can be used for fuel and soil mulch.

B. **The rounded sides** of the log, called "slabs", are the first pieces sent to the chipper as the log goes through the sawmill. This idealized picture shows the entire log being used for lumber, except for the slabs. Actually, as cutting continues, other pieces go to the chipper, including edgings, trim ends, and other parts of the log not usable as lumber. Each log presents different problems and can be handled differently.

C. **The outer portions** of the log have the fewest knots. This "clear" lumber is usually made into boards or planks varying in thickness from one to three inches.

D. **Toward the center** of the log, knots increase and the wood is less suitable for boards. Heavier planks, and square or rectangular beams are normally sawed from this section. The center of the log is used primarily for structural beams strong enough so that they are not weakened by knots. Knots are most frequent here because this is the oldest section of the tree. Branches that were removed during the early years of the tree's life left knots that were covered over as the tree grew outward.

Plywood is, in effect, a sandwich of thin wooden veneers. Veneer is made by "peeling," that is, holding a long blade against a rotating log. The wood is continuously peeled off, down to an eight-inch core. The core is then treated as though it were a small log. It can be made into lumber, and, of course, the rounded portions go to the chipper.

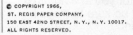

The terms board and lumber are often used loosely. Say "board" and you think right away of lumber; or the other way around, "lumber" and one thinks of a board, or perhaps the source of supply, the local lumberyard.

But both terms are a little more specific in the grading and classification of both the hard and softwoods. In general, the term lumber, or yard lumber, refers to individual pieces as cut from the log and dressed (planed, or surfaced) to a given width and thickness and cut to lengths of 8, 10, 12 ft. and so on up to the maximum length available. If the pieces are less than 2 in. thick and less than 8 in. wide they usually are classified as strips. If less than 2 in. thick and 8 in. or more in width they are classed as boards.

Pieces larger in sectional size than strips or boards are usually classified as *dimension* and *timbers:* Dimension lumber is 2 in. and less than 5 in. thick and any width normally supplied. Dimension lumber is commonly supplied as 2 x 4s, 2 x 6s, 2 x 8s, 2 x 10s and 2 x 12s. In sectional size timbers are 4 in. or more on the smaller dimension, as 4 x 6, 4 x 8 and so on.

All these classifications are commonly available in lengths from 6 or 8 up to 20 ft. or more in multiples of 2 ft. Thus to save stock the experienced purchaser of lumber who needs two 7-ft. lengths of 2 x 4, for example, buys one 14-ft. length rather than two 8 ft. lengths. All length dimensions are commonly cut slightly over to allow for trimming to the exact length required.

Lumber is sized as it comes from the saw and is commonly referred to as rough or rough-sawed. As it comes from the saw a 2 x 4 measures a full 2 x 4 in.; a 1 x 8 measures a full 1 in. thick and 8 in. wide. After surfacing (being run through a planer) the 1 x 8 is reduced to a thickness of ¾-in. and a width of 7⅝ in. The board is then referred to as being surfaced on all four sides, that is, on both faces and two edges (S4S). Likewise a rough-sawed 2 x 4 will measure 1⅝ x 3⅝ in. after surfacing.

Of course, there may be slight variations in the sectional dimensions due either to swelling or shrinkage.

Common lumber in both the hard and softwoods is priced and sold by the board foot. To visualize the meaning of the term "board foot" think of a piece (cut from a board) which measures 1 in. thick, 12 in. wide and 12 in. long in the rough. A strip 1 in. thick, 6 in. wide and 24 in. long also contains an equivalent volume of lumber, or 1 board foot. Likewise, a 2 x 4 - 12 ft. long contains 8 board feet.

Lumber is ordinarily graded into two main classifications, *select* and *common.* The select grade is sometimes referred to as clear, meaning it has few or no defects such as knots, checks or discolorations on at least one side of the board; any allowable defects on the opposite face can only be minor. None of these defects interfere in any way with use of the whole board in quality work. But the select grades in most of the common woods are also available in an order of decreasing quality and are designated as A, B, C and D. Many lumberyards combine the first two and refer to the grade as B and Better (B&Btr). If you specify this grade by symbol you'll generally get the best grade the dealer supplies. Some dealers in hardwoods supply a grade AA cut to specified lengths and widths and sold by the piece. Such stock is usually surfaced two sides (S2S) and comes clear with only very minor blemishes permissible on one side.

Common lumber has defects or blemishes that make it unsuited to any job where the project requires a high-grade finish on the exposed parts. However, allowable defects are such that they do not make the materials unsuitable for use as secondary (hidden) parts or as construction parts.

Common lumber is usually graded by number, 1, 2, and 3 being the standard gradings. Some species take gradings of 4 and 5, but are less commonly available. Of the first three No. 1 is, of course, the highest. Numbers 1 and 2 can be used in all suitable applications with no waste. But grade 3, also 4 and 5, usually must be cut to eliminate flaws such as loose knots and checks that would greatly weaken the piece for any use where appreciable stress is present.

Otherwise you should order the select grade for any inside work that requires staining and finishing or

finishing in the natural color. The lower grades of select stock will usually be suitable for a paint or enamel finish after assembling and sanding the parts smooth. An opaque finish can usually be depended on to conceal minor surface defects (after filling) and any discolorations that turn up on exposed parts. Quite naturally these rules do not apply when you select woods with normal surface defects, such as knotty pine or wormy cypress, where what are commonly regarded as blemishes in standard gradings are to be exposed and even emphasized with a clear finish or a stain finish in a light color.

Dimension lumber usually comes in only three grades, 1, 2 and 3. If for example you need a 2 x 4 to use in an exposed location where appearance is of first importance you should ask your dealer for No. 1. This piece will come to you clear and reasonably straight throughout its length.

A point to be kept in mind by the do-it-yourself lumber buyer is that some "softwoods" are actually classed as hardwoods. These are cut from broad-leaved (deciduous) trees and for this reason are classified as hard rather than softwoods. A good example is basswood, a fairly common wood of very close grain and fine texture especially suited to paint and enamel finishes. It has many of the characteristics of clear white pine and is just as easily worked with hand or power tools.

Still another point for do-it-yourselfers to remember: don't look for two or more boards of any common lumber exactly alike, or even nearly alike in texture or grain. You'll never find them. No two boards cut from the same tree or from any number of trees of the same species are ever precisely alike in surface detail, graining or color.

So when your project calls for parts of similar color and grain pattern, knot pattern, or whatever, that's what you specify or look for when your lumber dealer permits you to select from his stock—boards of *similar* color and grain pattern. These you can usually find just by looking over a relatively few pieces in the lumber rack.

Most lumber dealers will make up a special selection for you at a nominal extra charge. Just be sure to make it clear what you want.

When you order lumber, specify it correctly. If you decide you need 10 no. 2 white pine boards, measuring 1 x 8 in. and 8 ft. long, ask for: "10 8-ft. 1 x 8s, No. 2 white pine". Your shipping ticket likely will read: "10 8 1 x 8 No2 com pine 54 ft." The figure 54 is the total board feet in your order.

Tips on buying. Order the lowest grade that fits your needs. If you have a cooperative dealer, you can upgrade lumber yourself by sorting through the stacks; a No. 2 board, specially selected, sometimes will be as good as a select board.

You are charged for lumber by the *board foot*. To visualize a board foot, think of a piece of rough-sawed lumber measuring 1 in. thick, 12 in. wide and 12 in. long. A strip 1 in. thick, 6 in. wide and 24 in. long contains an equivalent volume of lumber—1 board foot. Likewise a 2 x 4 12 ft. long contains 8 board feet. See the chart below. If you buy any quantity of lumber, you'll be quoted a price per 1000 board feet.

Lumber in a yard neatly stacked for air drying. Notice how each board is stacked with spaced separators to allow free circulation of air.

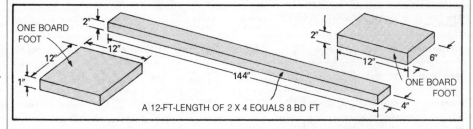

ONE BOARD FOOT — 2" — 12" — 12" — 1"

A 12-FT-LENGTH OF 2 X 4 EQUALS 8 BD FT — 144"

2" — 12" — 6" — ONE BOARD FOOT — 4"

STANDARD SIZES OF LUMBER

TYPE OF LUMBER	NOMINAL SIZE (in inches)		ACTUAL SIZE S4S AT COMM. DRY. SHP. WT. (in inches)	
	Thickness	Width	Thickness	Width
Dimension	2	4	1⅝	3⅝
	2	6	1⅝	5⅝
	2	8	1⅝	7½
	2	10	1⅝	9½
	2	12	1⅝	11½
Timbers	4	6	3⅝	5½
	4	8	3⅝	7½
	4	10	3⅝	9½
	6	6	5½	5½
	6	8	5½	7½
	6	10	5½	9½
	8	8	7½	7½
	8	10	7½	9½
Common boards	1	4	25/32	3⅝
	1	6	25/32	5⅝
	1	8	25/32	7½
	1	10	25/32	9½
	1	12	25/32	11½
Shiplap Boards	1	4	25/32	* 3⅛
	1	6	25/32	* 5⅛
	1	8	25/32	* 7⅛
	1	10	25/32	* 9⅛
	1	12	25/32	*11⅛
Tongued and Grooved Boards	1	4	25/32	* 3¼
	1	6	25/32	* 5¼
	1	8	25/32	* 7¼
	1	10	25/32	* 9¼
*—Width at face	1	12	25/32	*11¼

Courtesy Weyerhaeuser Sales Co.

TOTAL WOOD PRODUCTS FROM A TYPICAL LOG

FINISH ITEMS
(Lumber of good appearance and finishing)

SUITABLE FOR NATURAL FINISHES
Grade A
(practically free from defects)
Grade B
(allows a few small defects or blemishes)

SUITABLE FOR PAINT FINISHES
Grade C
(allows a limited number of small defects or blemishes that can be covered with paint)
Grade D
(allows any number of defects or blemishes which do not detract from the appearance of the finish especially when painted)

BOARDS
(Lumber containing defects or blemishes which detract from the appearance of the finish but suitable for general-utility and construction purposes)

SUITABLE WITHOUT WASTE
No. 1 Boards
(sound and tight-knotted stock; size of defects and blemishes limited; may be considered watertight lumber)
No. 2 Boards
(allows large and coarse defects; may be considered graintight lumber)

LUMBER PERMITTING WASTE
No. 3 Boards
(allows larger and coarser defects than No. 2 and occasional knot holes)
No. 4 Boards
(low-quality lumber admitting the coarsest defects, such as decay and holes)
No. 5 Boards
(must hold together under ordinary handling)

Properties of common woods

These data are based on results of experimental work at Forest Products Laboratory. Therefore entries and remarks are only average. As an example, pounds-per-cubic-foot are given for samples of dry wood. The figure can vary, even in samples cut from the same tree and reduced to the same moisture content. Figures under "Sanding" refer generally to grades of sandpaper that will not leave scratches on the surface when smooth-sanding as the final step. On some samples of wood, you may have to go to an even finer grade of paper to achieve desirable results. Figures given under the heading "Planing and Jointing" refer to cutting angles of edge tools that have been found generally best, especially for power tools with cutters such as a jointer or moulding head. Finishing data given for Douglas fir states under "Stain" that the color may be brown. This can be any shade of brown from light to dark. But few samples of fir, either of plywood or solid stock, are pleasing to the eye when stained—possible exceptions being a very light or very dark stain. This wood generally appears at its best when sealed, with a special sealer provided for the purpose, and painted or enameled. In entries "Oil" refers to a penetrating oil stain; "Wiping" refers to a wiping stain, usually an oil stain. Bleaching is not always necessary except, possibly, for uniforming the color of a given piece of wood.

Name of Wood	Weight Per Cubic Foot	Hardness	Planing and Jointing	Turning	Sanding	Natural Color	Usual Grain Figure	Stain Type	Stain Color	Filler Color	Bleach	Paint	Natural Finish	Remarks Note: NGR = Non-Grain Raising (Applies to stain)
Ash (U.S.A.)	35	Med.	Good 10-25	Fair	Best 2/0	White to Brown	Plain or Fiddleback	Any	Any	White or Brown	Yes	Yes. Fill First	Yes	A tough, grainy wood quite uniform in color. Bends quite easily when steamed. Will take stain, but finishes best in natural color
Basswood	24	Soft	Good 20-30	Poor	Poor 4/0	Cream	Very Mild	NGR	Red or Brown	None	Not Nec.	Yes	No	Light, softwood usually uniform in color. Fine texture, fairly strong, takes paint well. Used for drawing boards and as veneered core stock
Birch	39	Hard	Good 15-20	Good	Fair 4/0	Cream	Mild	Any	Walnut or Mahogany	Natural or Brown	Yes	Yes. Interior	Yes	Similar in texture to hard maple. Takes the maple finish well. Widely used in furniture construction. Fairly uniform color
Butternut	25	Soft	Good 10-25	Good	Fair 4/0	Heart: Amber Sap: Cream	Like Walnut	Water	Walnut or Oak	Medium Brown	Yes	No	Yes	Similar in grain and texture to black walnut. Relatively easy to work with hand and power tools, except as noted
Cherry	36	Med.	Best 10-25	Best	Best 4/0	Red to Brown	Good	Water	Red or Brown	Red to Black	No	No	Yes	One of the finest domestic cabinet woods. Fine texture, dense grain, often wavy or curly. Takes natural, stain, fine enamel finishes
Cedar (Aromatic Red)	23	Soft	Poor 5-15	Fair	Good 3/0	Heart: Red Sap: Cream	Knotty	None		None	No	No	Yes. Pref.	Universally used for cedar chests and clothes-closet linings, also novelties. Finishes best in its natural color
Chestnut	27	Soft	Good 15-20	Best	Best 3/0	Gray-Brown	Heavy Grain	Oil or Wiping	Red or Brown	Red or Brown	No	Yes	Yes	Rather coarse grained, often worm-holed. Used as picture frames and sometimes as random paneling. Machines well, takes novelty finishes
Cypress	29	Soft	Good 15-25	Poor	Fair 2/0	Heart: Brown Sap: Cream	Plain or Figured	Water, Oil or Wiping	Red or Brown	None	No	No	Yes	Tends to splinter when worked by hand or machine. Most durable in outdoor exposures. Will take natural or novelty finishes quite well
Elm (Southern)	34	Med.	Poor 15-20	Poor	Good 2/0	Brown to Cream	Heavy Grain	Water	Red or Brown	Dark Brown	No	Yes	Yes	A good furniture wood but difficult to work either by hand or machine. Takes stain fairly well. Some pieces attractively grained
Fir (Douglas)	26	Soft	Fair 10-25	Poor	Fair 3/0	Cream to Red	Plain or Wild	Wiping or Oil	Brown	None	No	Yes	No	Widely used in home construction, especially framing. Universally available as plywood in varying thicknesses. Best sealed and painted
Gum (Red)	33	Med.	Fair 10-20	Best	Fair 4/0	Heart: Br. Red Sap: Cream	Plain or Figured	Any	Red or Brown	Match Wood	Yes	Yes	Yes	Dense-grained wood, smooth texture. Occasional attractive figure in heartwood, easily worked. Widely used in furniture construction
Hickory	42	Hard	Good 10-25	Good	Best 2/0	White to Cream	Usually Straight	Water	Red or Brown	Brown	Yes	No	Yes	Among best domestic woods for steam bending, tool handles. Usually straight grained and of a fairly uniform color and texture
Holly	33	Hard	Good 10-25	Good	Best 3/0	Silver White	Mild	Water	Amber	None	Not Nec.	Yes	Yes	Similar to basswood in color and texture. Works easily. Can be stained. Once widely used in inlay and marquetry in early construction
Mahogany	35	Med.	Good 5-25	Best	Good 4/0	Brown to Red-Brown	Stripe	Water	Red or Brown	Red to Black	Yes	No	Yes	One of the choicest cabinet woods. Select pieces beautifully grained. Works easily. Takes both red and brown stains. An imported wood
Mahogany (Philippine)	33	Med.	Good 5-25	Good	Poor 3/0	Brown to Red-Brown	Stripe	Water or Wiping	Red or Brown	Red to Black	Yes	No	Yes	Similar to true mahoganies but coarser in grain and softer. Serves well as boat planking, also used as trim and in core-door construction
Maple	41	Hard	Fair 15-20	Good	Good 4/0	Cream	Varied	Water and Wiping	Maple	None	Yes	No	Yes	One of the best domestic hardwoods. Widely used in fine furniture construction, also as flooring, turnings, bowling pins
Oak (English Brown)	40	Hard	Best 10-20	Good	Good 2/0	Deep Brown	Plain, Flake or Swirl	NGR	Brown	Brown to Black	Yes	No	Yes	One of the finest of the oaks. An imported wood, most commonly available as veneer. Very attractively grained. Takes stains well
Oak (Red)	39	Hard	Best 10-25	Good	Best 2/0	Red-Brown	Plain or Flake	NGR	Green Toner	Brown	Yes	Yes	No	Perhaps the most common of the domestic oaks. Heavy, strong and tough. Open-grained, used in furniture where durability comes first
Oak (White)	40	Hard	Best 10-20	Good	Best 2/0	White to Light Brown	Plain or Flake	NGR	Brown	Brown	Yes	Yes	Yes	Perhaps the finest domestic oak of exceptional strength and durability. Beautiful graining when quarter-sawed. Takes fine finishes
Pine (White)	25	Soft	Good 10-25	Good	Fair 2/0	White to Cream	Mild	Water or Oil	Brown Only	None	No	Yes	No	One of the most popular woods almost universally used for trim, paneling and furniture. Perhaps the best all around domestic softwood
Poplar	29	Soft	Good 5-20	Good	Poor 4/0	White to Cream	Occ. Dark Stripe	NGR	Brown	None	No	Yes	No	Another of the most useful domestic softwoods. Widely used as a secondary wood in both early and late furniture construction
Redwood	29	Soft	Good 10-25	Fair	Poor 2/0	Red	Mild St. Grain	Red only for toning		None	No	Yes	Yes	An exceptionally durable softwood when used in outdoor applications as house siding, outdoor furniture, fencing, industrial applications
Sycamore	35	Med.	Poor 5-15	Good	Poor 3/0	White to Pink	Flake	Water	Amber or Brown	None	Seldom	Yes	Yes	Difficult to work with either hand or power tools. Beautiful, flaky grain when quarter-sawed. Most attractive in natural finish
Walnut	36	Med.	Good 15-20	Best	Best 4/0	Heart: Brown Sap: Cream	Varied	Water	Walnut	Brown to Black	Yes	No	Yes	Rated by most as the finest domestic cabinet wood. Used by best cabinetmakers from earliest times. Has every desirable feature

All about plywood

Panel Construction

Plywood panels are built up from sheets of softwood veneer glued together so that the grain of each ply is at right angles to the one adjacent to it. The veneers are united under high temperature and pressure with a resin glue that is completely waterproof, making the plywood suitable for use under conditions of extreme exposure to moisture.

Manufacture

The manufacturing process begins by cutting selected logs into peeler blocks either 8½ or 10½ ft long, depending on the desired length of the panel. Each peeler block is then conveyed to a barker where it is rotated against a steel claw that strips the bark from the block.

After the block has been barked it is moved to the lathe and centred in the chucks. As the block is rotated at a constant surface speed, the honed steel blade of the lathe is brought in contact with it, peeling a continuous sheet of veneer. A big peeler block can yield as much as a mile of veneer.

As veneer is produced it is directed to semi-automatic clippers that cut it into various widths. The clipper blade can also be actuated manually to remove defective pieces of veneer. The veneer then moves along a conveyor to the sorting area where it is graded and separated into stacks of heartwood and sapwood. This segregation is necessary because heartwood and sapwood have markedly different moisture contents and require different drying cycles.

Veneer is dried to approximately 5% moisture content within steam—or gas—heated ovens at temperatures ranging from 320° to 400°F. The speed at which the veneer moves through the dryer depends on the thickness of the veneer and whether it is heartwood or sapwood. After passing through the dryer, electronic moisture detectors mark all veneer in excess of 5% moisture content. This veneer is stacked separately and later re-dried.

After drying, the veneer is further sorted according to grade. Narrow strips are channelled to an edge gluer where veneer edges are trimmed and spread with glue before being fed to the edge gluer where the random widths are edge-butted into a continuous sheet as the gluelines are cured by a radio frequency field. This continuous sheet of veneer is then clipped into standard 54 or 66 in. widths.

Substandard veneer with oversize imperfections is channelled to patching machines where the imperfections are neatly replaced with sound wooden patches.

Sound veneer then moves to the glue spreader where the crossbrand veneers are uniformly coated with phenol formaldehyde resin glue and laid at right angles to the adjacent face and back veneers. This cross lamination accounts for plywood's exceptional two-way strength and dimensional stability. The phenol formaldehyde resin glue, when cured in the hot press, produces a completely water-and-boil-proof bond.

From the glue spreader, the veneer sandwiches go to the hot press, the key operation in the manufacturing process. Here, depending upon the thickness of the plywood panel, one or more sandwiches are loaded into each press opening. The press is then hydraulically closed and the panels subjected to a temperature of 300°F and a pressure of 200 psi which cures the glue.

After removal from the hot press, trim saws cut the plywood panels to the required dimensions, usually 48 by 96 in. Panel edges and panel ends are trimmed in consecutive operations.

If the panels are to be marketed as sheathing grades they pass directly to the grading operation. Panels produced as sanded grades pass to a sander where faces and backs are simultaneously sanded smooth.

Any minor imperfections remaining in the face and back veneers are repaired with wood inlays or synthetic filler before the panels are finally graded by skilled operators.

All grades of plywood produced by the plywood manufacturing members of the Council of Forest Industries of British Columbia are then edge-stamped with the registered certification mark COFI EXTERIOR before leaving the mill.

Grades of Plywood

COFI EXTERIOR plywood is manufactured in eleven appearance grades.

Grade names in general are based on the quality of the veneers used for the face and back of the panel. The four qualities of veneer are designated by the letters A (the highest grade), B, C Improved, and C (the lowest grade). The manufacturer, using these veneer grades in various combinations, can produce panels suitable for a variety of uses.

Veneer is often repaired to upgrade its quality. Repairs consist of wood patches and shims of various sizes and shapes which replace voids, knots and unsound wood; and synthetic wood-resin fillers which are used to fill small cracks, splits and other minor surface defects.

Panels with A or B grade face or back veneers are sanded to a smooth uniform finish. Sheating grades (that is, panels with C grade faces and backs) are unsanded.

Veneer Grades

A Veneer Smooth and sound. No knots, splits, pitch pockets, or other open defects. May contain a limited number of wood patches and synthetic filler repairs. Suitable for high quality paint finish.

B Veneer Solid surface free from open defects. May contain sound tight knots, tight splits, slightly rough grain, a limited number of wood patches and synthetic filler repairs and minor sanding and patching defects.

C Improved Veneer Solid surface with a limited number of minor open defects. May contain sound tight knots, rough and feather grain and wood patches and shims.

C Veneer May contain minor open defects, tight knots, and limited size knot-holes, pitch pockets, splits and worm or borer holes. Also permits rough and feather grain and wood patches and shims.

Size and Thicknesses

Plywood of all standard grades is usually manufactured in panels 48 in. wide by 96 in. long. Some mills also produce panels up to 60 in. wide and 120 in. long. In all sizes the face veneer may consist of one or more parallel pieces of neatly joined veneer, each of which is one unjointed piece lengthwise.

Panels longer than 120 in. up to any reasonable length are available with scarf joints. A scarf jointed panel consists of two panels glued together end to end along a tapered cut to form a single continuous panel. Scarf joints are made with waterproof thermo-setting phenol formaldehyde or melamine glue.

Nominal panel thicknesses for all standard grades of plywood are given below.

SCARF JOINT

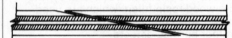

Storing and Handling

Plywood, like any other panel product, requires careful handling and storage. Despite its sturdy cross-laminated construction, face veneers, panel edges and panel corners are particularly vulnerable to damage and should always be protected.

Plywood is manufactured at a low moisture content and while small changes in moisture content will not appreciably affect its dimensions, large changes should be avoided since they may encourage checking of the face veneer with consequent impairment of its qualities as a paint base. It is good practice to store plywood which is to be used for interior finish under conditions that approximate those it will experience in service.

Points to watch when handling plywood are:

1. Store plywood panels level and flat.

2. Keep finish faces inward and cover stacks to protect from bumping and abrasion.

3. Protect panel edges and corners. This is especially important with tongue and groove plywood.

4. Carry panels on edge (always being careful not to bruise faces, edges and corners).

5. When plywood is used as a finishing material, deliver to job-site at the last possible moment.

6. Protect panels from sunlight, water or excessive humidity.

Sawing

Handsawing For handsaw work, panels should be sawn face (i.e. good side) up with the angle between saw teeth and panel surface as flat as possible. This prevents the face veneer splintering. Generally, an 8 or 10 point cross-cut saw or a 10 point panel saw gives the best results.

Hand Powersawing A sharp combination blade set to protrude no more than ½-in. and firm panel support will give excellent results with a hand power saw. Panels should be sawn face down.

Table Powersawing Panels kept face up on a table power saw are cut cleaner. A combination blade filed with less than normal hook is best for most work. The blade should be set to protrude no more than ½-in. In general, a blade of 10 in. diameter or more works best. A table extension will help in handling full sized panels.

Drilling

Hand brace and bit, power drill or drill press all work easily with plywood. Holes of large diameter are best cut with a brace and expansion bit rather than with a high-speed drill. For power drilling, spur bits give good results. Reversing the panel as soon as the bit point is through and completing the cut from the other side will ensure a clean cut without splintering.

Small holes are readily cut with either hand or powerdrills. As a general rule, the larger the hole the slower the drill speed.

Clean cuts can be obtained with all methods of drilling if the panel has firm support and is backed with scrap wood to prevent splintering.

Routing

Routers can be used to vee-groove, shiplap or rebate edges of panels. Special bits are available for moulding and chamfering. Use sharp bits and take care when working across panel. Deep cuts in panel edges should be made in two stages. For specific instructions, see router manufacturer's literature.

Bending

Plywood panels can easily be bent when dry into mild simple curves. The table below gives dry cold bend radii for the most common plywood thicknesses. As can be seen from the table, plywood can be bent more sharply when the bend is perpendicular to the direction of the face grain rather than across its width. These radii are based on panels selected at random with no regard to defects such as knots, patches and short grain. Without selection, a small percentage of panels bent to these radii may be expected to break. To obtain smaller radii, i.e. sharper curves, the panels must be soaked or steamed.

Saw-kerfing the back of the panel to make it bend more easily is not recommended if the plywood is to be used structurally. Compound curves are virtually unobtainable with plywood in panel form and should not be attempted.

Cold Bend Radii for Plywood

Plywood Thickness (in.)	Bending Radius Parallel to Face Grain (in.)	Bending Radius Perpendicular to Face Grain (in.)
¼	48	16
⁵⁄₁₆	60	24
⅜	84	36
½	108	72
⅝	148	96
¾	192	144

Interior Panelling

Sanded grades of plywood can be used as interior panelling applied directly to studs or to furring strips fastened to plaster, masonry or concrete walls. Plywood is simple to install and, with forethought, the joint pattern can be made very attractive.

A rhythmic, modular pattern generally gives the most pleasing effect. Fragmented, uneven patterns should be avoided because they tend to make rooms look smaller. Unbroken horizontal lines make rooms appear longer, while bold vertical lines give the effect of height.

The tendency in recent years has been to accentuate the joints between panels rather than trying to hide them since this greatly simplifies construction.

60

Edge Finishing

Planes used on plywood edges are working on grain that goes in both directions because of cross-lamination of the plies. For this reason a sharp plane with shallow set is recommended. A light jack plane will work well on most jobs and planing in from the ends towards the centre helps prevent end splinter.

Power tools will help get a smooth edge. A power saw alone can produce a smooth edge if the first cut is made more generous than is necessary and the edge is then cut to size with a hollow-ground blade. With a jointer it is best to feed the wood into the jointer head slowly. With a disc sander, feed the panel slowly against the sander at a slight angle so that the area of edge contact is on the downward side of the rotating disc.

Sanding

When finish-sanding the panel face, work with the grain using even pressure and regular strokes. Use fine sandpaper for the final easing and smoothing of the edges and for rubbing down between coats of paint.

Fastenings

Plywood can be fastened to framing materials and other materials can be fastened to plywood with a number of devices such as nails, staples, screws, bolts, clips, and glue. Of these, nails, staples, and glue are the most commonly used.

Nails

Nails are available in a variety of lengths, diameters, heads, points, shank styles and coatings. In Canada, nails are specified by the length and diameter of the wire used in their manufacture.

For most construction uses, common nails will be satisfactory. Where greater withdrawal resistance is required, such as in subflooring and underlayment nailing, ring thread or annularly grooved nails should be used. Coated nails are not generally used with plywood.

The length of nail for a specific purpose is determined by the thickness of plywood through which it must be driven. The following table gives recommended nail lengths for the thicknesses of plywood used in finish carpentry work.

Nails for Plywood used in Finish Carpentry

Plywood Thickness (in.)	Nail Length (in.) and Type
¼, ⅜	1½ casing or finishing
½	1½ casing or 2 finishing
⅝, ¾	2 casing or finishing

Staples for Plywood

Staples are similar in nature to nails and are often used interchangeably. Staples sizes conforming to the requirements of the National Building Code of Canada for plywood sheathing and subfloor attachment are given in the following table.

Plywood Thickness (in.)	Staple Length (in.)
⁵⁄₁₆ and ⅜	1½
½ to ¾	2

Maximum Spacing

6"oc along edges and 12"oc along intermediate supports
NOTES:
1. Staples shall be not less than 16 gauge with not less than ⅜" crown.
2. Staples shall be driven with crown parallel to framing.

Screws for Plywood

Screws are primarily employed to fasten plywood used in finish carpentry work, cabinetry, displays and boat building. Screw sizes for the most commonly used thicknesses of plywood together with the diameters of the screw shank clearance and pilot holes are given below.

Screws may be counter-sunk but care should be taken to avoid breaking the surface grain of the plywood panel.

In general, sheet metal screws hold better. Flathead screws set flush have more holding power than round-head screws of the same size. Under round head-screws, a washer will give extra strength.

Plywood Thickness (in.)	Screw Size (in.)	Shank Clearance (in.)	Pilot hole (in.)
¼	¾ No. 6	⁹⁄₆₄	¹⁄₁₆
⅜	1 No. 6	⁹⁄₆₄	¹⁄₁₆
½	1¼ No. 6	⁹⁄₆₄	¹⁄₁₆
⅝	1¼ No. 8	¹¹⁄₆₄	⁵⁄₆₄
¾	1½ No. 8	¹¹⁄₆₄	⁵⁄₆₄
	or 1½ No.10	³⁄₁₆	³⁄₃₂
	or 1½ No.12	⁷⁄₃₂	⁷⁄₆₄

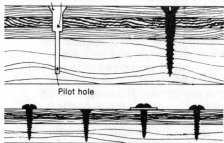

Counter sink   Shank clearance

Pilot hole

Bolts

These have only limited use in plywood construction, their use being mainly confined to fastening other materials to plywood.

Bolt holes should be ¹⁄₁₆-in. larger than the bolts since a tight fit requiring forcible driving of the bolts is not required. With common bolts, a washer or a metal plate or strap should be inserted between the plywood and the bolt head and between the plywood and the nut. Nuts should be tightened snugly but not so as to cause crushing of the wood under the washer, plate or strap.

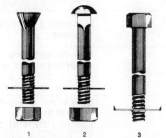

1. Plow bolts have flush heads with fins to prevent turning.
2. Carriage bolts normally are more useful with plywood than common bolts.
3. The speed nut system is a bolt with a self-locking nut of sheet metal.

Grommets and Inserts

Metal grommets and inserts are employed when plywood is used for removable panels. Several types are manufactured for this purpose.

1. Grommet is fitted with countersunk hole and crimped to form socket for removable wood screw.
2. Grommet designed for round head screw has slotted hole for panel adjustment.

Glues and Gluing

Glue is playing an increasingly important role in plywood construction, both in non-structural applications such as cabinets and built-ins and in structural uses such as plywood web beams and stressed skin panels.

The selection of the most suitable glue for a specific job depends upon the nature of the assembly, the workshop conditions during fabrication and the anticipated exposure. Glues are generally classified into three exposure or durability groups: waterproof; moisture-resistant; and dry bond or non-moisture-resistant. Interior contact bond adhesives are generally used to glue hard or textured surface materials such as formica or vinyl to plywood surfaces. One common application of this type of adhesive is to bond plywood panels to dry strapping or stud framing. The method is to apply the adhesive to the framing and on corresponding areas of the plywood. The adhesive is permitted to dry until no longer sticky. The plywood panel is then correctly positioned and pressed against the framing. To ensure the best possible bond, a 2 by 4 in. piece of lumber is placed on the plywood over the framing member and struck smartly with a mallet or hammer to secure the panel without nails, nail holes or hammer marks. Care must be taken to follow adhesive manufacturer's directions.

Pressure can be applied to secondary gluelines (i.e. gluelines other than the primary gluelines used in the manufacture of the plywood itself) by many methods, including weights, presses, clamps and nails. Whatever the method, it should be capable of exerting a pressure of 100 to 150 pounds per square inch of glueline area.

Weights, presses and clamps are often impractical for many gluing operations. In such cases, glueline pressure may be developed by nails; a technique known as nail-gluing. Nail sizes and spacings for various thicknesses of plywood are given in the following table and are suggested as a guide to nail-gluing.

Guide for Nail-Gluing

Plywood Thickness (in.)	Nail Length (in.)
¼, ⅜	1½ Common or Box
½ to ⅞	2 Common or Box
1, 1⅛	2½ Common or Box

Spacing

Nails shall be spaced not to exceed 3″ oc along each row for plywood up to ⅜″ thick or 4″ oc for plywood ½ in. and thicker. One row of nails shall be used for each 2″ width or part thereof of contact area to be glued. Rows shall be spaced such that the distance to the edge of the contact area is approximately half the distance between rows. Nails in adjacent rows shall be staggered to provide even glueline pressure and to reduce the danger of splitting the lumber.

Commonly used Glues for Working with Plywood

	Casein Glue	Urea Resin Glue	Resorcinol Resin Glue
Uses	Laminating, assembly of furniture, cabinets	General assembly work, some marine work, veneering, edge-gluing	Laminating, marine work, wood-plywood structural components
Advantages	May be formulated to have good water resistance, excellent gap filler. May be used at low temperatures and low pressures	High moisture resistance, does not stain, versatile, may be formulated to give very rapid set	Complete water resistance, may be used for joints exposed to extreme moisture conditions. Not subject to bacterial attack
Disadvantages	Stains, not completely water resistant, subject to bacterial attack (unless specially treated), hard on tools	Poor gap filler, not generally suited to outdoor exposure, affected by heat and water	Relatively expensive, dark colour. Hard on tools
Preparation	Mix cold with water-to-glue ratio as high as 2 to 1	Mix with water, usually an extender, and catalyst	Mix with catalyst (formaldehyde or paraformaldehyde)
Working Requirements	Dry wood (1 to 15% moisture content). Glue spread 40 to 60 lb wet glue per 1000 sq ft of glue line. Casein is a good gap filler and bonds may be made with little pressure. Assembly time from 20 minutes to 2 hours. Clamp time from 20 minutes to 12 hours. Cold setting temperature not less than 40°F	Dry wood (6 to 8% moisture content). Glue spread 40 to 70 lb wet glue per 1000 sq ft of glue line. Pressure 50 to 200 lb per sq in. Assembly time 5 to 20 minutes. Clamp time 2 to 6 hours. Cold setting temperature not less than 70°F	Dry wood (8 to 14% moisture content). Glue spread 40 to 70 lb per 1000 sq ft of glue line. Pressure 150 lb to 200 lb per sq in. Open assembly time not more than 10 minutes. Closed assembly time not more than 25 minutes. Clamp time 2 to 10 hours. Cold setting temperature not less than 70°F
NOTE: Clamp time (time under pressure) for all glues shown here may be varied according to working temperature. The higher the temperature, the less the time required to set the glue			
Composition	Alkaline dispersion of protein obtained from milk. Lime added in varying quantities to improve water resistance	A combination of urea and formaldehyde to which a catalyst is usually added to set the glue by polymerization	A combination of resorcinol and formaldehyde. Cure is effected by adding extra formaldehyde
Types	Low water resistance, medium water resistance, incorporated toxic for mould resistance	Cold press and hot press formulations, high frequency formulation	Cold or medium temperature formulations, high frequency formulation
Commercial Form	Powder	Powder or liquid	Liquid

NOTE: To achieve the optimum glue bond between members it is imperative that the glue manufacturer's recommendations in regard to lumber moisture content, shelf life, pot life, working life, mixing, spreading, assembly time, time under pressure, and ambient temperature be followed.

New plywood standards

GRADES AND USES

Grade of Plywood	Grade of Veneer			Typical Use
	Face	Inner Plies	Back	
Good Two Sides (G 2 S)	A	C	A	Where appearance is the prime consideration, with both sides of panel exposed to view, e.g., furniture, booth partitions, cabinet doors, etc
Good/Solid (G/Solid)	A	C	B	Where best appearing surface is required on one side with relatively good appearance on the other, e.g., doors, furniture, built-in fitments, kitchen cabinets, toys, etc
Good One Side (G 1 S)	A	C	C	Where good appearance of one side only is a prime consideration, e.g., panelling, soffits, sliding doors. For opaque paint finishes, etc
Solid Two Sides (Solid 2 S)	B	C	B	Same uses as Good Two Sides when finishing requirements are not as exacting, e.g., shelving, concrete forms.
Solid One Side (Solid 1 S)	B	C	C	Same uses as Good One Side when finishing requirements are not as exacting, e.g., floor underlay where sanded surface is desired. Suitable for concrete forms
Concrete Form 2 Sides	B	C	B	For concrete forms where a good, smooth surface is required and both plywood faces will be used for repetitive work
Concrete Form 1 Side	B	C	C	For uses where sanded material is not required, e.g., underlay with tile, linoleum or other flooring which does not require a sanded underlay
Sheathing	C	C	C	Excellent where hard finish is required, e.g., table tops, school furniture, lockers, bins, containers, tanks, signs, fixtures, boats, and displays. Ideal for concrete forms
Select Sheathing	C improved	C	C	For siding, soffits, panelling, built-in fitments, cabinets or any use requiring superior paint surface
High Density Overlay	B	C	B or C	Where strength and economy are required but sanded finish unnecessary, e.g., structural applications, such as roofing, wall sheathing, subflooring, single finish for farm structures, fences, utility and industrial buildings
Medium Density Overlay	B	C	B or C	For concrete forms where a good, smooth surface is required and only one plywood face will be used for repetitive work

NOMINAL PANEL THICKNESSES

Grade	Standard Thicknesses (in.)	Thicknesses Available On Special Order (in.)
Good Two Sides Good/Solid Good One Side Solid Two Sides Solid One Side	¼, ⅜, ½, ⅝, ¾	³/₁₆, ⅞, 1, 1⅛, 1¼
Concrete Form One – Two Sides	⅝, ¹¹/₁₆, ¾	None
High Density Overlaid	⁵/₁₆, ⅜, ½, ⅝, ¾	⅞, 1, 1⅛, 1¼
Medium Density Overlaid	¼, ⁵/₁₆, ⅜, ½, ⅝, ¾	
Select Sheathing Sheathing	⁵/₁₆, ⅜, ½, ⅝, ¾	⅞, 1, 1⅛, 1¼

Grades of Plywood

COFI EXTERIOR plywood is manufactured in eleven appearance grades. Grade names in general are based on the quality of the veneers used for the face and back of the panel. The four qualities of veneer are designated by the letters A (the highest grade), B, C Improved, and C (the lowest grade). The manufacturer, using these veneer grades in various combinations, can produce panels suitable for a variety of uses

Veneer is often repaired to upgrade its quality. Repairs consist of wood patches and shims of various sizes and shapes which replace voids, knots and unsound wood; and synthetic wood-resin fillers which are used to fill small cracks, splits and other minor surface defects.

Panels with A or B grade face or back veneers are sanded to a smooth uniform finish. Sheathing grades (that is, panels with C grade faces and backs) are unsanded.

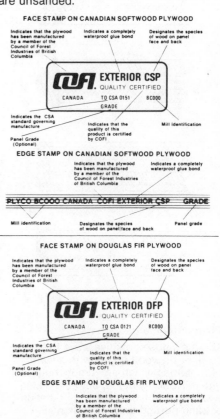

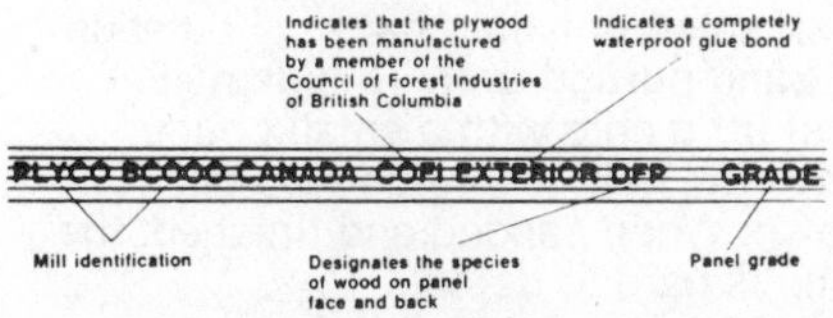

16 ways to hide plywood edges

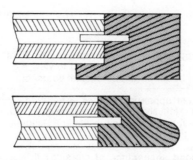

A problem from the beginning

The use of plywood presents the problem of how to hide laminated edges when exposed to view. Covering them with paper-thin wood tape, sold in rolls in a choice of woods and merely glued on, is one way. Being limited however, to plain square edges, this is not the answer when you prefer that the edges of a piece of furniture be shaped. But, as shown here, there are many ways you can add eye appeal to plain plywood edges and hide the laminates in doing so.

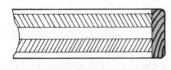

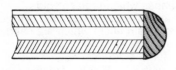

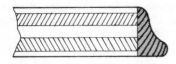

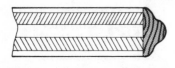

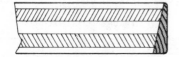

Plain butt-glue treatment

The drawings show five ways to treat straight plywood edges with a variety of moldings which are simply butt-glued. Not only glued, but also nailed with small finishing nails, with heads set and puttied over. To hide nails, first lift a chip with a small gouge, drive the nail, then glue chip back down. When sanded and finished, the chip is hard to detect.

Edging held with splines

With wide moldings, splines are often used to produce exceptionally strong joints. Here saw kerfs are run in both plywood and molding on a table saw and thin wood members are ripped to fit the kerfs. Plain solid stock may be applied to the edges and the members shaped afterwards. If the edge needs to be thicker than the plywood, additional strength can be gained by a rabbet. This, plus the spline and glue, produces a joint that can take a lot of punishment.

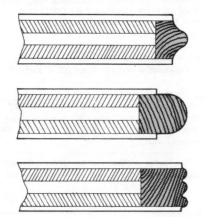

Moldings can be inserted in dadoes

The example above illustrate how the top and bottom surface veneers of the plywood itself can become part of the decorative edge. In each case a dado (groove) is made in the core laminations to a depth to suit the molding. In two examples the outer veneers form shoulders; in the other the depths of the groove, plus the molding shape, creates an edge where the veneers are held flush.

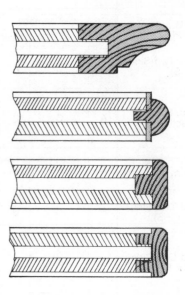

Tongue-and-groove joints are another way

Better than being just butt-glued, decorative edges applied with tongue-and-groove joints will not pull loose readily. The top and bottom examples differ from the others above in that tongues are cut in the plywood rather than the molding. The molding conceals the entire edge either by itself or by the addition of a veneer strip.

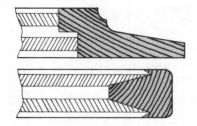

Examples of special treatment

The upper detail shows a wide, fancy picture-frame molding used to treat plywood edges by use of rabbet cuts. After the molding is glued in place, the top surface is sanded flush. The lower detail pictures a joint that perhaps is the strongest of all but requires special shaper cutters to form both groove and molding. You have the option of leaving the molding as is or shaping it.

How to work with plywood

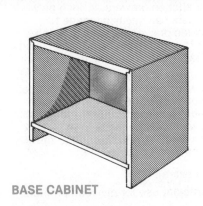

BASE CABINET

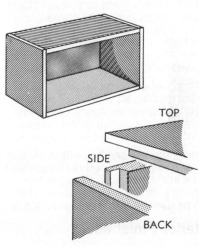

TOP

SIDE

BACK

FINISHING PLYWOOD EDGES

Even the most complicated task is easily learned if it is reduced to basics. And the most basic design in furniture making is the box. Master building a box and you're well on your way to tackle the most ambitious projects. For this reason we've listed many worthwhile hints for the hobby woodworker, the home handyman and the amateur carpenter; hints that are already possessed by the skilled carpenter.

Most projects are variations of these two basic boxes

Hanging Cabinet

Joints are butt or single rabbet. Ends of cabinet show no end grain; weight is at right angles to the nails.

Base Cabinet

Top joints are mitered or double rabbeted. Bottom is dadoed in for extra strength. No end grain shows; bottom is set up for toe room.

Back Panel

For both boxes the back panels are set into rabbets for strength and rigidity. Fastened with glue and nails, ¼-inch plywood is strong enough for most projects.

Corner Joint Details

Fir plywood is without equal for cabinets, cupboards and built-ins because no framing is required in most cases. Shown are joint details for cabinets.

Glue for Joints

Glue is the commonest means of joining fir plywood in cabinet work. Water-soluble, cold-setting adhesive of the urea-formaldehyde type is easy to work with. Glue is best applied with a brush for small jobs and with a proper spreader for large areas.

Glued joints should fit together snugly. Blocks under clamp jaws will help prevent bruising of the veneer. If sawdust is thrown on glue that squeezes from the joints, it will absorb moisture and help when glue is to be peeled off.

Finishing Plywood Edges

If exposed plywood edges are to have a paint finish they can be treated with spackle or wood filler and finished without trim. An attractive natural

edge finish can be produced by filling end grain with tinted putty or pastewood filler and rounding the edges slightly. (Note: If plywood is to be stained or rubbed down with paint tint to show grain use water-soluble or oil-soluble putty compounds for filling nail heads or other defects. Some acetone based putties seal grain so wood cannot absorb stain. This leaves a light unstained mark on the finished job. Under solid paint any good putty is recommended.) The sanded edge is then sealed and finished. Edges may also be finished by application of various mouldings as shown.

SHELF INSTALLATION

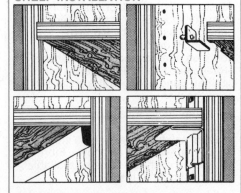

Shelf Installation

Where shelves form part of the cabinet structure, the rabbeted construction is recommended. If desired the exposed edge can be hidden by an applied moulding.

Lipped Doors

Most lipped cabinet doors are cut from ¾-inch stock but sometimes small lipped doors are made with ½-inch plywood. Lipped or rabbeted doors are labour savers because lip covers joint between door edge and cabinet frame and means this joint need not fit with great accuracy.

One method to obtain a lipped door is to join two pieces of ⅜-inch plywood together so that the face piece is larger by the width of the lip.

Flush Doors

A variety of hinges are available for flush doors. In general it is best to avoid hinges that depend entirely upon screws set in the end grain of the plywood.

SLIDING DOORS

66

Sliding Doors

All sizes of sliding doors can be made from plywood. Simplest is a ¼-inch panel that slides between two wooden stops. It is used for small doors on alternate open and closed storage such as in bookshelves or cabinet. Sand edges of the panel and soap the slot.

For completely closed storage, by-passing panel doors are required. They can slide between three stops or in two dadoed slots as shown. Fibre tracks and channels are also available and are simple to install.

Solid panels of ¾-inch plywood are used for larger sliding doors. Full-sized wardrobe doors are best made with ¼-inch plywood glued to both sides of a frame of 1 inch lumber stock.

Full size doors require rolling hard-ware and are generally hung from the top. Several good types of top-hung nylon and other wheels and metal

DRAWER DETAILS

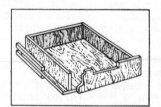

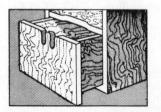

tracks are available in single and double track sizes.

Drawer Details

Typical plywood drawers, drawer pulls and sliding mechanisms are illustrated here.

In general ½-inch plywood is suitable for back and sides of a drawer with ¼-inch plywood used for the bottom and ⅝—inch for the front. Sides and bottom fit best if the front is rabbeted with a table saw to accommodate them.

One way to achieve a rabbeted effect in drawer front construction is to screw and glue two ⅜-inch thick pieces of plywood together so that the inner piece is shorter and narrower to take in the drawer sides and the bottom.

Paint Finishes

Conventional wall and woodwork paints and enamels may be used successfully on plywood. Best results are obtained when the panels are primed well, and high grade paints and enamels are used.

Texture Paints

Textured surfaces may be obtained by priming with regular undercoat followed by a heavy coat of stippling paint.

Water-thinned Paints

Before application of water-thinned paints, the plywood should be sealed with a clear resin, shellac, or a flat white paint to prevent grain raise. The paint is then applied according to manufacturer's directions.

For kitchen drawers, ¼-inch plywood dividers can easily be made to provide drawer sections that can contain cutlery, baking utensils and other kitchen equipment.

If edges of drawer bottoms and drawer runners are waxed or soaped, smooth operation of the drawer is readily achieved. Drawer runners can conveniently be made from ¾ X ¾ inch wood strips attached to the sides of the cabinet.

Hardware

Particular use for plywood projects:

Plywood lends itself to popular "Lazy Suzan" construction for corners. "Lazy Suzan" hardware can be purchased and, depending on the type installed, details for the revolving shelves can be easily worked out.

A variety of cabinet door catches are on the market, all of which can be used with plywood doors. On p. 48 some typical catches of the types available. Many others are equally efficient.

Sliding shelves can be built in several ways. A simple method is to purchase metal shelf hardware. Wooden shelf supports can be installed or shelf slots can be dadoed into the cabinet sides.

Interior Finishes

Painting procedures for finishing plywood are not different from those used to finish other wood. A variety of attractive finishes is possible.

Bleached or "Blond" Finish

The "bleached" effect is obtained with a preliminary white undercoat.

1. Apply one coat thinned white undercoat.
2. Before tacky, wipe down or dry-brush to desired tone by following the grain.
3. Sand lightly and apply one coat white shellac or flat varnish.

Stain Finish

If considerable grain contrast is desired, the surface may be stained without preliminary treatment. However, if a more subdued effect is preferred, the surface should be sealed with a clear resin sealer or thinned white shellac prior to application of the stain. The stained surface is then protected with coats of shellac or varnish.

Hardboard

Types and Sizes of Hardboard

Sizes and thicknesses shown are those generally available at lumber and building materials dealers, or which can be ordered through dealers. Some special sizes may not be listed. If you need a size not listed, check with your dealer.

Nominal Thickness (inches)	Sizes
Standard hardboard	
1/8 and 3/16	4 x 4, 4 x 7, 4 x 8, 4 x 9, 4 x 10, 4 x 12, 4 x 16
1/4	4 x 4, 4 x 7, 4 x 8, 4 x 10, 4 x 12, 4 x 16
5/16	4 x 4, 4 x 8, 4 x 9, 4 x 10, 4 x 12
Panel hardboard	
3/16 and 1/4	4 x 8, 4 x 10, 4 x 12, 4 x 16
Underlayment	
1/4	4 x 3, 4 x 4
Standard, both faces smooth	
1/8	5 x 8, 5 x 16, 4 x 8, 4 x 16
3/16	5 x 8, 5 x 16, 4 x 7, 4 x 8, 4 x 16
Perforated hardboard (standard and tempered)	
1/8	4 x 4, 4 x 8
1/4	4 x 8
Tempered hardboard	
1/8 and 3/16	4 x 4, 4 x 7, 4 x 8, 4 x 9, 4 x 10, 4 x 12, 4 x 16
1/4	4 x 4, 4 x 8, 4 x 10, 4 x 12, 4 x 16
5/16	4 x 8, 4 x 9, 4 x 10, 4 x 12
Black tempered hardboard	
1/8 and 1/4	4 x 4, 4 x 8, 4 x 10, 4 x 12
Tempered, both faces smooth	
1/8 and 3/16	4 x 4, 4 x 8, 4 x 10, 4 x 12
1/4	4 x 4, 4 x 8, 4 x 10, 4 x 12
5/16	4 x 8, 4 x 10, 4 x 12
Die-cut filigree hardboard	
1/8	16" x 6, 2 x 4, 2 x 6, 4 x 8
Hardboard tile panels	
1/8	4 x 4, 4 x 8, 4 x 10, 4 x 12, 4 x 16
Embossed Hardboard	
1/8	4 x 4, 4 x 6, 4 x 8, 4 x 12, 4 x 16
1/4	4 x 7, 4 x 8, 4 x 10
Concrete form hardboard	
3/16 and 1/4	4 x 8, 4 x 12

Siding (in panels)
(Thickness and lengths available vary with design and with manufacturer)

7/16	4 x 6, 4 x 7, 4 x 8, 4 x 9, 4 x 10, 4 x 12, 4 x 16

Siding (lap)
(Thickness and lengths and widths vary with design and manufacturer)

1/4, 5/16, 7/16	9", 12", 16", 24" widths 8, 12, 16-ft. lengths

In 1924, William Mason invented hardboard while seeking a use for the vast quantity of wood chips left as waste behind the nation's sawmill operations. Experimentally, he reduced the chips to their component fibers in a roaring blast of steam that removed impurities and left each wood fiber encased in lignin, the natural bonding agent of wood.

He made mats of the damp wood fibers, felting them together with their own coating of lignin. Then he applied heat and pressure to remove the moisture and to reweld the fibers. He expected to produce a soft insulating material. To his surprise, he made a smooth, tough, grainless panel—the world's first hardboard.

Since that time, hardboard has become a standard material for home construction, remodeling, repair, furniture making and craftwork. Its industrial uses increases each year because, while it has most of the characteristics of wood, it has some additional advantages.

The surface of hardboard is dense and smooth, ready for finishing as soon as it is applied. There is no grain, so there is no tendency for the finish to check. The panels are equally strong in all directions and there are no knots or other imperfections. Hardboard will not splinter or crack, it can be curved, fastened with any fastener, and easily worked with ordinary tools.

Standard Hardboard, the basic material, is light brown and has a fairly hard, smooth surface on one side and a rough screen impression on the other. It is recommended for most interior uses, such as partitions, ceilings and cabinets. It should not be used where there is excessive moisture or where subjected to considerable abrasion.

Tempered hardboard is impregnated with a special compound which produces a much harder wearing surface, increases the strength, and reduces moisture absorption. Tempered hardboard is a deeper brown, is suitable for interior and exterior use, and can be used where the humidity is high as in bathrooms or basements. If there is a doubt as to which kind to order, play it safe and order tempered. It will cost a little more but will wear much better.

Black-tempered hardboard is identical to tempered hardboard except that it is treated with a black dye at the time of manufacture. It is suitable only where a flat-black effect is desired.

Panel hardboard is somewhat denser than standard hardboard, but not as dense as tempered. It is chiefly intended for use in ceilings, walls and soffits, where high strength and hardness are not critical factors. It has good resiliency, and is finished smooth on one side.

Underlayment is manufactured specifically for use over wood floors or subfloors to provide an extremely smooth, flat surface upon which to lay linoleum, tile or carpeting.

Hardboard smooth on both sides is available in both standard and tempered types, for applications where both sides may be seen.

Hardboard tile panels are exceptionally hard, with a very low water-absorption rate. They are scored to give the appearance of 4-in. wall tiles, and are used primarily in bathrooms, kitchens and laundry areas, where a tile effect is desired.

Embossed hardboard is a tempered material with a patterned surface that is produced by embossing the finished side. A very popular finish looks like fine-grain leather. Other finishes, such as Travertine marble, are available and new patterns are frequently introduced. Embossed finishes are used mostly in wall paneling and in furniture making, but offer the homeowner a fine opportunity to achieve decorative effects.

Filigree hardboard is a die-cut panel for interior use, available in several patterns. The filigree effect is excellent in screens, room dividers, ceiling installations, and any place where an unusual design effect is desired.

Concrete-form hardboard is specially tempered for use in building forms for pouring concrete. Because it can be bent to make smooth curves, it is useful in making unusual, irregular or free-form shapes. It imparts a smooth finish to the concrete.

Hardboard siding is available in a number of designs and types. There is a minimum of waste in using this material, which produces a smooth surface, free of knots and checks.

It can be purchased unfinished, prime-coated, or in colors.

Perforated hardboard is a special wall panel developed for its decorative effect and its utility. Holes, 3/16-in. in diameter are drilled in it on 1/2-in. and 1-in. centers. A variety of wire hangers can be pushed into these holes to hold tools, kitchen implements, pictures, etc.

Pre-finished hardboard, coated with plastic or other materials, finished to look like fine hardwood paneling, is available for wall paneling or furniture finishing.

See the Chart on page 67 to find the range of sizes and thicknesses of hardboard panels that are commonly available. Note especially that there are "short" and "long" panels— longer or shorter than the standard 8-ft. lengths. These are easier to use and more economical in finishing rooms, for example, with 7, 9 or 10-ft. ceilings. These lengths may not be stocked by all dealers.

Hardboard is carried by most lumber and building-supply dealers. Many will cut a panel to size on request, but they may charge you on the basis of the next 24-in. multiple, regardless of where the cut is made.

Use Ordinary Tools

Ordinary woodworking tools can be used on all hardboards. The material is easily cut with a relatively fine-toothed saw. Coping, keyhole and compass saws also can be used. In sawing hardboard, always saw with the finished surface toward you. This produces a sharp, clean edge.

For cutting with power saws, a cross-cut or combination semi-high-speed or high-speed-steel blade is best. If you intend to do considerable cutting of hardboard, use a carbide-tipped blade.

Twist drills are better than auger bits for use with hardboard. Drilling should be done from the finished surface, not the screened side.

Hardboard panels can be bent to simple, one-directional curves. The material in its "cold dry" state can be "wrapped" around a curved framework—such as the frame of a curved cabinet—if the radius is not too small. Begin by fastening one end of the hardboard to the frame. Then bend the panel, and nail every few inches curing the bending to hold the curve.

For sharper bends, the hardboard panels should be soaked in cold water for a minimum of 40 minutes, or scrubbed with water on the screened side and stacked for a day or more to permit the moisture to be absorbed. If only one panel is to be bent, apply wet rags or newspapers to the screened side for the same period.

Almost any type of nail, wood screw, bolt, staple or rivet can be used to fasten hardboard. Always nail at right angles to the panel. Don't try to toenail hardboard, and don't drive nails too close to the edge of the panel. Always nail the center of the panel first (except in following curves), toward the edges. Don't nail closer than 3/8-in. to the panel edges.

Every hardboard joint must have solid support behind it. Don't use the hardboard itself as a nailing base. Nails won't hold satisfactorily in it.

Hardboard paneling can be installed with contact cement. Apply cement to the furring strips or framing members and to the paneling, and wait until it is dry. Carefully put the panel in place, setting it right the first time, since it will be difficult or impossible to move the paneling once the two cemented areas are in contact.

One-eight-inch hardboard is often used to provide a new surface for cracked plaster walls. The hardboard can be nailed through the old plaster to the studs. If the plaster is sound enough to hold it, the hardboard can be applied with waterproof tile cement or contact cement. After cementing the panels complete the job with finishing nails, starting at the center of each panel and working toward the edges.

One-eighth-inch hardboard should always be used over a solid, continuous surface. Other thicknesses may be fastened to furring strips, joists, studs or other framing members not more than 16-in..on centers.

If you intend to panel a large area with hardboard, it is a good idea to scrub the screened side of the panels with water and stack the panels back to back for a day or two before fastening them in place. This will cause a slight swelling in the hardboard and prevent trouble at the seams later.

When installing hardboard panels against a masonry wall, above or below grade, install a vapor barrier, such as polyethylene film or aluminum foil, over the framing members first.

Never butt two panels of hardboard tightly against each other. If the panels absorb moisture and swell, something will have to give—and usually a buckle appears at the joint. Leave a slight space at the joint to avoid this problem.

Finishing Hardboard

Almost any kind of finish that is suitable for wood is also suitable for hardboard, and finishes can be applied with a brush, roller or spray gun.

In painting or enameling, a three-coat application is recommended. Apply a good primer or sealer as a first coat, followed by an undercoater and one or two coats of paint.

When hardboard is used out of doors, all edges must be carefully sealed and protected with at least three coats of paint or enamel.

MINIMUM BENDING RADII (in inches)

Thickness Of Stock	Cold Dry Bends		Cold Moist Bends	
	Smooth Side Out	Smooth Side In	Smooth Side Out	Smooth Side in
Standard Hardboard				
1/8	12	10	7	5
3/16	18	16	10	8
1/4	27	24	15	12
5/16	35	30	22	18
Panel Hardboard				
3/16	20	18	12	10
1/4	30	27	18	15
Both Faces Smooth				
1/8	10		7	
3/16	16		12	
Tempered Hardboard				
1/8	9	7	6	4
3/16	16	14	9	6
1/4	25	22	14	10
5/16	35	30	20	16
Tempered, Both Faces Smooth				
1/8	10		7	
3/16	16		12	
Embossed Finishes				
1/8	10		7	

Moldings –
the finishing touch

No matter where located, moldings are a basic of design, an element to be utilized in a wide range of applications. Without moldings almost any structure, anything with dimension, is little more than a box shape with stark overhangs and uninteresting square corners.

A molding adds something both elemental and decorative, the finishing detail.

Traditional architecture utilizes a range of applied moldings both inside and outside the structure; inside as a finishing detail in a room, such as picture molding; a coved mold in the corner where wall meets ceiling; as a baseboard with quarter-round and as door and window trim with stops having one molded edge. Outside you see moldings in various forms under cornices, around sash frames and around and over door frames.

Common applied moldings are combinations of curves, reverse curves and plane surfaces generally worked on the face, corners and edges of both hard and softwood lumber. As a rule these shapes come in the form of strips varying in width and thickness and are sold by the lineal foot.

Common among the applied moldings are the simple cove and quarter-round shapes which are cut on small square or rectangular strips. The former shape is ordinarily used as trim under an overhanging member such as a mantel, shelf or similar application. The latter you'll see forming the trim where a baseboard meets flooring. Of course, there are variants in the application and shape of these forms which are commonly known as bed moldings.

Crown and cove moldings are similar in that both shapes are usually cut on one face of stock varying in width from 2 or 3 in. to 5 in. or more in the standard sizes.

These moldings, usually intended to span a right-angle corner, are cut at a 45-deg. angle and the adjacent corners are trimmed at 90 deg. to the 45-deg. corners, the flats serving as "stops" for the curves cut on the face.

Cove moldings are commonly cut with a single concavity on the face, often the full width of the stock, but these also are cut in combinations of concavity and reverse curve.

Common crown moldings consist of variations of reverse-curve and cove cuts in combination on the same face of the stock. They come in standard widths from about 1½ in. up. Like the cove moldings, crown moldings in the larger sizes are designed to span a corner.

Half-round moldings, of which there are various sizes, generally are applied as nosings, that is, are nailed or otherwise fastened to square edges to serve either a practical or decorative purpose.

Stops commonly range in thickness from ⅜ to ½ in. and in widths up to 2 in. or more. These usually come with a reverse-curve molding on one corner but there also are variants of the shapes available. Some are supplied with only one corner slightly rounded to a uniform radius. Stops are used mainly in door and window framing and are ordinarily attached with small finishing nails having the heads set below the surface and the holes puttied flush. On the finest work the stops are attached with ovalhead screws, the heads being countersunk flush or turned down on plated washers.

Other shapes which classify as moldings are full rounds, screen moldings, chair rails, window stools and corner beads to name a few of the many shapes. Some of these are not so commonly used in present-day construction but most are still available as replacements. Full rounds in larger sizes are often utilized as stair rails. A variant (although it does not classify as molding) is the well-known dowel, which is regularly supplied 36 in. long.

If you've ever made screen frames you've used one of the several forms of screen moldings and you'll see many of the other forms illustrated in nearly all old work and occasionally in newer structures.

All the illustrations, which are end views of the shapes, show only one size. But, of course, many of the moldings come in several widths and thicknesses to adapt them to various types of work.

Patterns and sizes

CROWNS

WP 49 11/16" x 3 5/8"

WP 52 11/16" x 2 3/4"

WP 60 11/16" x 1 3/4"

WP 74 11/16" x 1 3/4"

COVES

WP 85 11/16" x 1 3/4"

WP 86 11/16" x 1 5/8"

BEDS

WP 90 3/4" x 1 1/8"

WP 93 3/4" x 3/4"

QUARTER ROUNDS

WP 103 1 1/16" x 1 1/16"
WP 105 3/4" x 3/4"
WP 108 1/2" x 1/2"
WP 110 1/4" x 1/4"

HALF ROUNDS

WP 123 5/16" x 5/8"
WP 124 1/4" x 1/2"

BASE SHOE

WP 126 1/2" x 3/4"

SHELF EDGES

WP 142 1/4" x 3/4"

WP 144 1/4" x 3/4"

BRICK MOLDINGS

WP 175 1 1/16" x 2"

WP 180 1 5/16" x 2"

DRIP CAPS

WP 187 1 1/16" x 2"
WP 188 1 1/16" x 1 5/8"

WP 196 11/16" x 1 3/4"
WP 197 11/16" x 1 5/8"

CORNER GUARDS

WP 201 1 3/8" x 1 3/8"

WP 202 1 1/8" x 1 1/8"

WP 203 1 3/8" x 1 3/8"

WP 205 1 1/8" x 1 1/8"

WP 206 3/4" x 3/4"

SHINGLE MOLDINGS

WP 207 11/16" x 2 1/2"
WP 208 11/16" x 2"
WP 210 11/16" x 1 5/8"

WP 212 11/16" x 2 1/2"
WP 213 9/16" x 2"

HAND RAILS

WP 230 1 5/16" x 1 11/16"

WP 231 1 5/8" x 1 3/4"

ROUNDS

WP 232 1 5/8" x 1 5/8"
WP 233 1 5/16" x 1 5/16"
WP 234 1 1/16" x 1 1/16"

S4S STOCK

WP 236 1 5/8" x 1 5/8"
WP 237 1 5/16" x 1 5/16"
WP 238 1 1/16" x 1 1/16"
WP 239 3/4" x 3/4"

WP 246 3/4" x 2 3/4"
WP 248 3/4" x 1 3/4"
WP 249 3/4" x 1 5/8"
WP 251 3/4" x 1 3/8"
WP 254 1/2" x 3/4"

PICTURE MOLDING

WP 273 11/16" x 1 3/4"

LATTICE

WP 265 9/32" x 1 3/4"
WP 266 9/32" x 1 5/8"
WP 267 9/32" x 1 3/8"
WP 268 9/32" x 1 1/8"

BACK BAND

WP 280 11/16" x 1 1/16"

PLY CAPS

WP 294 11/16" x 1 1/8"

WP 296 3/4" x 3/4"

BASE CAPS

WP 163 11/16" x 1 3/8"

WP 167 11/16" x 1 1/8"

CASING AND BASE

WP 301 11/16" x 2 1/2"
WP 306 11/16" x 2 1/4"

WP 315 11/16" x 2 1/2"

WP 316 11/16" x 2 1/4"

STOPS

WP 816 7/16" x 1 3/8"
WP 818 7/16" x 1 1/8"
WP 820 7/16" x 7/8"

WP 846 7/16" x 1 3/8"
WP 848 7/16" x 1 1/8"
WP 850 7/16" x 7/8"

WP 876 7/16" x 1 3/8"
WP 878 7/16" x 1 1/8"
WP 880 7/16" x 7/8"

WP 906 7/16" x 1 3/8"
WP 908 7/16" x 1 1/8"
WP 910 7/16" x 7/8"

WP 936 7/16" x 1 3/8"
WP 938 7/16" x 1 1/8"
WP 940 7/16" x 7/8"

MULLION CASING

WP 978 3/8" x 1 3/4"

WP 983 3/8" x 1 3/4"

CASING AND BASE

WP 321 11/16" x 2 1/4"

WP 324 11/16" x 2 1/4"

WP 327 11/16" x 2 1/4"

WP 351 11/16" x 2 1/2"
WP 356 11/16" x 2 1/4"

WP 361 11/16" x 2 1/2"
WP 366 11/16" x 2 1/4"

WP 376 11/16" x 2 1/4"

WP 329 11/16" x 2 1/4"

WP 444 11/16" x 3 1/2"

WP 412 11/16" x 3 1/2"
WP 432 9/16" x 3 1/2"
WP 433 9/16" x 3 1/4"

WP 620 9/16" x 4 1/4"
WP 622 9/16" x 3 1/2"
WP 623 9/16" x 3 1/4"

WP 452 11/16" x 2 1/2"
WP 472 9/16" x 2 1/2"

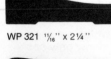

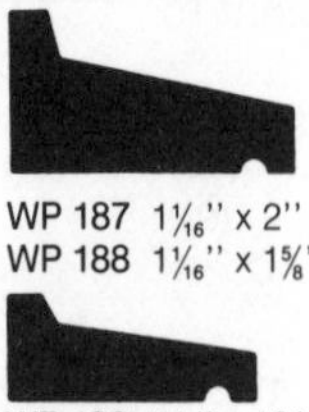

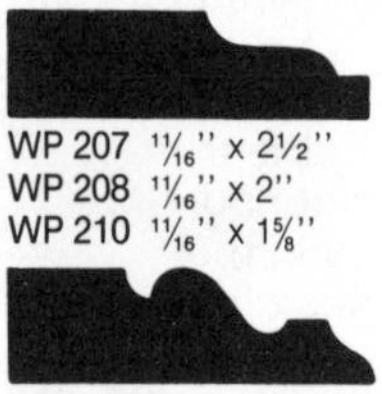

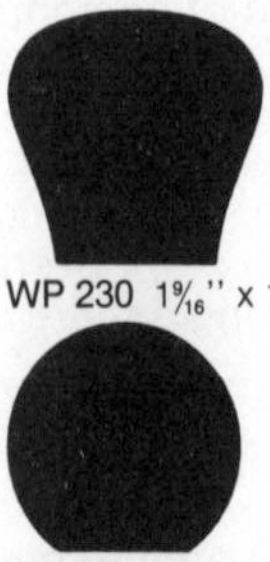

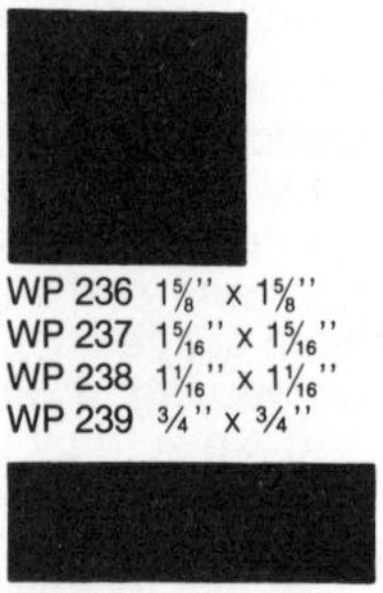

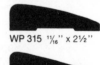

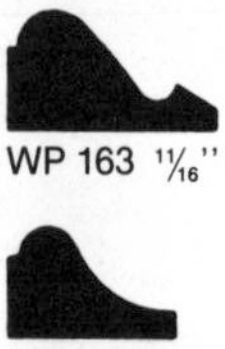

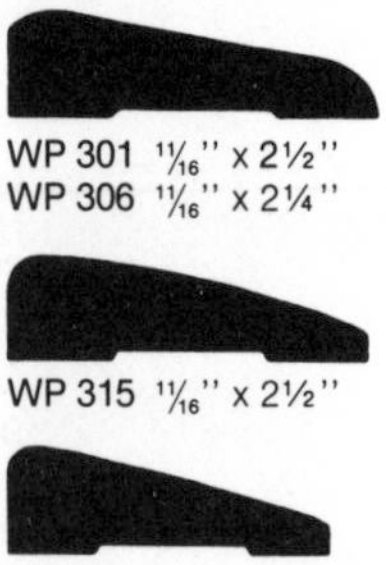

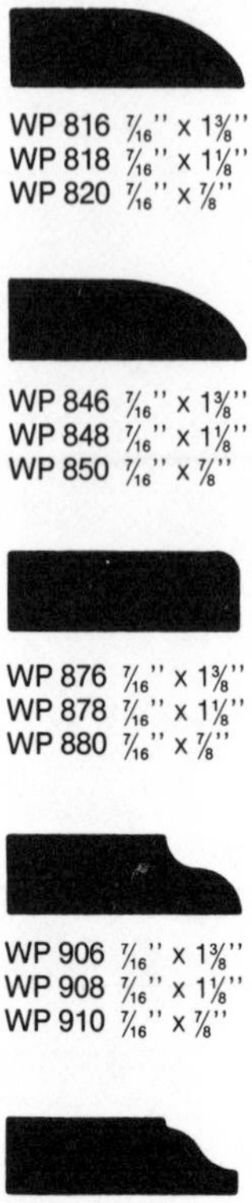

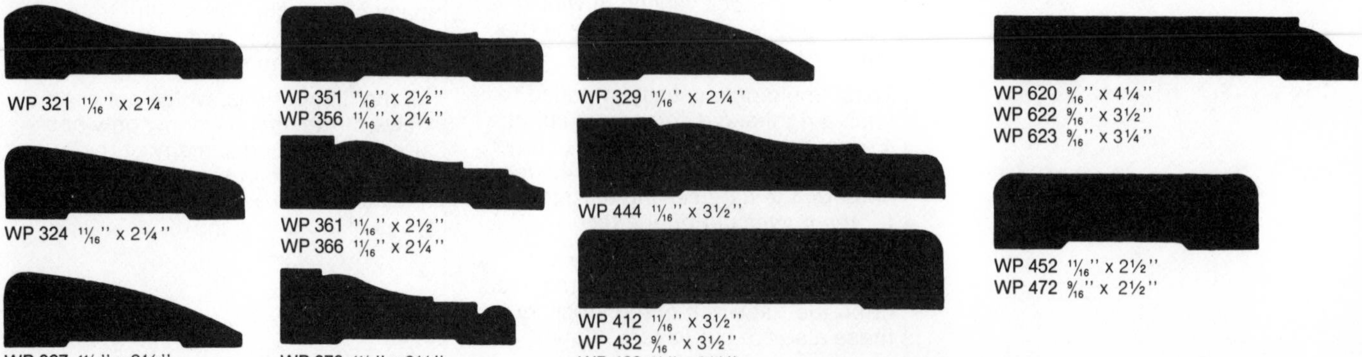

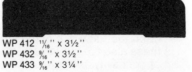

Work magic with moldings

Make no mistake about it, your molding job will look only as good as the workmanship you put into it. How accurately joints fit and nails are placed reveal just how much effort was supplied. Get in the habit of using sharp saws only. A dull saw — no matter how great your patience and effort — is almost certain to produce unsightly, amateurish-looking joints.

The first rule is never to guess at miter cuts — always use a miterbox. It is important to remember this rule or you will waste a lot of molding by making miter cuts in the wrong plane.

When installing moldings around outside corners the ends are mitered and it's the usual practice to cut the two members just slightly over at the mitered ends. This assures a tight fit and should there be slight shrinkage of the wood, or movement of the framing due to shrinkage, the mitered joint will remain a tight fit.

In the case of cove or crown moldings around the ceiling of a room, you should remember that while outside corners are generally mitered, inside corners should always be coped — you should never miter both. If you do, the inside ones will later open up when the wood shrinks, making a poor joint.

Coping is the term applied to cutting the reverse shape of one molding to coincide with the profile contour of the adjoining molding when the two are butted together.

Transferring the reverse shape to the molding can pose a perplexing problem. However, there's a simple stunt to follow that will give you a near-perfect fit every time. The line of cut is actually "marked" by placing the molding in the miterbox and sawing the end at a 45-degree angle. Here you will notice that the molding is set in the miterbox in the same position as it will be installed — the part that fits flat against the wall is placed flat against the back of the box.

The very edge of the 45-degree cut establishes the line of cut which is now carefully followed with a coping saw held at right angles to the face of the molding. This way you will have a perfect joint.

Where all corners of a room are inside corners, only one end of each molding is coped, the other end is simply sawed off square to butt into the corner. Moldings that fit between walls should not be forced; rather they should be cut slightly under. A coped joint — like all molding joints — should be installed with glue as well as nails.

How to miter and cope moldings

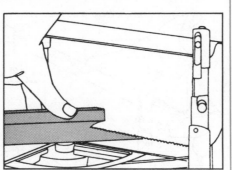

Set miterbox saw at 45° to make miter cuts. Always hold molding securely while doing the cutting.

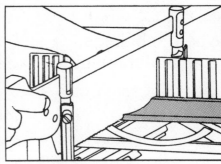

To cope a joint, first make the miter cut to the exact length desired as shown above.

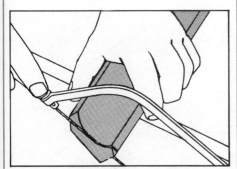

Next, with coping saw held at 45° angle, follow miter line (profile) to cut out wedge-shape piece.

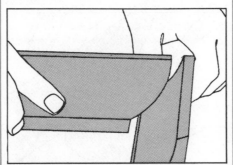

Test-fit the coped molding against piece of molding to which it will butt.

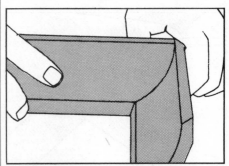

If necessary, use block plane and sandpaper to assure tight-fitting joint. Glue and nail to fasten.

How to do blind nailing

72

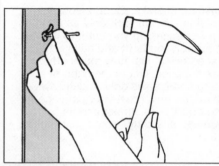

Carefully gouge up a small sliver of wood that's wide enought to conceal the finishing-nail head.

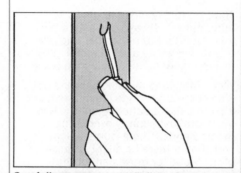

Carefully swing sliver out of way, then drive in the nail. Next step is to set the nailhead.

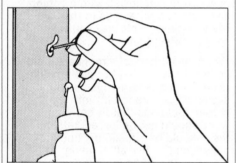

Apply white glue to the sliver and push it into place. Immediately wipe off any glue ooze-out.

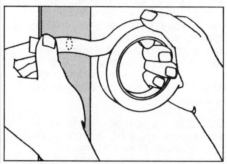

Press on a piece of masking tape to hold the sliver in place until the glue is completely dry.

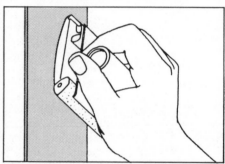

After glue is dry, remove masking tape and touch up the blind spot with a fine-grit sandpaper.

Where moldings meet at right angle

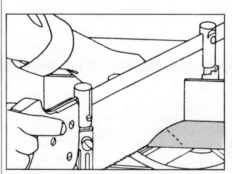

Two 45° cuts are made to create point with length equal to half-width of the molding.

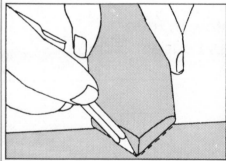

Use the piece as the pattern for laying out the cuts to be made on the piece it will join.

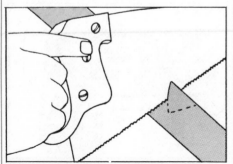

Following the lines, use a finetooth, cross-cut saw to make the cutout on the mating molding.

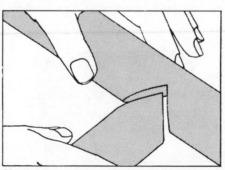

Check joint for fit. If you made the cuts carefully, joint should be practically invisible.

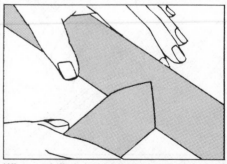

When satisfied with the joint, use glue and toenail several brads through one mold into other.

Wood joints

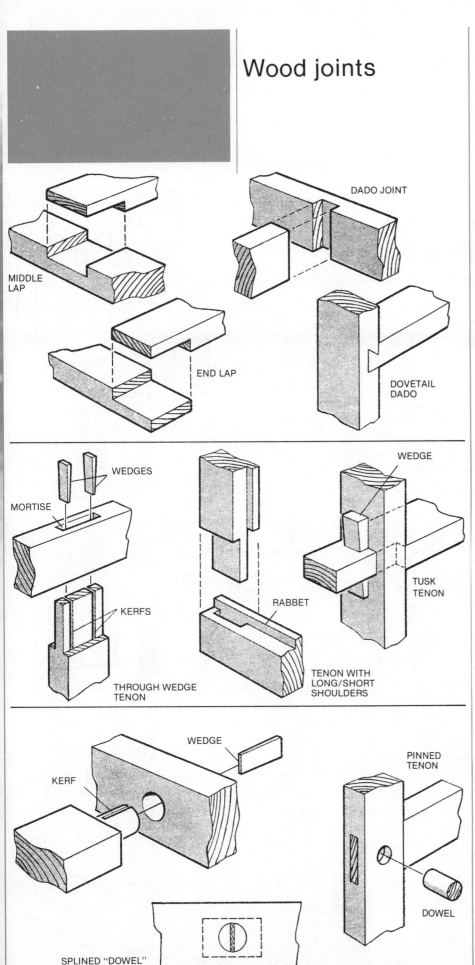

DADO JOINT

MIDDLE LAP

END LAP

DOVETAIL DADO

WEDGES

MORTISE

KERFS

THROUGH WEDGE TENON

WEDGE

RABBET

TENON WITH LONG/SHORT SHOULDERS

TUSK TENON

WEDGE

KERF

PINNED TENON

DOWEL

SPLINED "DOWEL" TENON JOINT

Do you know the difference between a cogged joint and a tusk joint, between a bare-face tenon and a dovetail dado?

A working knowledge of the many different ways wood members may be fitted to one another will help in determining the best, most practical joinery to use in assembling any project you build. Some of the joints shown here are simple to make; others are more involved. You'll notice that a few are partly self-fastening. All 28 have their place in good, sound furniture construction. The one you pick will depend on the project itself. Often you have a choice, one joint being as strong as the other.

Many of the joints shown — half-lap, dado, rabbet, spline, open mortise and plain butt — can be made easily on a table saw alone. This is partly so also when making a mortise-and-tenon joint, except that the mortise part of the joint requires a drill press equipped with a mortising attachment. Here a bit turning inside a hollow square chisel removes the waste as the chisel squares up the corners.

A mortise, blind or exposed, is similarly formed when done by hand. A row of overlapping holes is first made within the mortise outlines, then a regular chisel and mallet are used to do the squaring. General practice in making a mortise-and-tenon joint is to cut the tenon first, then the mortise. Likewise, the cheek cuts on a tenon are generally made after the shoulder cuts.

Exact spacing of mating holes and square drilling are important steps in making strong dowel-fastened joints. Even greater strength is had when the dowels themselves have spiral grooves in them. Such grooves give glue additional holding power.

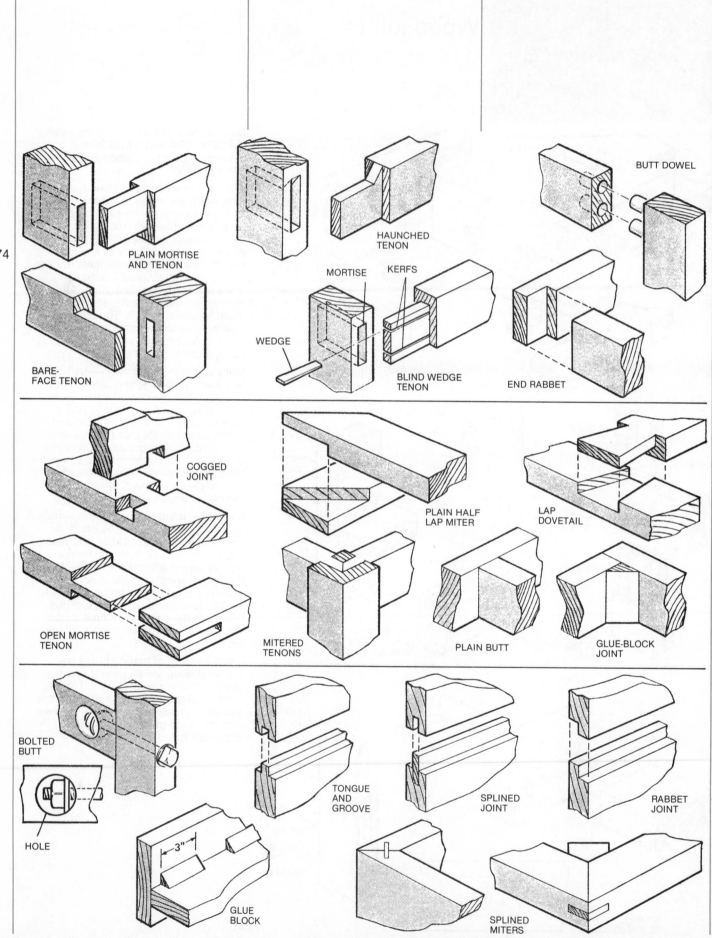

74

PLAIN MORTISE
AND TENON

HAUNCHED
TENON

BUTT DOWEL

BARE-
FACE TENON

WEDGE

MORTISE

KERFS

BLIND WEDGE
TENON

END RABBET

COGGED
JOINT

PLAIN HALF
LAP MITER

LAP
DOVETAIL

OPEN MORTISE
TENON

MITERED
TENONS

PLAIN BUTT

GLUE-BLOCK
JOINT

BOLTED
BUTT

HOLE

TONGUE
AND
GROOVE

SPLINED
JOINT

RABBET
JOINT

3"

GLUE
BLOCK

SPLINED
MITERS

12 ways to attach legs

Your choice of methods for attaching legs depends on the piece of furniture and its style. If you're building a simple modern chest or slab table, you can get by with purchased legs that screw into their own mounting plates. But if you're reproducing or refurbishing a period piece, you'll most likely have to go to hand joinery.

The dozen methods sketched on these pages cover most means of attaching legs to rails and aprons or flat undersides. Say you want to build a workbench that won't jiggle or "walk" when you plane stock or do some hammering. For this, use the butt joint with a drawbolt to join the legs to the rails of the frame. You'll get a job that will take the roughest usage — EVEN WITHOUT BRACING OR GLUING.

In making a cabinet or table with turned legs, use rails-to-legs joints with mitered, wedged or draw-pinned tenons.

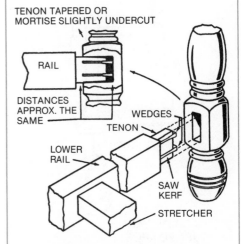

TENON SHOULD NOT BE MORE THAN ONE THIRD WIDTH OF LEG STOCK

MITERED TENON

RAIL

LEG

RAIL

1 MORTISE-AND-TENON JOINT WITH MITERED TENONS

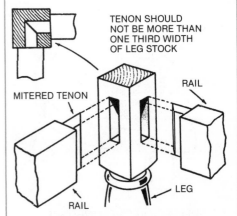

TENON TAPERED OR MORTISE SLIGHTLY UNDERCUT

RAIL

DISTANCES APPROX. THE SAME

WEDGES

TENON

LOWER RAIL

SAW KERF

STRETCHER

2 MORTISE-AND-TENON JOINT WITH WEDGED TENON

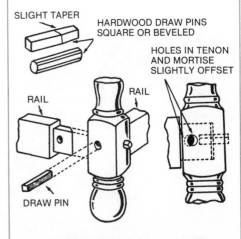

SLIGHT TAPER

HARDWOOD DRAW PINS SQUARE OR BEVELED

HOLES IN TENON AND MORTISE SLIGHTLY OFFSET

RAIL

RAIL

DRAW PIN

3 MORTISE-AND-TENON JOINT DRAW-PINNED

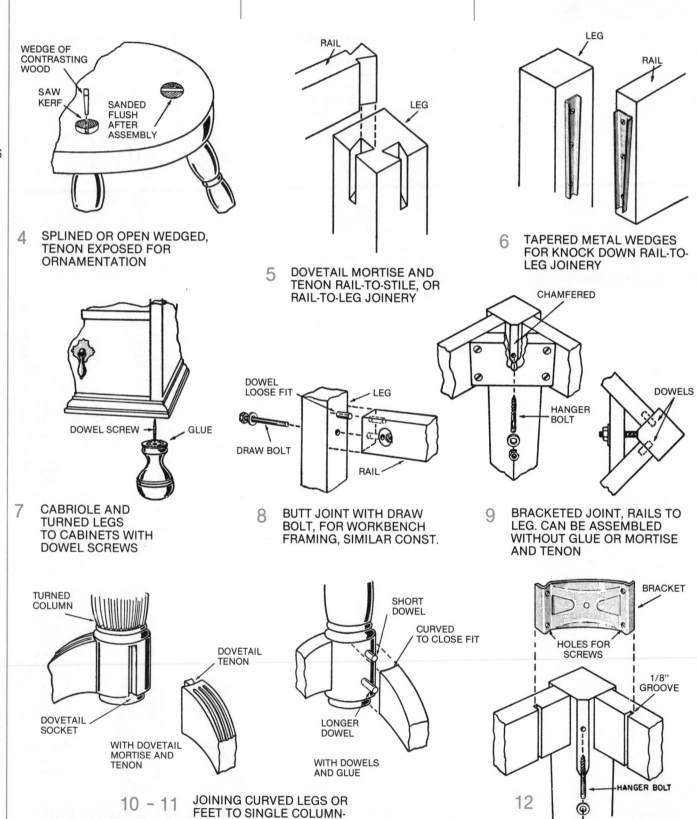

4 SPLINED OR OPEN WEDGED, TENON EXPOSED FOR ORNAMENTATION

WEDGE OF CONTRASTING WOOD

SAW KERF

SANDED FLUSH AFTER ASSEMBLY

RAIL

LEG

5 DOVETAIL MORTISE AND TENON RAIL-TO-STILE, OR RAIL-TO-LEG JOINERY

LEG

RAIL

6 TAPERED METAL WEDGES FOR KNOCK DOWN RAIL-TO-LEG JOINERY

DOWEL SCREW

GLUE

7 CABRIOLE AND TURNED LEGS TO CABINETS WITH DOWEL SCREWS

DOWEL LOOSE FIT

LEG

DRAW BOLT

RAIL

8 BUTT JOINT WITH DRAW BOLT, FOR WORKBENCH FRAMING, SIMILAR CONST.

CHAMFERED

HANGER BOLT

DOWELS

9 BRACKETED JOINT, RAILS TO LEG. CAN BE ASSEMBLED WITHOUT GLUE OR MORTISE AND TENON

TURNED COLUMN

DOVETAIL SOCKET

DOVETAIL TENON

WITH DOVETAIL MORTISE AND TENON

SHORT DOWEL

CURVED TO CLOSE FIT

LONGER DOWEL

WITH DOWELS AND GLUE

BRACKET

HOLES FOR SCREWS

1/8" GROOVE

HANGER BOLT

10 – 11 JOINING CURVED LEGS OR FEET TO SINGLE COLUMN-TWO WAYS

12

The glue used for any job should be a little stronger than the wood that forms the joint. *Polyvinyl (white)* glue is perhaps easiest to use, but is not as strong as some other glues. Don't use excessive pressure when clamping polyvinyl. *Plastic resin* is extremely strong, and leaves an almost invisible glue line, but it requires heavy clamping pressure. *Casein* is good choice for oily woods such as teak and pitch pine, and shrinks very little in drying. *Resorcinol glue* is waterproof, but never apply it at temperatures lower than 70°. *Contact cement* is the choice for applying any sheet material to a wood base, but *don't spray it on!* It's highly flammable. *Epoxy* is not a good choice for wood joints (wood inhibits its curing) but may be useful in cementing metal or plastic to wood.

WOODWORKERS' GLUING CHART

TYPE OF WORK	GLUE FOR LOW-COST WATER-RESISTANT JOINT (In order of preference)
All general gluing of hard and softwoods	Plastic resin glue Casein glue Polyvinyl glue
Particle and chip boards to wood	Plastic resin glue Casein glue Contact cement Polyvinyl glue
Plywood to decorative plastic laminates	Casein glue Contact cement Plastic resin glue
Laminating heavy framing members	Casein glue
Veneering, inlays, cabinet work	Plastic resin glue (extended) Polyvinyl glue
Bonding oily woods (teak, pitch pine, osage, yew)	Casein glue (sponge surface with dilute caustic soda solution 1 hour before gluing)
End-wood joints, mitered joints, scarf joints	Polyvinyl glue Casein glue (heavy mix)
Loose-fitting joints, relatively rough surfaces	Polyvinyl glue Casein glue (heavy mix)
Doweling	Plastic resin glue Polyvinyl glue
Hardboard to plywood, wood or itself	Plastic resin glue Casein glue Polyvinyl glue Contact cement
Porous materials, such as linoleum and canvas to wood	Plastic resin glue Casein glue Contact cement
Plastics, metal and foil to wood	Epoxy glue

Glues and adhesives

Introduction

We've come a long way from the flour-and-water paste we once used to paste up our scrap books. The Space Age is brewing up some fierce new adhesives to replace the old glue pot. In the home the variety of glues available makes it possible to make and mend almost everything. New cements are reducing the use of traditional fasteners such as nails, and it is no longer unusual to find many recreation rooms held together by adhesives alone.

Why the Need for the Many Different Varieties of Adhesives?

No single adhesive can do all types of bonding work—on all types of material. There really is no such thing as a "Universal" adhesive. Vegetable, mineral, animal and synthetic adhesives all have different characteristics on different kinds of bonding jobs.

Many of the new glues are fully as strong as claimed, but there are some jobs they simply won't do. Many of them are designed for adhering very specific materials together. Contact Cement, Household Cement, Epoxy Glue etc. are more or less multi-purpose glues and are good for general repairs.

Choosing the Right Glue for the Job

The trick to choosing the right glue is to know which glue is right for which surface; to know how much strength is required, and whether your glue can provide it; and to know if your glue has the right characteristics (waterproof, heat resistant, quick setting, etc.) for the job. Perhaps several will have the qualities you need. It is then that you should decide on the basis of cost and ease of use. For example, using an epoxy which is fairly expensive and tricky to work with, to glue paper together would be like hiring a cab to take a book next door.

In choosing an adhesive for the job, the first consideration should be the materials you are trying to bond. It makes a great difference. For example, paper is an extremely porous material and you can stick paper to paper with paste or mucilage, but when you attempt to bond paper to metal you are up against an entirely different problem, metal being quite non-porous.

Wood to wood, two porous surfaces, presents no great problem. Plastic resin glue and waterproof marine glue do a fine job here. But when you start bonding wood to glass or wood to metal you are dealing with another set of circumstances and here, epoxy might be the answer.

Gluing and Clamping

It's a safe bet that though all the king's horses and all the king's men couldn't put Humpty Dumpty together again, the *right glue* could make those mends! The variety and versatility of glues and adhesives available today make is possible for you to fix most things around the house—from chairs to stairs, chandeliers to wood veneers, and lots more! But you do need to follow certain rules in gluing and mending procedures:

- You must select the right glue for the materials you're repairing.
- You must know whether the glue will hold the pieces together without clamps or weights or some form of pressure, or whether clamps are a *must*.
- You need to study the nature of the glue. Read instructions on the container. Some glues give off vapors or fumes that are dangerous to inhale (the so-called airplane glues that children have been known to sniff for "kicks"). Other glues *cannot be used in the presence of any flame—including stove pilot lights and lighted cigarettes. The danger from these is explosion and fire.* Some glues must be mixed, and others will not take hold effectively if you're working in the cold or in rooms with temperatures below 50 degrees Fahrenheit. If you're repairing wood, don't start a project in a room or shed that may go from warm to very cold overnight—while the glue is drying. (Furniture glues usually require a temperature of 75 degrees Fahrenheit for twenty-four hours, and, according to the experts, the wood itself should be about the same temperature.)

For details on types of glue and how to use them, consult the chart opposite, see our suggestions on various ways to put pressure on your mending projects, and take our tips on gluing techniques.

Glue Chart

Characteristics

ACRYLIC RESIN GLUE

A two-part glue (liquid and powder). Drying and setting times are controlled by the proportions of liquid to powder. Extremely strong bond is made when glue dries—it takes a weight of 3 tons to break the glued joint apart!

ALIPHATIC RESIN GLUE

Comes ready to use; looks like heavy cream. Advantage of this glue is that it can be "dyed" or precolored with watersoluble dyes to match the material being repaired. It's water-resistant but *not* waterproof.

BUNA-N BASE ADHESIVE

Made from synthetic rubber; tan in color; sold in tubes or bottles. Its great virtue is that, like rubber, it's flexible yet strong.

CASEIN GLUE

The old reliable glue, made from milk. It comes as a light beige powder which you mix with water. The glue is not waterproof, but it is moisture-resistant, and has long been used on outside jobs. The unmixed powder will last for as long as two years.

CLEAR CEMENT OR PLASTIC CEMENT

Dries clear, sets quickly (in about 10 minutes) with some pressure put on the joint, but the cement takes 24 to 48 hours to set completely. Waterproof except on wood and *some* plastic surfaces; it will discolor wood and *some* plastics. *Most cements are flammable before they're dry. The fumes are toxic and dangerous.* When gluing plastic, use the cement best suited. Styrene glues are usually best for rigid plastics; vinyl glues best for flexible plastics.

CONTACT CEMENT

Bonds on contact and needs no clamping. *Most contact cements are flammable, and the fumes are toxic.* But some types (for kitchen-counter laminating) are water-based; use these if you're working in a room with a pilot light. Don't use contact cements on copper, brass, bronze, or manganese.

Uses

ACRYLIC RESIN GLUE
Special glue for very special jobs. Good for heavy-duty repairs to objects immersed in water (such as boats), but useful in the home, too. Sticks to almost anything, including metal and wood. Good for filling gaps or cracks in objects that hold or are in water.

ALIPHATIC RESIN GLUE
Good general wood glue. It is water-resistant enough to be used for various indoor and covered-porch furnishings.

BUNA-N BASE ADHESIVE
Special glue for bonding two materials with a flexible joint between them. This glue will bond *anything to anything*, allowing ample back-and-forth movement.

CASEIN GLUE
A good furniture glue. This also works as a gap filler in wood that's cracked. Can be used outdoors. It makes a strong bond when it's set.

CLEAR CEMENT OR PLASTIC CEMENT
Good for most plastics (but check the package directions; some plastics resist gluing). Also good for wood, metal, paper, glass, ceramics. Fine for jewelry repairs.

CONTACT CEMENT
The best adhesive to use for bonding plastic laminates (such as plastic counter tops), linoleum, leather, or synthetic rubber, to wood. Good for china. Good for replacing tiles. Can be used with metals, *except* copper, bronze, brass, manganese.

Special Directions

ACRYLIC RESIN GLUE
Must be mixed. Be sure to follow directions on container to get proper proportions for the job you're doing. Drying and setting controlled by the amounts mixed: for example, 3 parts of powder to 1 of liquid will set in about 5 minutes at 70 degrees Fahrenheit. Changing these proportions will allow for faster or slower drying and setting.

ALIPHATIC RESIN GLUE
Will hold light weight, small jobs together without clamping, but you should hold the mend in place for a minute or two to be sure it's dried.

BUNA-N BASE ADHESIVE
When this glue is used on porous materials, the moving parts can be assembled while the glue is wet. But when you want a flexible joint between two nonporous materials (such as two pieces of metal), apply the glue, let it dry, then soften it with heat just before bringing the parts together. Don't put *newly* glued items on good tabletops, etc., because the solvent in the glue may mar their finish.

CASEIN GLUE
Can be worked with in any temperature above freezing.

CLEAR CEMENT OR PLASTIC CEMENT
Roughen nonporous surfaces to be mended. Clamp the joined pieces while cement is drying for a tight, firm bond. Some types (such as the ones used on model airplanes) give a good-enough bond if the pieces are held together for 15-20 seconds. *Be sure to work in a well-ventilated room. Don't work near flame (including stove pilot light or lighted cigarette).*

CONTACT CEMENT
Coat both surfaces generously, and allow to dry before joining them. Drying takes from ¼ to ½ hour, but you must finish the job in 2 hours. Once the glued surfaces touch they're impossible to adjust, so these must be aligned exactly before you join them. Be sure that the temperature in the room is at least 65 degrees Fahrenheit or the bond will be weak. Complete drying time requires 8 hours to several days, and surfaces to be joined must be absolutely dry or they will come apart. *Be sure to work in a well-ventilated room. Don't work near flame (pilot light on stove or lighted cigarette) unless you're sure the contact cement you're using is water-based.*

Characterics	Uses	Special Directions
EPOXY GLUE Provides a very strong bond, but not a flexible one. Doesn't shrink when it hardens. Is waterproof and heat-resistant; mends made with epoxy can be washed in a dishwasher, after the glue has set. The mixture must be used quickly. Clamp the repair while the glue cures. A little heat from a light bulb will shorten the curing time. If you work in low temperatures (50 degrees or less) the epoxy will not harden. Normal curing is ½ to 8 hours. (A new type of epoxy hardens in 5 minutes.) It's expensive, so use glue sparingly—for the job that needs this type of strength, waterproofing, and heat-resistance.	Good to use on metals and china. Also good for ceramics, glass, pottery, porcelain, marble, concrete, brick, most plastics (some resist gluing), rubber, cloth, and wood.	Must be mixed *exactly* so follow the instructions on the container. Usually, equal proportions of resin and hardener are called for. Mix these thoroughly (too little mixing and the mend will come apart). Wait 5 minutes and mix again. Be sure to get the epoxy into all cracks and crevices on each surface. Be sure surfaces are dirt-and-grease-free. Use a thin coat of glue. Roughen all nonporous surfaces (such as metal) to make a better grip for the glue.
HIDE GLUE The traditional *hot glue* of the cabinetmaker. Comes in two forms—solid flakes or strips, or liquid. Sets overnight. Not waterproof. The solid types must first be soaked, then heated, and mixed with the proper amount of water. You must use it quickly. Your best bet is probably the *liquid* type. The liquid glue is ready to use and allows plenty of working time.	If you're a purist and want to do repairs on fine furniture, this is an excellent glue for the job.	In all cabinetwork and furniture repairs, surfaces should be carefully prepared. All the old glue should be scraped from joints, then the surfaces given a soaking in warm vinegar and water to remove vestiges of old glue. Dry the surfaces to be joined, roughen them a little, wipe clean, then apply thinnest possible coat of glue. Let it soak into the pores of the wood for a few minutes, then join and *clamp tightly* overnight.
POLYVINYL RESIN GLUE OR WHITE GLUE Dries quickly and doesn't stain. Is nontoxic, nonflammable. It requires little pressure and only short clamping time. Comes ready to use, usually in a squeeze bottle. Doesn't support great stress for long periods. A recent type of this glue is washable but not waterproof.	Good for paper, wood, cloth, leather, and other porous materials.	Not to be used on bare metal—causes corrosion. Sets fully in 72 hours, and when the work is clamped, the glue will give you a stronger bond.
RESORCINOL RESIN GLUE Comes in 2 parts: a syrupy resin and a powder; these are mixed. Completely waterproof, and is stronger than wood.	Fine for outdoor furniture and for items immersed in water—such as boats (even toy boats).	Temperature of surroundings must be at least 70 degrees Fahrenheit. Will set in 8 hours in these conditions and in 1½ hours at 100 degrees Fahrenheit. Bonding strength increases for next 6 weeks. Keeps indefinitely.
RUBBER-BASE ADHESIVE Comes in tubes and cans (for large-scale projects). It's usually black, sticks to most things, can be used on nonporous materials if there's a way for the solvent to evaporate.	Economy all-purpose adhesive. Can be used to caulk roofs, and will hold wall panels to brick or concrete. Can also be used to seal seams underwater.	Though this will glue wood to wood, there are other adhesives (see above) that are better for the job. When used for caulking, let this glue harden, then paint it and the seam will be less visible. You can make cleanups (of hands or tools) with kerosene (but be careful when you use kerosene—a flammable material).
STEEL AND ALUMINUM GLUES **(Plastic Steel, Plastic Aluminum, Furnace Cement)** Most of these adhesives come in squeeze tubes. Best used as fillers for cracks. The furnace cement (Quick Metal) is actually used to repair furnaces and hardens like steel.	For patching metal cracks and for bonding two metals together. The furnace cement is best to use where fireproof mending is needed, but big or tricky metalwork on stoves, etc. is something you should consult a blacksmith about.	Be sure to follow directions for each type of metal sealer or bonder.
NEUTRAL LIBRARY PASTE **(Also called Book-Binder's Paste)** Made of white flour and water. Is acid-free and thus is used for mounting art works.	The ideal paste recommended for original paintings and art works to be mounted and framed. Available at art supply stores.	Keeps well for a few days in cool temperatures. Discard it when it "sours".

Clamping and clamps

Repair projects that use glue almost always require pressure to set the mend. The surest and most professional way to exert this pressure is with various kinds of clamps. The basic types are available at hardware stores. You may want to use several clamps for one job, *or* you may use various sizes of one type of clamp for various repair jobs.

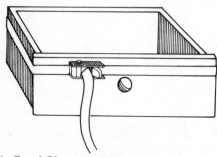

1. **Band Clamps.** These come in canvas or steel bands, and work like a belt that you pull tightly around your waist. They are indispensable for bringing strong pressure on irregular surfaces. The band encircles the work, is pulled tight through a self-locking device (like the buckle on a stretch belt), and is released with a flick of the fingers. You can buy the band clamp with four steel corners for special repairs on items like picture frames.

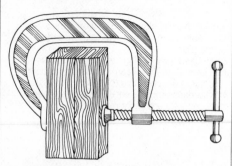

2. **C Clamps.** So called because they're shaped like the letter C. C Clamps come in about two dozen different sizes. You'll find the C clamp right for most of the gluing and clamping work you do. To use the clamp, insert the repair in the jaws of the clamp, then tighten the screw.

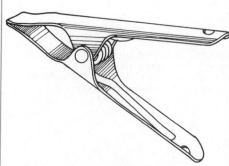

3. **Spring Clamps.** These look and operate like the clothespins you use to hang up your laundry, but they're made of steel, not wood, and their springs are stronger and grip the work more tightly than clothespins. Their tips are coated with plastic to protect fine finishes. These "extra hands" are good for many types of repairs: they'll hold the screening for your screen door in place, tautly, while you tack it to the frame. They'll do the same for canvas, plastic, metal, and wood, when you're gluing these or nailing them into place.

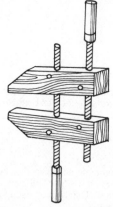

4. **Hand Screws.** These clamps have jaws made of wood, and are able to hold various shapes—including round shapes and irregular ones. Good for metal-, plastic-, fabric-gluing, and perfect for furniture repairs.

Other Ways to Put Pressure on Glued Repairs

Don't fret if you have no fancy clamps handy. You can improvise and exert pressure in a number of ways (some simple and obvious, others a little trickier) with items around the house.

A Stretch-Elastic Belt. Use this the same way you'd use a store-bought band clamp.

Clothesline and a Wood or Metal Stick or Bar. Make a tourniquet to hold the glued joints together. It's just like the tourniquet described in your First Aid kit. Wrap clothesline around the mend, then tighten the rope by turning the stick. Wedge the stick in place. (But remember to protect fine furniture finishes by padding under the rope with clean cloth.)

Clothespins or Stationer's Clips. Use these the way spring clamps are used.

Various Weights. A stack of books can weight down a glued joint.

Two sacksful of marbles, beads, or lead shot, tied together and slung over an awkward join (a cup handle, for instance) will put pressure on the two surfaces of the mend.

Weather stripping can be used for making splints.

Tips on Gluing

If the object you're planning to mend is a treasure and you're not confident about your glue know-how, take the item to an expert. If you are patient and eager to do the work yourself, follow these procedures:

Consult the Glue Chart. Select the glue, then use a scrap of material similar to what you're mending. Test the glue, after it dries, in these ways (depending on the material you're mending):

1. Try to pull the joined pieces apart with your hands. There should be no give at all.
2. Try to bend the joint. If the material is rigid, the mend should not bend.
3. Drop the glued test piece. If there are any breaks, these should be *new* ones, and not along the lines of the earlier break.
4. Soak the mended scrap in water: it should not come apart.
5. Boil the test piece in water. If your mending job survives this test, you know the particular glue you're using for, say, a piece of chinaware will hold and stand up under washing and regular use.

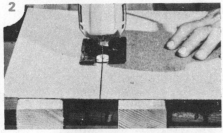

Plastic laminates

You can beautify your home with durable, long-lasting installations laminated plastic on sinktops, vanities, tables ... almost any flat surface. For professional-looking results, simply follow the step-by-step procedures

1 - Preparing the Surface.

For application to new plywood or particle-board: Simply make sure surface is clean, dry and smooth, with no holes or voids.

2 - Cutting the Laminate

With hand saw: Use fine tooth saw with low angle stroke to avoid chipping the laminate. Saw with decorative side *up.*

With circular power saw: Saw with decorative side of sheet *down.* Hold saw firmly against sheet.

With thin shears: Cut with decorative side of sheet *up.* Cut oversize to allow for possible chipping along the cut edge.

Always: Firmly support the laminate sheet as close to the line of cut as possible.

Always: Cut ⅛" to ¼" oversize. After sheet is firmly glued to base material, trim off excess with router or file.

3 - Applying the Adhesive

With a clean paint brush or roller, apply an even coat of contact cement to the back of the laminate sheet... and another coat to the wood surface to which it is to be glued. Be sure to get *complete* coverage on both surfaces. Allow the glue to dry, Read the label on the adhesive can carefully for specific instructions on application, drying time, room temperature, etc.

Note: Bare wood is often porous enough to absorb some of the adhesive. In such cases, apply a first coat of adhesive to the wood surface and allow it to dry.

4 - Applying Laminate to the Surface

Once the two cemented surfaces touch, the contact cement bonds immediately and no further adjustment of position is possible. Therefore, you *must* position the sheet *exactly* before the glue surfaces touch. This is best done by the following method:

Cut several pieces of heavy brown wrapping paper. Place them on the wood surface so they overlap each other and completely cover the glued area. Place the laminate sheet on the paper. Position it for perfect fit. Pull the first piece of paper out a few inches at a time, gently pressing the laminate to the wood as you go. Then remove the remaining paper sections.

5 - Applying Pressure

When the sheet is in place and the paper removed, apply heavy pressure to the surface to create a strong and lasting bond. Start in the center and work toward the edges. Cover every square inch of the surface. Use a three inch hand roller with all the pressure you can apply. For hard-to-reach areas, hold a smooth block of wood on the surface and tap it firmly with a hammer. Remove excess cement from the surface by rubbing with your fingers.

6 - Finishing the Edges

This methods is commonly used.

- Edge banding with laminate. This is the preferred method for finishing the flat, vertical edges of sink, counter and other tops. Just follow this step-by-step procedure:
- For best appearance, nail 1½" or 2" wide strips of the ¾" plywood or particleboard to the underside of exposed edges, to provide a finished edge approximately 1½" thick. Sand to make sure the strip and the original edge form a smooth, flat surface.
- Cut a strip of the laminate sheet a minimum of ¼" wider and longer than the edge to be covered.
- Coat the wood edge twice and the back of the laminate strip once with adhesive as explained in point 3. Allow to dry, then apply the strip and roll with firm pressure. (Or use block and hammer.)
- Trim excess laminate flush with top and bottom of the wood surface. Use router with flush trimming bit or block plane and hand file.

After finishing edge band, apply laminate sheet to the top as explained in point 4. Trim off excess material. Bevel edge joint, using router with 22½° bevel trimming bit, or hand file.

4
Wood finishing

Having spent much time in planning, cutting and assembling your project — make sure your patience sees you through to the "finish".

For much of your earlier efforts can be spoiled quickly by a finish that feels rough to the touch, a paint job which peels and blisters, or a stain that just doesn't match.

Besides, by paying close attention to proper sanding and finishing procedures, you may yet save the day for a project that didn't come off exactly as planned. Because a good finish can hide a multitude of do-it-yourself mistakes.

Sanding from start to finish

Good finishing begins with good sanding. On new work sanding brings out the best in the wood. On old work which has been previously finished sanding should do two things: preserve the aged color of the wood and smooth the surface to take a new finish. Working from new-rough or old-rough is a repeat-step procedure, using sandpaper from coarse to fine through several successive steps. This applies to both hand and power sanding. In power-sanding new work you may produce an acceptable surface in three successive steps. In hand sanding it may take as many as five successive steps, using five grades of sandpaper, to end up with a surface of equal quality. Each time over must remove the "scratch" marks of the step preceding, as otherwise these marks, will show under any finish.

On old work preservation of the color, or patina, of fine woods usually is desirable. Take off the old finish, either transparent or opaque, with a wash-off type remover. Then sand lightly with a medium to fine grade paper and note results closely as you go. Don't use a hand scraper or power sander to remove the finish on old work when you wish to preserve the aged color. Finish with the finest grade of paper.

The best test you have of smoothness is simply to draw your forefinger lightly over the sanded surface diagonally or at right angles to the direction of sanding. Thus you can detect any minor depressions, or even slight roughness. Give these places, if any, a little more attention. But be careful not to cut through that old color acquired only by the aging of the wood.

New work can be handled a little more vigorously. If you are hand-sanding and you discover any slight ups and downs on the surface, make a special sanding block from a 5-in. length of 2 x 4. Cut the ends at an angle of 5 degrees or so, cut a strip of sandpaper to the exact width of the block and to such length that the ends will fold up on the ends of the block where each can be attached with tacks. Don't pad with felt.

Purpose of such a block is to cut down the high spots, ridges and the like and level the surface the first time over. Use a uniform pressure, overlap each stroke about one fourth the width and be especially careful not to round the edges of the work-piece. Don't allow the block to over-run the edges more than about one-fourth its length or width. If there are knots in the surface, to be retained as a decorative feature of the grain, re-member these usually are of a differ-ent texture, harder than the sur-rounding wood, causing the abrasive to cut somewhat slower. Such areas usually call for a few extra strokes in each sanding step to hold them flush. Keep a close watch when sanding certain softwoods having a coarse, flat grain. There may be especially soft areas which tend to cut down faster, producing a surface of low ridges and shallow hollows. Changing sanding strokes to a slight angle with the grain usually disposes of this problem. Keep a close check on progress with the finger-tip test.

Pad sanders are of two types, orbital and straight line, and are used mainly for the finish steps with the finer grades of sandpaper

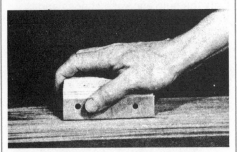

Unpadded sanding block usually saves time and work on rough surfaces. It cuts down high spots, sands out hollows and leaves a true surface

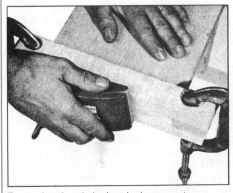

To sand end grain by hand, clamp waste strips to work as pictured. This not only keeps end square but prevents rounding edges. Or, use an unpadded block

"Shoeshine" sanding is usually best for rounding corners and sanding turnings. Method maintains desired radius and leaves smooth surface

Something new in "sandpapering". Per-forated sheet metal forms edges that cut in all directions. Sheet is self-cleaning, removes stock very fast

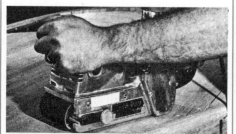

For boat-hull sanding there's nothing quite like a portable belt sander of husky size with a belt at least 3 in. wide. It saves hours of labor

Should the project you are working on be of veneer construction, either plywood or solid-core type, either old or new, be especially careful not to over-run the edges and cut down to the core stock. On new work the veneers used are likely to be quite thin, usually only about ¹⁄₂₈-in., and may have already been machine-sanded, so you haven't much of the veneer left for the finishing steps.

On older work the veneers are usually thicker, but as a rule they've been sanded pretty thoroughly when prepared for finishing.

One disadvantage of the unpadded block is its tendency to score the work more deeply than will a padded block and also it may tilt and slightly ridge the work along the length of the strokes if you don't keep close tab on the uniformity of the pressure you are applying. But it does level the work the first time over, cuts down the more resistant areas, such as knots and vertical grain, and in the end it's a timesaver. After using an unpadded block the first time over most crafts-men go to the padded block (the bottom of the block padded with felt or other soft, flexible material) or they use a flexible rubber block such as supplied by manufacturers of sand-paper. Some even prefer to wrap the sandpaper around a piece of thick, hard felt for the final finish sanding. But in using flexible blocks of any type one should keep in mind that they have a tendency to round the edges and corners of any workpiece which is narrower than the block. For such work, also sanding end grain, a small unpadded block is generally best, especially if the finished job calls for sharp, straight corners with no waves or wobbles.

As a rule blocks don't work well on any type of curved surface that must

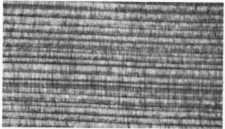

On open-grained woods, such as oak, sanding at a slight angle with grain will prevent enlarging pores

With few exceptions sanding should be done with the grain, even though latter is at angle with workpiece

be hand-sanded. Some types of straight moldings can be sanded quite accurately with flexible blocks but on moldings having irregular or curved shapes such as those on scalloped edges, one generally finds it best to cut sandpaper into small squares, fold once over and use the thumb or forefinger as the "block". Such a simple method is quite effective and much faster than one might suppose. Wear a glove or finger cot if there's much of this kind of thing to do.

The "shoeshine" method of sanding usually works best on turnings, either in the lathe immediately after turning to finish size or with the workpiece held in a vise, or on turnings already assembled, as in old pieces or unfinished furniture. Just tear or cut strips of cloth-backed abrasive from ½ to 1 in. wide, pass the strip around the work and pull on the ends in a back-and-forth stroke. When sanding in this fashion in the lathe operate the machine at a slower speed and keep the abrasive strip moving back and forth and simultaneously along the work to prevent undue heating and discoloration of the wood. As a rule you use only the medium to fine grades of abrasives in shoeshine sanding, but you use descending grades from medium to fine to eliminate scratches as you go.

Hand sanding from medium to fine grade is usually done with a felt-padded block unless surface is rough or ridged. Strokes should follow grain and overlap slightly as sanding progresses

Only the bulb and vase shapes and the concavities of turnings should be sanded by the shoeshine method. Don't pass the strip over narrow beads as it tends to flatten them; use instead a fine V-file or 3-cornered file, touching it lightly to the work in a back-and-forth stroke and rolling it simultaneously to retain the curvature of the bead. In many cases a strip of sandpaper wrapped around a dowel of small diameter is handy for getting into flutes, round-bottom cuts, also on straight moldings where short-radius shapes are involved. Spread glue on the dowel and wrap the sandpaper strip diagonally with the meeting edges of the strip butted, not overlapped.

How to Clean Sandpaper

Sometimes there's trouble with the finer grades of paper clogging or glazing, especially on woods of resinous content, or on "oily" woods such as teak. Usually you can clean the abrading surface effectively with a brush having metal bristles; a brush of the type used for cleaning suede shoes is just the thing. When sanding old work preparatory to refinishing, residues of old fillers may tend to glaze the sandpaper and resist cleaning with the brush. When this

84

For hand-sanding curves of short radius, a sheet of sandpaper folded several times is quite effective. Flexibility of folded "pad" allows it to follow contour of surface without digging in or scoring too deeply

Disc sander of swiveling type makes short work of truing a butt joint such as that pictured. Disc cuts very fast and leaves a smooth, swirl-free surface. Use only light, uniform pressure

problem develops just spill a little turpentine onto the work surface. This will usually cut the glaze and "resharpen" the abrasive. The turps will evaporate quickly and won't discolor the wood, but one should keep in mind that turpentine is rather highly flammable, that there is always some hazard in its use. Move the job outdoors when possible or have your home fire extinguisher handy. And don't smoke.

Once the initial rough sanding has been finished go to a finer grade of sandpaper, a grade that will remove the scratch marks of the first, and then continue the step-by-step procedure, going to a finer grade of abrasive each time, until the finger test turns up a glass-smoothness over the entire surface. Many craftsmen dampen the sanded surface after initial sandings from coarse to medium grades of sandpaper.

Dampening the surface raises the grain, causes surface fibers to stand vertically, or near vertically. In this position they are easily cut off in the next step. On very fine work this procedure is often carried through several steps, to properly condition the wood for a "piano" finish.

Sanding by Machine

Machine sanding with a portable electric sander is much the same thing except that it's faster and requires a little closer attention to control of the tool. Generally a portable belt sander is best for average work on flat surfaces, one having a 3-in., or wider, belt being somewhat easier to control when using fast cutting abrasives in the coarser grades. If the surface to be sanded is in reasonably good condition, no digs, gouges, dips, or ridges, then use of a coarse-grade abrasive may not be necessary. Make sure that the belt you use tracks properly when in place on the sander and be sure to check to see that it's running in the right direction. All sander belts are marked with an arrow indicating the direction they are to be run.

Start the sander before lowering it onto the surface to be sanded and keep it moving after contact in slow, back-and-forth strokes much the same as in hand sanding, the strokes overlapping slightly and working either to right or left. Don't allow the unit to stop on the surface, even for an instant, and be especially careful to prevent it from tipping sidewise. If the unit is stopped momentarily, or permitted to tilt slightly, the coarser-grade abrasives can cut through thin veneers in the wink of an eye, or form a depression that's difficult to sand out. Just as in hand sanding with a block, be doubly alert to avoid overrunning the edges and ends of the work.

Don't bear down on a belt sander. Usually the weight of the unit is sufficient to keep the belt cutting freely. If it seems necessary to urge it a little, as in sanding end grain perhaps, bear down only very lightly and keep close watch of results. Bearing down heavily may cause the belt to heat unduly and glaze, thereby greatly reducing its efficiency. Once the surface has been leveled satisfactorily— use that finger test again—change to a finer grade belt, continuing to step down until you finish with the finest belt.

Pad sanders are of two types, the terms, or names, used referring to the action of the pad. In the orbital type the pad moves in a circular stroke. On the second type known as the straight-line sander the pad moves in a straight, back-and-forth stroke. On some later-model pad sanders the stroke can be changed from straight to orbital as desired. Pad sanders are generally used for the finishing steps with finegrade abrasives as they are capable of sanding to a very smooth surface.

In general, stance is of some importance in both hand and machine sanding. Some prefer to stand at the side of the work when hand sanding as they can keep pressure and stroke more uniform on a relatively large surface. Working with a portable belt sander can be done in much the same position. Hand pressure is not necessary with the power unit, leaving the hands free to control direction and limits of the stroke. On some woods, especially those with a coarse, open grain, you'll get a somewhat smoother job by directing the strokes slightly diagonal to the grain through all the steps from coarse to fine. This will be true of both hand and power sanding. Also, it's advisable to do a little experimenting to determine the grades of sandpaper that do the best job from start to finish on a given wood.

Choose the right abrasive

In Selecting an Abrasive

There are six minerals and two backings from which to choose. The secret of a good finishing job is choosing the right combination. Among the minerals, *flint* is the least durable and least expensive. *Garnet* is slightly better, but don't use it in a power sander. *Aluminum oxide* is a synthetic, good for all-around use.

Silicon carbide, another synthetic, shiny black in color, is good for wet sanding of primers, undercoats and floors. *Emery cloth,* a dull black, is used for light polishing and for removing rust and scale from metal. *Crocus cloth,* made of iron oxide, comes in only one grade—very fine— and gives metal a mirror-like finish.

Paper backings are available in A, C, D and E weights, increasing in weight (thickness) in that order. *Cloth* backing comes in X and J weights, with the heavier X weight preferred for most machine-sanding jobs around the house.

Sanding guide

The grade shown for each operation is intended as a starting guide only. You may find that a grade coarser or finer is preferred depending upon the condition of the surface to be sanded.

Note: Grades are based on hand sanding. If a power tool is used start one grade finer.

Wood		Alumide Paper	Garnet Paper	Flint Paper	Waterproof Paper	How to do it
Surface Preparation	Removing Old Finish	Coarse Medium	Coarse Medium	Coarse Medium		Sand until old finish, shallow scratches, burn marks, etc., are removed.
	Bare Wood	Fine	Fine			Sand until completely smooth.
Finish Coats (Finish coats must be thoroughly dry before sanding)	After staining	Ex Fine	Ex Fine			Sand lightly to wisk off raised wood fibres.
	After sealer coat	Ex Fine	Ex Fine			Scuff lightly until perfectly smooth and "bright spots" are dulled.
	Sanding between varnish or lacquer coats				240A	Sand dry until smooth. Wipe clean.
	Final Finish Dull-Gloss				320A	Sand wet until desired finish is achieved. Apply furniture cleaner.
	Semi-Gloss				400A	Follow dull-gloss procedure.
	High-Gloss					After semi-gloss operation rub with compound until all sanding marks are removed. Apply quality furniture polish.
	Enamel					Do not sand.

Metal		Alumide Paper		Water proof Paper	Emery Cloth	How to do it
Surface Preparation	Removing old finish, rust spots, etc.	Coarse Medium			Coarse Medium	Sand until bare metal is exposed.
	Bare metal	Fine			Fine	Sand until surface is smooth and clean.
Finish Coats (Finish coats must be thoroughly dry before sanding)	After primer coat	Ex Fine		240A 320A		Sand wet or dry until perfectly smooth. Wipe clean.
	After enamel coat					Rub with compound. Wax and polish.
	If additional coat is desired			400A		Sand lightly until glossy finish is removed and surface is smooth.

Storage and Handling

The recommended Conditions for Storing Coated Abrasive Products are:
Temperature: 18-21 Degrees C.
Relative Humidity: 45% - 50%

BELTS

Hang belts on pegs not less than 3'' in diameter. Small belts may be stored in the original cartons.

SHEETS

Store sheets flat on shelves. Keep grading information to the front for easy identification.

ROLLS

Large rolls should be laid on their sides to prevent uneven moisture absorption. Do not stack large rolls. Small rolls may be stacked.

DISCS

Discs should be placed flat with a weight on top of them to prevent curling. Keep in original cartons until ready for use.

The finish really does it

Many craftsmen like the finishes that come in spray cans, especially opaque finishing materials, but others stick by the conventional equipment for spray application. Both are fast and economical

When finishing knotty pine or other knotty woods it's best to seal knots with a thin coat of white shellac to prevent undue absorption or "bleeding"

If the brush sheds bristles (and all brushes do), be sure to flick off the loose bristles that otherwise will adhere to the finished surface

That's right! The finish really does it. But the finish can be no better than the surface over which it is applied.

You've spent hours of fun dreaming up a shop project of your very own, selected the best woods the market affords, lavished weeks, maybe months of spare time on joinery that matches that of the professionals.

Now all that's left to do is the finishing, and time is wasting.

It's at this point that one must guard against any tendency to hurry the job—skimp a little here and there, yield to that pressing urge to slap on a finish so you can see at last what the job is going to look like.

If you examine your project closely you may see a few sanding marks here and there, planer marks still showing, sharp edges and corners, a roughness in places.

These defects will show under any transparent finishing materials, even under some opaque finishes. You can't finish a sharp corner; the finish won't stay on it. You can't conceal those ripply planer marks with half a dozen top coats, and visible sanding scratches left by coarser grades of abrasives are not the mark of a master craftsman.

Usually it takes only a few minutes more. You'll be secretly if not openly admiring your own special project and you'll be looking at it for a long time to come, so instead of putting up with those little irritating defects let's take a few minutes more and produce surfaces that will take a top-rate finish.

Usually this means sanding and more sanding, a little more here, a touch or two there, a delicate rounding of exposed edges—until both surface and edge feels really s-m-o-o-t-h to the tip of your finger.

If you're working with a wood having oblique graining—that is, grain that meets the surface at an angle—brush off the dust frequently and examine the surface closely in good light. The mill planer will often chip such surfaces slightly here and there leaving tiny, wedge-shaped holes that are difficult to see even after a careful dusting. But you must catch them if the surface is to take that perfect finish.

Now that you have a satisfactory surface for finishing, keep in mind that any clear finishing material will darken the wood somewhat by changing its light-reflecting properties. By dampening the smoothed surface of a piece of scrap from the project you can get a good idea how the wood will look when finished in its natural color.

Apply Sealer

Although some of the new finishing materials act as a sealer and top coat, it's often advisable to apply a sealer as the initial coat if the wood is of a soft, absorptive texture. Some finishing materials are supplied as a separate sealer, or base coating, and a recommended top coating. Some are compounded to "build" on the surface, such as the natural varnishes and various synthetic clear finishes. Others are combinations of special oils designed to penetrate deep into the wood. These are applied to bare wood with no top coating.

Before you set up a finishing schedule determine whether or not you will use stain or finish in the natural color. If staining seems desirable, run several test panels of stain colors to check color range and tonal depth, using smoothed scrap from the project. Allow the stained panels to dry so you see the true colors.

Artist's color will mix with most sealers, and combining the two usually makes a good stain-sealer combination. The sealer serves as the penetrating vehicle to carry the stain into the wood. Or, use the prepared non-grain-raising stains if you prefer and follow with a sealer as a base coat.

On open-grained woods such as oak and walnut you can use the top coats as the filler, thus eliminating a separate filler entirely. The process is commonly used in hand-finishing gunstocks but can be applied to other small projects as well, especially where the wood is to be finished in the natural color or by light staining. It's done by repeat applications of top coat and a sanding between coats across the grain. The procedure is calculated to remove nearly all the coating each time, leaving only the pores of the wood filled. After the finish "builds" to a smooth surface it is rubbed down with either very fine steel wool or a prepared rubbing compound.

Exploiting the beauty of the grain is one of the main reasons for finishing finer cabinet woods in their natural colors or with light staining. So, assuming that you are to finish a close-grained wood such as birch, maple or cherry, you might set up a finishing schedule something like this:

- Brush or spray a non-grain-raising (commercially prepared) stain of desired color and wipe lightly if necessary to attain desired tone.

Some craftsmen use a coarse, lintless fabric for applying wiping stains. In many instances this method gives better control of the color depth

Hold your finishing brush like this and don't bear down on it unduly. Held in this way, a brush releases its load in a smooth, uniform film

Allow to dry at least 30 min.

- Brush or spray a sealer. (Lacquer or white shellac can also be used if thinned to proper consistency). Allow ample drying time.
- Smooth lightly with 6 or 8-0 abrasive; dust off.
- If sealer shows any uneven absorption, apply a second coat, sand and dust as before.
- Spray or brush two top coats, sanding lightly between the first and second applications. Allow to dry thoroughly.

- Rub to a satiny finish with fine steel wool (3-0 or finer), pumice-stone paste or a rubbing compound.

This is a simple, basic finishing schedule which may be altered for any special condition. For example, you can substitute what is known as a "sanding sealer" for regular sealer, lacquer or white shellac. Also as a finishing top coat you can substitute a rubbed-effect varnish or lacquer. This product dries to a soft, satiny sheen and requires no rub-down if protected from dust while drying.

For an open-grain wood such as walnut, oak or mahogany a basic schedule might be set up as follows:

- Brush or spray a stain of desired color and allow to dry.
- Brush or spray a thinned "wash" coat of white shellac or lacquer.
- Sand very lightly with fine abrasive. Dust.
- Tint a prepared filler slightly darker than the stain, thin to brushing consistency and lay onto the surface with one-way strokes of the brush. Allow to dry flat (about 15 min.) then rub off across the grain with a coarse fabric.
- Sand lightly and dust.
- Brush or spray sanding sealer (you can use regular sealer but wipe off any excess after 10 to 15 min.).
- Sand the sealer satin-smooth to remove any dust flecks and any tiny air bubbles. Dust off.
- Brush or spray two coats of finish of your choice—lacquer, synthetic natural varnish.
- Sand very lightly, then rub satin-smooth with a rubbing compound or 4-0 steel wool.

Always make sure the preceding coat of any finishing material is thoroughly dry before applying a succeeding coat.

You'll get a better job by spraying any of the materials except filler. Usually a suitable sprayer can be rented from your paint dealer. Where possible tip the piece so that the wet material is applied on a horizontal surface. Where you must apply on a vertical surface take special care to prevent sags and drips at the edges.

Here are tips in brush handling that will help you when finishing those more difficult surfaces such as paneled doors. The procedures detailed apply to the application of both clear and opaque finishing materials; also to application on either a vertical or horizontal surface. Be especially careful to prevent the finishing materials from collecting in corners or sagging on a vertical surface. Strike the brush "dry" and pick up any excess before it sets. Then be sure to brush out to a smooth film of a uniform thickness. Always brush with the grain on finishing strokes. Avoid edge drips

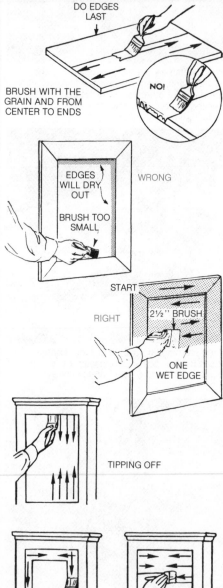

DO EDGES LAST

BRUSH WITH THE GRAIN AND FROM CENTER TO ENDS

NO!

EDGES WILL DRY OUT

BRUSH TOO SMALL

WRONG

START

RIGHT

2½" BRUSH

ONE WET EDGE

TIPPING OFF

CUTTING IN

CROSS-BRUSHING

88

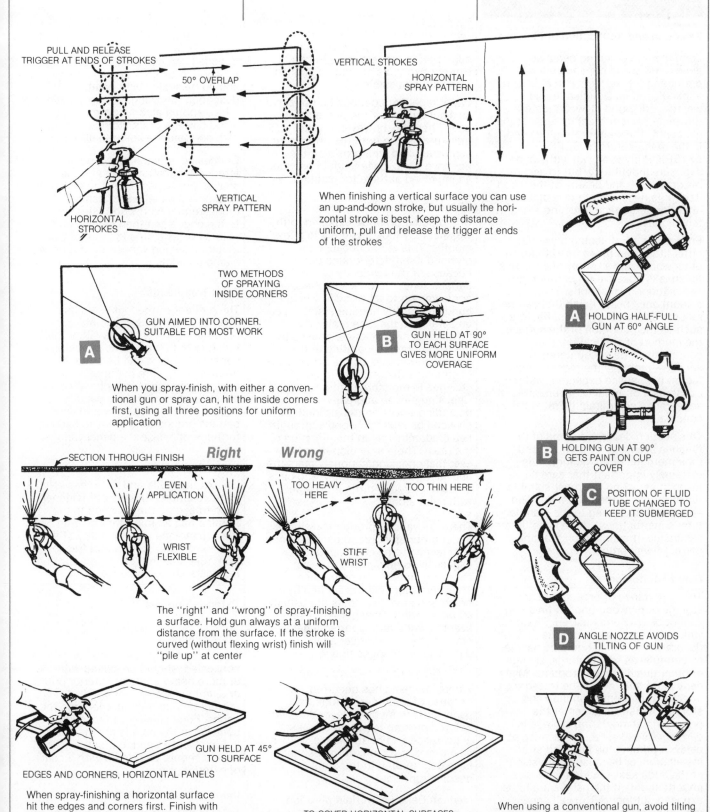

PULL AND RELEASE TRIGGER AT ENDS OF STROKES

50° OVERLAP

VERTICAL SPRAY PATTERN

HORIZONTAL STROKES

VERTICAL STROKES

HORIZONTAL SPRAY PATTERN

When finishing a vertical surface you can use an up-and-down stroke, but usually the horizontal stroke is best. Keep the distance uniform, pull and release the trigger at ends of the strokes

TWO METHODS OF SPRAYING INSIDE CORNERS

A GUN AIMED INTO CORNER. SUITABLE FOR MOST WORK

B GUN HELD AT 90° TO EACH SURFACE GIVES MORE UNIFORM COVERAGE

When you spray-finish, with either a conventional gun or spray can, hit the inside corners first, using all three positions for uniform application

A HOLDING HALF-FULL GUN AT 60° ANGLE

B HOLDING GUN AT 90° GETS PAINT ON CUP COVER

C POSITION OF FLUID TUBE CHANGED TO KEEP IT SUBMERGED

SECTION THROUGH FINISH   *Right*   *Wrong*

EVEN APPLICATION

WRIST FLEXIBLE

TOO HEAVY HERE

TOO THIN HERE

STIFF WRIST

The "right" and "wrong" of spray-finishing a surface. Hold gun always at a uniform distance from the surface. If the stroke is curved (without flexing wrist) finish will "pile up" at center

D ANGLE NOZZLE AVOIDS TILTING OF GUN

GUN HELD AT 45° TO SURFACE

EDGES AND CORNERS, HORIZONTAL PANELS

When spray-finishing a horizontal surface hit the edges and corners first. Finish with horizontal strokes, triggering the gun at each edge

TO COVER HORIZONTAL SURFACES START AT NEAR END

When using a conventional gun, avoid tilting more than 50-60 deg. Or change angle of the nozzle for horizontal or overhead surfaces

Finishing
softwood plywood

Selection and Application of Finishes

Long life and enduring beauty of almost any wood depends upon protecting the surface with a properly applied coating. Douglas fir and western softwood plywood require the same basic protection against the elements. The waterproof glue used in the manufacture of COFI EXTERIOR plywood will withstand exposure indefinitely, but to assure maximum life and beauty of the wood itself it is necessary to give close attention to surface finishing techniques.

Procedures for finishing plywood differ little from those used to finish other woods and a variety of attractive finishes is possible for both interior and exterior applications. There is seldom one "best" finish that can be recommended for plywood. Factors such as the condition of the surface, the method of application, the conditions to be encountered in service—probably the most important factor, the service expected, and the economics of initial cost versus appearance and durability must be considered.

This section describes some of the finishes available for plywood and their methods of application. It is extremely important that care be taken in selecting the most suitable finish for the purpose intended and applying it according to the manufacturer's instructions. There is no better assurance of satisfaction than the correct finish properly applied.

Care and Storage.

The importance of proper care and storage of plywood prior to finishing cannot be over-emphasized. Plywood which will become part of the decorative scheme should be handled as carefully as trim material, sidings or other quality finish products. Many early paint failures can be traced directly to improper handling and storage. Moisture can enter the panel prior to finishing during storage in damp or humid areas, or because of delay in priming the plywood after installation, or because of omission of the edge seal. (The latter two are important only if the panels are to be exposed outdoors.) Thus all panels should be stored in a cool, dry place out of the sunlight. They should be

well covered if left outdoors during construction. The prime coat and edge seal for panels intended for exterior exposure should be applied as soon as possible.

Water repellent coatings do not serve as a substitute for the prime paint coat. They will, however, retard moisture pickup until the prime coat can be applied and, providing they do not have a wax base, should provide an improved surface for painting.

Checking

Unprotected plywood exposed to the weather may look unsightly in a few months. This is not because the plywood itself deteriorates but because of the tendency of the surface veneer to check; a phenomenon common to all wood in which hundreds of tiny hairline cracks open up parallel to the face grain. These tiny cracks or checks are caused by the wood fibres separating at the growth boundaries as the fibres swell or shrink as the result of rapid changes in moisture content. Checking has no appreciable degrading effect on the strength of plywood because plywood's strength lies predominantly in the direction of the grain. There's no disputing however that checking seriously mars the appearance of the plywood, and once it has occurred is difficult to hide with paint alone.

There are various products available under proprietary brand names that are claimed to be compounded especially to help plywood resist checking and reduce grain raise. These products can be applied by brush or spray. Two coats are usually recommended. They penetrate and seal the wood and reportedly help stabilize the face veneer against dimensional changes due to moisture.

Where checking has occurred because of improper storage, the panel surface must be reconditioned before finishing to obtain the best appearance and performance. This is also true of old paint surfaces that have deteriorated to the point of needing renewal.

Medium Density Overlaid plywood is not susceptible to checking because of its resin-fibre overlay.

Exterior and Interior Edge Treatments

Exposed and concealed edges of plywood in exterior applications should be sealed with paint as described following. Exposed panel edges should also be covered with wood battens or mouldings fastened with corrosion-resistant nails.

Concealed edges of plywood in interior applications need not be sealed. For appearance, the end grain of exposed panel edges can be hidden either with wood filler applied to the edges and then sanded and painted or with an edge trim of wood moulding, wood veneer, or proprietary clamp-on edging.

Joint Treatments

The tendency in recent years has been to accentuate the joints between plywood panels rather than trying to hide them. This simplifies construction and can be quite attractive. Joints are commonly accentuated in naturally finished panels and frequently in painted panels. Butted joints covered with battens or moulding are also used to further emphasize the panelizations.

Fastenings

On exterior walls and in excessively damp locations, the type of fastener used to secure the plywood to the framing has an important bearing on the appearance and durability of the finish. For long service and freedom from rust staining, corrosion-resistant fasteners should be used.

Exterior Finishes

Edge Sealing

All plywood edges, exposed or concealed, should be sealed with one or more heavy coats of exterior primer or aluminum-based paint. This prevents moisture migration into the edges. Edge sealing can readily be done when the panels are in a stack. In unusually damp locations, backs of panels should be primed with a coat of exterior primer.

Paint

Paint is not recommended for application to the standard grades of plywood used in exposed locations. *Under severe exposure conditions, checking of the surface veneer may cause paint deterioration.* When a paint finish is desired, the use of Medium Density Overlaid (MDO) plywood is recommended. The smooth, uniform surface provides just the right tooth for paint, allowing the paint resins to firmly grip the surface to give excellent durability, exceeding that of paint finishes on ordinary wood. Paint flows evenly and smoothly, penetrating the surface uniformly resulting in more attractive appearance and more efficient paint use. Painting recommendations are as follows:

Surface Preparation
Medium Density Overlaid plywood needs no surface preparation. No presanding or sealer coats are required. However, it is important that the surface has been dry for at least 48 hours and is completely clean before application of paint.

Prime Coat
Any good primer, properly formulated and designed for exterior exposure, may be used with satisfactory results. The limitations may be listed as follows:

1. Strict adherence to the paint manufacturer's recommendations.

2. Compatibility of the prime coat to top coat must be considered. In this respect the use of flexible film-forming primers, such as some of the latex or oleoresinous based formulations, are not recommended when they are to be top coated with a hard film-forming paint. The reverse, however, does not normally present a problem, i.e., hard film-forming primer over-coated with a softer, more flexible film-forming finish coat.

Top or Finish Coat
Nearly all good quality paints formulated for exterior finish are acceptable. As with the prime coat, the manufacturer's recommendations must be followed, and the compatibility of the top coat to the primer must be considered.

With the advent of the many new synthetic resins and combinations thereof, it is an almost insurmountable task to evaluate all systems and formulations relative to their performance on Medium Density

Overlaid plywood. However, experience and testing to date permits the following more specific recommendations:

For exterior exposure such as in agricultural, residential, marine and sign applications, the best results have been obtained with self primed long or medium oil alkyd finishes and enamels, vinyl alkyd enamels and phenolic enamels applied over medium or long oil alkyd primers.

Most latex paints of the styrene-butadiene, acrylic and polyvinyl acetate emulsion type have also exhibited satisfactory results whether self primed or applied over alkyd primers.

Systems not recommended are self primed blister resistant titanium paints, polyvinyl acetate homopolymer latexes, lacquers, and paints containing zinc oxide.

If non-overlaid plywood has been used and a paint rather than a stain finish is desired, top quality exterior paint should be applied as follows:

Prime the panels carefully front and back with oil-base undercoat or aluminum-base paint. If aluminum-base paint is used as a primer ensure that it is of the type specified for wood and not for general purposes or metals. Ensure that the undercoat and subsequent coats seal the edge grain. A three coat finish with an intermediate coat of undercoat (but not aluminum-base paint) mixed half and half with finish colour will look best. For the final coat apply the paint unthinned.

Low lustre and porous type paint systems which permit the capillary flow of moisture through the paint film should not be used because the frequent wetting and drying of the plywood surface will lead to abnormally early checking and paint failure.

Refinishing Painted and Checked Plywood

A satisfactory repaint system for refinishing checked plywood is an exterior acrylic latex paint formulated for wood applied in two coats over a compatible oil-base primer. Although some of the open checks may still be visible, this flat finish tends to mask the checks and presents a satisfactory appearance. Checks will probably reappear as moisture changes cause

the face veneer to work, but the paint system will maintain its bond without showing the typical curling and flaking of an oil paint. The procedure is as follows:

1. Thoroughly wire brush the old paint surface and sand if necessary to provide a smooth surface for repainting. (If paint deterioration is well advanced, it may be advisable to remove all the flaking paint down to the bare wood.) Old paint can also be removed by liquid paint removers, scraping or special paint removing tools.

2. Wipe off dust and excess chalk.

3. Apply a brush coat of oil-base primer.

4. When dry, apply two coats of acrylic latex paint.

For better appearance and performance, the open checks may be filled with any suitable synthetic patching compound (a number of which are available under specific brand names) and the surface re-painted with latex paint as described above. The plywood should be thoroughly dry to ensure that existing checks are fully open to the filler. If carefully applied, the compound will fill the open checks and, after sanding, provide a smooth, void free surface for repainting. Plywood refinished by this method and exposed to severe weather conditions will eventually show some surface roughness as the filler is forced out of the checks by the repeated working of the fibres of the face veneer, and paint failure may eventually occur as a result of this movement.

Stain

A stain finish is ideal for unsanded plywood panels exposed to the weather. A heavy-bodied stain is particularly recommended and will provide an attractive finish requiring little maintenance.

Stains are available which have considerable hiding power but do not obscure the plywood grain. Creosote base stains penetrate deep into the plywood, producing rich lively colours that enhance grain beauty but leave little or no surface film to crack and blister. Stains containing water repellents are thought to be useful in deferring checking.

Stains are among the easiest of finishes to apply. The usual requirements for a clean, dry surface apply. Successive coats should be allowed to dry before the next coat is applied. One—or two—coat systems should be used depending upon the manufacturer's recommendation and the pigmentation in the stain (penetrating stains usually require two coats). Since colour uniformity depends upon equal pigment distribution, stains should be thoroughly mixed before application and from time to time during application.

Checking in stained plywood usually occurs during the first six months of outdoor exposure. With heavily pigmented dark stains, best results are obtained by applying a first coat and allowing any checking to occur, then six months or so later a second coat can be applied so that the checks are filled with stain. When the stain weathers or fades so that refinishing is indicated, little or no surface preparation is needed.

Prestained specialty plywood siding products in a variety of colours are available from some manufacturers.

Stain cannot be used successfully on overlaid plywood. Sanded panels may be stained if desired.

Clear Finishes

Clear finishes for exterior exposure have been found to be generally unsatisfactory and are not recommended for use on plywood. Clear coatings quickly fail because of the lack of protective pigments and thus require constant and costly maintenance.

Textured Coatings

Proprietary surface coatings containing fibrous or granular materials in a liquid vehicle are available for use over plywood and have proven more satisfactory for exterior use than conventional paints. It is claimed that certain types of textured coatings are highly resistant to alkali and acid conditions and are not susceptible to the aggressive atmospheric conditions found in industrial and coastal areas. Service life of 10 to 20 years is claimed for some types. Coatings of this nature which completely conceal and protect the plywood appear to be one of the best methods of finishing plywood for exterior exposure and their use is recommended.

Overlays

There are a number of overlays and coatings suitable for exterior use with plywood. The most common of these, are fibreglass and Neoprene-*Hypalon,*

Surface Preparation

Plywood for interior applications usually will be one of the sanded or textured grades and will require little surface preparation other than to ensure that the surface is thoroughly clean and that all blemishes have been filled with wood filler and sanded smooth. Whenever practicable, fill the plywood edge grain before painting. Always use fine sandpaper and sand with the grain, never across it. Do not paint over dust or spots of oil or glue. When the plywood is to be painted, all knots and pitch streaks should be spot-primed with sealer. For best results always use good quality paints and follow the paint manufacturer's instructions.

Paint and Enamel

Conventional wall and woodwork paints and enamels may be used. For surfaces which will be cleaned frequently, use washable paints or enamels. First, brush on flat paint or enamel undercoat. Thin if desired. Second, apply a second coat of undercoat tinted to shade of finish coat. For gloss finish mix equal parts flat undercoat and gloss enamel for second coat. Third, apply final coat as it comes from can. A two-step finish without second undercoat may be used as an alternative.

Interesting textured surfaces may be obtained by priming as above, followed by a heavy coat of stippling paint. Use brush, roller or sponge to texture. When using water-thinned paint, first seal plywood with clear resin sealer, shellac or flat white oil paint, then paint according to manufacturer's instructions for a sealed surface.

Natural Finishes

For an easy, inexpensive blonde finish, first apply coat of interior white undercoat thinned so grain pattern shows through. Tint if colour is desired. Second, apply clear shellac, flat varnish or lacquer.

Attractive and economical one-coat stain waxes are also available in various colours. If a dark stain is preferred, first apply coat of clear resin sealer to subdue grain contrast.

A luxurious light stain glaze can be obtained as follows: First apply white undercoat thinned with equal parts of turpentine or paint thinner. Wipe or dry brush for more grain show through. Second, apply one coat thinned white shellac or clear resin sealer. Third, to provide colour, apply interior undercoat or enamel thinned as in step one. Wipe or dry brush to proper colour tone. Fourth, apply one coat of flat varnish. Rub down with steel wool for added lustre.

Wood painting

Wood as a Material

Wood is a noble material which lends itself to such a large number of uses that it would be presumptuous to attempt to enumerate them. Its abundance in some areas, its resistant qualities and its stability, the ease with which it can be worked, its beautiful coloring and grain are among the characteristics which dictate its uses—framing, cabinet work, cladding, floors, furniture, etc.

Why Finish Wood

As may be seen from very old constructions, wood is a long lasting material. Yet, to prolong its useful life, it should be protected against wear, against soiling as well as from various other agents, dampness that causes warping and induces rotting, insects that attack it, mildew that disfigures it, weather that erodes it, fire that destroys it. Thus wood finishes are chosen according to use, and also according to the characteristics of the wood species and to the final appearance desired.

Various Types of Finishes for Wood

Finishing methods should first be selected according to the exposure, exterior work or interior finishing.

The service conditions or the function of the surface, floors, wall cladding, doors, furniture, etc. are the next considerations.

Finally, transparent or natural finishes are treated differently from opaque finishes.

Common Species of Wood

Wood is a temperamental material and its characteristics vary with the species as well as with origin, conditioning, and type of cut. Various species differ in natural color, grain or figure, pore size, hardness, density and porosity.

Woods are usually classified as **hard wood** or **soft wood** according to whether they come from leaf trees or from evergreen trees. The actual hardness and density do not necessarily fit this classification but most important in respect to finishing are porosity, pore size and the presence of natural colorants and resins.

A Few Species in Common Use:

English Name	French Name	Type of grain	
		Open	Closed
African Mahogany (Samara)	Gabon, Okoumé	X	
Ash	Frêne	X	
Aspen	Tremble		X
Basswood (linden)	Tilleul		X
B. C. Fir (Douglas Fir)	Sapin de Colombie		X
Beech	Hêtre	X	
Birch	Bouleau		X
Cedar	Cèdre		X
Cherry	Cerisier		X
Chestnut	Châtaignier	X	
Cypress	Cyprès		X
Elm	Orme	X	
Fir	Sapin		X
Hickory	Noyer blanc	X	
Mahogany	Acajou	X	
Maple	Erable		X
Oak	Chêne	X	
Pine	Pin		X
Poplar	Peuplier		X
Redwood	Séquoia		X
Rosewood	Palissandre (Bois de rose)	X	
Spruce	Epinette		X
Teak	Teck	X	
Walnut	Noyer	X	
Wild cherry (birch)	Merisier		X

Grades and Quality

Woods are classified in several grades according to their appearance, color, knots, imperfections or faults. Only the finest qualities lend themselves to transparent and painstakingly applied finishes.

Wood cuttings

The pores, the number and size of the annual growth rings depend on the way wood has been cut: plain sawn boards have a flat grain and quarter sawn show edge grain. Wood may also be sliced (as for veneers) or split (shingles).

Surface texture varies according to whether the lumber has been left rough sawn, bleached, dressed or sanded.

Plywood is made from thin sheets of wood glued together to give panels that are strong in spite of their thinness.

Surface Preparation Prior to Finishing

Proper surface preparation is most important for durable and satisfactory finishing of wood and deserves particular attention in interior finishing.

Any surface to be painted, varnished or stained must be sound, dry, clean and free from dust, grease, wax or any contaminant that might affect adhesion of the coatings.

Moisture should not be more that 12% as measured with a moisture meter. Since the degree of humidity in wood reaches a balance with moisture in the air, it may vary with ambient conditions. Wood should thus be protected from rain and from contact with moist ground. Wood may also absorb water from different materials in contact with it, as plaster, mortar, concrete.

Resin knots and veins of resinous woods must be sealed with shellac or a vinyl knot sealer. It is best to wash off excess gum with turpentine or to burn it with a torch if darkening of the wood is of no consequence. Alumimum paint is not recommended as a knot sealer.

Colored Woods

Some species of wood, like redwood or western red cedar contain natural colorants that are water soluble and may bleed through light tint latex paints to give brownish stains. These woods should be primed with primers recommended for these woods.

Treated Woods

When the exact nature of the products used to treat wood is not known, a preliminary test should be made to check compatibility of the finishes to be used.

Stains

When stains are only superficial (pencil marks, contact with other building materials), they should be removed by scraping or sanding. Deeper stains require bleaching treatment.

Mildew stains are removed with javel water or a concentrated solution of trisodium phosphate.

Oil, grease and tar stains are removed with paint thinner, taking care not to spread the stains to larger areas.

Iron stains are bleached with a solution of oxalic acid (poisonous).

Copper stains are usually difficult to remove from wood. Chemicals used for bleaching should be removed completely by rinsing with plenty of water and the wood should then be allowed to dry thoroughly.

Filling and Patching

Nail holes, open joints, cracks and minor defects should be filled only after the coat of sealer or primer has dried. Under a clear finish, use a compound tinted the same color as the wood. Never use oil putty under latex paints for interior. For exterior work, do not use crack fillers or cements meant for interior use.

Where the defects are greater, replace the defective wood parts rather then try to fill with compounds.

Roughness

Always sand with the grain of the wood. Start with coarse grades of sandpaper and then move to finer grades so as not to leave scratches. Dust thoroughly after sanding, then wipe with a tack rag, a lintless cloth specially treated to attract dust. A tack rag can be made by soaking a piece of cloth in dilute varnish then wringing almost dry.

Exterior Work

Requirements

When finishing exterior wood, surface preparation need not be as thorough as for interior work; what really matters is to have sound wood that is clean and dry and to make sure that it will remain dry by taking the necessary precautions.

Only materials of recognized quality should be used, applied under favorable conditions and in a sufficient thickness right from the start for effective and long lasting protection against the elements.

The moisture problem

Problems of peeling, blistering and mildew growth are due to moisture, mainly that coming from the interior of buildings.

- Use nothing but dry, well seasoned wood.

- Seal all assembly joints and when possible apply a prime coat to the back of all woodwork to prevent water absorption through capillary action. Paint the top and bottom of doors.

- Caulk all openings (windows) to prevent water infiltration.

- Avoid contact of the wood with the earth; lower row of boards on walls, stairs, sills, etc. When contact with the earth cannot be avoided, as with fence posts, impregnate the wood with a preservative that will retard rotting. Always design wood work so that rain water will drain off easily.

- Provide adequate ventilation of the interior of buildings and of the air space in the walls to prevent water condensation that causes paint failure. Vents should be large enough, in sufficient number, well placed and not obstructed.

Durability of Transparent Finishes

Varnish

Without any protection whatsoever, wood exposed to weather soon loses its natural color and turns grey. Various finishes are used to keep the natural beauty of wood but unfortunately, with most commonly used woods such as pine, cedar or redwood, varnishes are relatively short lived. The actinic rays of the sun (the ultra-violet rays) have a damaging effect both on the coating and on the substrate (wood). Phenolic resin varnishes have a reasonably good resistance to this and when modified with colorless ultra-violet filtering agents, may provide good durability. It is very important to apply a sufficient number of coats, at least three, so that the agents may have maximum effect, as well as to proceed with refinishing before the films are affected to any great extent.

Sealers

Sealers are of little value in protecting wood against weathering since they only provide very thin coatings. Thus a colorless and neutral base meant for preparing stains should not be used as is for exterior use.

Oils

Linseed oil, particularly when thinned, penetrates the wood and can protect it from water damage. But oil deteriorates quickly in the sun, it remains slightly sticky and holds dust and finally, constitutes an excellent medium for the growth of mildew which produces the blackish look of oiled wood.

Some oil compositions, like Scandinavian finish with a wood preservative and water repellent, do not provide satisfactory protection for any reasonable length of time, since they provide very thin coatings.

Stains

Pigmented wood stains will provide satisfactory protection to exterior wood because their pigments check the damaging rays of the sun. To preserve the natural color of wood, the color of stain that matches the color of the wood as closely as possible should be selected. Wood stains are penetrating and bind to the wood. They wear by erosion without peeling and applying fresh coats is never a problem.

What you should know about paint brushes

Paint-brush quality and spreadability are largely determined by the number and length of the bristles. When dipped about $\frac{1}{3}$ the length of the bristles in pigmented finishing materials such as paints and enamels, a quality brush will pick up just the right amount and lay it on a vertical or horizontal surface in a smooth film of uniform thickness without sags, runs, drips, or brush marks.

Pro painters, decorators and restorers are sticklers for quality and they generally pick a brush by points, keeping always in mind the purposes for which it is to be used. A painter will want a brush with plenty of "body" and fairly long bristles that will pick up and carry a good load of paint at each dip and hold it to a uniform film thickness throughout a long, sweeping stroke. Decorators who prefer a brush to roller application will look for much the same characteristics in the brush they use to apply oil-base or water-soluble paints or enamels to interior walls and woodwork.

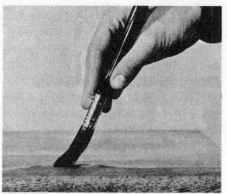

Always brush off an edge, as otherwise you'll have trouble with drips. It helps to give the brush a slight twist at an edge.

Such brushes usually come with natural (animal) bristles or with bristles made from synthetic materials such as nylon. Bristles of the best brushes of either type have "flagged" ends, or tips, the term referring to the outer ends of the bristles which are "split", or divided, to form a number of hair-like projections. On the animal bristle these are a natural characteristic of those selected for the manufacture of brushes. On the synthetic bristles, such as those made from nylon, the flags are produced artificially.

For application of the free-flowing, quick-drying finishes and stains used

On vertical surfaces you flow the material on smoothly with a fairly fast sweep of the brush, using a light but uniform pressure.

Pressure on the brush largely determines the amount of material laid on a surface. Bristles of this brush are cut wedge-shape, forming a "chisel edge".

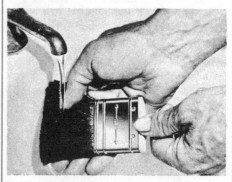

Brushes used in water-soluble materials are easily cleaned in tap water. Work the bristles gently with thumb and fingers to make sure all finishing materials have been washed away.

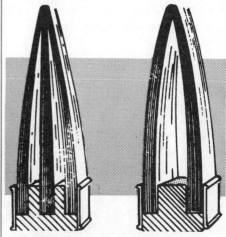

See the difference between two and three rows of bristles in paint brushes. High-quality brushes are usually made with three rows of bristles in the filler block which is a part of the handle.

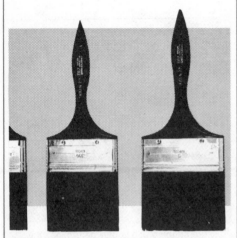

A few of the many widths of brushes which are available.

by the home craftsman, refinisher and restorer, a softer brush with a little less "spring" usually is best. Quality brushes for this work are made with soft, flexible bristles selected from the pelts of such animals as the goat, sable, badger and others. These brushes, in the top grades, usually are full-bodied and the bristles are trimmed to a wedge shape, forming what is commonly referred to as a chisel edge. This shape of the edge makes it possible to lay, or "cut", a sharply defined line of finishing material with the corner, or edge, of the brush without forming a bead. The chisel edge also enables the user to spread a uniform film of finishing material without brushing out or working back over the material laid on in a one-direction brush stroke.

One quick check to determine quality in a brush is to spread the bristles with the thumbs and forefingers. This will determine the body, or density, of

the bristles and whether they are inserted in the filler block — a part of the handle — in two or three rows. Once parted, the bristles should spring back into position when released. There should be a minimum of loose bristles in a new brush, although a few loose bristles are not necessarily an indication of poor quality. As a rule the best brushes have three rows of bristles in the filler block.

In your paint dealer's brush racks you'll see brushes for just about every purpose, in varying widths and lengths of bristle and in quality ranging from the cheap, use-once-and-throw-away

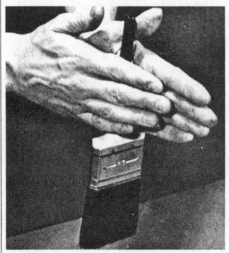

Two steps you should take to condition a brush before you use it. First, suspend it in linseed oil for 24 to 36 hrs. Then remove excess oil by twirling the handle between the palms. Wash in solvent.

brush, usually in a narrow width, to the top-quality product with long, springly bristles having flagged ends.

Perhaps the most commonly used

widths range from 1 to 4 in., with the "specials" running both narrower and

A strike wire on the container is always handy.

wider. For painting exterior siding the 4-in. brush is probably the most commonly used with a 1-in. brush at hand for painting sash and other more intricate work, For laying on stains, sealers, shellacs, varnishes, lacquers and other synthetics most finishers will select a 1½ to 2-in. brush for large surfaces and a 1-in., or even a ½-in. brush, for the fine detail work. The widths are only suggestive, not arbitrary. The large, wide brush will carry more finishing material and cover a larger area with a minimum of brushing, either when applying paints and enamels or laying on clear finishing materials. But the large, wide brush can't be used to advantage for painting, or "cutting in", sash or handling other close detail work. Much the same rule of thumb applies to interior decorating with paint and the brush-application of clear finishing materials.

Here's a quick check of brush quality. Bristles should be full-bodied, resilient; should spring back when released.

Seal a knot with shellac after finish-sanding the wood, and be sure to clean the brush with alcohol immediately after use.

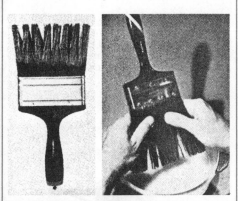

Using the side of the brush on a narrow surface causes the bristles to "finger". There's no practical cure.
As the final step in cleaning, work solvent into the heel of the brush with the fingers.

Avoid "joining" strokes whenever possible. Strokes should be continuous.

Brush always from wet to dry.

New brushes should be conditioned before use, as otherwise the individual bristles will absorb finishing materials and stiffen. This lessens normal resiliency and spreadability. It is the common practice to suspend the brush (if necessary drill a small hole through the handle to take a wire support) in a can or brush-keeper containing sufficient linseed oil (boiled) to cover the bristles when the brush is supported in the can. Allow the bristles to remain in the oil for 24 or 36 hrs. Then hold the brush inside the can or other container and twirl the handle between the palms to remove excess oil. Dip in turpentine and continue to twirl in this manner until all oil has been removed.

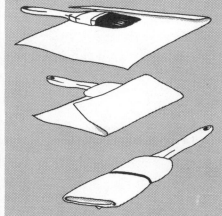

Many finishing materials will harden in bristles in an hour or less. If you must leave a job unfinished, wrap the brush tightly in aluminum foil.

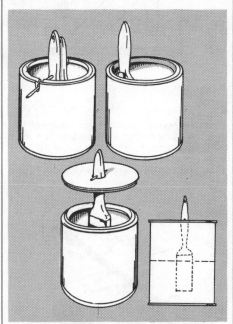

Brushes can be stored safely for a limited time in a keeper you can easily make yourself from a 1-gal. can with a friction lid. Fill the can with sufficient linseed oil to fully cover the bristles. Add a little pure turpentine and cover with plastic wrapping or aluminum foil.

Don't permit finishing materials or paint to harden *in* the brush. If you must leave a job unfinished and you are using a finish that hardens within an hour, then clean the brush thoroughly in a solvent sometime within that hour. There are special solvents for reclaiming brushes in which finishes or paints have hardened, but avoid their use whenever possible by cleaning the brush promptly. Use the correct solvent: lacquer reducer (thinner) for brushes used in lacquers; turpentine or synthetic solvents for the common clear finishes and paints; and alcohol for brushes used to apply shellac.

To store brushes for long periods of time do a thorough job of cleaning in solvent, running a brush comb through the bristles to straighten them. Then wrap in oiled paper, the wrapping so made that it excludes air and extends up onto the handle where it can be sealed with tape.

Clean bristles occasionally with wire brush and a brush comb to remove any paint residues.

PART V

Practical ideas

Practical ideas can save you time and money. Usually it's the little ideas that count, ideas gathered over many years of practical experience by tradesmen and do-it-yourselfers alike. Since you're bound to come across some situations where a few practical ideas could help you on your way to success and satisfaction, we've selected a few we hope you'll find useful.

While most circular saws are equipped with a depth scale, a lot of craftsmen will still use a rule to set the depth of cut. Here you may find a marking gauge better than a rule since the adjustable head provides a stop.

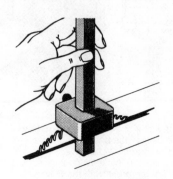

Cement 1/8-in.-thick plastic strips along one edge of a triangle to make a combined T-square and triangle.

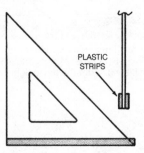

PLASTIC STRIPS

When a door binds at the top or bottom, you can correct the fit without planing by cutting off portions of one hinge barrel and inserting washers of the same thickness at the opposite end of each barrel to level the door.

When sharpening a saw, protect the tips of your fingers by slipping a rubber bulb from a medicine dropper over the free end of the three-cornered file. This fingertip grip can easily be removed whenever necessary.

Use the shank end of an old drill as a center punch when mounting a hinge, to produce perfectly aligned holes.

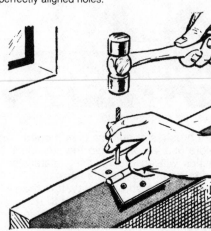

Here's a way to fasten your miterbox to a sawhorse and have it easily removable. Simply mount loose-pin butt hinges on the box and horse, or replace the pins in standard butts with cotter pins.

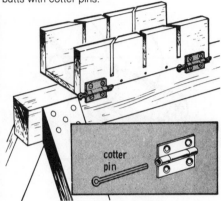

cotter pin

Prevent skinned knuckles when sawing firewood by tacking pieces of inner tubing over the ends of the crossed uprights of the log cradle.

PADDING

A ¼-in. plywood panel replacement for the regular cross braces makes your ladder more rigid and easier to carry.

¼" PLYWOOD

HAND GRIPS

To add a scraper to a hammer, just mount a short section of saw blade on the top of the head as shown. It's great for quickly removing concrete scale from construction form boards.

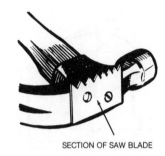

SECTION OF SAW BLADE

This collapsible sawhorse made from a length of 2 x 4 and ¾-in. plywood is strong, but comes apart easily for storage.

1" x 1" CLEATS

2 x 4

¾" PLYWOOD LEG

You'll always have solder handy if you wind it on a typewriter ribbon spool and mount it on the top of your soldering gun with a bolt and wing nut.

Steel wool makes an efficient throwaway grit catcher for the exhaust chute on your bench grinder.

STEEL WOOL

Shelves for your garage can be made by boring holes in the studs for ½-in. pipe. Fasten the shelves with pipe straps.

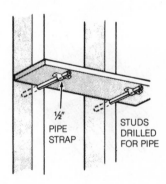

½" PIPE STRAP

STUDS DRILLED FOR PIPE

This squaring guide built from scrap lumber lets you crosscut squarely to a layout mark, without having to guide the saw along a line.

Practical ideas

This handy holder for a single-edge razor blade can easily be made by cutting a deep notch in one end of a large cork, then gluing the cork to a shop wall, or a cabinet door.

You can find the center of a dowel of any diameter by using a center finder of the dimensions shown.

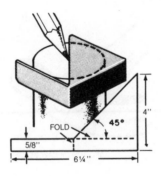

No more nicked fingers if you make this holder for a double-edge razor blade. Slit a short piece of tubing and insert the blade. The blade will stay put in the tubing when you squeeze it.

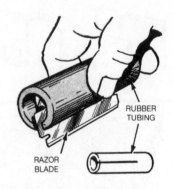

Make a glue brush from a paper clamp and a scrap of window screen.

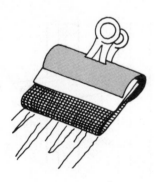

Use a jacknife with a large blade as a sliding wedge to hold the saw kerf open when ripping long boards.

Skidproof feet for an artist's triangle can be made by cutting small pieces of pencil eraser and gluing them to the triangle.

This homemade pitch-gauge attachment clamps to the end of your level. Bend it from sheet metal, as shown, and solder a hex nut to the upper surface of the lower section of the gauge.

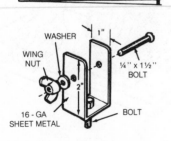

A thick leather strip with a cut-out makes a fine vise-jaw pad.

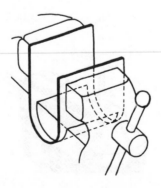

Have trouble keeping track of thumbtacks in your shop? Here's a good idea to keep them handy. Buy a large cork and mount it in a convenient place. Then whenever you find a thumbtack, stick it on this holder.

When installing traverse rods, make a simple cardboard template to assure proper alignment of all supports with the windows.

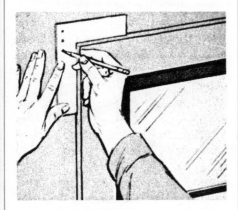

A tiny twist drill can be straightened quickly if you chuck it in a hand drill and then snug a metal-jaw vise on it just enough so that it still turns. Grasp the drill firmly enough to put a little side pressure on the bit and crank it slowly.

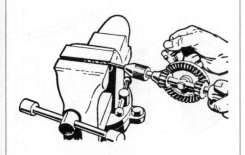

If you lose the cap to a plastic glue bottle, a slip-on pencil eraser makes an excellent substitute since it fits the spout exactly. The eraser can also be used to spread the glue.

Wire-size twist drills are easily bent if you are not careful. To straighten one don't hammer it like a nail. Instead place the drill between two blocks of wood and roll it back and forth. The drill will be straight again.

Looking for a simple tool holder for use on a ladder? Round up a juice or beer can, partially cut the top, bend it back into a hook and hang the can from a rung of the ladder.

Filing flat surfaces on small parts can be done accurately if discarded hacksaw blades are clamped along the layout lines. The part is filed down to the blades, which limit the depth of the cut.

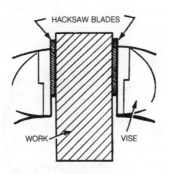
HACKSAW BLADES
WORK   VISE

One motor can move around in your shop if you mount it on a board with half a pair of loose-pin hinges screwed to the edge. The other half of the hinge is mounted on the tool bench. The pivoting weight puts tension on the belt.

101

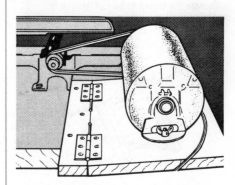

A quickie marking gauge can be made from a section of hacksaw blade anchored in a slot through a wood block. The teeth provide a wide selection of notches that hold a pencil right on target.

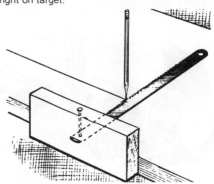

When working to a close dimension you need a fine, flat point on the pencil for accurate scribing. Cement an emery board to the handle of your try square and you'll have a handy means of renewing that worn point quickly.

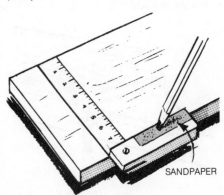
SANDPAPER

Practical ideas

Working outdoors with a ladder and need a sawhorse to trim a board or two, remember this simple stunt: Place a scrap board on the second rung of the ladder in the manner shown so it rests at an angle to form a sawbuck. In this position, the slanting board will cradle the board to be cut when it is placed against the ladder.

BOARD

Save time and labor when you are making cabinet drawers by placing a 1/16-in. insert between two 1/8-in. dado blades. The 5/16-in. groove that is cut will make it easy to insert the 1/4-in. plywood drawer bottom and will allow for expansion of the wood.

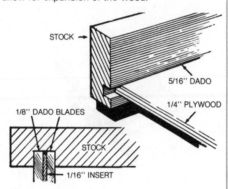

STOCK
5/16" DADO
1/4" PLYWOOD
1/8" DADO BLADES
STOCK
1/16" INSERT

A corner clamp will hold small stock firmly while you glue and brad box joints. Just cut 3/4 x 1-in. slots on the centerlines of a hardwood block. Use Tee-nuts and bolts as clamps.

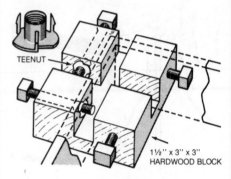

TEENUT

1½" x 3" x 3"
HARDWOOD BLOCK

Drawer pulls and the handles of cabinet doors will hold tightly if you insert a sandpaper washer between the handle and face of the drawer. Glue the washer in place and then tighten the screw.

SANDPAPER-WASHER GLUED TO KNOB

ABRASIVE SIDE

A kerf wedge prevents binding when sawing thin panels. It's a shingle nail driven into a small block of wood which can be inserted above the saw when the cut is deep enough.

You don't have to buy special shelf brackets when adding an extra shelf to kitchen cabinets. Just use two screw eyes at each end of the shelf, turning them into the side pieces as shown.

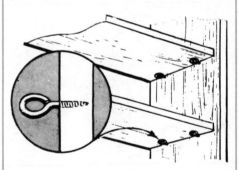

Drive two large staples into one edge of the bench to support the bolt and bore a hole in the top of the bench to take one of the legs when the bolt is swung into position. Position the hole so that the bolt will be at right angles to the edge of the bench when it's swung over to act as a stop.

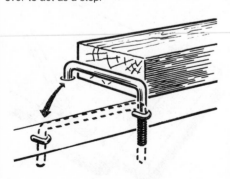

A notched piece of brass is better than the driver that comes with glazier points because it holds the point flat against the glass and keeps it from bending up when being tapped in place.

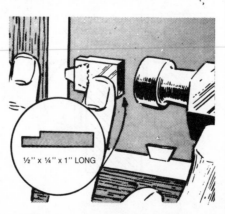

½" x ¼" x 1" LONG

A scrap of insulation board slipped into your shirt pocket and used as a pincushion is especially handy when you're up on a ladder using brads and tacks.

A spare sanding belt doubles as a sanding block if you slip it over a pair of blocks, hinged with tape, to fit inside.

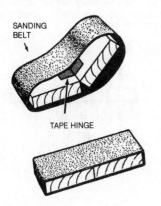

SANDING BELT

TAPE HINGE

A palm-size sanding block can be made by cutting slits in the end of 3½-in. piece of 1 x 2 stock. Use No. 6 screws to clamp the sandpaper.

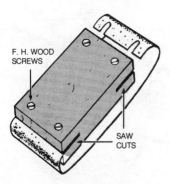

F. H. WOOD SCREWS

SAW CUTS

To make a scrap box from a cardboard carton, trim the flaps and glue them over a length of heavy wire.

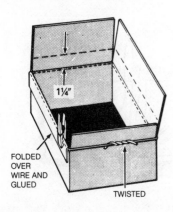

1¼"

FOLDED OVER WIRE AND GLUED

TWISTED

Drilling holes in round stock calls for a V-block. This one is made by making right angle cuts down the center of a hardwood block. Angle iron screwed to the block provides a true surface.

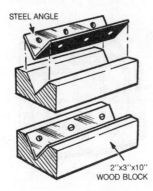

STEEL ANGLE

2"x3"x10" WOOD BLOCK

A sanding block for smoothing round edges can be made from a piece of cove or bed molding of a width that matches the work. Either glue or thumbtacks hold the sandpaper in place.

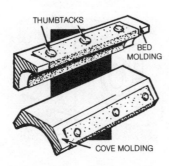

THUMBTACKS

BED MOLDING

COVE MOLDING

To make a hold-down block for use when grooving dowels on a bench saw, cut a V-shaped notch in one edge of a piece of 1-in. stock and line it with abrasive paper. Adjust the saw fence to center the dowel over the blade.

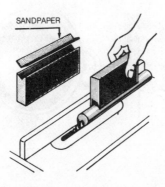

SANDPAPER

To toenail a stud, drive the head of a horizontal nail into the sill.

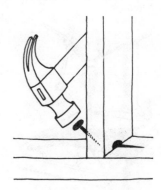

Loose screws in a door hinge may be tightened by wrapping them with several layers of cellulose tape. When the screw is reinserted, the tape will be pressed into the threads, giving a snug fit.

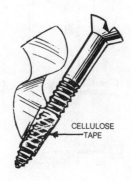

CELLULOSE TAPE

Bore a hole through a corrugated corner fastener and your bench, drop in a shingle nail, and you have a removable bench stop.

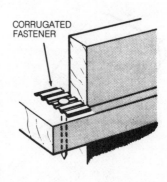

CORRUGATED FASTENER

Practical ideas

104

A nonslip surface for your drill-press table can be made from a section of inner tube. Stretch the tube over the table and cut a hole in it over the center hole in the table for the drill to pass through.

Handy hooks soldered to the outside of a can in which you store bolts will hold nuts and washers, and make it easy to locate the size you want. Use 1/8-in. welding rod or coat-hanger wire to form the hooks.

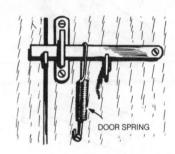

Barn doors and other outbuildings that have thumb latches will lock with a more positive action if a coil spring is attached to the latch bar. The downward pull keeps the bar from jumping out of the notch in the striker when door slams.

You'll find that the jaws from toolmaker's clamps make excellent straps for mounting work on a drill-press table or the face plate of a lathe.

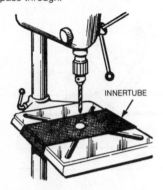

By setting a screw eye into the slot of a hasp on a storage chest or bin, you can prevent the hasp from falling over the staple every time you close the lid.

When welding small butt joints, it's often hard to hold the pieces together for a good weld, while providing a grounding circuit for the arc welder. A clever way is to secure the pieces with C-clamps to a large horseshoe.

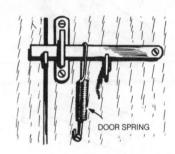

The striking strip on a matchbook makes a good substitute for an oilstone when sharpening modeling knives.

When the setscrew holding a doorknob works loose, wrap the screw with a turn of cello-phane tape before replacing it. The tape will tighten the grip between threads.

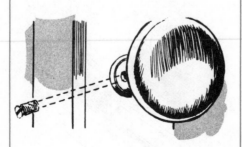

A small magnet on the end of a piece of twine will prevent fumbling in the pocket of your carpenter's apron for small nails and brads. Pin the free end of the twine to the apron.

When drilling a hole for a bolt, use an adjustable end wrench as a simple substitute for calipers.

When your open-end wrench is too big, insert a washer to "adjust" the jaw for a snug fit.

To shorten a spring that is too long for your purposes, just slip it over a bolt or rod large enough to fit snugly inside and use a file to cut the spring at the desired spot.

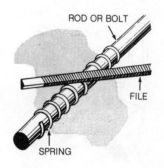

ROD OR BOLT

FILE

SPRING

Choosing the right drill for a bolt is no problem if you use the nut to test the bits for size.

If you don't have an offset screwdriver handy you can improvise one by fastening a washer to a long bolt with two nuts.

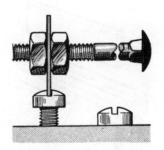

A broken file renews the grip of your vise. Weld two sections to straddle plates.

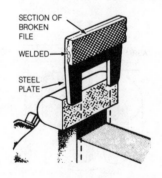

SECTION OF BROKEN FILE

WELDED

STEEL PLATE

To make a square joint when bending angle iron, mark the axis, strike a line at right angles to show the thickness of the leg, scribe 45-deg. lines from the intersection and cut and bend the gap shut.

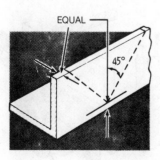

EQUAL

45°

For more grip when applying plaster or stucco to a smooth surface, install a number of protruding staples on the surface. Just place a thin piece of wood under the gun when you're driving the staples.

STAPLE

An improvised drill rack can be made from cardboard and thumbtacked to the wall.

CORRUGATED CARDBOARD

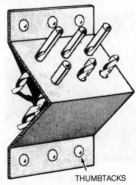

THUMBTACKS

Practical ideas

How do you edge-plane short boards on a sawhorse? It's simple as can be if you make the adjustable stop shown here. Bend a length of steel rod to form the stop, then drill holes for the legs in the crossmember of the horse.

To enlarge a hole slightly, fold a strip of abrasive paper or cloth so that it is a little longer than the diameter of the hole and slip this into a slot cut in the end of a steel rod. Then chuck the rod in your drill.

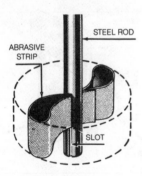

Dowels driven into the underside of your workbench serve as extra fingers to hold bags open when collecting sweepings.

To find the rough center of a rod or dowel, seat a scrap of angle with a square inside corner across the end. A slot in one side adapts the angle to various diameters. Scribe lines along the edge nearest the rod's center, turning the rod each time.

Hold short boards for edgeplaning with wood cleats nailed about ¾-in. apart on your sawhorse. Blocks nailed at the slot ends serve as stop-blocks.

A grooved ruler attached to the edge of your workbench is a handy accessory for measuring dowels and holding them while sawing.

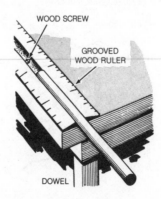

Quick renewal of the abrasive strip on a sanding block used for sanding tiny parts is made easy with a press-on clamp in the form of a rectangular cut-out to fit the block.

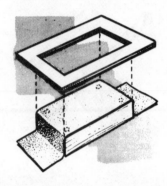

This sawhorse jig supports long boards being cut on a table saw.

To build a jig for scoring dowels to be glued, drill a series of holes in a hardwood block. Drive No. 6 x ¾-in. roundhead wood screws through the edge so they project enough to score 1/16 in. deep. Twist the dowels through twice.

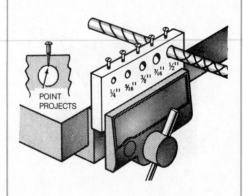

A carton shelf hung from studs in your garage is a handy place to store oilcans, small tools, gloves and other necessities. Just cut tabs as shown and nail them to the studs.

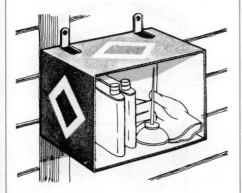

A glass door knob that becomes loose is easy to make tight again. Simply remove the knob from the door, pour sand into the gap between the ferrule and glass. Then flow glue on top of the sand while supporting the knob.

SAND-AND-GLUE

A disposable dustpan is the perfect tool for cleaning up spilled food or other moist materials. To make one, cut an aluminum-foil pie plate in two, leaving two thirds for a pan and one third for a scraper.

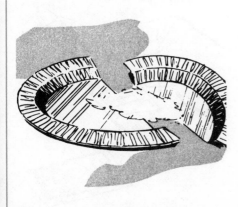

On workshop equipment which is frequently assembled and disassembled, speed the process by grinding away several threads on the ends of the bolts. The nuts will then slip freely on the bolt end. When the threads are engaged, a fast spin tightens the nut.

BOLT

THREADS GROUND OFF

Cable lamps from switch boxes can be put to work to serve as neat toolholders for screwdrivers, chisels and other thin tools. Just mount them on the wall or fasten them to pegboard.

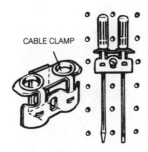

CABLE CLAMP

Use an old hacksaw blade to make a straight edge for tearing masking tape. Notch the ends, and then mount it on the tape roll with a rubber band through a soda straw.

For perfect alignment when mounting a hinge, use a screwdriver with a blade which matches the diameter of the holes. Two taps mark the center.

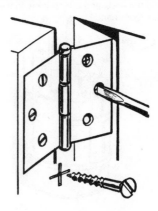

Use pre-positioned bolts recessed in your bench top to mount seldom-used tools, such as a pipe vise.

A long-lasting acid brush for use in soldering jobs can be made by slitting the chisel end of a slip-on pencil eraser to form acid-holding "bristles". (Rubber is almost acid-proof.)

Practical ideas

This brush holder is made by folding a length of coathanger wire double and slipping two ¼-in. tubing spacers over it. Flatten the spacers and spread wires between them, then bend the ends and attach them to the can with rubber bands.

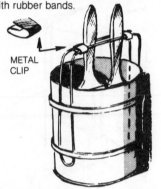

METAL CLIP

Cleaning paint brushes will take less time if you cover the metal ferrule with masking tape before you begin the job. Just pull off the tape and throw it away.

When storing a wet paintbrush temporarily in a plastic bag, it will remain flexible longer if you force the air out of the bag. To do this, immerse the lower part of the bag in water, then tie it tightly.

Protect the bristles of your paint brush between coats by inserting the handle through a slit in a plastic coffee can lid and suspending in solvent.

Maintain that chisel edge on your paint-brushes by clamping the bristles in a large paper clip, as shown. This will also provide a hanger for suspending the brushes from hooks or nails.

A swing-up holder fastened to your paint can with a large rubber band will keep the paint from skidding off your stepladder.

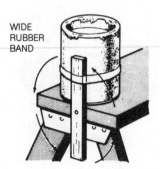

WIDE RUBBER BAND

A perfect strainer for paint can be made by prying off the rim of a coffee can and crimping it as shown, then using this to stretch cheesecloth over the can.

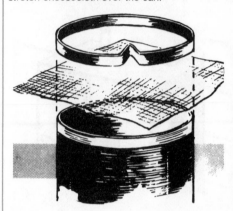

A pipe cleaner makes a good throw-away liner for the rim of a paint can. When the job's completed, lift it out and replace the lid.

PAINT

This shaping sheath for old brushes holds the bristles together and prevents them from splaying outward after cleaning. Make it by folding a sheet of stiff plastic to fit the brush and stapling the side. Place it on the brush by slipping it over the handle.

PART VI

101 Plans
that you can build

109

On the following pages are shown
101 plans of useful around-the-house
projects subdivided under 10
different headings.

Each heading, in turn, features several
projects, complete with detailed plans,
instructions and material list.

To get started, simply turn to the
heading of interest to you.

For plan index see page 287.

Mr. Chips 101 Plans is a "fun" book designed for the home handyman who wants to improve his skills and techniques by doing — rather than just reading. For Mr. Chips 101 Plans features a selection of the most popular do-it-yourself projects I've built on TV over the past few years.

I've classified and grouped each project under a major heading so that the reader will find several projects requiring different skill levels under the heading "Patio-Garden Furniture", for instance. This way the reader can start with a simple project first, before he moves on to something more ambitious.

Because I've built each project before, the reader can judge by my photographs and plans how each particular project would fit in best with his needs. Then, working from my detailed plans and my exact material lists, disappointments and wastage are kept to a minimum as the reader knows beforehand what the finished project should look like and what he'll need in materials.

I've enjoyed selecting these projects for you and hope you'll enjoy building them as much as I did.

Sincerely,

Mr. CHIPS

1
Kitchen

1 DRY SINK   112

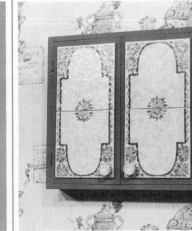

4 SPICE RACK   116

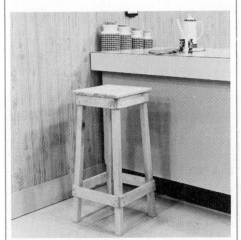

2 KITCHEN STOOL   114

5 WALL HUNG DISH CABINET   118

3 CUTTING BOARD   115

6 KNIFE HOLDER   119

1
dry sink

112

Designed to look like a sink cabinet to fit in with your kitchen decor, this dry sink gives you the extra work and storage space you need — without upsetting the overall appearance of your kitchen.

INSTRUCTIONS:

(1) Cut parts and make up base. Rout moulding into (C) and (D).
(2) Make parts and assemble side panels and install. Nail on (A).
(3) Install shelf and parts (J) and (O).
(4) Lay out, cut and assemble to sections (E), (F), (G), (H) and install.
(5) Attach moulding (P).
(6) Make up doors and install.
(7) Attach pulls and catches.
(8) Mixture of ⅔ boiled linseed oil and ⅓ turpentine, rubbed in makes an excellent finish.

MATERIAL LIST:

(A)	1 Pc.	¾" x 16" x 28"	Plywood
(B)	1 Pc.	¾" x 16" x 28"	Plywood
(C)	1 Pc.	¾" x 5" x 38"	Pine
(D)	2 Pcs.	¾" x 5" x 17"	Pine
(E)	1 Pc.	¾" x 6" x 28½"	Pine
(F)	2 Pcs.	¾" x 6" x 16½"	Pine
(G)	1 Pc.	¾" x 4" x 26½"	Pine
(H)	1 Pc.	¾" x 1½" x 26½"	Pine
(J)	2 Pcs.	¾" x 1½" x 25"	Pine
(K)	1 Pc.	¾" x 13" x 26½"	Pine
(L)	2 Pcs.	¾" x ¾" x 13"	Pine
(M)	2 Pcs.	¾" x 1¼" x 14"	Pine
(N)	1 Pc.	¾" x 1¼" x 26½"	Pine
(O)	1 Pc.	¾" x 1½" x 24¼"	Pine
(P)	1 Pc.	¾" x 1¼" x 64"	Pine Moulding
(Q)	1 Pc.	¼" x 25½" x 28"	Plywood

Side Panels:

(A)	2 Pcs.	¾" x 1½" x 24¼"	Pine
(B)	4 Pcs.	¾" x 2½" x 24¼"	Pine
(C)	4 Pcs.	¾" x 2½" x 12"	Pine
(D)	2 Pcs.	¼" x 12" x 20¼"	Plywood

Doors:

(A)	4 Pcs.	¾" x 2" x 21¼"	Pine
(B)	4 Pcs.	¾" x 2" x 9¼"	Pine
(C)	2 Pcs.	¼" x 9¼" x 18¼"	Plywood

Misc.: Hinges, pulls, catches, nails, glue, wood filler, sandpaper.

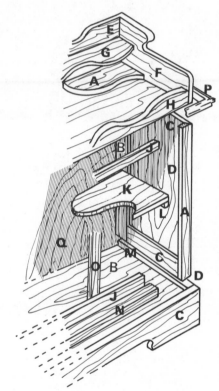

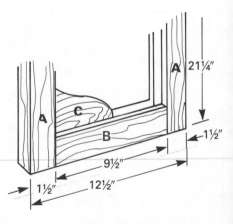

DOOR SIZE 12½" x 21¼"

Verify all measurements before cutting

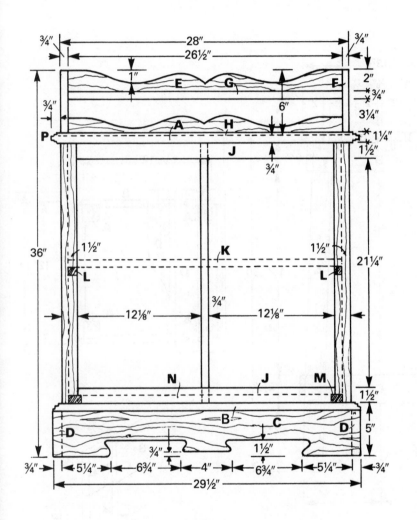

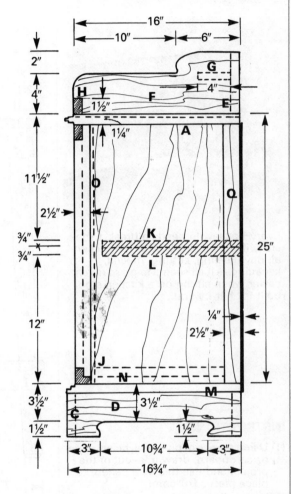

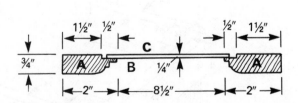

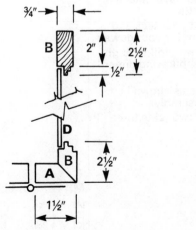

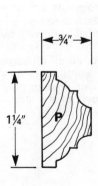

2
kitchen stool

Every housewife needs a break. Especially if she has to stand in the kitchen all day. Peeling, cutting, mixing, kneading — it all seems to go so much easier when sitting on a kitchen stool built for her by you.

INSTRUCTIONS:

(1) Using a piece of plywood, heavy paper or cardboard, draw a layout of the project and use this as a pattern to place pieces (A) onto.

(2) You will see by the material list that the parts are all about 1″ longer than required. This will allow you to cut the angles after you have obtained them from your pattern.

(3) When you have cut your legs and crossrails, drill them for your dowels.

(4) Make sure you do not drill through existing dowels by following dimensions in circle (A).

(5) Round off all edges as shown in drawing, before assembly.

(6) Paint, stain or give two (2) to three (3) coats of shellac.

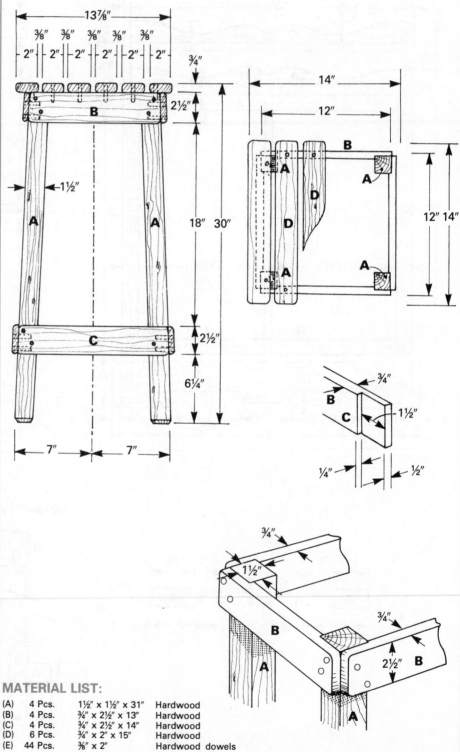

MATERIAL LIST:

(A)	4 Pcs.	1½″ x 1½″ x 31″	Hardwood
(B)	4 Pcs.	¾″ x 2½″ x 13″	Hardwood
(C)	4 Pcs.	¾″ x 2½″ x 14″	Hardwood
(D)	6 Pcs.	¾″ x 2″ x 15″	Hardwood
(E)	44 Pcs.	⅜″ x 2″	Hardwood dowels

3
double sink cutting board

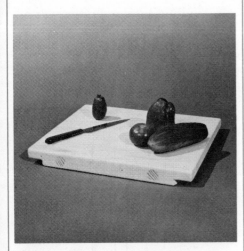

Want to do something special for the woman in your life? Then build her this nifty cutting board she'll really appreciate. Now she can cut up all kinds of tempting ingredients for those super sandwiches you love to eat.

INSTRUCTIONS:

(1) You will need approximately 11 linear feet of 1½" x 1½" hardwood (birch).

(2) Cut these pieces a little longer than actually required to allow for final trimming.

(3) Make yourself a jig so that all holes will be equally spaced; drill ⅜" dia. holes on six of them.

(4) On the two outside pieces first drill ¾" holes about 1" deep to receive nuts, washers and plugs. Then drill ⅜" dia. holes right through for rods.

(5) Assemble pieces on rods, using a small amount of glue. Using a socket wrench, tighten up nuts, making sure that you have equal spaces on each end for plugs.

(6) Insert plugs and then proceed to cut to final length and rout edges — sand all surfaces smooth.

(7) Make template as indicated on drawing and cut check on under side of board.

(8) You may wish to make your board smaller or larger; if so change dimensions accordingly.

Verify all measurements before cutting

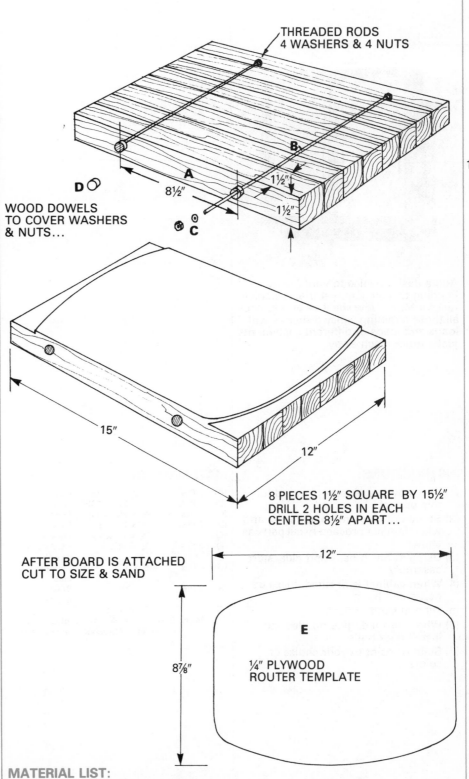

THREADED RODS
4 WASHERS & 4 NUTS

WOOD DOWELS
TO COVER WASHERS
& NUTS...

A
8½"

B

D

C

1½"
1½"

15"

12"

8 PIECES 1½" SQUARE BY 15½"
DRILL 2 HOLES IN EACH
CENTERS 8½" APART...

AFTER BOARD IS ATTACHED
CUT TO SIZE & SAND

12"

8⅞"

E

¼" PLYWOOD
ROUTER TEMPLATE

MATERIAL LIST:

(A)	8 Pcs.	1½" x 1½" x 15"	Hardwood
(B)	2 Pcs.	5⁄16" dia. x 10½"	Threaded steel rod
(C)	4 Pcs.	5⁄16" nuts and washers	
(D)	4 Pcs.	¾" dia. x ½" wood plugs (¾" dowel)	
(E)	1 Pc.	¼" x 8⅞" x 12"	Plywood

4
spice rack

Add a dash of spice to your life by building this elegant, yet practical spice rack for Mom. Now she'll be able to cook all those tempting, spicy dishes — with loads and loads of different condiments just a quick reach away.

INSTRUCTIONS:

(1) You may use pine or plywood for this project.
(2) Study drawing and material list and when familiar proceed to cut parts as shown.
(3) Using 1" finish nails and glue, start assembly.
(4) When cabinet is finished, make up doors and hang.
(5) Fill and sand project.
(6) When finished, glue on tiles and install door pulls.
(7) Stain or paint to your choice of colors.

MATERIAL LIST:

(A)	2 Pcs.	½" x 2¾" x 15"	Pine
(B)	2 Pcs.	½" x 2¾" x 13½"	Pine
(C)	2 Pcs.	⅜" x 2¼" x 14¼"	Pine
(D)	2 Pcs.	½" x 7" x 13"	Pine
(E)	1 Pc.	⅛" x 14" x 15"	Plywood
(F)	3 Pcs.	¼" x 14¼"	Hardwood dowel
(G)	4 Pcs.	6" x 6"	Ceramic tiles
(H)	2 Prs.	1" x 1½"	Brass hinges
(J)	—	Door pulls	

Misc.: Ceramic tile glue, wood glue, nails, wood filler, sandpaper, paint or stain.

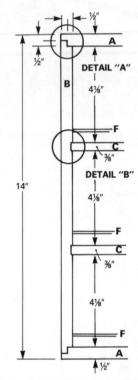

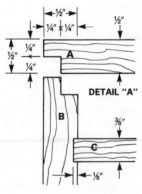

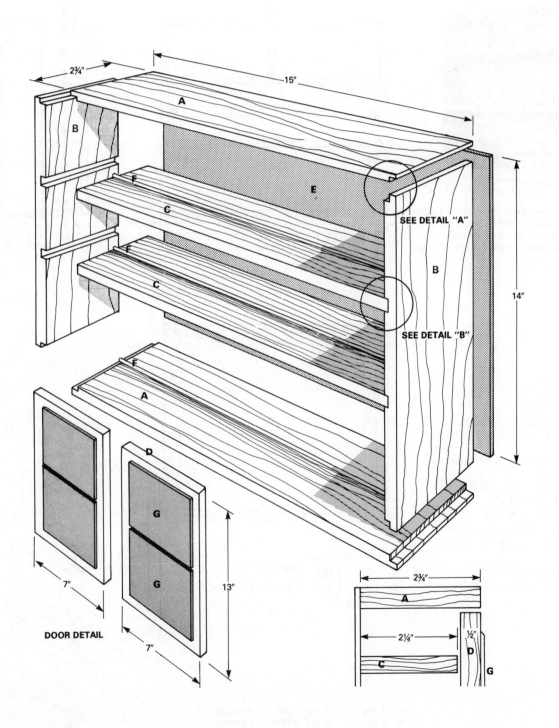

2¾"

15"

A

B

SEE DETAIL "A"

F

E

C

B

F

C

14"

SEE DETAIL "B"

F

A

D

G

G

G

G

7"

13"

DOOR DETAIL

7"

2¾"

A

2¼"

½"

C

D

G

5
wall hung
dish cabinet

Old style charm and a more relaxed pace of life find expression in this wall hung dish cabinet. It's a real labor of love which extends a warm welcome to all at dinner time.

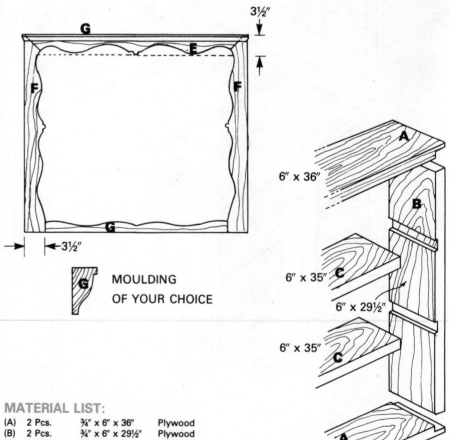

MOULDING
OF YOUR CHOICE

INSTRUCTIONS:

(1) You will require one piece of plywood ¾" x 36" x 36" and one piece ¼" x 36" x 48".
(2) Cut parts as per drawing and material list.
(3) Make dado cuts in pieces (B) and rabbet cuts in pieces (A).
(4) Using glue and nails, assemble unit.
(5) Nail and glue on back panel (D).
(6) Lay out and cut pieces (E) and (F) and attach.
(7) Fill and sand all nail holes.
(8) Paint or stain to your choice of colors.

MATERIAL LIST:

(A)	2 Pcs.	¾" x 6" x 36"	Plywood
(B)	2 Pcs.	¾" x 6" x 29½"	Plywood
(C)	2 Pcs.	¾" x 6" x 35"	Plywood
(D)	1 Pc.	¼" x 30" x 36"	Plywood
(E)	1 Pc.	¼" x 3½" x 36"	Plywood
(F)	2 Pcs.	¼" x 3½" x 30"	Plywood

6
knife holder

Got odds and ends lying about? Some scrap lumber, too? Well, don't throw it out. Build this handsome knife holder. And eliminate the constant kitchen-drawer scramble to find the right knife just when you really need it.

INSTRUCTIONS:

1. The materials for this project will most likely be found in your shop scrap box.
2. I obtained the steel balls from a rear axle bearing at a local garage, which are preferable, but wooden balls can be used, such as beads.
3. When cutting pieces (D) be sure that the angle is the same on all of them.
4. Place part (B) in position on part (A) and nail and glue.
5. Follow carefully dimensions on drawing, and using glue and nails attach to (A).
6. Place steel bearings in slot and nail and glue covers (E) in place.
7. Fill and sand and paint or stain to your choice of colours.

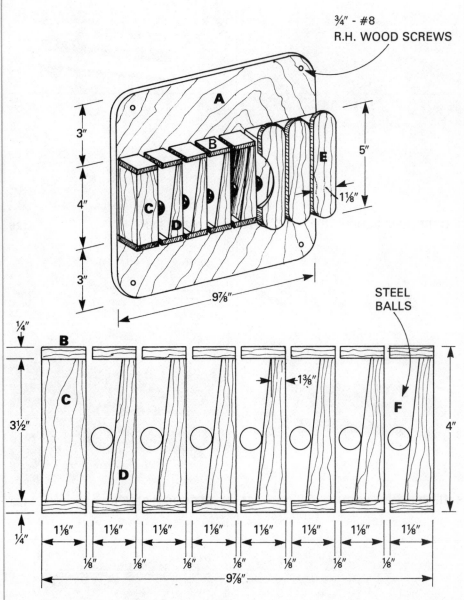

MATERIAL LIST:

A.	1 Pc.	¼″ x 9⅞″ x 10″	Plywood
B.	2 Pcs.	¼″ x ¾″ x 9⅞″	Pine
C.	1 Pc.	¾″ x 1⅛″ x 3½″	Pine
D.	7 Pcs.	¾″ x ¾″ x 3½″	Pine
E.	8 Pcs.	¼″ x 1⅛″ x 5″	Pine
F.	7 Pcs.	½″ or ⅝″ diameter wooden or steel balls.	
	Misc.:	Small nails, wood filler, sand-paper, paint or stain and 4 — 1″ #8 R.H. screws.	

Verify all measurements before cutting

7 COBBLER'S BENCH 122

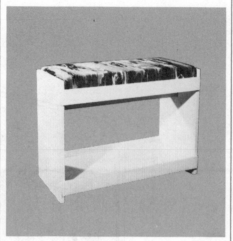

10 VANITY BENCH 126

13 GRECIAN BENCH 132

8 TELEPHONE BENCH 124

11 BEDROOM BENCH 128

14 STORAGE BENCH 134

9 BED TRAY 125

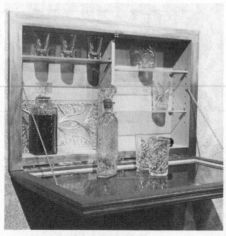

12 PICTURE FRAME BAR 130

15 FIRESIDE BENCH 136

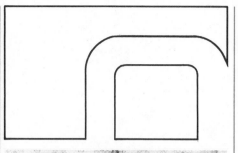

2
Bars
tables
benches

16 ONE DRAWER NIGHT TABLE 138

19 STACK TABLES 141

22 FOLDAWAY TABLE 146

17 KNOCKDOWN TABLE 139

20 POKER TABLE 142

23 COFFEE TABLE 148

18 CIRCULAR TABLE 140

21 BAR COFFEE TABLE 144

24 GAME TABLE 150

7
cobbler's bench

122

Shining shoes, and keeping paste and cloth under control, is a cinch with this design. It's very utilitarian and very attractive. It's also a very practical tool to teach youngsters how to earn their pocket money around the house.

INSTRUCTIONS:

(1) Cut 2 x 4 to rough length and making sure that edges are square, glue them together. When set sand smooth and make layout from drawing and cut out. Layout and cut legs and assemble pieces. When these pieces are done assemble the leg sections and then attach this assembly to main section. Proceed from drawing and cut and assemble top section and attach to top of main section.

(2) Cut and assemble drawer parts. Do not make them too tight.

(3) Set and fill all nail holes and imperfections in wood and sand smooth.

(4) Stain or paint to your choice of colours.

MATERIAL LIST:

A.	4 Pcs.	1¾" x 3¾" x 42"	Pine
B.	4 Pcs.	1¾" x 5¼" x 12"	Pine
C.	2 Pcs.	¾" x 2¾" x 17"	Pine
D.	2 Pcs.	¾" x 2¾" x 9"	Pine
E.	2 Pcs.	¾" x 2¾" x 12"	Pine
F.	1 Pc.	¾" x 8" x 16"	Pine
G.	1 Pc.	¾" x 7" x 10"	Pine
H.	1 Pc.	¾" x 9" x 13"	Pine
J.	3 Pcs.	¾" x 3¾" x 8"	Pine
K.	3 Pcs.	¼" x ¾" x 3¾"	Pine
L.	2 Pcs.	¾" x 3¾" x 4¾"	Pine
M.	4 Pcs.	½" x 3¾" x 7½"	Pine
N.	2 Pcs.	½" x 3⅛" x 3¾"	Pine
P.	2 Pcs.	⅛" x 4" x 7⅜"	Pine
Q.	2 Pcs.	1" hardwood knobs.	
Misc.:		Finish nails, screws, glue, wood filler, sandpaper, paint or stain of your choice.	

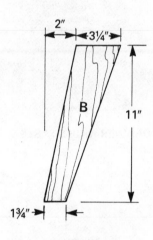

LEG DETAIL

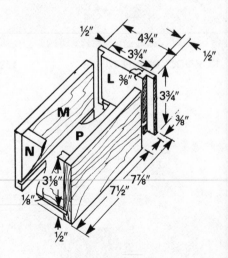

DRAWER DETAIL

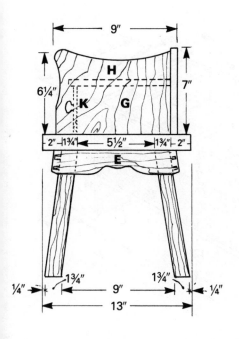

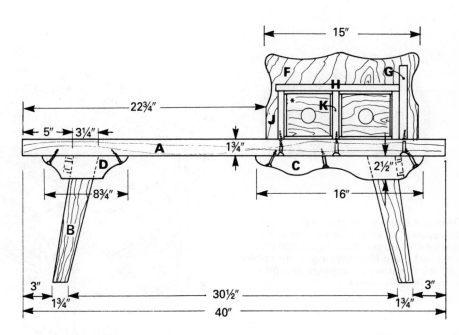

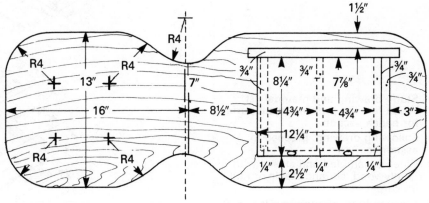

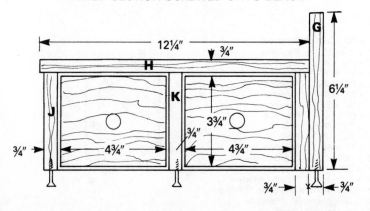

DRAWER SECTION SCREWED ONTO BENCH

*DRAWERS (2)
DO NOT MAKE
THEM TOO TIGHT

8
telephone bench

This is the ultimate conversation piece —
because a lot of conversations will be
held on it. Super attractive, comfortable,
and just plain chat-inviting. A must-have
gift for talkative youngsters and other
den-talk enthusiasts.

INSTRUCTIONS:

(1) Study drawing and material list.
     When familiar proceed to cut parts
     for bench section.
(2) Following drawing, proceed to
     assemble.
(3) When assembled and closed with
     ⅛" plywood, cut and staple or nail
     on carpet.
(4) Proceed to make upper section and
     cover with plastic laminate.
(5) Paint shelf and uncarpeted under
     side of bench.

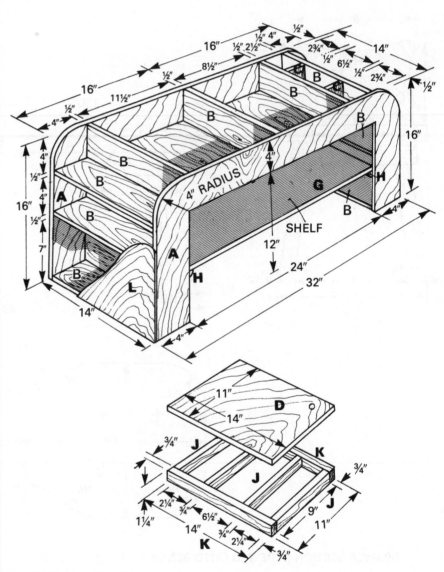

MATERIAL LIST:

(A)	2 Pcs.	½" x 16" x 32"	Plywood
(B)	10 Pcs.	½" x 4" x 13"	Plywood
(C)	2 Pcs.	½" x 2½" x 4"	Plywood
(D)	1 Pc.	½" x 11" x 14"	Plywood
(E)	2 Pcs.	½" x 2¼" x 8½"	Plywood
(F)	2 Pcs.	⅛" x 6½" x 8½"	Plywood
(G)	1 Pc.	¾" x 14" x 24"	Plywood
(H)	2 Pcs.	¾" x ¾" x 14"	Plywood
(J)	4 Pcs.	¾" x 1¼" x 9½"	Pine
(K)	2 Pcs.	¾" x 1¼" x 14"	Pine
(L)	2 Pcs.	⅛" x 14" x 48"	Plywood
(M)	1 Pc.	16" x 66"	Red Carpet
(N)	1 Pc.	12" x 60"	Grey Carpet
(O)	1 Pc.	16" x 18"	Plastic Laminate
	Misc.:	Contact cement, white glue, 1½" finish	
		nails, sandpaper, ⅜" staples or	
		¾" common nails, paint.	

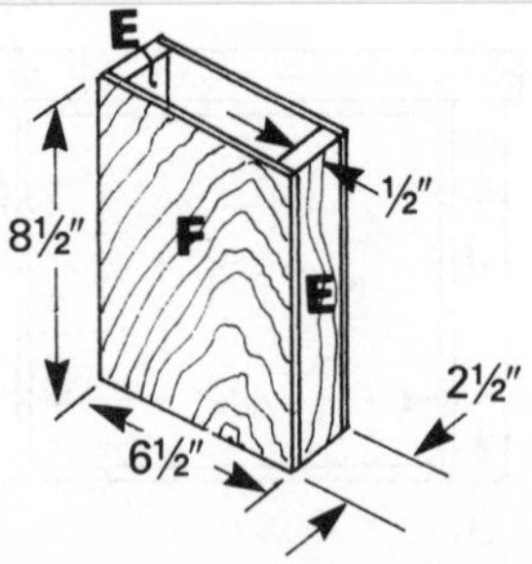

9
bed tray

Now you can have your breakfast in bed without having to worry about messy spills every time you butter the toast or stir the coffee. Just a small job, designed to make your Sunday mornings a bit more enjoyable.

INSTRUCTIONS:

(1) Study drawing and material list and when familiar, proceed to cut parts as per material list.

(2) Cut piece (A) and then cut rough lengths (C) and (D).

(3) When (C) and (D) are made, use ½" x 19 gauge nails and glue to attach to piece (A).

(4) Cut, nail and glue piece (B) to piece (A).

(5) Make layout for legs and cut parts.

(6) Glue these parts together and clamp.

(7) Round off all edges and sand.

(8) Attach legs to (B) with hinges with proper size screws.

(9) Set and fill all nail holes and imperfections, then sand.

(10) Stain, paint or varnish to your choice.

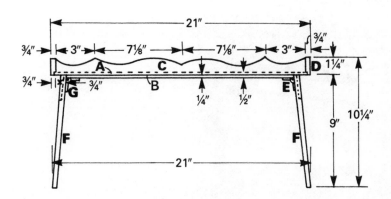

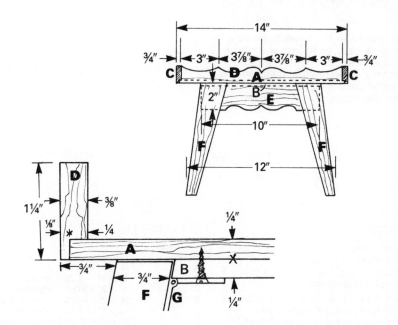

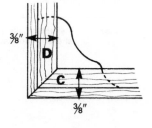

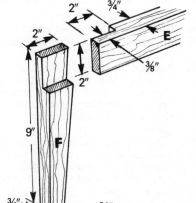

MATERIAL LIST:

(A)	1 Pc.	¼" x 13¾" x 20¾"	Plywood
(B)	1 Pc.	¼" x 10" x 18"	Plywood
(C)	2 Pcs.	⅜" x 1¼" x 22"	Pine
(D)	2 Pcs.	⅜" x 1¼" x 15"	Pine
(E)	2 Pcs.	¾" x 2" x 11"	Pine
(F)	4 Pcs.	¾" x 2" x 10"	Pine
(G)	4 Hinges	1½" x 1½"	
	Misc.:	Small finishing nails, glue, wood filler, paint, stain or varnish.	

10
vanity bench

A simple variation from the basic box, this design is easy to follow and reaps a handsome reward. Enlist Mom's aid when you get to making the cushions. Her sense of color and her experience with different materials can help you greatly.

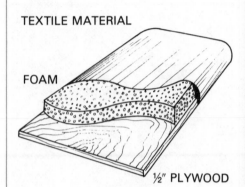

TEXTILE MATERIAL

FOAM

½" PLYWOOD

SEAT DETAIL

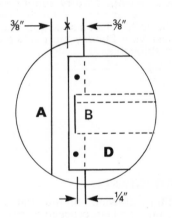

⅜" ⅜"

A B

D

¼"

DETAIL "A"

INSTRUCTIONS:

1. You will require a ¾" x 30" x 48" piece of plywood to cut pieces A, B, C, plus a piece ½" x 12" x 25" to cut piece F for cushion bottom.
2. When you have cut these pieces as per drawing and material list, proceed to cut dados as shown in sketch A.
3. When dados are cut, nail and glue together pieces A and B.
4. Nail and glue in place piece C.
5. Cut pine pieces D and nail and glue in place.
6. Set and fill all nail holes and any imperfections and also edges of plywood with wood filler and when dry sand smooth. Give a coat of shellack and paint to your choice of colours.
7. Cut plywood cushion base and place foam on it and cover with your choice of material. Staple this material to bottom of cushion base.
8. The base can be secured by 1¼" screws from underside of piece B if desired but is not necessary.

MATERIAL LIST:

Part No.	Pieces Req.	Dimensions	Type of Wood
A	2	¾" x 11½" x 18½"	Plywood
B	2	¾" x 11½" x 25"	Plywood
C	1	¾" x 2" x 24½"	Plywood
D	4	⅜" x 2¼" x 25¼"	Pine or Birch
E	1	½" x 11¼" x 24¼"	Plywood
F	1	2" x 11¼" x 24¼"	Foam rubber
G	1	20" x 30"	Textile or simulated leather
Misc.:		1½" finish nails, glue, wood filler, shellac, sandpaper and paint.	

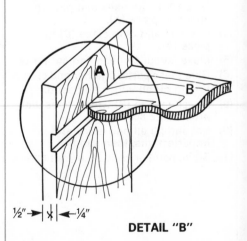

A

B

½" ¼"

DETAIL "B"

Verify all measurements before cutting

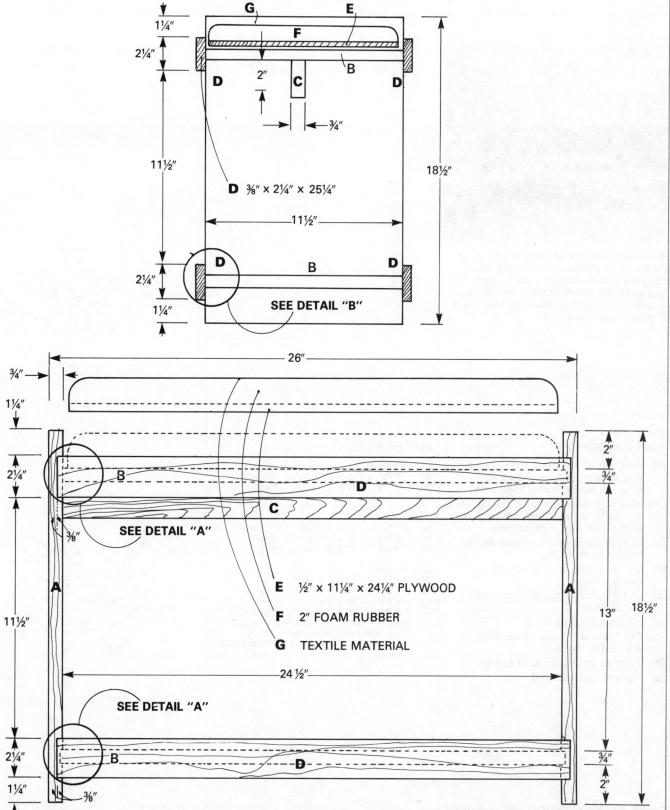

1¼″

2¼″

G

E

F

2″

C

D

B

D

11½″

D ⅜″ × 2¼″ × 25¼″

11½″

18½″

2¼″

D

D

B

D

1¼″

SEE DETAIL "B"

26″

¾″

1¼″

2″

¾″

2¼″

B

D

⅜″

C

SEE DETAIL "A"

A

A

E   ½″ × 11¼″ × 24¼″ PLYWOOD

F   2″ FOAM RUBBER

G   TEXTILE MATERIAL

11½″

24 ½″

13″

18½″

SEE DETAIL "A"

2¼″

B

D

¾″

1¼″

⅜″

2″

11
bedroom bench

Another useful variation of the basic box. Holds extra blankets, is foam-pillow covered and rolls about on casters. If sitting down when putting on shoes gives you a happier slant on life, build this one right away.

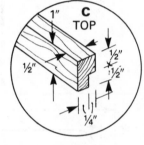

DETAIL "A"

INSTRUCTIONS:

(1) Proceed to cut parts for leg sections and assemble, using glue and small finishing nails; then sand.

(2) Make up shelf section and locate and attach to leg sections, using glue and 1" #6 steel F.H. screws.

(3) Cut ½" plywood top panel and glue, then nail on to legs.

(4) Cut to length and attach top pieces (B).

(5) Cut moulding (C), glue and nail around top.

(6) Fill and sand unit.

(7) Cut foam to fit and cover with a suitable material.

(8) Paint to your choice of colors.

(9) Casters are optional.

MATERIAL LIST:

Top Section:
(A)	1 Pc.	½" x 16" x 28"	Plywood
(B)	2 Pcs.	¾" x 1½" x 24"	Pine
(C)	10 Lin ft.	¾" x 1"	Pine

Shelf Section:
(A)	1 Pc.	¼" x 15" x 24"	Plywood
(B)	2 Pcs.	¾" x 1" x 24"	Pine
(C)	3 Pcs.	¾" x ¾" x 14"	Pine

Leg Section:
(A)	4 Pcs.	¾" x 2" x 13½"	Pine
(B)	4 Pcs.	¾" x 1" x 14½"	Pine
(C)	4 Pcs.	¾" x 1" x 1¼"	Pine
(D)	4 Pcs.	½" x 13½" x 15½"	Plywood

Misc.: 1 — set of 2" casters, nails, glue, wood filler, sandpaper.
1 — Pc. 2" x 15½" x 27½" foam rubber.

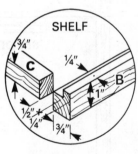

DETAIL "B"

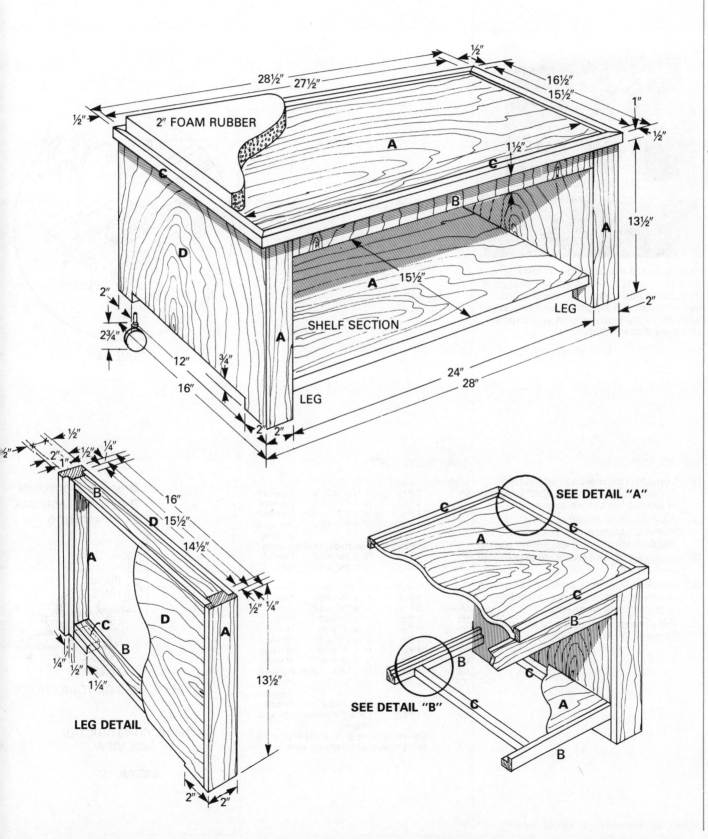

½"

28½" 27½" 16½"
15½"

½" 1"

2" FOAM RUBBER ½"

A 1½"

C C

B 13½"

D

A 15½" A

SHELF SECTION LEG

2" A 2"

2¾" 24"

12" ¾" 28"

16" LEG

2" 2"

LEG DETAIL

½"
2" ¼"
2" 1" ½"
B
16"
D 15½"
A 14½"
½" ¼"
C
B
D
¼" ½"
1¼"
13½"

2" 2"

SEE DETAIL "A"

C C

A

C

B

SEE DETAIL "B"

B

C

A

B

12
picture frame
bar

130

You've heard of wall-safes hidden behind pictures... but a bar? Well, not everyone has stocks and bonds he needs to hide — but you can still surprise your friends with other treasures when you expose this well-stocked bar.

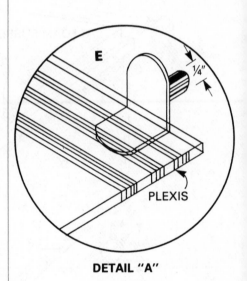

DETAIL "A"

INSTRUCTIONS:

(1) Construct cabinet as indicated on drawing. Drill holes for shelf brackets in pieces (B) before assembly.

(2) Glue and nail together parts for frame and when dry, miter cut them to length and assemble frame.

(3) Glue picture and laminate to piece (F) and install.

(4) Install piano hinge on frame and then attach to cabinet frame. Install support arms or chains.

(5) Cut plexiglass shelves to fit. Stain or paint to your choice.

MATERIAL LIST:

Cabinet Construction parts

(A)	2 Pcs.	½" x 4" x 28¾"	Plywood
(B)	3 Pcs.	½" x 4" x 16¼"	Plywood
(C)	1 Pc.	⅛" x 17¼" x 28¾"	Plywood
(D)	3 Pcs.	¼" x 4" x 13½"	Plexiglass or glass
(E)	12 Pcs.	Adjustable shelf supports	
(F)	2 Pcs.	¾" x 1⅝" x 32"	Pine
(G)	2 Pcs.	¾" x 1⅝" x 20"	Pine

Frame Construction parts

(A)	4 Pcs.	¾" x 1⅝" x 32"	Pine
(A—A)	4 Pcs.	¾" x 1⅝" x 20"	Pine
(B)	2 Pcs.	¾" x ¾" x 32"	Pine
(B—B)	2 Pcs.	¾" x ¾" x 20"	Pine
(C)	1 Pc.	⅞" x 1½" x 10'	Molding
(D)	1 Pc.	½" x ½" x 10'	Molding
(E)	1 Pc.	¼" x ⅜" x 10'	Molding
(F)	1 Pc.	½" x 16¼" x 28¾"	Plywood
(G)	1 Pc.	16¼" x 28¾"	Plastic laminate
(H)	1 Pc.	16¼" x 28¾"	Picture
(J)	1 Pc.	1½" x 28" piano hinge and screws	

Contact cement, glue, wood filler, nails, sandpaper, support chains, paint or stain.

D ½" x ½" MOULDING
G PLASTIC LAMINATE
F ½" PLYWOOD

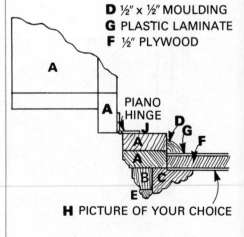

H PICTURE OF YOUR CHOICE

**FRAME CONSTRUCTION
SIDE VIEW**

DETAIL "B"

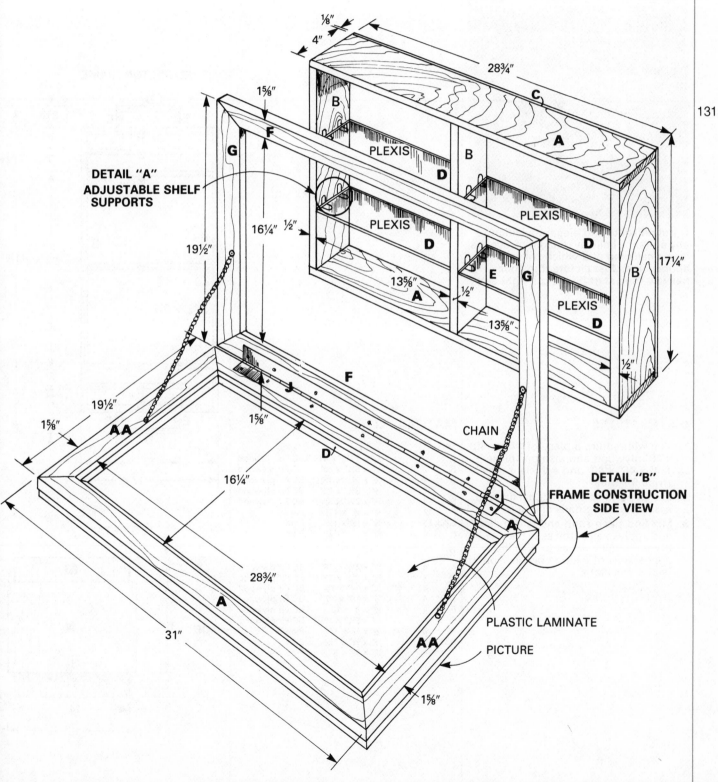

DETAIL "A"
ADJUSTABLE SHELF
SUPPORTS

DETAIL "B"
FRAME CONSTRUCTION
SIDE VIEW

PLEXIS

CHAIN

PLASTIC LAMINATE

PICTURE

13
grecian bench

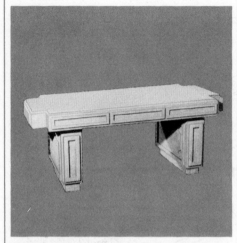

A truly distinct and elegant addition to any entrance hallway. A labor of love that is eye-catching and which will be appreciated. Just picture it in your hallway, then start building it right away.

INSTRUCTIONS

1 You will require a piece of 1/2" x 48" x 48" plywood and also one piece 1/4" x 48" x 48" and sufficient pine strips for trim.
2. Cut all parts as per material list and assemble using nails and glue.
3. Mix fine clean sand and latex paint and apply to all surfaces to the texture of your choice, so as to give the appearance of a stone bench. Apply with a wet cloth.

MATERIAL LIST:

bench

A	1	¼" x 17½" x 41½"	BC Fir plywood
B	2	½" x 3¼" x 36"	BC Fir plywood
C	7	½" x 3¼" x 16½"	BC Fir plywood
D	2	½" x 3¼" x 12"	BC Fir plywood
E	4	½" x 2¼" x 3¼"	BC Fir plywood
F	12	⅜" x ½" x 11⅜"	Pine
G&J	16	⅜" x ½" x 1½"	Pine
H	4	⅜" x ½" x 11"	Pine

leg

K	4	½" x 2½" x 16"	BC Fir plywood
L	4	½" x 2½" x 13"	BC Fir plywood
M	4	¼" x 14" x 16"	BC Fir plywood
N	4	½" x 10" x 15"	BC Fir plywood
P	4	½" x 3" x 10"	BC Fir plywood
Q	4	¼" x 5½" x 10½"	BC Fir plywood
R	8	½" x ¾" x 14"	Pine
S&U	16	½" x ¾" x 7½"	Pine
T	8	½" x ¾" x 3"	Pine

BENCH TOP FRAME

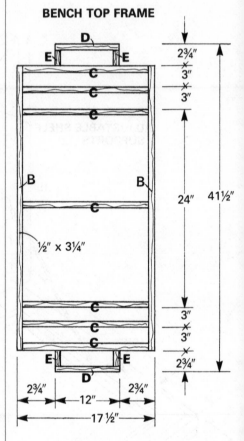

LEG DETAIL

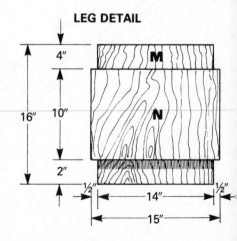

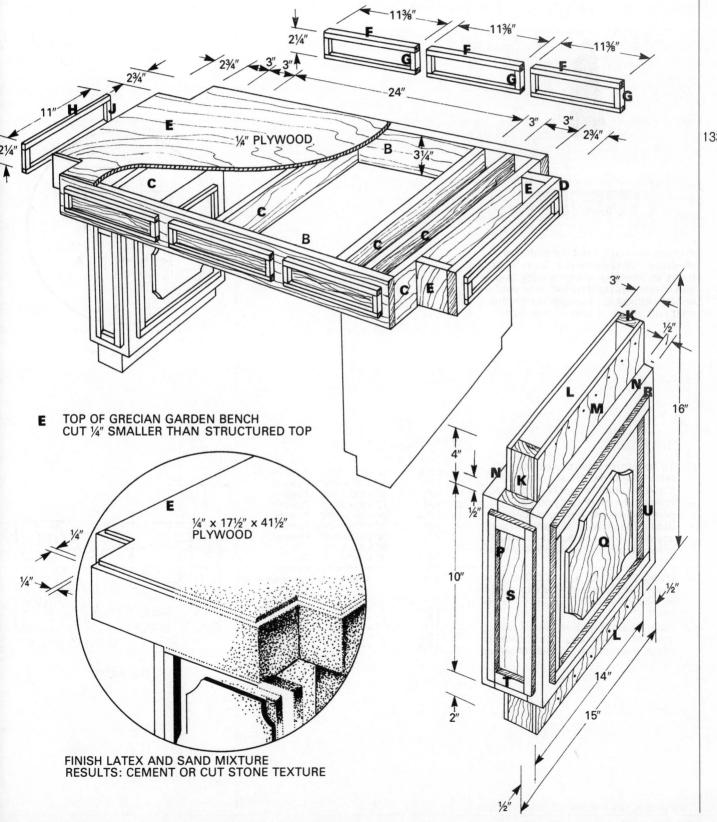

2¼"

11⅜" 11⅜" 11⅜"

F F F

G G G

24"

2¾" 2¾" 3" 3"

3" 3"

2¾"

11" 2¼"

H J

¼" PLYWOOD

B 3¼"

C

C

C

B C E D

C E

E TOP OF GRECIAN GARDEN BENCH
CUT ¼" SMALLER THAN STRUCTURED TOP

E

¼"

¼"

¼" x 17½" x 41½"
PLYWOOD

FINISH LATEX AND SAND MIXTURE
RESULTS: CEMENT OR CUT STONE TEXTURE

3"

½"

K

L N B

M

16"

4"

N K

½"

10"

P

Q U

S

½"

L

T

2"

14"

15"

½"

14
storage bench

Winters are easier to take with this mudroom storage bench. Gives Mom a break by keeping wet or muddy boots and overshoes right by the door. And wet winter clothes dry out quicker on the coat rack which is part of this plan.

INSTRUCTIONS:

(1) To construct both pieces you will require approx. 1½ sheets of ¾" plywood and ½ sheet of ½" plywood. Proceed to mark out parts on plywood sheets before cutting to obtain best use of material. When satisfied, proceed to cut to dimensions shown on drawing and material list.

(2) Using glue and 1½" and 2" finish nails assemble parts and when finished fill all nail holes and imperfections and sand.

(3) Before painting, give one or two coats of shellac and sand between coats. Paint to your choice of colors.

MATERIAL LIST:
Storage Bench

(A)	2 Pcs.	¾" x 18" x 28"	Plywood
(B)	1 Pc.	¾" x 16" x 31½"	Plywood
(C)	1 Pc.	¾" x 5¾" x 34½"	Plywood
(D)	1 Pc.	¾" x 3" x 36"	Plywood
(E)	2 Pcs.	¾" x 10" x 15¾"	Plywood
(F)	1 Pc.	½" x 15¾" x 34½"	Plywood
(G)	1 Pc.	½" x 28" x 35¼"	Plywood
(H)	1 Pc.	¾" x 1½" x 34½"	Pine
(J)	2 Pcs.	¾" x 1½" x 17½"	Pine
(K)	1 Pc.	¾" x 17½" x 34½"	Plywood
(M)	1 Pc.	1½" x 30" Piano hinge and screws	

Hat and Coat Rack

(A)	2 Pcs.	¾" x 9" x 14"	Plywood
(B)	1 Pc.	¾" x 8½" x 35"	Plywood
(C)	1 Pc.	½" x 14" x 35½"	Plywood
(D)	1 Pc.	½" x 5½" x 34½"	Plywood
(E)	5 Pcs.	¾" x 4½"	Hardwood dowel

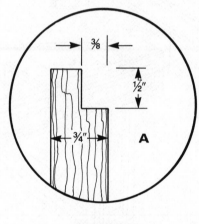

DETAIL "A"

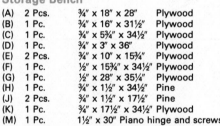

DADO FOR SHELF

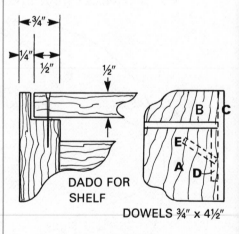

DOWELS ¾" x 4½"

DETAIL "B"

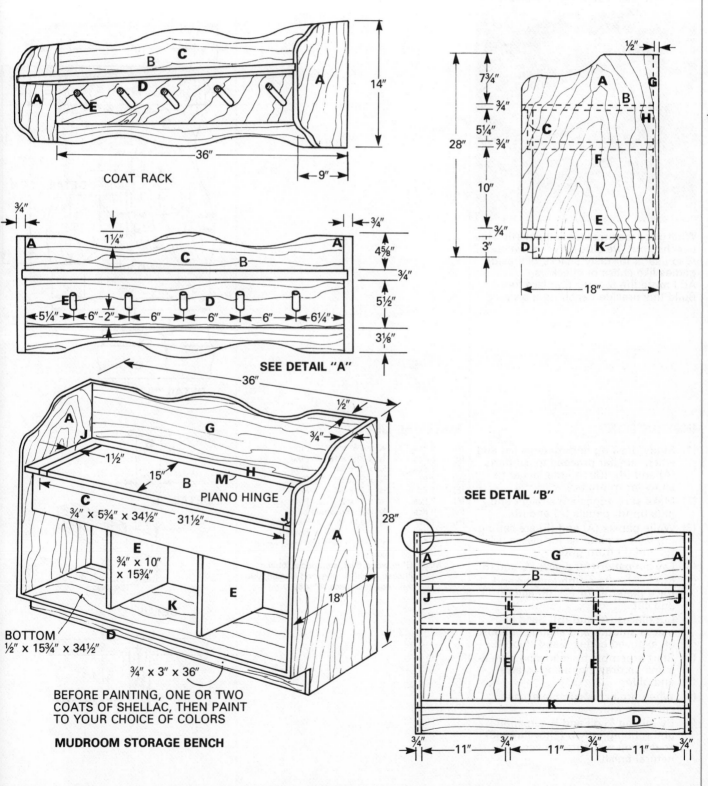

COAT RACK

SEE DETAIL "A"

SEE DETAIL "B"

BOTTOM
½" x 15¾" x 34½"

¾" x 3" x 36"

BEFORE PAINTING, ONE OR TWO
COATS OF SHELLAC, THEN PAINT
TO YOUR CHOICE OF COLORS

MUDROOM STORAGE BENCH

PIANO HINGE

¾" x 5¾" x 34½"

E
¾" x 10"
x 15¾"

15
fireside bench

What good is a fireplace without a fireside bench to put "ye olde brew" down upon? Also useful for tasty snacks, or fireside games like chess or checkers.
Add more life to your fireplace fun.
Build this fireside bench right away.

INSTRUCTIONS:

(1) Study drawing and material list and when familiar proceed to cut parts (A) and (B). (Cut a little longer to allow for trimming).

(2) Make sure edges are straight and glue up for panels (A) and (B).

(3) While panels (A) and (B) are setting up, lay out patterns for pieces (C), (E) and (F) from grid.

(4) Lay out pattern for pieces (A) and (B).

(5) Cut lumber to rough lengths and trace patterns for (C), (E) and (F) and cut.

(6) Cut pieces (A) and (B). Sand all pieces smooth and slightly bullnose all exposed edges. Sand smooth.

(7) Start assembly by following dimensions on drawing, using screws and glue.

(8) When project is complete, sand carefully with grain.

(9) By mixing ⅔ oil and ⅓ turpentine and rubbing in two (2) or three (3) coats, you will obtain a very nice natural finish.

Verify all measurements before cutting

MATERIAL LIST:

(A)	4 Pcs.	¾" x 3½" x 36"	Pine
(B)	8 Pcs.	¾" x 3½" x 16"	Pine
(C)	2 Pcs.	¾" x 3" x 34"	Pine
(D)	2 Pcs.	¾" x 3" x 12"	Pine
(E)	1 Pc.	¾" x 3" x 34"	Pine
(F)	2 Pcs.	⅝" x 1" x 2½"	Pine
(G)	8 Pcs.	⅜" dia. screwhole plugs	
(H)	1 Pc.	⅜" dia. x 10"	Hardwood dowel
(J)	36 Pcs.	1¼" No. 8 flat head steel wood screws	

Misc.: Glue, wood filler, sandpaper, boiled linseed oil. (If ¾" plywood is used, you will require a piece 36" x 60").

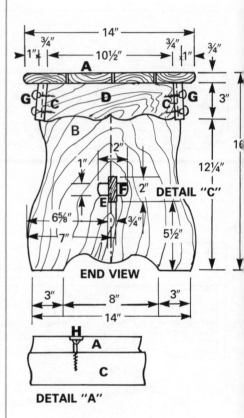

END VIEW

DETAIL "C"

DETAIL "A"

DETAIL "B"

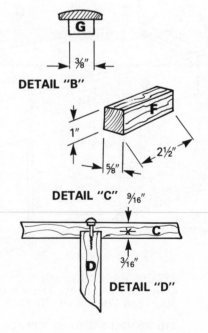

DETAIL "C"

DETAIL "D"

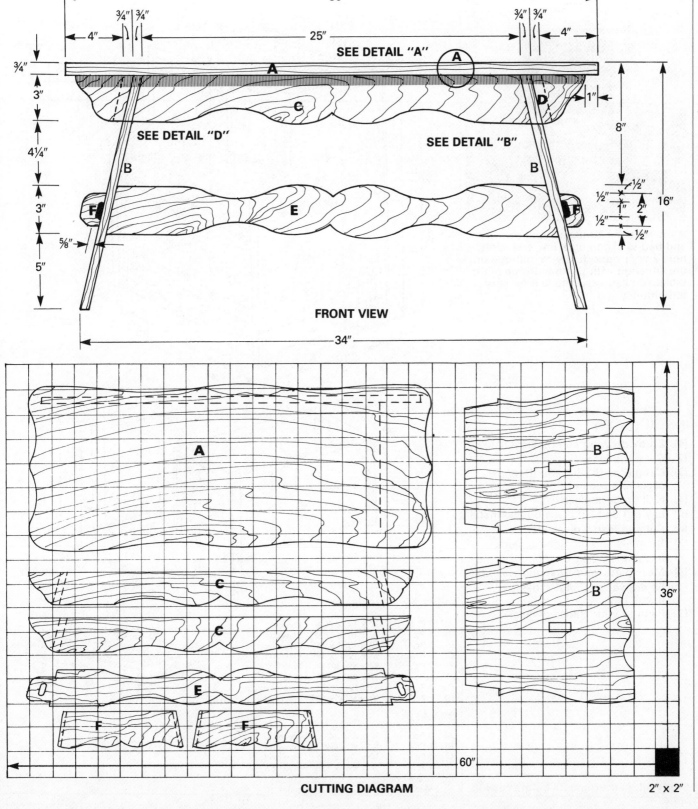

36"

¾" ¾"

4"   25"   ¾" ¾"   4"

SEE DETAIL "A"

A

¾"

3"

A

C

D

1"

8"

4¼"

SEE DETAIL "D"

SEE DETAIL "B"

B

B

3"

F

E

F

½"
½"
1"
2"
½"
½"

16"

⅝"

5"

FRONT VIEW

34"

A

B

C

C

B

36"

E

F

F

60"

2" x 2"

CUTTING DIAGRAM

16
one drawer night table

If you recently furnished your own home and had to skimp on a few essentials, here's your opportunity to improve on the situation with this handsome night table. You can easily build it for very little money.

INSTRUCTIONS:

(1) Study drawing and material list.
(2) Cut parts for side.
(3) Cut pieces (B), (C) and (D) and assemble cabinet.
(4) Nail on back piece (H).
(5) Lay out and cut piece (F) and install.
(6) Cut and install piece (E).
(7) Set nails and fill. Sand project.
(8) Install moulding on top.
(9) Make parts for drawer and assemble.
(10) Fit drawer so that it slides well. Install pull.
(11) Paint to your choice of color.

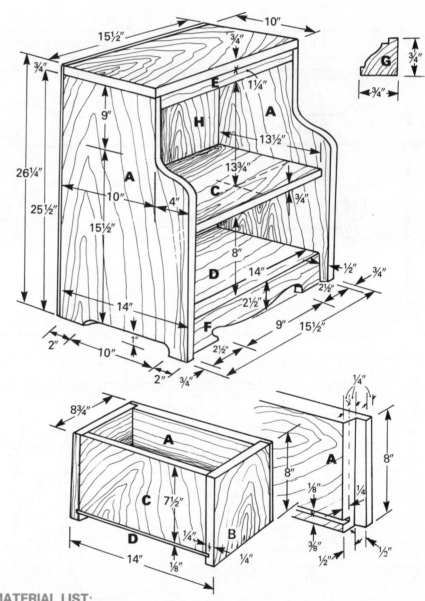

MATERIAL LIST:

(A)	2 Pcs.	¾" x 14" x 26¼"	Plywood
(B)	1 Pc.	¾" x 10" x 15½"	Plywood
(C)	1 Pc.	¾" x 13½" x 14"	Plywood
(D)	1 Pc.	¾" x 12¾" x 14"	Plywood
(E)	1 Pc.	¾" x 1¼" x 14"	Pine
(F)	1 Pc.	¾" x 2½" x 14"	Pine
(G)	1 Pc.	¾" x ¾" x 40"	Pine moulding
(H)	1 Pc.	⅛" x 15½" x 25¼"	Plywood

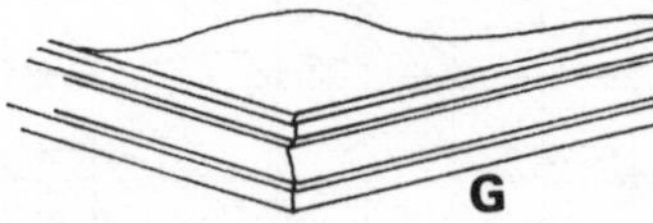

DRAWER:

(A)	1 Pc.	¾" x 8" x 14"	Plywood
(B)	2 Pcs.	½" x 8" x 8½"	Plywood
(C)	1 Pc.	½" x 7½" x 13"	Plywood
(D)	1 Pc.	⅛" x 8¼" x 13½"	Plywood
(E)		Drawer pull	

Misc.: Wood filler, sandpaper, paint.

17
knockdown
table

Unexpected supper guests or larger than usual dinner crowds are easier to handle with a storable knockdown table close at hand. A very practical and worthwhile project for home handymen who enjoy entertaining.

INSTRUCTIONS:

(1) You will require 1½ sheets of ¾" x 4' x 8' plywood.
(2) Study drawing and when familiar proceed to cut plywood.
(3) Build frame (E) and (D), nail and glue to piece (A).
(4) Nail and glue piece (F) to edges of piece (A).
(5) Lay out and cut slots in pieces (B) and (C).
(6) Cut angle iron brackets and drill holes for screws and bolts, then attach to pieces (C) as shown on drawing.
(7) Assemble unit.
(8) Set and fill all nail holes. Sand.

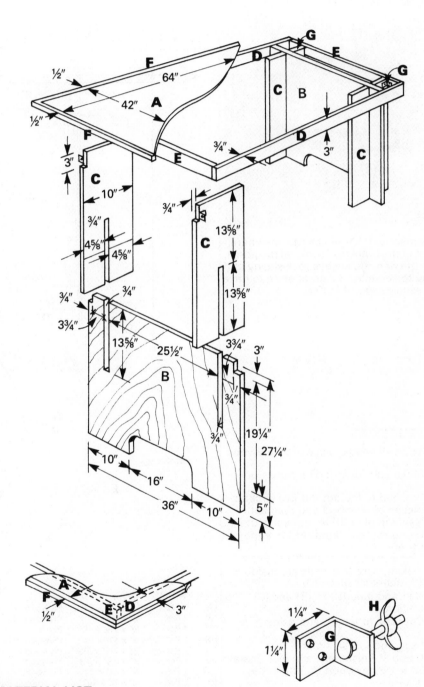

MATERIAL LIST:

(A)	1 Pc.	¾" x 42" x 64"	Plywood
(B)	2 Pcs.	¾" x 27¼" x 36"	Plywood
(C)	4 Pcs.	¾" x 10" x 27¼"	Plywood
(D)	2 Pcs.	¾" x 3" x 58"	Plywood
(E)	2 Pcs.	¾" x 3" x 34½"	Plywood
(F)	20 Lin. ft.	½" x ¾"	Pine
(G)	4 Pcs.	1¼" x 1¼" x 1¼"	Angle iron
(H)	4 Pcs.	1¼" carriage bolts	
	Misc.:	Nails, glue, wood filler and paint.	

18
circular table

A handsome table which fits anywhere. Use it in the breakfast nook, on the porch, or in the den. It's always rock-steady and ready to serve. And a great place to have that second cup of coffee.

INSTRUCTIONS:

(1) You will need a piece of ¾" plywood 4' x 5'.
(2) Make your own radius rod as per sketch.
(3) Proceed to lay out the five circular pieces of plywood and then cut.
(4) Nail and glue (D) to underside of (A).
(5) Using router, round off top edge of (B) and (C).
(6) Nail and glue (B) and (C) together, making sure that nails are inside of 12" diameter piece (D).
(7) Nail and glue (D) to (B) and (C) section.
(8) Cut tube to length and using glue and 1" common nails, join tube to base and top sections.
(9) Using 1" finish nails and glue, install ¼" x 1½" plywood around edge of table.
(10) Set all nails and fill holes and imperfections with wood filler and sand.
(11) Give one or two coats of shellac and sand.
(12) Paint to your choice of colors.
(13) Apply vinyl.
(14) If you find table too light, put a few pounds of sand in tube before closing to add more stability.

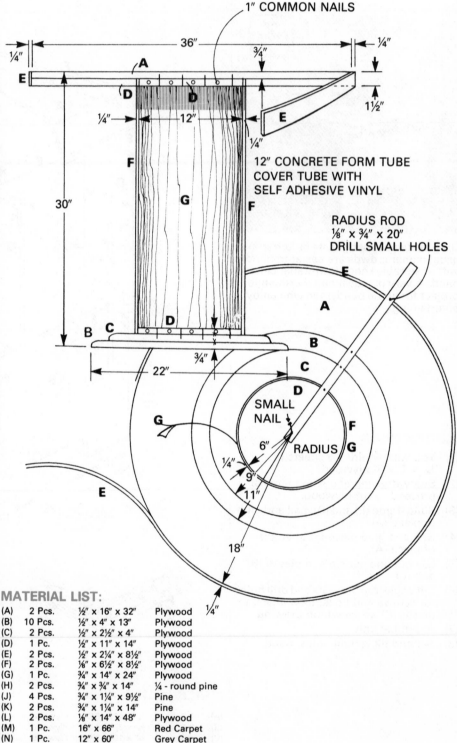

MATERIAL LIST:

(A)	2 Pcs.	½" x 16" x 32"	Plywood
(B)	10 Pcs.	½" x 4" x 13"	Plywood
(C)	2 Pcs.	½" x 2½" x 4"	Plywood
(D)	1 Pc.	½" x 11" x 14"	Plywood
(E)	2 Pcs.	½" x 2¼" x 8½"	Plywood
(F)	2 Pcs.	⅛" x 6½" x 8½"	Plywood
(G)	1 Pc.	¾" x 14" x 24"	Plywood
(H)	2 Pcs.	¾" x ¾" x 14"	¼ - round pine
(J)	4 Pcs.	¾" x 1¼" x 9½"	Pine
(K)	2 Pcs.	¾" x 1¼" x 14"	Pine
(L)	2 Pcs.	⅛" x 14" x 48"	Plywood
(M)	1 Pc.	16" x 66"	Red Carpet
(N)	1 Pc.	12" x 60"	Grey Carpet
(O)	1 Pc.	16" x 18"	Plastic laminate
Misc.:		Contact cement, white glue, 1½" finish nails, sandpaper, ⅜" staples or ¼" common nails, paint.	

Verify all measurements before cutting

19
stack tables

When serving coffee or snacks in the living room, pull out these stack tables to prevent accidental spills or messy surprises. That way, you can enjoy yourself and concentrate on having a good time entertaining your guests.

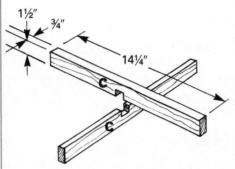

CIRCLE FOR TABLE TOP 14″
LEG SUPPORTS 14¼″
CENTERED SO LEGS ARE
⅛″ FROM TABLE TOP...

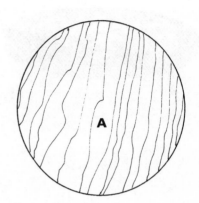

INSTRUCTIONS:

(1) Using a good grade of pine, proceed to cut 4 pieces for tops as shown in drawing. Sand edges carefully.

(2) Cut 16 pieces for the legs and following drawing, cut to length, taper and sand.

(3) Cut cross pieces and half lap them and using glue and 1¼″ screws, attach to under side of table tops.

(4) Lay tops on flat surface and attach legs using 1¾″ screws and a small amount of glue.

(5) Sand off all sharp edges and install screw hole plugs.

(6) Give coat of orange shellac and sand lightly.

(7) Give one or two coats of clear shellac and sand between coats.

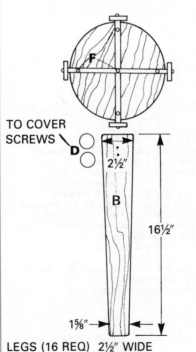

TO COVER SCREWS

LEGS (16 REQ) 2½″ WIDE
TAPERING TO 1⅝″ WIDE
AT BOTTOM ¾″ THICK 16½″ LONG

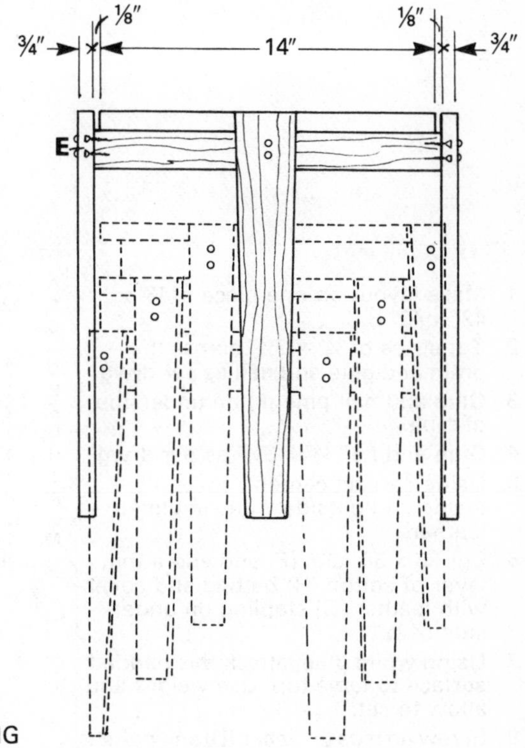

MATERIAL LIST:

(A)	4 Pcs.	¾″ x 14″ diameter Pine
(B)	16 Pcs.	¾″ x 2½″ x 16½″ Pine
(C)	8 Pcs.	¾″ x 1½″ x 14¼″ Pine
(D)	32 Pcs.	⅜″ Cabinet maker's screw hole plugs.
(E)	32	1¾″ - #8 F.H. steel wood screws.
(F)	20	1¼″ - #8 F.H. steel wood screws.

Wood filler, sandpaper, orange shellac.

Verify all measurements before cutting

20
poker table

If you play poker just for the fun of it, then building this poker table isn't going to cost you very much money. A fun project for the advanced do-it-yourselfer who would like to try his hand at something different.

INSTRUCTIONS:

1. Make layout on one piece of ½" x 42" x 42" B.C.
2. Cut strips of ¼" x 2¼" across the grain and glue and nail as per drwg.
3. Glue and nail pine (F) on underside of table.
4. Glue and nail ½" x 3½" as per drwg.
5. Using contact cement, cover all inside and outside with simulated leather.
6. Cut ¼" x 34" dia. (E) and add a thin layer of cotton (H) batting and cover with leather (G) stapling on underside of ¼".
7. Using white glue, attach this padded surface to table top. Use weight and allow to set.
8. Screw on legs to pieces (D) and paint.
9. Make up 6 ash tray dividers and cover with leather.
10. Leave these dividers loose so that you can vary the amount of players at one time.

MATERIAL LIST:

A. 1 Circular piece ½" x 33¾" dia. Plywood
B. 22 Lin. ft. ¼" x 2¼" Plywood.
C. 1 Circular piece ½" x inside dia. 34¼" outside dia. 41¼".
D. 2 Pcs. ½" x 3½" x 38" B.C. Plywood.
E. 1 Circular piece ¼" x 34" dia. B.C. Plywood.
F. 2 Pcs. ¾" x 1¾" x 33¾" Pine or Plywood.
G. 1 Piece 54" x 72" simulated leather.
H. 1 Piece Quilt Batting 36" x 36".
J. 1 Set of 27" tapered legs.
K. 6 Pcs. ½" x 4" x 8".
L. 12 Pcs. ¼" x 3¼" x 1¼" (Cover With Leather).
M. 1 Qt. contact cement.
Nails and paint for legs — Glue.

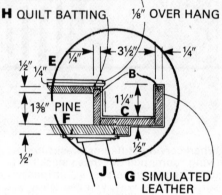

DETAIL "A"

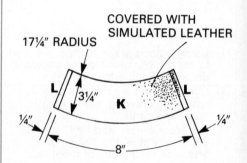

TOP VIEW

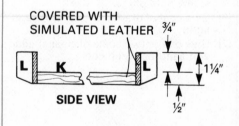

SIDE VIEW

DETAIL "B"

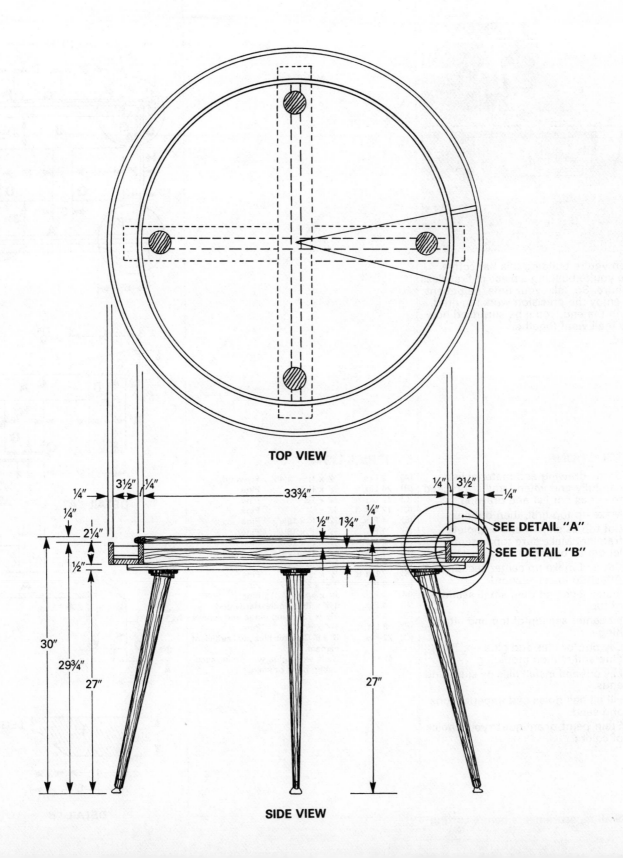

TOP VIEW

¼" 3½" ¼" 33¾" ¼" 3½" ¼"

¼" ½" 1¾" ¼"

2¼" SEE DETAIL "A"

½" SEE DETAIL "B"

30"

29¾"

27" 27"

SIDE VIEW

21
bar coffee table

144

When you're building this bar coffee table you're building a piece of first class furniture. So, take your time, be patient and enjoy the precision work required. Yet, in the end, you'll be surprised how easy it all went together.

INSTRUCTIONS:

(1) Study drawing and material list carefully and when familiar proceed to cut as per list and drawing.

(2) Make up top first, then bottom.

(3) Cut top as shown and complete framing. Make sure top is same length as bottom.

(4) Cut and make up center section. Attach to lower section.

(5) Install legs and then small sections of top.

(6) Fit center section of top and attach hinge.

(7) Lay out for tiles and glue on. Then glue and nail on moulding.

(8) Lay out and install tiles on sides and ends.

(9) Fill all nail holes and imperfections and sand.

(10) Stain, paint, or antique to your choice of colors.

MATERIAL LIST:

(A)	2 Pcs.	½" x 19¾" x 45"	Plywood
(B)	24 Lin. ft.	¾" x 1½"	Pine
(C)	12 Lin. ft.	¾" x 1⅜"	Pine
(D)	12 Lin. ft.	¾" x ¾"	Pine
(E)	4 Pcs.	¾" x 1" x 18¼"	Pine
(F)	1 Pc.	¾" x 1" x 18⅛"	Pine
(G)	1 Pc.	¾" x 1" x 23½"	Pine
(H)	2 Pcs.	½" x 13" x 26"	Plywood
(J)	2 Pcs.	½" x 13" x 17"	Plywood
(K)	7 Lin. ft.	½" x ½"	Pine
(L)	8 Pcs.	1½" x 2½" x 7"	Pine
(M)	1 Pc.	½" x ¾" x 25"	Pine
(N)	4 Pcs.	1¾" x 15" spindles	Hardwood
(O)	1 Pc.	1½" x 25" Piano hinge and screws	
(P)	9 Lin. ft.	³⁄₁₆" x ½"	Pine
(Q)	22 Pcs.	6" x 6" Ceramic tiles plus sufficient cement.	
Misc.:		Nails, wood glue, wood filler, sandpaper, paint or stain.	

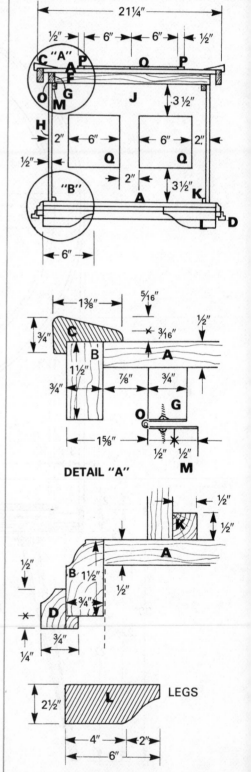

DETAIL "A"

DETAIL "B"

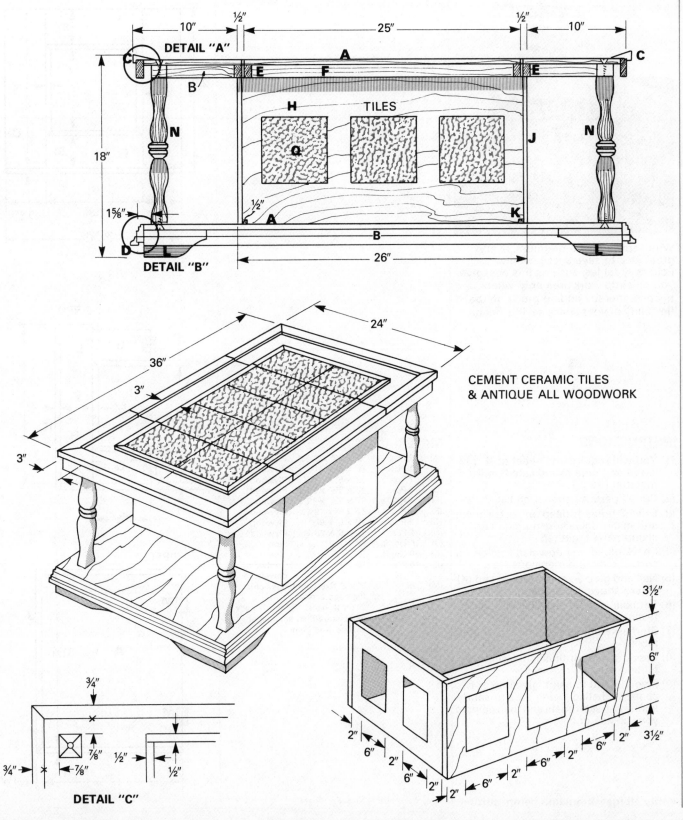

DETAIL "A"

DETAIL "B"

10″ ½″ 25″ ½″ 10″

A

C E F E C

B

H TILES J

18″ N Q N

1⅝″

½″ A K B

D L L

26″

24″

36″

3″

3″ CEMENT CERAMIC TILES
& ANTIQUE ALL WOODWORK

¾″
7/8″ ½″
¾″ 7/8″ ½″

DETAIL "C"

3½″

6″

3½″

2″ 6″ 2″ 6″ 2″
6″ 2″ 6″ 2″
6″ 2″

22
foldaway table

When space is at a premium, every great idea to save space counts. Foldaway tables, such as this one, give you an extra work area only when needed, thereby adding much to the flexibility of your space saving needs.

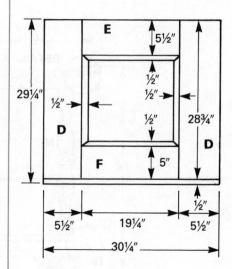

INSTRUCTIONS:

(1) You will require one sheet of ¾" plywood and pine as indicated on material list.

(2) Cut all parts as shown on list.

(3) Drill ⅜" holes 1" deep on parts shown and insert dowels using glue and clamp parts together.

(4) Check glued and doweled section for correct overall dimensions.

(5) Nail and glue on pine parts (J) and (K) where shown on drawing.

(6) Set nails and fill all holes and imperfections and sand.

(7) Start assembling sections to complete table.

(8) Check quality of finished assembly, fill and sand as required.

(9) If you intend to paint, give one or two coats of shellac, being sure to sand lightly between coats and then paint to your choice of colors.

MATERIAL LIST:

(A)	2 Pcs.	¾" x 23" x 31¾"	Plywood
(B)	1 Pc.	¾" x 6" x 31¾"	Plywood
(C)	2 Pcs.	¾" x 5" x 28¾"	Plywood
(D)	2 Pcs.	¾" x 5½" x 28¾"	Plywood
(E)	1 Pc.	¾" x 5½" x 19¼"	Plywood
(F)	1 Pc.	¾" x 5" x 19¼"	Plywood
(G)	2 Pcs.	¾" x 5" x 9½"	Plywood
(H)	2 Pcs.	¾" x 5" x 28¾"	Plywood
(J)	16 Lin. ft.	¾" x 1⅛"	Pine
(K)	40 Lin. ft.	½" x ¾"	Pine
(L)	16 Pcs.	⅜" x 2"	Hardwood dowels
(M)	8	2" x 3" fixed pin hinges plus flat head screws	
	Misc.:	2" finish nails, 1½" finish nails, glue, woodfiller, sandpaper, shellac and paint.	

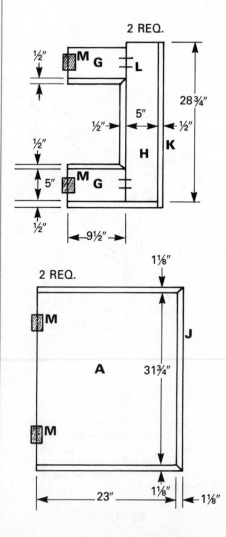

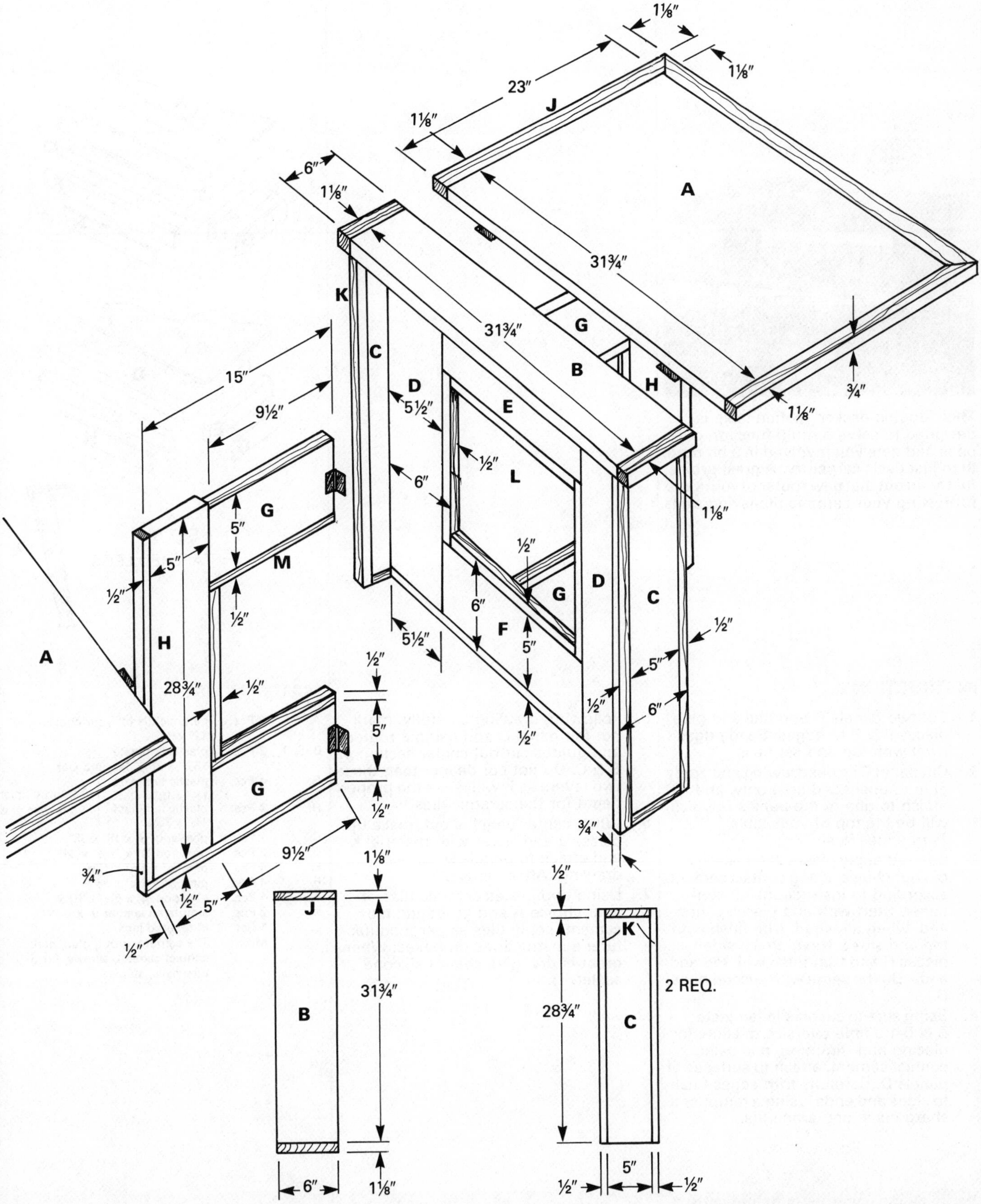

1⅛″
1⅛″
23″
J
1⅛″
A
6″
1⅛″
31¾″
K
31¾″
G
C
B
H
¾″
1⅛″
15″
D
5½″
E
9½″
½″
L
6″
1⅛″
G
5″
½″
5″
M
D
½″
6″
G
C
½″
½″
H
F
5½″
5″
5″
A
28¾″
½″
½″
5″
6″
½″
½″
G
½″
¾″
9½″
1⅛″
½″
¾″
½″
5″
J
K
½″
2 REQ.
31¾″
B
28¾″
C
6″
1⅛″
5″
½″
½″

23
coffee table

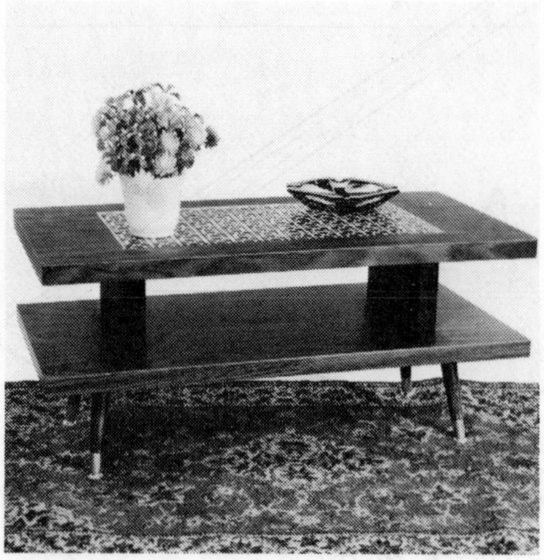

This "double-decker" coffee table is designed to serve a multi-function purpose and gets you involved in a bit more than just basic carpentry. A great project for trying out that new router of yours and for testing your ceramic tile-laying skills.

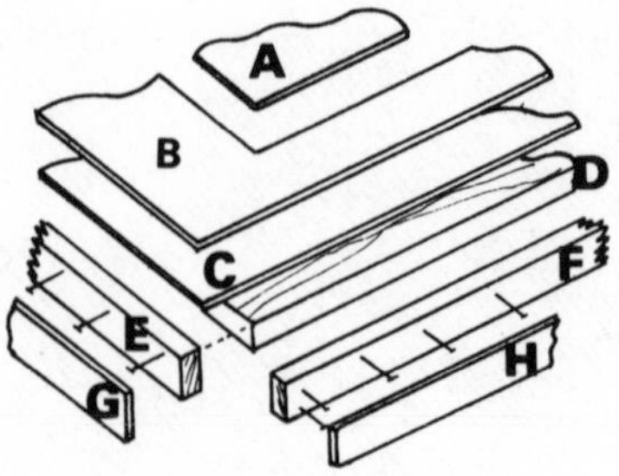

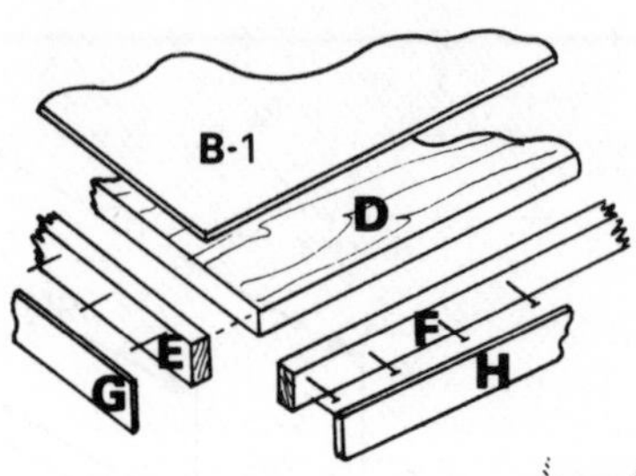

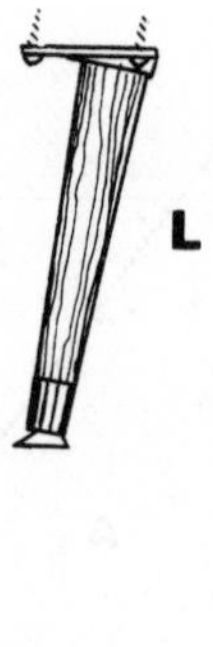

INSTRUCTIONS:

1. Cut two panels D and nail and glue pieces F & E to edges. Sand edges level with top and set nails.
2. Cut panel C as per drawing and apply glue to unshaded area only, and attach to one of the panels D which will be the top of your table. Trim edges flush.
3. Cut and apply plastic laminate of your choice, using contact cement, according to instructions on container. Start with end pieces G first and, when attached, trim flush with top and sides. Next, attach side pieces H and trim flush with top and ends. Do the same with second panel D.
4. Being sure to cut plastic laminate B & B-1 a little oversize to allow for placing and trimming, and using contact cement, attach to surfaces of panels D. Carefully trim edges flush to sides and ends, using a router or a sharp plane and a fine file.
5. Following drawing carefully, mark out top panel D and using a router and guides cut out center section of B & C. Do not cut deeper than these two layers as it will leave the proper depth for the ceramic tiles.
6. When center panel is out, make up pieces J and cover with material K and attach to panels D, as per drawing. Attach legs L.
7. Using two pieces ceramic tiles of your choice A and grout and tile cement, apply tiles as per manufacturer's instructions on boxes. When grout is dry, give coat of silicone sealer.

MATERIAL LIST:

A.	2 Pcs.	ceramic tile (of your choice) 12″ x 12″.	
B.-B.-1	2 Pcs.	plastic laminate 18½″ x 36½″ Moreno Oak.	
G.	4 Pcs.	plastic laminate 1⅝″ x 18¼″	Textured finish o your own choic
H.	4 Pcs.	plastic laminate 1⅝″ x 36¼″	
C.	1 Pc.	plywood ⅛″ x 18″ x 36″	
D.	2 Pcs.	plywood ¾″ x 16½″ x 34½″	
E.	4 Pcs.	pine ¾″ x 1¼″ x 16½″	
F.	4 Pcs.	pine ¾″ x 1¼″ x 36″	
J.	4 Pcs.	plywood ¾″ x 6½″ x 10½″	
K.	2 Pcs.	simulated leather 9″ x 24″	
L.	1 Set	8″ tapered legs.	
	Misc.:	Tile cement, grout, glue, nails, contact cement, screws, furniture nails, staples	

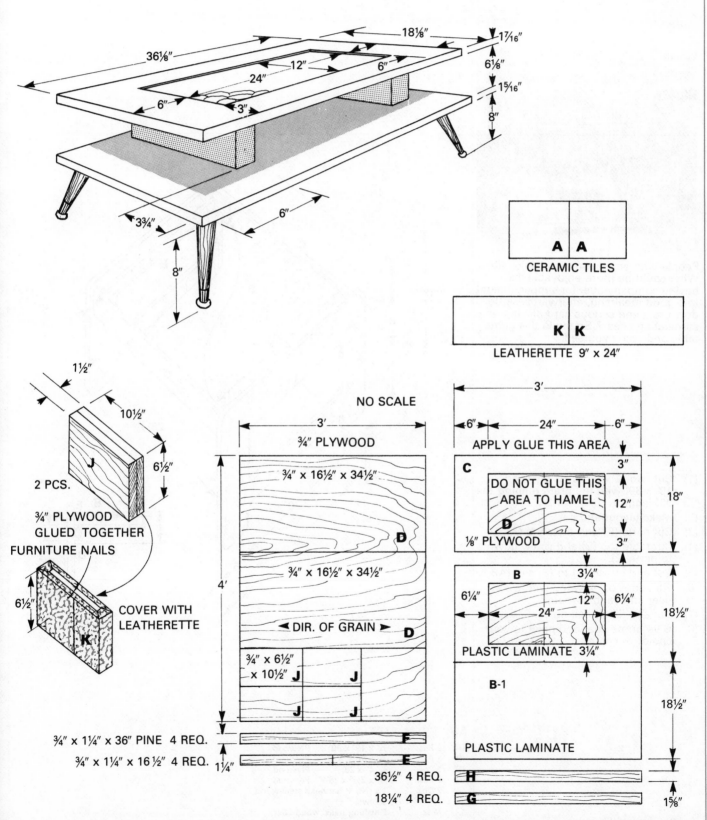

36⅛″ 18⅛″ 1⁷⁄₁₆″
12″ 6″ 6⅛″
24″ 1⁵⁄₁₆″
6″ 3″ 8″
3¾″ 6″
8″

CERAMIC TILES
A A

LEATHERETTE 9″ x 24″
K K

1½″
10½″
6½″
J
2 PCS.
¾″ PLYWOOD GLUED TOGETHER
FURNITURE NAILS
6½″
K
COVER WITH LEATHERETTE

NO SCALE

3′
¾″ PLYWOOD
¾″ x 16½″ x 34½″
D
¾″ x 16½″ x 34½″
4′
◄ DIR. OF GRAIN ► D
¾″ x 6½″ x 10½″ J J
J J

¾″ x 1¼″ x 36″ PINE 4 REQ. F
¾″ x 1¼″ x 16½″ 4 REQ. E 1¼″
36½″ 4 REQ. H
18¼″ 4 REQ. G 1⅝″

3′
6″ 24″ 6″
APPLY GLUE THIS AREA
C 3″
DO NOT GLUE THIS AREA TO HAMEL 12″ 18″
D 3″
⅛″ PLYWOOD
B 3¼″
6¼″ 24″ 12″ 6¼″ 18½″
PLASTIC LAMINATE 3¼″
B-1 18½″
PLASTIC LAMINATE

24
game table

People who enjoy company, enjoy life.
What could be more enjoyable than
having company over for supper, delight
in a good meal and, afterwards, settle
down to some serious card playing or
stimulating chess? So, build this game
table and enjoy yourself.

INSTRUCTIONS:

(1)   Cut two (2) pieces ¾″ plywood
      19″ x 30″ with the grain running the
      30″ length.
(2)   Make layout and cut.
(3)   Cut parts (D) and attach to (A).
(4)   Cut table top (B) and screw down
      to parts (E).
(5)   Cut and attach (C) to (B) and (A).
(6)   Fill edges of plywood with wood
      filler and sand smooth.
(7)   Set and fill all nail holes. Sand.
(8)   Give prime coat and paint to your
      choice of colors.

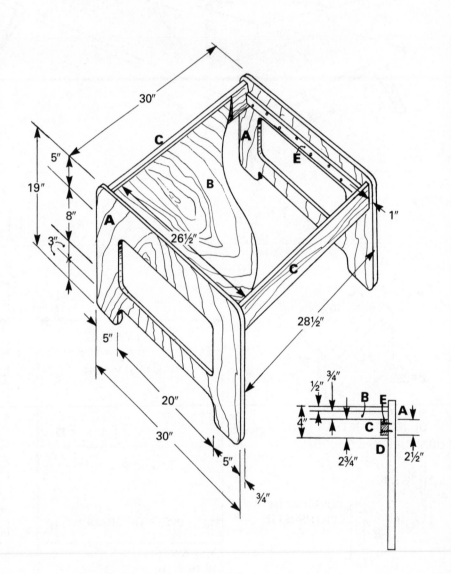

MATERIAL LIST:

(A)	2 Pcs.	¾″ x 19″ x 30″	Plywood
(B)	1 Pc.	¾″ x 26½″ x 28½″	Plywood
(C)	2 Pcs.	¾″ 4″ x 28½″	Plywood
(D)	2 Pcs.	¾″ x 2½″ x 26½″	Plywood
(E)	2 Doz.	1¼″ No. 8 flat head steel wood screws.	
Misc.:		Finishing nails, wood filler, sandpaper and paint.	

3
Desks

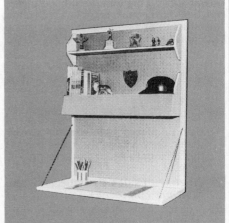

25
desk and chair

As soon as the kids start to outgrow their home-built toy chests and swing sets, it'll be time again for Dad to haul out his power tools. This time he'll build this practical study desk, complete with chair, for budding archaeologists, space scientists and engineers.

INSTRUCTIONS: chair

(1) Using a piece of plywood or heavy paper, draw side view layout and use this as a pattern for assembling chair.
(2) When both sides are done, join both sides with pieces (E).
(3) Proceed to install seat slats by drilling ¼" hole, ¼" deep.
(4) Using screws and glue attach seat slats.
(5) Same procedure for back slats.
(6) Plug all holes in seat and back by gluing in short length of ¼" dowel.
(7) When glue is dry, use belt sander to sand down.
(8) Sand chair and use your choice of finish.

MATERIAL LIST:

(A)	2 Pcs.	¾" x 2½" x 32"	Pine
(B)	2 Pcs.	¾" x 2½" x 15¾"	Pine
(C)	2 Pcs.	¾" x 2½" x 14¼"	Pine
(D)	2 Pcs.	¾" x 1¾" x 12¼"	Pine
(E)	2 Pcs.	¾" x 1¾" x 12"	Pine
(F)	4 Pcs.	¾" x 2½" x 14½"	Pine
(G)	4 Pcs.	¾" x 2½" x 14½"	Pine
(H)	16 Pcs.	⅜" diameter cabinet maker's screwhole plugs.	
	Misc.:	¼" dowel, 2 doz. 1¼" No. 6 flat head screws, wood filler, glue, sandpaper, stain or paint.	

Verify all measurements before cutting

INSTRUCTIONS: desk

(1) Carefully read drawing and material list and when familiar, proceed to cut lumber.
(2) If you use pine, you will have to make up panels by gluing and attaching drawer slides with screws.
(3) All screws should be installed from inside desk.
(4) When assembled set nails and fill. Sand any imperfections.
(5) Make up drawer parts and assemble.
(6) Install drawer pulls.
(7) Finish to your choice.

MATERIAL LIST:

(A)	1 Pc.	¾" x 15" x 36"	Pine or Plywood
(B)	3 Pcs.	¾" x 14" x 28¾"	Pine or Plywood
(C)	1 Pc.	¾" x 2½" x 20½"	Pine or Plywood
(D)	1 Pc.	¾" x 2½" x 21¾"	Pine or Plywood
(E)	1 Pc.	¾" x 1" x 32½"	Pine
(F)	3 Pcs.	¾" x 1" x 11¼"	Pine
(G)	10 Pcs.	¾" x 1" x 13¼"	Pine
(H)	1 Pc.	¾" x 2½" x 11¼"	Pine or Plywood
(J)	1 Pc.	¾" x 3¾" x 12¾"	Pine or Plywood
(K)	1 Pc.	⅛" x 12½" x 28¼"	Plywood

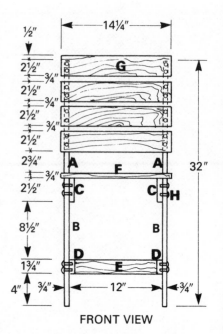

FRONT VIEW

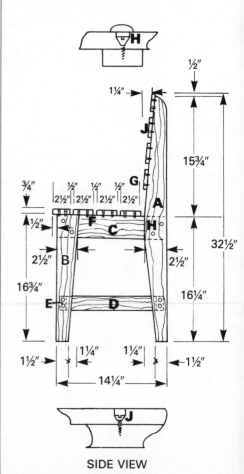

SIDE VIEW

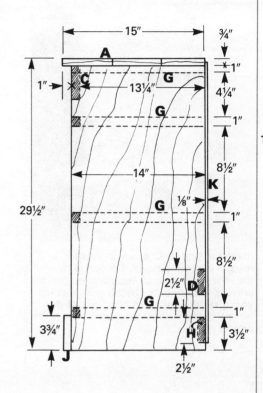

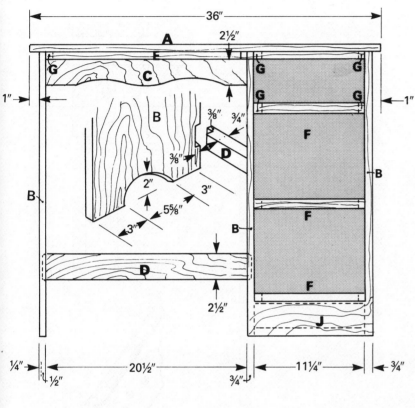

153

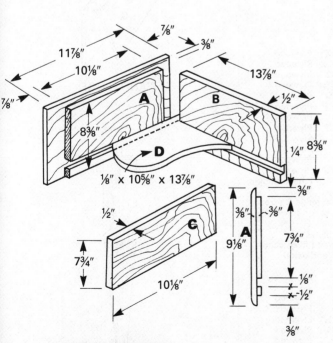

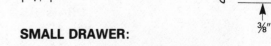

LARGE DRAWERS:

(A) 2 Pcs.   ¾″ x 9⅛″ x 11⅞″   Pine or Plywood
(B) 4 Pcs.   ½″ x 8⅜″ x 13⅞″   Pine or Plywood
(C) 2 Pcs.   ½″ x 7¾″ x 10⅛″   Pine or Plywood
(D) 2 Pcs.   ⅛″ x 10⅝″ x 13⅞″   Plywood

SMALL DRAWER:

(A) 1 Pc.   ¾″ x 4⅞″ x 11⅞″   Pine or Plywood
(B) 2 Pcs.   ½″ x 4⅛″ x 13⅞″   Pine or Plywood
(C) 1 Pc.   ½″ x 3½″ x 10⅛″   Pine or Plywood
(D) 1 Pc.   ⅛″ x 10⅝″ x 13⅞″   Plywood
(E) 3 Decorative drawer pulls.
(F) 3 Doz. 1¼″ No. 6 flat head wood screws.
(G) Misc.:   Nails, glue, wood filler, sand-
                paper, stain or paint.

26
bedroom desk

Ideal for sleepless executives and mystery novel writers. Comes in handy, too, for balancing cheque books, private correspondence or anything important you'd rather not have lying about the house. In short, it's your own corner of the world.

INSTRUCTIONS:

(1) You will require 1 sheet of ¾" plywood, 1 piece 4' x 4' x ½" plywood and 2' x 5' x ⅛" plywood.

(2) Cut parts for cabinet section as per drawing and list and assemble.

(3) Cut parts and assemble drawers.

(4) Cover all horizontal edges with moulding and vertical edges with ⅛" x ¾".

(5) Fill all nail holes and imperfections and sand. Give coat of shellac and when dry sand lightly and paint.

MATERIAL LIST:

(A)	2 Pcs.	¾" x 15⅞" x 27"	Plywood
(B)	1 Pc.	¾" x 6⅞" x 42"	Plywood
(C)	1 Pc.	¾" x 15⅞" x 42"	Plywood
(D)	1 Pc.	¾" x 15⅞" x 41¼"	Plywood
(E)	2 Pcs.	¾" x 9⅞" x 15⅞"	Plywood
(F)	2 Pcs.	¾" x 6½" x 15⅞"	Plywood
(G)	2 Pcs.	¾" x 4" x 15⅞"	Plywood
(H)	1 Pc.	¾" x 13¾" x 39"	Plywood
(J)	1 Pc.	⅛" x 27" x 42"	Plywood
(K)	1 Pc.	¾" x ¾" x 40½"	Pine
(L)	10 Pcs.	½" x 5½" x 9"	Plywood
(M)	1 Pc.	½" x 5½" x 20¾"	Plywood
(N)	40 Lin. ft.	¾" x ¾"	Pine moulding
(O)	6 Lin. ft.	⅛" x ¾"	Pine
(P)	1 Pc.	1½" x 39" Piano hinge & screws.	
(Q)	6 —	Decorative pulls for drawers & desk cover.	
(R)	4 —	18" Legs and plates	
	Misc.:	Finish nails, wood filler, sandpaper, shellac and paint.	

DRAWERS:

(A)	3 Pcs.	¾" x 4" x 12⅞"	Plywood
(B)	6 Pcs.	½" x 4" x 15¾"	Plywood
(C)	3 Pcs.	½" x 3½" x 11⅞"	Plywood
(D)	3 Pcs.	⅛" x 12⅜" x 15½"	Plywood
(E)	2 Pcs.	¾" x 5¾" x 9"	Plywood
(F)	4 Pcs.	½" x 5¾" x 15¾"	Plywood
(G)	2 Pcs.	½" x 5¼" x 8"	Plywood
(H)	2 Pcs.	⅛" x 8½" x 15½"	Plywood

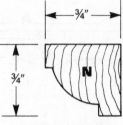

PINE MOULDING

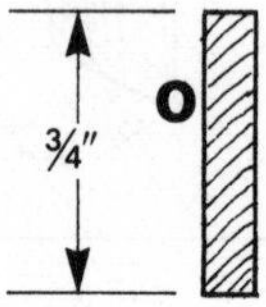

PIANO HINGE

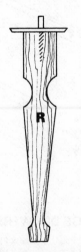

LEG AND PLATE

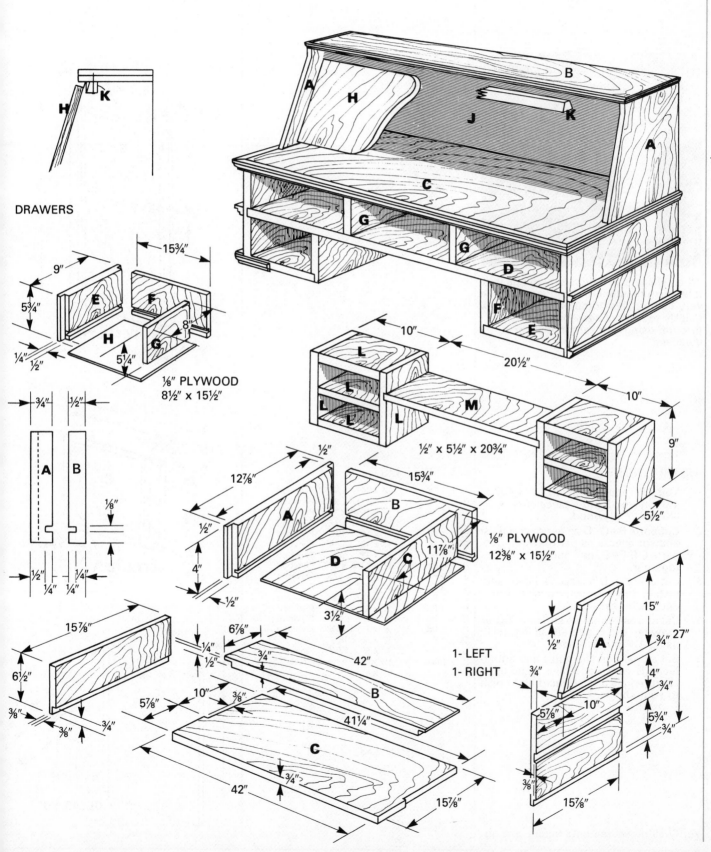

DRAWERS

H K

A B H

E F

H G

8"

9"

15¾"

5¾"

¼" ½"

5¼"

⅛" PLYWOOD
8½" x 15½"

¾" ½"

⅛"

½" ¼"
¼" ¼"

A B

15⅞"

6½"

⅜" ¾"
⅜"

5⅞" 10"

⅜"
½"

6⅞"
¼"
½"
¾"

42"

41¼"

C

42"

15⅞"

¾"

B

C

D

A

B

12⅞"

15¾"

½"

4"

½"

11⅞"

3½"

1- LEFT
1- RIGHT

10"

20½"

L

L

L

L

L

L

M

10"

9"

5½"

½" x 5½" x 20¾"

⅛" PLYWOOD
12⅜" x 15½"

A

15"

27"

4"

¾"

½"

¾"

¾"

10"

5⅞"

5¾"

⅜"

15⅞"

A
H
J
K
B
C
G
G
D
F
E

When space is at a premium, things that fold, push together or disappear come in very handy. This home office folds back quickly to cabinet size once you're through using it. Ideal for apartment dwellers.

INSTRUCTIONS:

1. You will require a piece of ½" x 4'0" x 4'0" plywood and a piece of ¾" x 4'0" x 4'0" plywood.

2. Cut parts B+C+D as per material list and cut checks as per drawing. Cut parts L-E-F+G, nail and glue together.

3. Cut check in D to receive hinge and install. Same procedure for A. Cut and install base J+K.

4. Cut and assemble leg structure as per drawing. Cut H and attach leg to H, using 1½" piano hinge.

5. Set all nails and fill holes and imperfections with wood filler. Sand all sharp edges and surfaces and finish to your choice.

MATERIAL LIST:

A.	1 Pc.	¾" x 14¾" x 19¼"	Plywood
B.	1 Pc.	¾" x 14¾" x 27"	Plywood
C.	1 Pc.	¾" x 10¾" x 14¾"	Plywood
D.	1 Pc.	¾" x 14¾" x 16¼"	Plywood
E.	1 Pc.	¾" x 12" x 18¼"	Plywood
F.	1 Pc.	¾" x 12" x 17¾"	Plywood
G.	1 Pc.	¾" x 12" x 14¾"	Plywood
H.	1 Pc.	¾" x 17¾" x 27"	Plywood
J.	2 Pcs.	¾" x 2¼" x 17¼"	Plywood
K.	2 Pcs.	¾" x 2¼" x 11"	Plywood
L.	2 Pcs.	½" x 18¾" x 27"	Plywood
M.	1 Pc.	½" x 11" x 23¼"	Plywood
N.	1 Pc.	½" x 2½" x 9"	Plywood
P.	2 Pcs.	⅛" x 11" x 23¼"	Plywood
Q.	1 Pc.	½" x ¾" x 15½"	Pine
U.	1 Pc.	¾" x ⅞" x 17¾"	Pine
	Misc.:	1½" piano hinge, screws, bars, etc.	

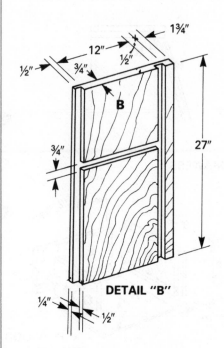

DETAIL "B"

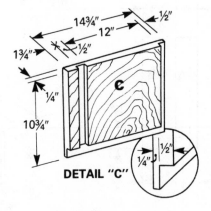

DETAIL "C"

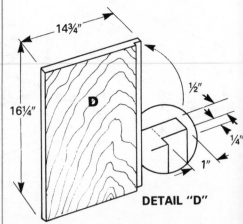

DETAIL "D"

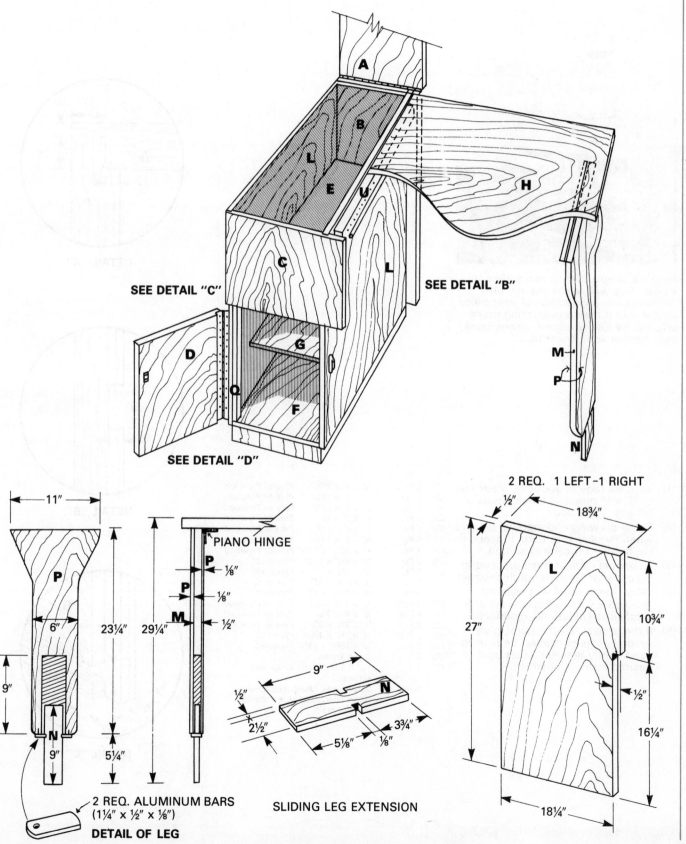

SEE DETAIL "C"

SEE DETAIL "B"

SEE DETAIL "D"

2 REQ. 1 LEFT–1 RIGHT

11″

PIANO HINGE

P   ⅛″

P   ⅛″

M   ½″

23¼″   29¼″

9″

N

9″

6″

5¼″

2 REQ. ALUMINUM BARS
(1¼″ × ½″ × ⅛″)

DETAIL OF LEG

9″

N

½″

2½″

5⅛″   3¾″

⅛″

SLIDING LEG EXTENSION

½″   18¾″

L

27″   10¾″

½″

16¼″

18¼″

28
wall telephone office

Here's a simple idea to make life a bit easier. This wall telephone not only enhances the appearance of your office or den, but it makes everything more efficient by having phone, phone book, etc., right at your finger tips.

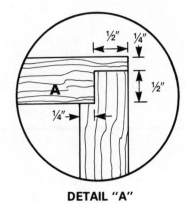

DETAIL "A"

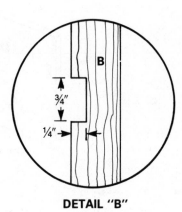

DETAIL "B"

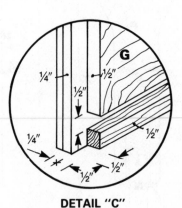

DETAIL "C"

INSTRUCTIONS:

(1) You will require about 16 linear feet of ¾" x 9" pine and small pieces of ½" and ¼" plywood.

(2) Study drawing and material list and when familiar with both, proceed to cut lumber for cabinet section.

(3) Assemble cabinet, then proceed to cut parts for tilt-out bin and construct.

(4) When bin is fitted and installed, proceed with the drawers. Fill and sand all nail holes and imperfections.

(5) If the project is left natural, give several coats of shellac. Be sure to sand lightly between coats until desired lustre is obtained.

MATERIAL LIST:

(A)	2 Pcs.	¾" x 9" x 23¾"	Pine or Plywood
(B)	2 Pcs.	¾" x 9" x 20¼"	Pine or Plywood
(C)	1 Pc.	¾" x 9" x 22¾"	Pine or Plywood
(D)	1 Pc.	¾" x 9" x 15"	Pine or Plywood
(E)	1 Pc.	¾" x 4½" x 9"	Pine or Plywood
(F)	1 Pc.	¾" x 9" x 11¼"	Pine or Plywood
(G)	1 Pc.	¾" x 10¾" x 14½"	Pine or Plywood
(H)	2 Pcs.	½" x 6¾" x 14½"	Plywood
(J)	1 Pc.	½" x 9¾" x 11"	Plywood
(K)	1 Pc.	½" x 6¾" x 11"	Plywood
(L)	1 Pc.	¼" x 10¼" x 12"	Plywood
(M)	2 Pcs.	¾" x 4" x 10¾"	Pine or Plywood
(N)	4 Pcs.	½" x 4" x 7¾"	Pine or Plywood
(O)	2 Pcs.	½" x 3¼" x 9¾"	Pine or Plywood
(P)	2 Pcs.	¼" x 7¾" x 10¼"	Plywood
(Q)	1 Pc.	¼" x 20¾" x 23¾"	Plywood
(R)	3	Small knobs	
(S)	1	1½" x 10¾" Piano hinge and screws.	
	Misc.:	Screw eyes, chain, finish nails, wood filler, sandpaper, shellac, paint or stain.	

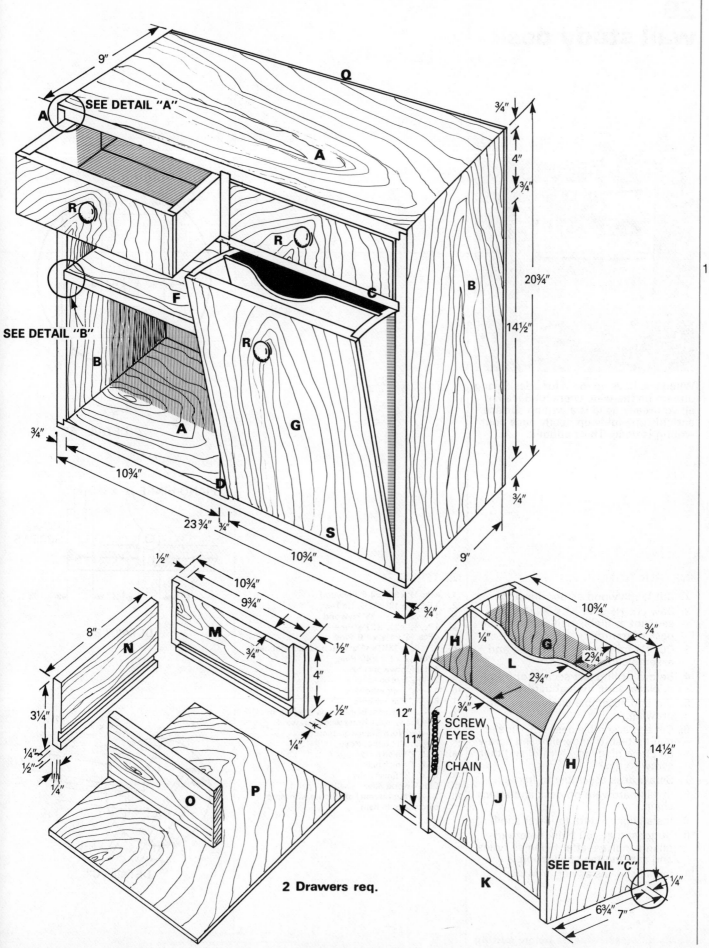

SEE DETAIL "A"

A

A

Q

¾"

4"

¾"

20¾"

14½"

B

B

R

R

C

F

SEE DETAIL "B"

B

R

A

G

¾"

10¾"

D

23¾" ¾"

S

10¾" 9"

¾"

½"

10¾"

9¾"

N

M

8"

3¼"

4"

½"

¼" ½"

¾"

½"

¼"

¼"

O

P

2 Drawers req.

10¾" ¾"

H ¼" G

L 2¾"

2¾"

12"

¾"

11"

SCREW
EYES

CHAIN

J

H

14½"

K

SEE DETAIL "C"

¼"

6¾" 7"

29
wall study desk

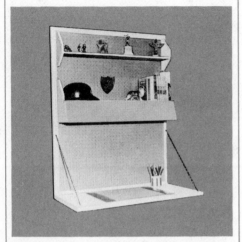

When you have no room for a desk, hang one up on the wall. Literally! Because all you really need is a writing surface, and this one folds up neatly once your writing is done. Think about it.

INSTRUCTIONS:

1. Cut ½" plywood as per drawing.
2. Saw cut 1½ with ⅛" x ⅜" slot, if saw not available nail pegboard on back of frame.
3. Cut 1½ framing on 45 degree and assemble locking each.
4. Before nailing last section of frame in place, slide in pegboard.
5. Cut and assemble shelves, as per drawing.
6. Cut and assemble desk top. Glue and nail tin test to underside and screw on piano hinge to ¾" x 1¼" and then screw to desk.
7. Screw desk assembly to frame.
8. Install hardware on desk and attach chain.
9. Install light fixture to lower shelf.
10. Suggest that you paint before installing shelves, after filling all holes and sanding the shellacking.
11. Install shelves as per drawing.

MATERIALS:

1. 1 Pc. ½" x 3'0" x 4'6" Plywood
2. 1 Pc. ½" x 18" x 37½" Tin Test
3. 1 Pc. ¼" x 6½" x 35" Plywood
4. 1 Pc. ¾" x 1¼" x 37½" Pine
5. 4 Pcs. ¾" x 1½" x 4'6" Pine
6. 1 Pc. ⅛" x 35¾" x 45¾" Untempored pegboard.
7. 4 Pcs. ¼" x 1¼" x 40" Pine.
8. 4 Ft. Lightweight chain
9. 2 — ³⁄₁₆" Eye bolts
10. 4 — ³⁄₁₆" Toggle bolts
11. 6 — ³⁄₁₆" Flat washers
12. 1 — Length brass piano hinge ¾" x ¾" x 36"
13. 3 — Doz. ¾" No. 4 Brass wood screws
14. 4 — 1½" No. 8 Steel wood screws
15. 1 — Small hook and eye
16. ½ Lb. 2" finish nails
17. ½ Lb. 1" finish nails
18. ½ Lb. 1½" finish nails
19. Glue - wood filler - shellack - paint
20. 1 — 24" fluorescent light fixture with lamp cord and pull chain

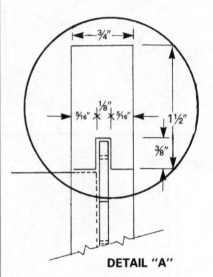

DETAIL "A"

PIANO HINGE ¾" x ¾"

1¼" #8 SCREWS

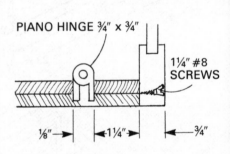

DETAIL "B"

1¼" x ¾" x 37½"

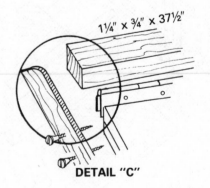

DETAIL "C"

Verify all measurements before cutting

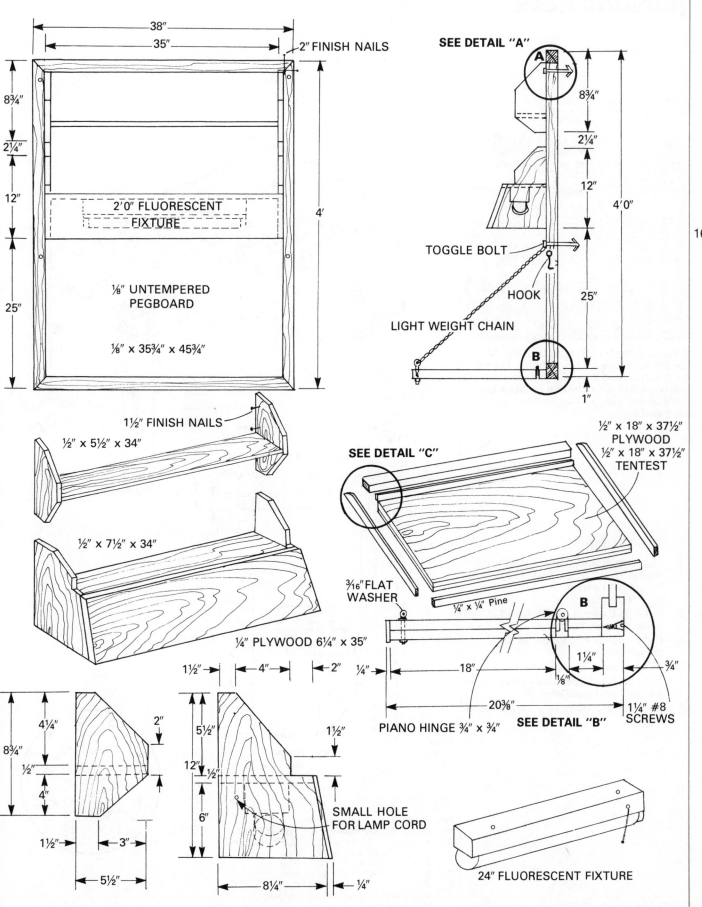

38"

35"

2" FINISH NAILS

8¾"

2¼"

12"

4'

2'0" FLUORESCENT FIXTURE

⅛" UNTEMPERED PEGBOARD

⅛" x 35¾" x 45¾"

25"

SEE DETAIL "A"

A

8¾"

2¼"

12"

4'0"

TOGGLE BOLT

HOOK

25"

LIGHT WEIGHT CHAIN

B

1"

1½" FINISH NAILS

½" x 5½" x 34"

½" x 7½" x 34"

¼" PLYWOOD 6¼" x 35"

½" x 18" x 37½" PLYWOOD
½" x 18" x 37½" TENTEST

SEE DETAIL "C"

³⁄₁₆" FLAT WASHER

¼" x ¼" Pine

B

1¼"

⅛"

¾"

18"

20⅜"

1¼" #8 SCREWS

PIANO HINGE ¾" x ¾"

SEE DETAIL "B"

1½"

4"

2"

¼"

4¼"

2"

8¾"

½"

4"

1½"

3"

5½"

5½"

1½"

12"

½"

6"

8¼"

¼"

SMALL HOLE FOR LAMP CORD

24" FLUORESCENT FIXTURE

30
parsons desk

Classic elegance. Simple to build. Much depends on the choice of finish. Doubles as a handy food server when entertaining party guests. Or could be pressed into service for a host of other uses. Build one and see.

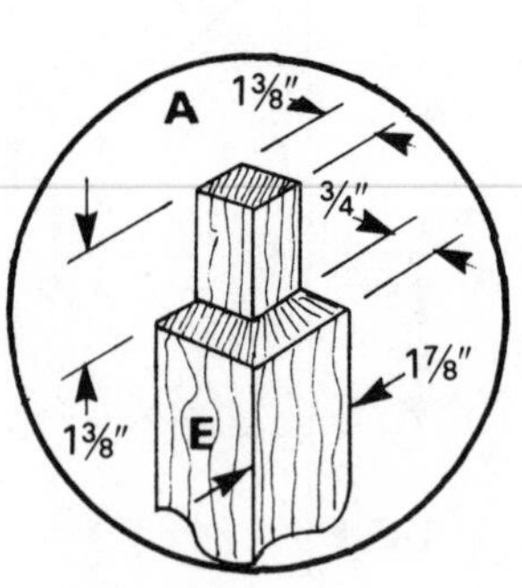

INSTRUCTIONS:

1. Cut parts B and C and cut ¼" x ½" rabbet check as per sketch B. Cut to length with a miter box and nail and glue together.
2. Cut legs E as per sketch A and install using glue and nails.
3. Cut pieces D and install as per drawing.
4. Cut and install ½" plywood top.
5. Set and fill all nail holes and imperfections and sand smooth.
6. Shellack and paint to your choice of colours.

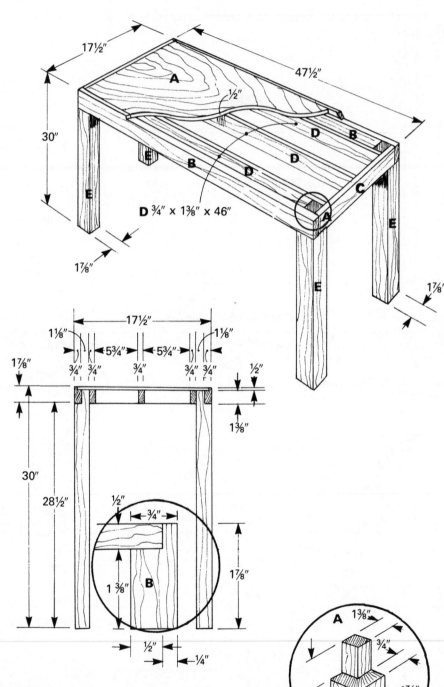

D ¾" x 1⅜" x 46"

MATERIAL LIST:

Part No.	Pieces Req.	Dimensions	Type of Wood
A	1	½" x 17" x 47"	BC Fir Plywood
B	2	¾" x 1⅞" x 48"	Pine
C	2	¾" x 1⅞" x 18"	Pine
D	3	¾" x 1⅜" x 46"	Pine
E	4	1⅞" x 1⅞" x 29½"	Pine

Misc.: Nails, glue, woodfiller, shellack, sandpaper, paint

4
Planters

31 WISHING WELL PLANTER   164

32 PLANTER   166

33 HANGING PLANTER LAMP   167

34 WINDOW BOX   168

35 PORTABLE PLANTER   170

36 LAMINATED PLANTER   172

37 FLOWER POT HOLDER   173

38 FLOWER CART   174

39 FLOWER POT TREE   176

31
wishing well
planter

One of those little, unusual do-it-yourself projects that can take up quite a few afternoons until it's done just right. But what a pleasure to behold when it's finished. It's a real attention getter which will win you many compliments.

INSTRUCTIONS:

(1) Study drawing and material list, then proceed to cut parts (A), (B) and (C).

(2) Assemble above and then cut parts (D) on a 45° angle and nail and glue onto box section.

(3) Cut and roll edges on parts (E) and (K) and glue on surface of box section.

(4) Cut parts (G) and (H) and make two small frames for roof section.

(5) Cut parts for balance of roof structure and assemble.

(6) Cut parts (F) and drill holes to locate roller (O).

(7) Install parts (F) and using ¼" dowels, install roller and handle.

(8) Set all nails and fill, then sand project and paint.

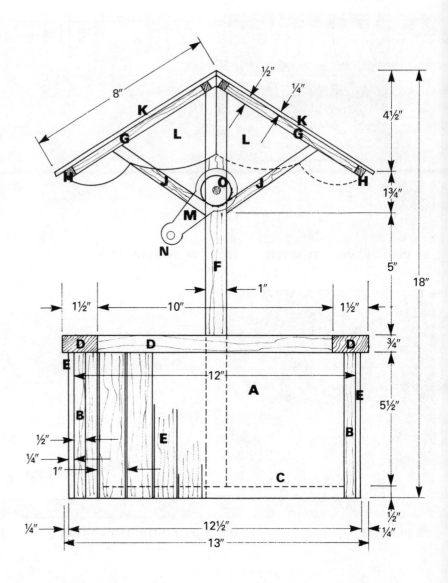

MATERIAL LIST:

(A)	2 Pcs.	½" x 6" x 12"	Plywood
(B)	2 Pcs.	½" x 6" x 11"	Plywood
(C)	1 Pc.	½" x 11" x 11"	Plywood
(D)	4 Pcs.	¾" x 1½" x 14"	Pine
(E)	48 Pcs.	¼" x 1" x 6"	Pine
(F)	2 Pcs.	1" x 1" x 16½"	Pine
(G)	4 Pcs.	½" x ½" x 6¾"	Pine
(H)	4 Pcs.	½" x ½" x 11"	Pine
(J)	4 Pcs.	½" x ½" x 6"	Pine
(K)	22 Pcs.	¼" x 1" x 8"	Pine
(L)	2 Pcs.	¼" x 5" x 13"	Plywood
(M)	1 Pc.	¼" x 1½" x 3½"	Plywood
(N)	3 Pcs.	¼" x 3"	Hardwood dowel
(O)	1 Pc.	1¼" x 9½"	Hardwood dowel
Misc.:		Glue, nails, woodfiller, sandpaper and paint.	

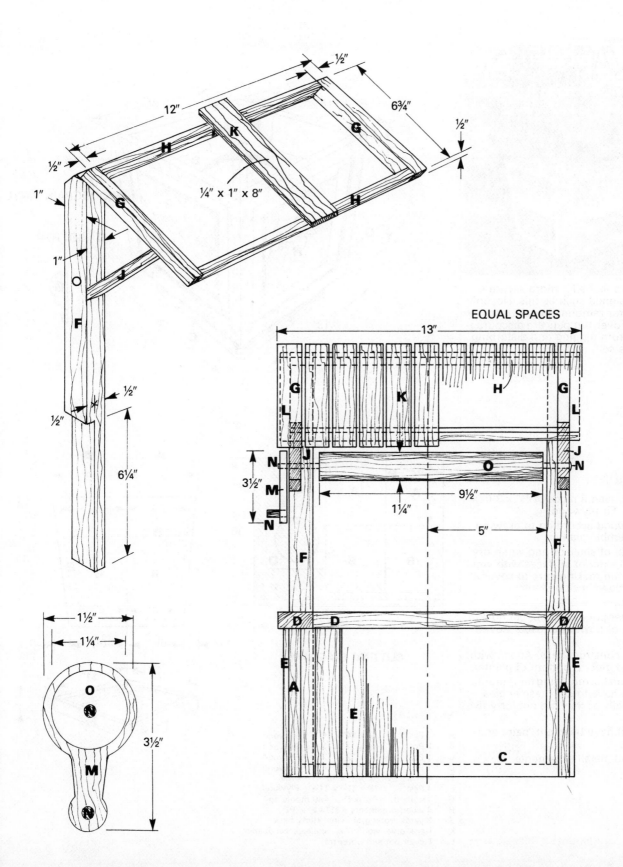

½"

12"

6¾"

½"

K

H

G

¼" x 1" x 8"

½"

1"

G

H

1"

O

J

F

½"

½"

6¼"

EQUAL SPACES

13"

G

K

H

G

L

L

J

J

N

O

N

M

3½"

9½"

N

1¼"

5"

F

F

D

D

D

E

E

A

A

E

C

1½"

1¼"

O

N

M

3½"

N

32
planter

Indoor plants feel a lot more secure in planters designed such as this. Not only is it harder for rambunctious kids to knock them over, but pets are discouraged as well from digging and disturbing the precious soil.

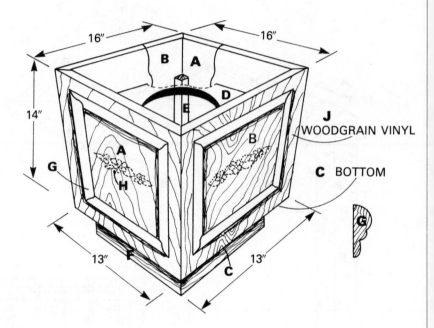

WOODGRAIN VINYL

C BOTTOM

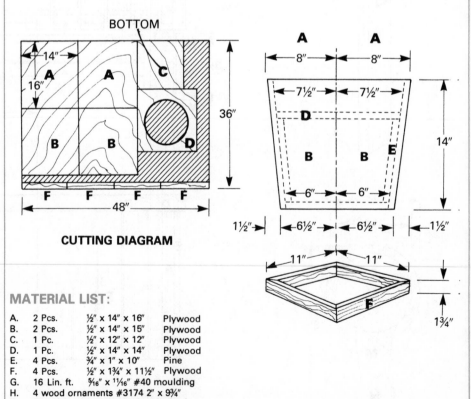

CUTTING DIAGRAM

INSTRUCTIONS:

1. You will need a piece of ½" x 3'0" x 4'0" B.C. Fir plywood.
2. Cut plywood according to drawing and assemble planter.
3. Give coat of shellack and when dry cover all exterior surfaces with vinyl wood grain making sure to cover at least 5" down inside planter.
4. Install supports E.
5. Cut flower pot support D, cut hole to suit size of flower pot used. Cover with vinyl.
6. Cut and construct base. Attach with nails and glue to bottom of planter.
7. Cut and install moulding temporarily. You will have to cut these angles individually as they are not forty five degrees.
8. When all have been cut, paint and reinstall.
9. Paint and install ornaments.

MATERIAL LIST:

A.	2 Pcs.	½" x 14" x 16"	Plywood
B.	2 Pcs.	½" x 14" x 15"	Plywood
C.	1 Pc.	½" x 12" x 12"	Plywood
D.	1 Pc.	½" x 14" x 14"	Plywood
E.	4 Pcs.	¾" x 1" x 10"	Pine
F.	4 Pcs.	½" x 1¾" x 11½"	Plywood
G.	16 Lin. ft.	⁵⁄₁₆" x ¹¹⁄₁₆" #40 moulding	
H.	4 wood ornaments #3174 2" x 9¾"		
J.	3 yards wood grain vinyl sticky back		
K.	Nails, glue, wood filler, shellack, sandpaper		
L.	Flower pot and water tray.		

33
hanging
planter lamp

When it comes to thinking up unusual shapes and patterns, this design is way out in front. Your skill and patience will produce a conversation piece visitors are bound to admire. Yet it costs so little to build.

INSTRUCTIONS:

(1) This project consists mostly of lamp fixture parts and can be found in most hardware stores.

(2) The planting pots can be found in nursery departments of large stores. You may use any other type of pot that you desire as long as you adapt pieces (B) to fit around the outside.

(3) Obtain some ⅜" thick hardwood and following the drawing proceed to make pieces (B) and (C).

(4) Evenly space (B) around pot as per drawing and secure to (C) with screws. Same for bottom pot.

(5) Install electrical parts.

(6) Connect top and bottom with about 6" of chain.

(7) Suggest you put your plants in before connecting top and bottom.

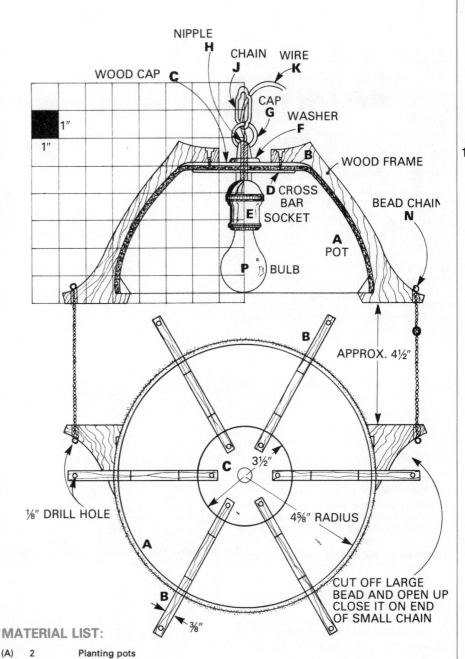

MATERIAL LIST:

(A)	2	Planting pots
(B)	12 Pcs.	⅜" x 2½" x 9" Ash or Oak
(C)	2 Pcs.	⅜" x 3½" dia. Ash or Oak
(D)	1	Cross Bar
(E)	1	Short socket
(F)	1	Washer
(G)	1	Cap and Ring
(H)	1 Pc.	1" long ⅛" running thread pipe nipple to connect cap and socket
(J)	—	Swag Lamp chain and hooks
(K)	—	Lamp wire
(L)	1	Line switch (optional)
(M)	1 Doz.	½" #4 flat head brass wood screws
(N)		12" of Large size bead pull chain
(O)		36" of Small size bead pull chain
(P)	1 —	Appliance light bulb
(Q)		Sandpaper, stain or paint.

L LINE SWITCH (OPT.)

M ½" - #4 F.H. BRASS SCREWS

Verify all measurements before cutting

34
window box

Here's a window flower box with a difference! This one goes inside the house — so you can try your green thumb almost from your easy chair...Great, too, for avoiding mosquito bites come weeding time.

INSTRUCTIONS:

(1) You will require approximately 16 linear feet of 1" x 12" pine shelving.

(2) Study drawing and material list and when familiar proceed to lay out parts on pieces of heavy kraft paper or cardboard.

(3) When layout is completed, cut out paper and use these as patterns to mark up wood for cutting.

(4) Cut out parts and make temporary assembly.

(5) When satisfied with assembly, dismantle and sand all pieces.

(6) Assemble parts, using glue and screws.

(7) Sand off all sharp edges and fill all imperfections with wood filler and when dry, sand.

(8) You may stain or paint to your choice of colors or you may give two (2) or three (3) coats of shellac, being sure to sand lightly between coats.

MATERIAL LIST:

(A)	2 Pcs.	¾" x 9" x 36"	Pine
(B)	1 Pc.	¾" x 7⅝" x 32"	Pine
(C)	2 Pcs.	¾" x 7½" x 10"	Pine
(D)	2 Pcs.	¾" x 8" x 23"	Pine
(E&F)	1 Pc.	¾" x 4¼" x 30¾"	Pine
(G)	4 Pcs.	¾" x 2¾" x 12"	Pine
(H)	4 Pcs.	¼" x ¾" x 1¾"	Pine
(J)	16 Pcs.	⅜" diameter screwhole plugs	
(K)	20	1¼" #8 Flat head wood screws	
(L)	Misc.: White glue, wood filler, sandpaper and paint or stain.		

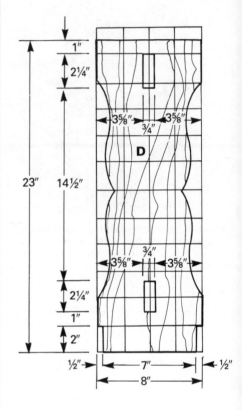

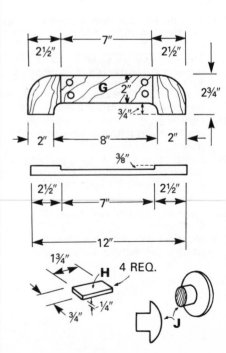

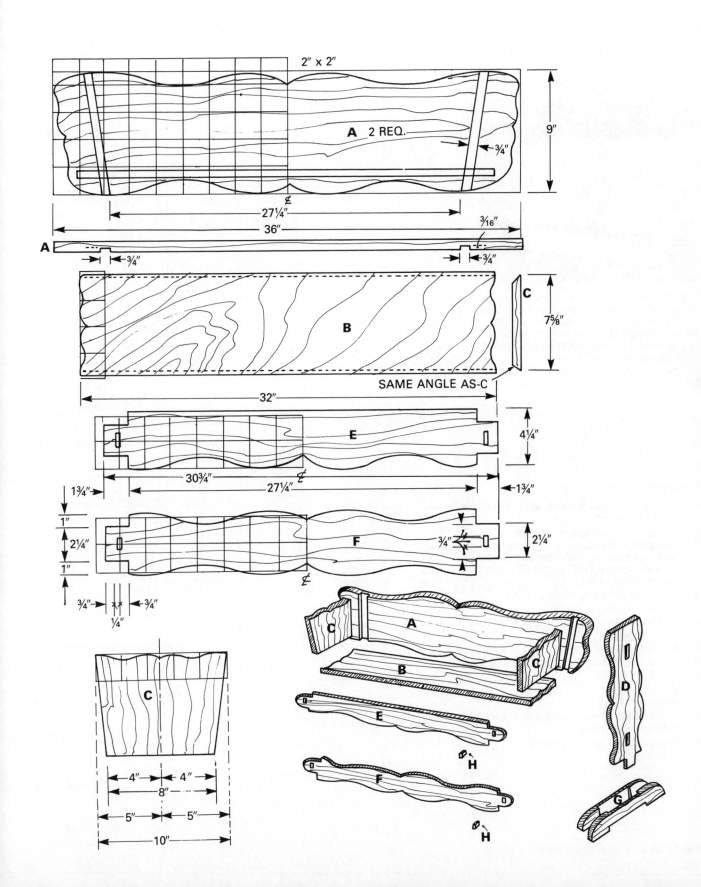

2" x 2"

A   2 REQ.

9"

¾"

27¼"

36"

³⁄₁₆"

A

¾"   ¾"

C

B

7⅝"

SAME ANGLE AS-C

32"

E

4¼"

30¾"

27¼"

1¾"   1¾"

1¾"

1"

2¼"

F

¾"

2¼"

1"

¾"   ¾"

¼"

C

4"   4"

8"

5"   5"

10"

A

C

C

B

D

E

H

F

H

G

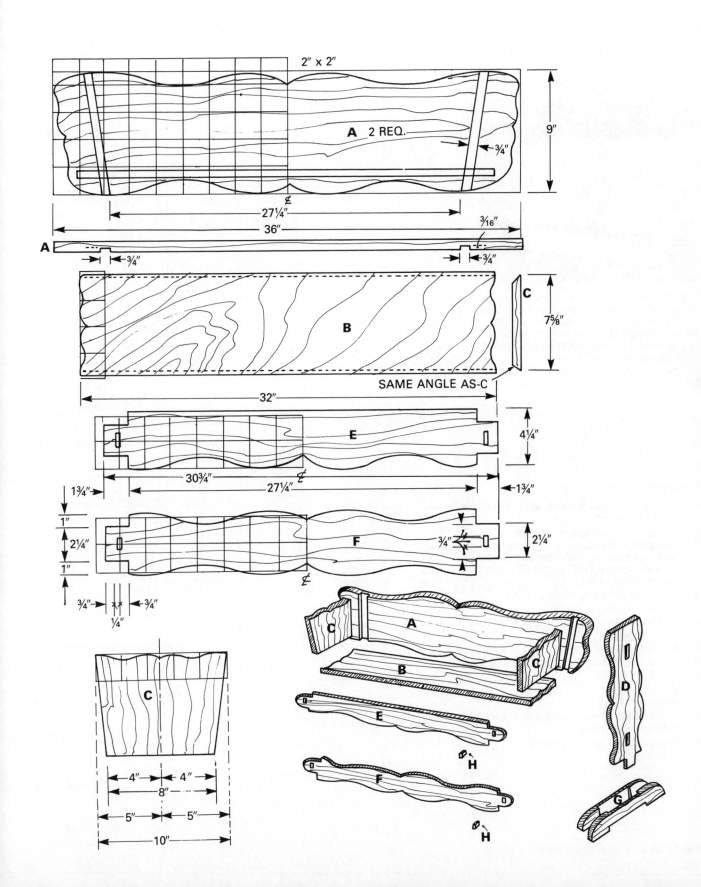

35
portable planter

This portable planter is a real blessing for constant room re-arrangers. No need to slip discs or strain unused muscles, as this design features built-in casters for ease of moving. So you can change your decor in minutes.

INSTRUCTIONS:

1. You will require a piece of ½″ x 3′0″ x 6′0″ plywood.
2. Cut pieces A to length and from top dimension measure in ¾″ on bottom and mark angle. Transfer this angle to level square and use on all subsequent angle cuts.
3. Cut ends B and bottom C and using nails and glue, assemble.
4. Following drawing, cut and assemble bottom section.
5. Cut legs as per drawing and install.
6. Finish off by cutting and installing top trim J + H.
7. Attach casters + ornamental mouldings.
8. Set and fill all nail holes and imperfections and sand.
9. Paint to your choice of colours.

MATERIAL LIST:

A.	2 Pcs.	½″ x 8″ x 35¾″	Plywood
B.	2 Pcs.	½″ x 8″ x 9½″	Plywood
C.	1 Pc.	½″ x 8″ x 33¼″	Plywood
D.	1 Pc.	½″ x 10½″ x 35¾″	Plywood
E.	2 Pcs.	½″ x 1½″ x 35¾″	Plywood
F.	3 Pcs.	½″ x 1½″ x 9½″	Plywood
G.	4 Pcs.	¾″ x 2½″ x 20″	Pine
H.	2 Pcs.	¾″ x 1″ x 37″	Pine
J.	2 Pcs.	¾″ x 1″ x 12″	Pine
K.	1 Set of casters		
L.	Ornamental wood mouldings of your choice.		
	Misc.: Screws, nails, glue and paint.		

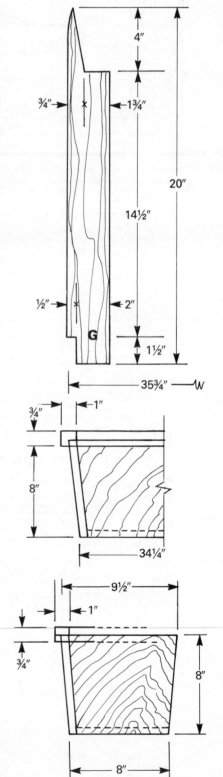

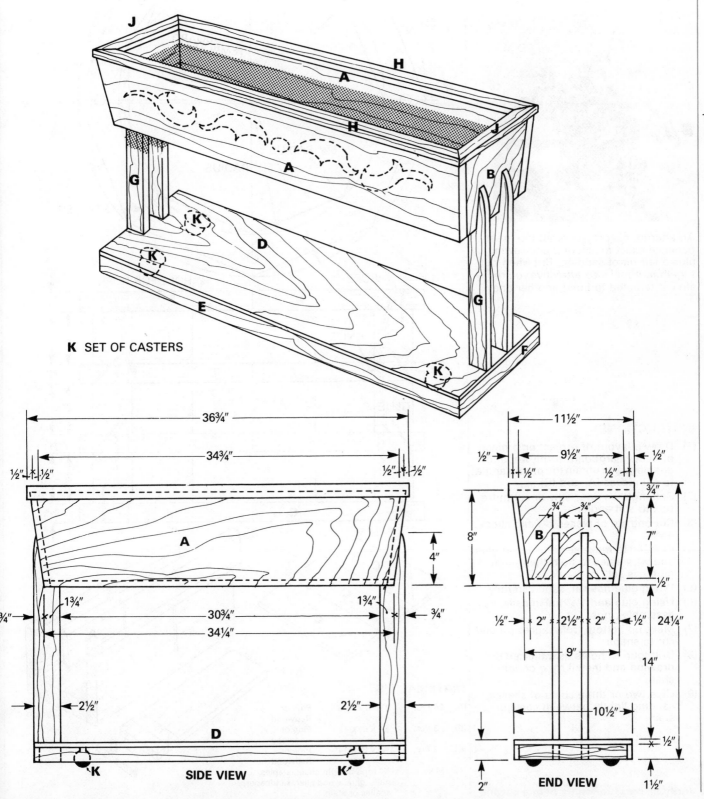

K SET OF CASTERS

36¾"

34¾"

½"— ⇥↢ 1½"   ½"—⇥—½"

A

4"

¾"—   1¾"   1¾"   ¾"

30¾"

34¼"

2½"   2½"

D

SIDE VIEW

11½"

½"   9½"   ½"

¾"

¾"   ¾"

B

8"   7"

½"

½"— ⇥ 2" — ⇥ 2½" ⇥ 2" —½"   24¼"

9"

14"

10½"

½"

2"   1½"

END VIEW

36
laminated
planter

An afternoon's project requiring great patience exact measuring and sawing, plus a fair bit of sanding. But when put together, it looks so attractive you're almost tempted to build another one.

INSTRUCTIONS:

(1) Draw a layout of project on a piece of heavy cardboard or plywood to enable you to obtain the proper angle to cut pieces (A) and (B).

(2) Set angle on your saw or cut mitre box to suit angle.

(3) Cut one set of pieces (A) and check angle.

(4) Proceed to make sections using glue and ⅜" staples to hold them until glue has set.

(5) When glue has set, sand carefully.

(6) Using glue and 1½" finish nails, assemble rings.

(7) Make up bottom from pieces (C) and cut to shape.

(8) Drill four ¼" holes as indicated on drawing and install rope or light chain.

(9) Give two or three coats of shellac, sanding lightly between coats, or stain.

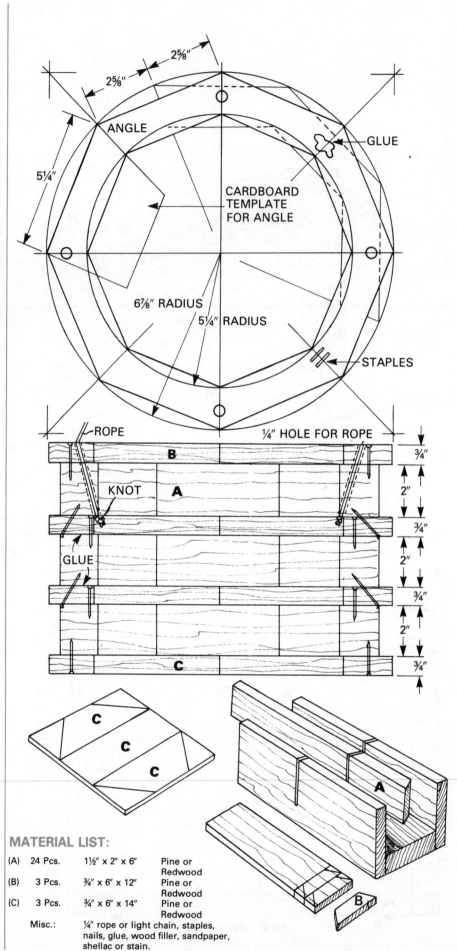

MATERIAL LIST:

(A)	24 Pcs.	1½" x 2" x 6"	Pine or Redwood
(B)	3 Pcs.	¾" x 6" x 12"	Pine or Redwood
(C)	3 Pcs.	¾" x 6" x 14"	Pine or Redwood
	Misc.:	¼" rope or light chain, staples, nails, glue, wood filler, sandpaper, shellac or stain.	

37
flower
pot holder

Here's a design taken straight from the sturdy egg crate. Enlarged, and improved upon, it can hold from 12 to 18 flower pots — depending on the size you choose. Great practice project for that new router you're itching to try out.

INSTRUCTIONS:

(1) Cut three pieces (A) and tape them together and lay out cuts to be made.
(2) Cut pieces (B).
(3) Sand all parts.
(4) Cut pieces (C).
(5) Using white glue and nails, assemble unit.
(6) Set nails and fill. Sand.
(7) Paint or stain to your choice.

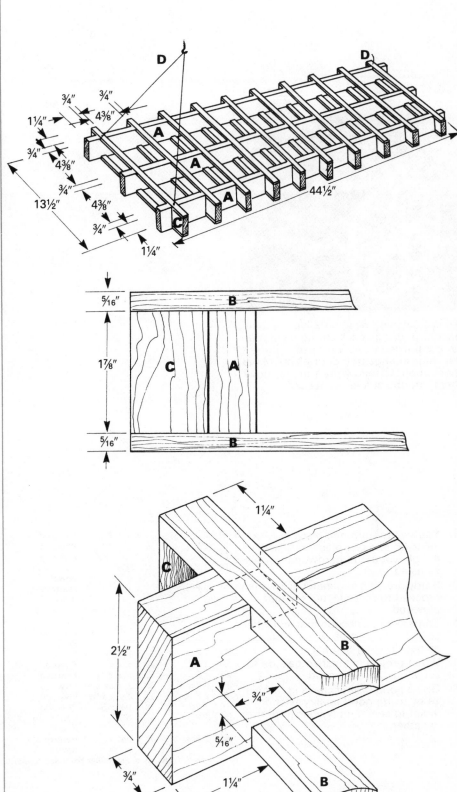

MATERIAL LIST:

(A)	3 Pcs.	¾″ x 2½″ x 44½″	Pine
(B)	18 Pcs.	5⁄16″ x ¾″ x 13½″	Pine
(C)	18 Pcs.	¾″ x 1¼″ x 1⅞″	Pine
(D)	12 Lin. ft.	No. 5 sashcord or lightweight chain.	

Verify all measurements before cutting

38
flower cart

An eye-catching design to liven up any backyard. Brings back strong memories of less hurried days. Very useful for sunshine outings of indoor plants. Move them about to follow the sun , or move them into the shade, as needed.

INSTRUCTIONS:

(1) You will require one piece of ½" x 36" x 48" and one piece of ¾" x 48" x 48" plywood and hardwood dowels as listed.

(2) Study drawing and material list, then proceed to make layout on your plywood.

(3) Construct box section first and when completed, start on wheel structure as per drawing and list.

(4) When project is finished be sure to set all nail, fill and sand.

(5) Give a good primer coat and complete by using good quality exterior paint to seal the plywood from the weather.

MATERIAL LIST:

(A)	2 Pcs.	½" x 6" x 32"	Plywood
(B)	2 Pcs.	½" x 5" x 19"	Plywood
(C)	1 Pc.	½" x 19 x 25"	Plywood
(D)	1 Pc.	¾" x 21½"	Hardwood dowel
(E)	2 Pcs.	¼" x 1¾"	Hardwood dowel

Wheel Section:

(A)	2 Pcs.	¾" x 23½" x 23½"	Plywood
(B)	2 Pcs.	¾" x 12" x 12"	Plywood
(C)	1 Pc.	¾" x 10½" x 17½"	Plywood
(D)	1 Pc.	¾" x 6" x 6"	Plywood
(E)	1 Pc.	¾" x 5" x 22½"	Plywood
(F)	6 Pcs.	¾" x 3" diameter	Plywood
(G)	2 Pcs.	½" x 2½" x 17½"	Plywood
(H)	2 Pcs.	½" x 1½" x 6"	Plywood
(J)	1 Pc.	¾" x 26½"	Hardwood dowel
(K)	2 Pcs.	¼" x 1¾"	Hardwood dowel

Misc.: Glue, nails, woodfiller, paint, sandpaper.

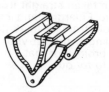

Flower box

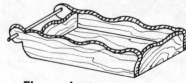

Wheel structure

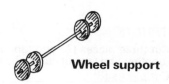

Wheel support

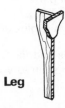

Leg

Wheel detail

Verify all measurements before cutting

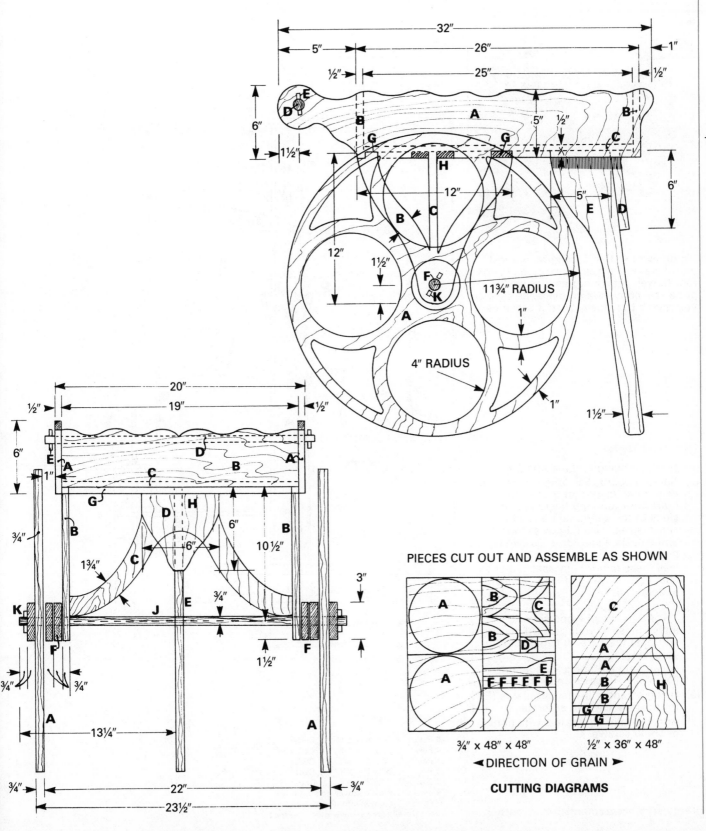

PIECES CUT OUT AND ASSEMBLE AS SHOWN

¾" x 48" x 48"   ½" x 36" x 48"

◄ DIRECTION OF GRAIN ►

CUTTING DIAGRAMS

39
flower pot tree

It's unusual — that's for sure. But lest you mistake it for a clothes rack, hang up four flower pots and presto — you've got a real conversation piece. Be sure you give it the sturdy base it deserves.

INSTRUCTIONS:

(1) Study drawing and material list.

(2) Cut four boards 5'6" long and using a center line layout on these boards, mark your tapering lines on both sides of the center line and when satisfied nail two (2) pieces together and cut. Do same for other two (2) pieces.

(3) Nail these four (4) pieces together as shown on drawing. Plane and sand as required.

(4) Layout and cut supports (B). Using 1½" #8 flat head wood screws, attach these to your post (A) making sure that they are 90 degrees to the vertical post.

(5) Locate and cut holes for supports (D). Make supports and install.

(6) Using a center line layout pieces (E) for baskets, cut and assemble.

(7) Attach chains to baskets with hooks or small screws.

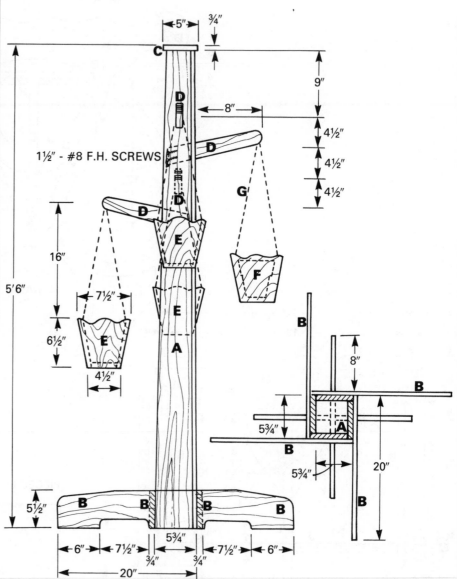

1½" - #8 F.H. SCREWS

MATERIAL LIST:

(A)	4 Pcs.	¾" x 6" x 5'6"	Cedar
(B)	4 Pcs.	¾" x 6" x 1'8"	Cedar
(C)	1 Pc.	¾" x 5" x 5"	Cedar
(D)	4 Pcs.	¾" x 2½" x 12"	Cedar
(E)	20 Pcs.	½" x 7" x 8"	Cedar
(F)	4 —	Plastic flower pots and trays	
(G)	50 Ft.	Lightweight chain	
Misc.:	Small screws, nails, glue, sandpaper		

Verify all measurements before cutting

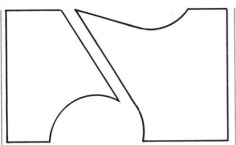

5
Music center

40 RECORD CABINET   178

41 RECORD STORAGE HASSOCK   180

42 FOOT STOOL STORAGE   182

43 CHILD'S WALL SYSTEM   184

44 STEREO WALL UNIT   186

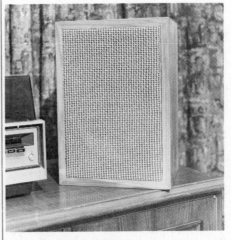

45 SPEAKER CABINET   188

40
record cabinet

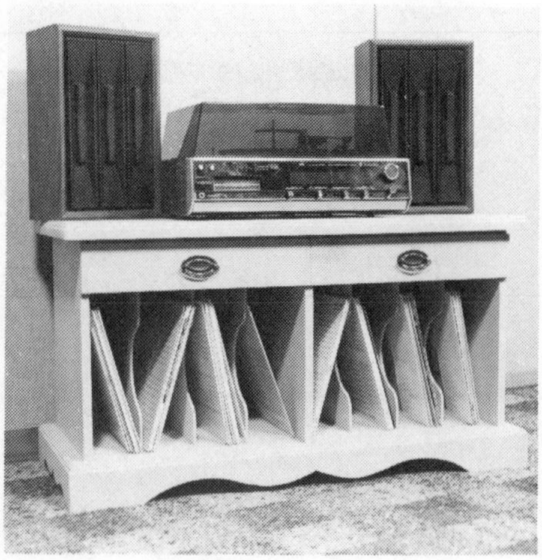

Here's a super attractive way to get your electronics all together. Holds records galore and is an ideal place to display all that stereophonic equipment you've been assembling. Let's you test your router and sabre saw skills, too.

INSTRUCTIONS:

(1) You will require a piece of ¾" x 4' x 5' plywood, and a piece of 30" x 40" x ½" plywood, 10 linear feet of 1" x 3" pine and approximately 30 linear feet of 1" x 2" pine, some ¼" plywood and ⅛" plywood as indicated on material list.

(2) Study drawing and material list and when familiar proceed with cutting and assembly.

(3) When cabinet section is finished proceed with drawers.

(4) Fill all imperfections and nail holes and sand.

(5) Stain or paint to your choice of colors.

MATERIAL LIST:

(A)	2 Pcs.	¾" x 16½" x 40½"	Plywood
(B)	2 Pcs.	¾" x 14⅞" x 18"	Plywood
(C)	1 Pc.	¾" x 14⅞" x 18"	Plywood
(D)	2 Pcs.	½" x 14⅞" x 18⅞"	Plywood
(E)	2 Pcs.	¾" x 3½" x 43" (oversize)	Pine
(F)	2 Pcs.	¾" x 3½" x 19"	Pine
(G)	2 Pcs.	¾" x 1¼" x 43"	Pine
(H)	2 Pcs.	¾" x 1¼" x 19"	Pine
(J)	3 Pcs.	¾" x 1⅛" x 37½"	Pine
(K)	4 Pcs.	¾" x 1⅛" x 13⅜"	Pine
(L)	1 Pc.	⅛" x 18" x 39"	Plywood
(M)	16 Pcs.	⅛" x 4⅜" x 12"	Plywood
(N)	6 Pcs.	¼" x 12" x 13¼"	Plywood

Drawers:

(A)	2 Pcs.	¾" x 3⅞" x 19½"	Plywood
(B)	4 Pcs.	½" x 3⅛" x 14⅞"	Plywood
(C)	2 Pcs.	½" x 2¾" x 17⅜"	Plywood
(D)	2 Pcs.	⅛" x 14⅞" x 17⅜"	Plywood
(E)	2 —	Drawer pulls	
(F)	Misc.:	Nails, glue, wood filler, sandpaper, stain or paint.	

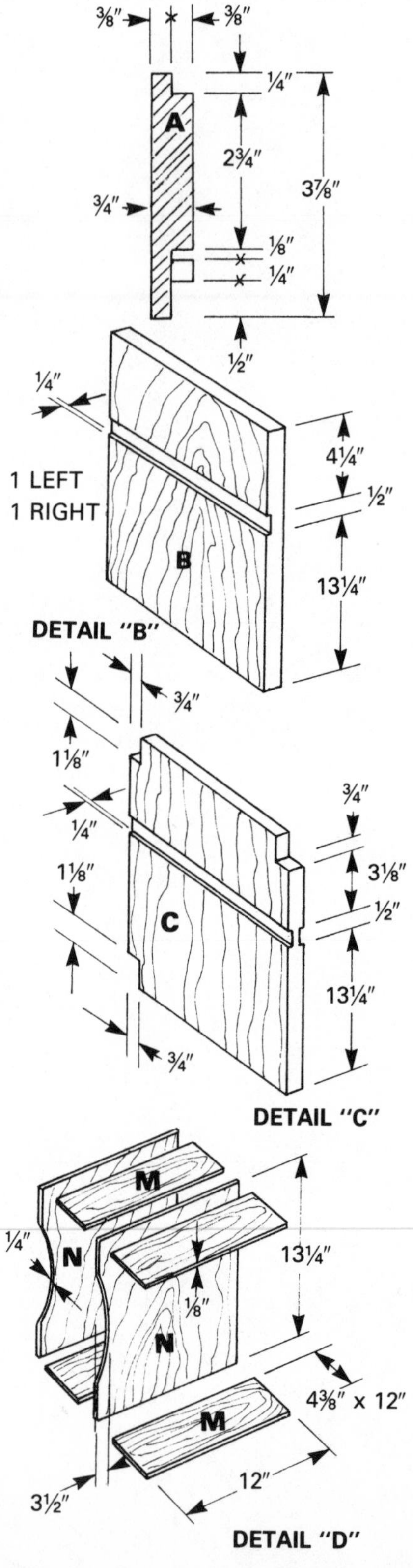

⅜"
⅜"
¼"
A
2¾"
3⅞"
¾"
⅛"
¼"
½"
¼"
4¼"
1 LEFT
1 RIGHT
½"
B
13¼"
DETAIL "B"
¾"
1⅛"
¾"
¼"
1⅛"
3⅛"
½"
C
13¼"
¾"
DETAIL "C"
M
¼"
N
13¼"
⅛"
N
4⅜" x 12"
M
12"
3½"
DETAIL "D"

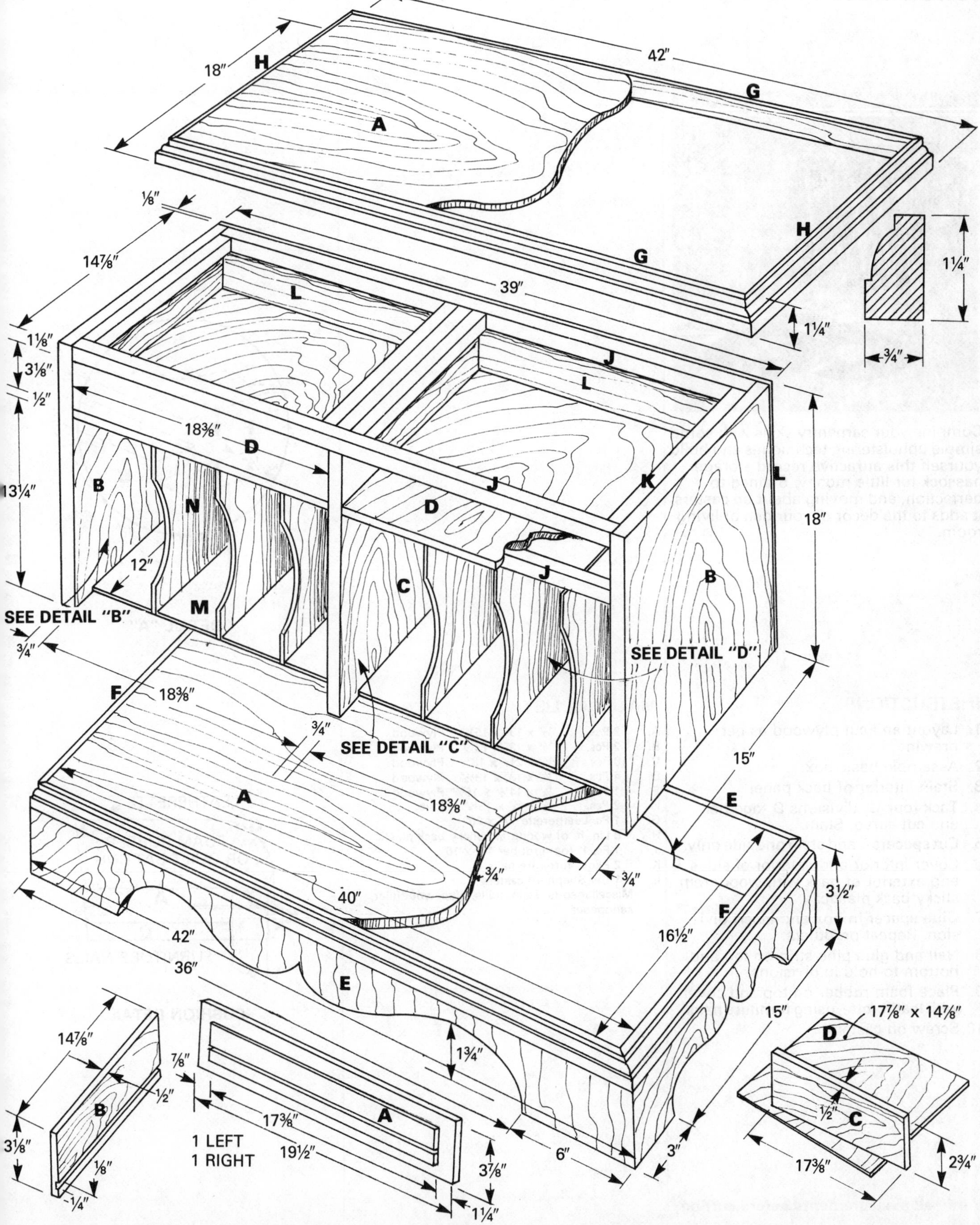

42″
18″
H
A
G
⅛″
14⅞″
G
39″
H
1¼″
1¼″
¾″
L
1⅛″
3⅛″
½″
J
L
18⅜″
D
13¼″
B
N
J
K
L
D
18″
12″
C
J
B
M
SEE DETAIL "B"
¾″
SEE DETAIL "D"
F
18⅜″
¾″
SEE DETAIL "C"
15″
A
18⅜″
E
¾″
¾″
3½″
40″
F
42″
16½″
36″
E
15″
17⅞″ × 14⅞″
D
1¾″
14⅞″
⅞″
½″
B
17⅜″
A
½″
C
3⅛″
1 LEFT
1 RIGHT
19½″
6″
3″
17⅜″
2¾″
⅛″
3⅞″
¼″
1¼″

41
record storage hassock

Combine your carpentry skills with some simple upholstering techniques and build yourself this attractive record storage hassock for little money. Stained to perfection, and moving about on casters, it adds to the decor of your den or living room.

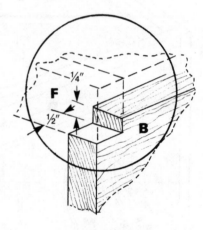

DETAIL "A"

INSTRUCTIONS:

1. Layout and cut plywood as per drawing.
2. Assemble basic box.
3. Stain interior of back panel.
4. Tack four ¼" divisions D together and cut curve. Stain.
5. Cut spacers C and stain one side only.
6. Cover interior and exterior of sides, and exterior of back with woodgrain sticky back plastic.
7. Glue spacer in box and insert division. Repeat on others.
8. Nail and glue pine strip on top and bottom to hold in divisions.
9. Place foam rubber on top and cover with leatherette, using furniture nails.
10. Screw on casters.

MATERIAL LIST:

A.	2 Pcs.	½" x 13" x 15¾"	Plywood
B.	2 Pcs.	½" x 13" x 13½"	Plywood
C.	10 Pcs.	¼" x 2¾" x 13"	Plywood
D.	4 Pcs.	¼" x 13" x 13½"	Plywood
E.	1 Pc.	¼" x 14½" x 15¾"	Plywood
F.	2 Pcs.	½" x ¾" x 15¾"	Pine
G.	1 Pc. Leatherette 17" x 20"		
H.	6 Lin. ft. of woodgrain sticky back plastic		
J.	1 Pc. 1" foam rubber 14" x 16"		
K.	2 Pkgs. furniture nails		
L.	1 Set Shepherd casters		

Miscellaneous: stain, nails, glue, woodfiller, sandpaper.

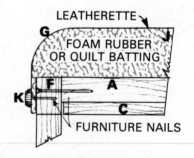

CUSHION DETAIL

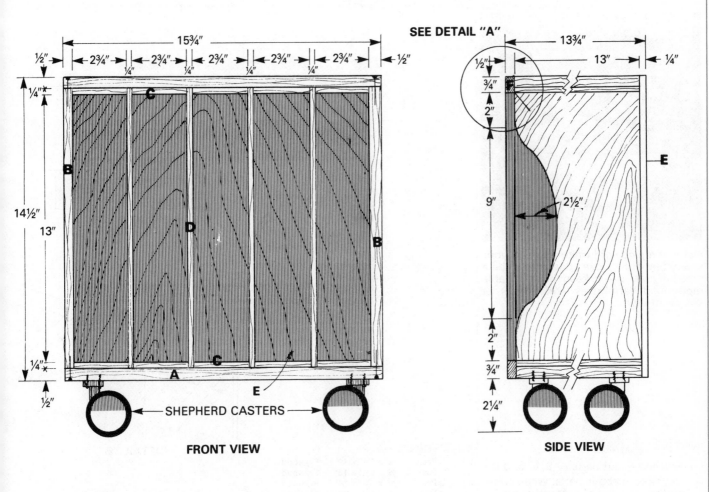

SEE DETAIL "A"

15¾″
½″ 2¾″ ¼″ 2¾″ ¼″ 2¾″ ¼″ 2¾″ ¼″ 2¾″ ½″

¼″
14½″
13″
¼″
½″

C
B
D
B
A
C
E

SHEPHERD CASTERS

FRONT VIEW

13¾″
13″ ¼″
½″
¾″
2″
9″
2½″
2″
¾″
2¼″

E

SIDE VIEW

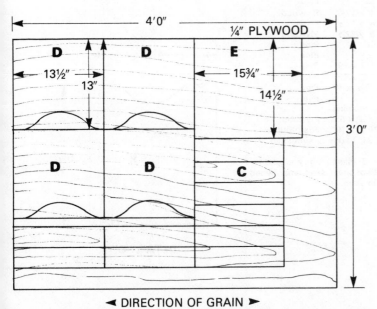

4′0″
¼″ PLYWOOD
D D E
13½″
13″ 15¾″
14½″
3′0″
D D
D D C

◄ DIRECTION OF GRAIN ►

CUTTING DIAGRAMS

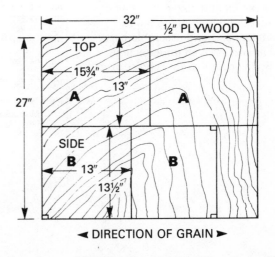

32″
½″ PLYWOOD
TOP
15¾″
27″ 13″
A A
SIDE
B 13″ B
13½″

◄ DIRECTION OF GRAIN ►

42
foot stool
storage

Not just a piece of furniture to rest your weary feet on. It's been designed to be a tape bar as well — to keep those valuable tapes out of harm's way. And in the order you want them.

INSTRUCTIONS:

(1) Proceed to cut parts A, B, C, and D.
(2) Cut slots in above parts. When completed, nail and glue together and install bottom D.
(3) Install divisions P and nail on ¼" x ¾" x ½" pine strips on top to hold in divisions.
(4) Make lid and cover with fabric.
(5) Attach lid with piano hinge.
(6) Make parts and assemble base.
(7) Fill and sand all imperfections.
(8) Stain or paint to your choice of colors.

MATERIAL LIST:

(a)	2 Pcs.	¾" x 5¾" x 19"	Plywood
(b)	2 Pcs.	¾" x 5¾" x 15"	Plywood
(c)	3 Pcs.	½" x 5¼" x 14½"	Plywood
(d)	1 Pc.	½" x 14" x 17½"	Plywood
(e)	2 Pcs.	¾" x 4" x 17½"	Plywood
(f)	2 Pcs.	¾" x 4" x 12½"	Plywood
(g)	2 Pcs.	¾" x 3" x 12½"	Plywood
(h)	6 Lin. ft.	¼" x ¾"	Pine
(j)	4 Lin. ft.	¼" x ½"	Pine
(k)	2 Pcs.	¾" x 1½" x 19"	Pine
(l)	2 Pcs.	¾" x 1½" x 15"	Pine
(m)	1 Pc.	½" x 15½" x 19"	Pine
(n)	6 in. ft.	½" x ½" round molding	Pine
(p)	44 Pcs.	³⁄₁₆" x 4¼" x 5¼"	Plywood
(q)	1 Pc.	2" x 15½" x 19"	Foam Rubber
(r)	1 Pc.	30" x 36" Textile or simulated leather.	
(s)	1 Pc.	1½" x 17" Piano hinge and screws.	

Misc.: Short length of chain, sandpaper, wood filler, nails, paint or stain.

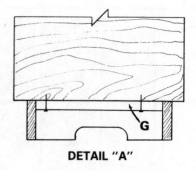

DETAIL "A"

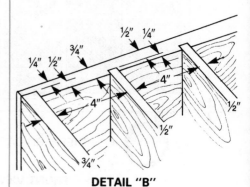

½" ¼"
¾"
¼" ½"
4"
4"
½"
½"
¾"

DETAIL "B"

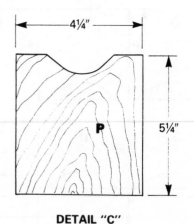

4¼"

P

5¼"

DETAIL "C"

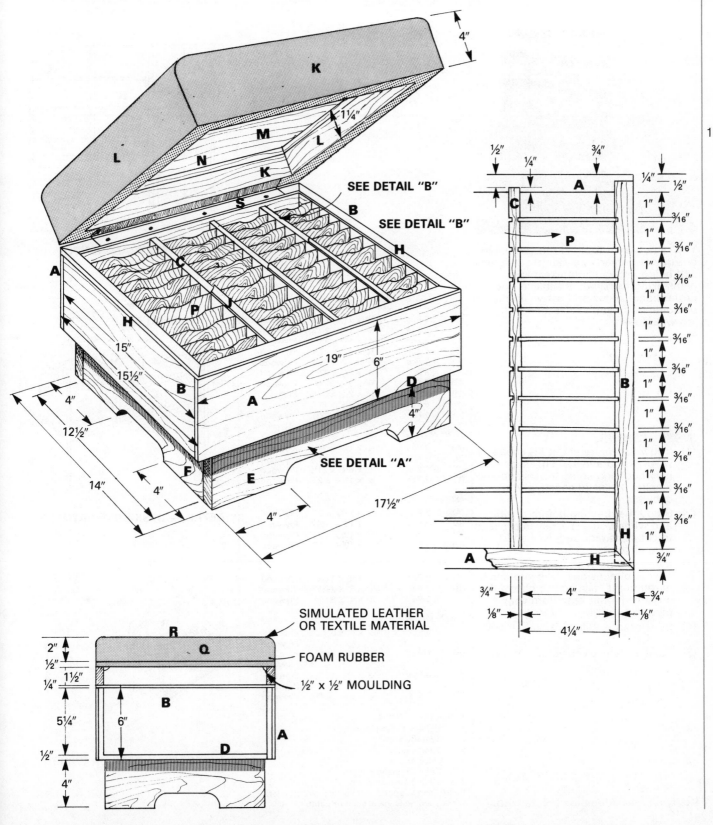

4"

K

1¼"

M

L

L

N

K

SEE DETAIL "B"

SEE DETAIL "B"

S

B

H

A

C

P

J

H

15"

19"

6"

15½"

B

D

A

4"

4"

12½"

F

E

SEE DETAIL "A"

14"

4"

4"

17½"

½"

¼"

¾"

¼"

½"

C

A

1"

3⁄16"

P

1"

3⁄16"

1"

3⁄16"

1"

3⁄16"

1"

3⁄16"

1"

3⁄16"

B

1"

3⁄16"

1"

3⁄16"

1"

3⁄16"

1"

3⁄16"

1"

3⁄16"

H

1"

¾"

A

H

¾"

4"

¾"

⅛"

⅛"

4¼"

SIMULATED LEATHER
OR TEXTILE MATERIAL

R

Q

2"

½"

¼" 1½"

FOAM RUBBER

½" x ½" MOULDING

B

5¼"

6"

A

½"

D

4"

43 child's wall system

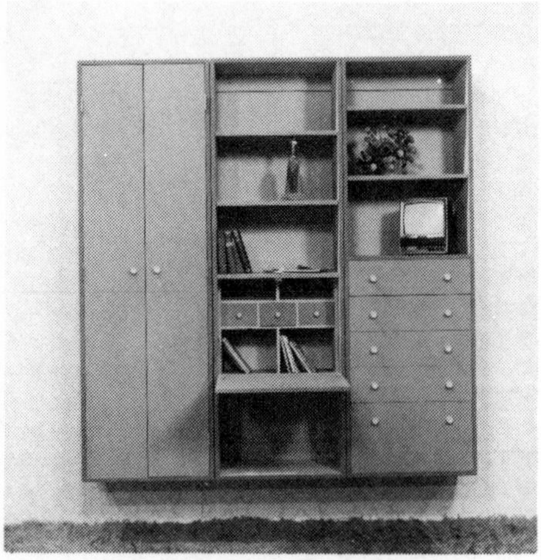

You're not goint to build this project in one day. However, by sticking to the plans and being finicky about exact and painstaking work, you'll achieve true professional status and derive immense personal pride and satisfaction from a job well done.

INSTRUCTIONS:

(1) You will require about 3½ sheets of ¾" plywood and 1½" sheets of ¼ plywood, and some miscellaneous smaller pieces to construct the 3 cabinets.

(2) Study the drawing before cutting and when you are satisfied proceed to cut parts required. Nail and glue all joints.

(3) If you should wish to change the overall dimensions, take into consideration the best size to obtain the most economic cuts from your plywood.

(4) Be sure to set all nails and fill and sand.

(5) Paint or stain to your choice of colors.

Verify all measurements before cutting

MATERIAL LIST FOR A, B, C:

(A)	6 Pcs.	¾" x 11¾" x 72"	Plywood
(B)	6 Pcs.	¾" x 11¾" x 23¼"	Plywood
(C)	5 Pcs.	¾" x 11" x 23"	Plywood
(D)	6 Pcs.	¾" x 11" x 22⅜"	Plywood
(E)	2 Pcs.	¾" x 11" x 70⅝"	Plywood
(F)	3 Pcs.	¼" x 24" x 72"	Plywood
(G)	6 Pcs.	¾" x 3" x 22½"	Plywood
(H)	6 PCs.	¾" x 2½" x 22½"	Pine
(H-H)	6 Pcs.	¾" x 2½" x 6"	Pine
(J)	1 Pc.	¾" x 18" x 22½"	Plywood

Drawers (A)

(A)	3 Pcs.	¾" x 7½" x 22½"	Plywood
(B)	6 Pcs.	½" x 6¾" x 11⅜"	Plywood
(C)	3 Pcs.	½" x 6⅜" x 21½"	Plywood
(L)	3 Pcs.	⅛" x 11⅜" x 22"	Plywood

Drawer (A-A)

(A)	1 Pc.	¾" x 11¾" x 22½"	Plywood
(B)	2 Pcs.	½" x 11" x 10⅝"	Plywood
(C)	1 Pc.	½" x 10⅝" x 21½"	Plywood
(D)	1 Pc.	⅛" x 10⅝" x 22"	Plywood

Desk Compartment

(A)	2 Pcs.	½" x 8" x 17¼"	Plywood
(B)	2 Pcs.	½" x 8" x 21½"	Plywood
(C)	3 Pcs.	½" x 4" x 8"	Plywood

Desk Drawers

(A)	3 Pcs.	½" x 4" x 6 13/16"	Pine or Plywood
(B)	6 Pcs.	½" x 4" x 7¾"	Pine or Plywood
(C)	3 PCs.	½" x 3⅝" x 5 13/16"	Pine or Plywood
(D)	3 Pcs.	⅛" x 6 5/16" x 7¾"	Plywood

Misc. Hardware

6 1½" x 3" Brass hinges
6 Butterfly bolts
8 Drawer pulls
3 Wood knobs
1 Pc. 1½" x 22" piano hinge
2 Folding arm supports
Roll-ti shelf supports and ferrules. Wood filler, sandpaper, nails, glue, stain or paint.

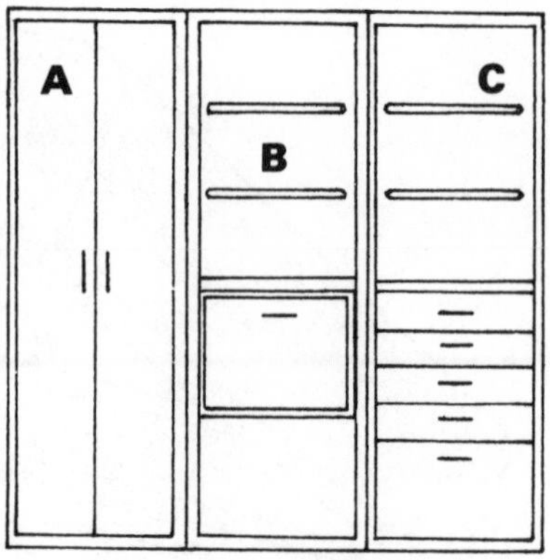

UNIT ARRANGEMENT

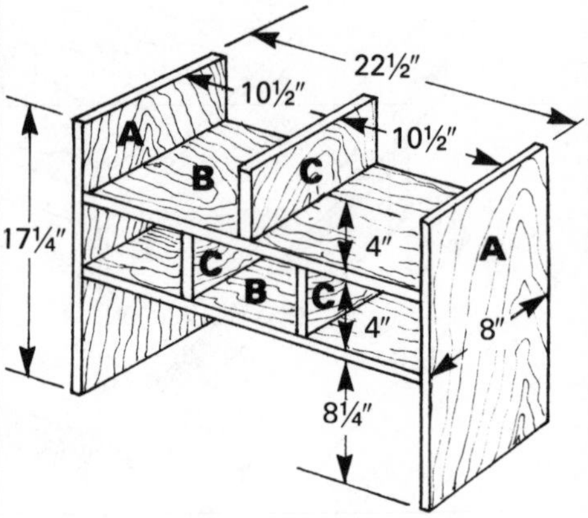

DETAIL — DESK COMPARTMENT

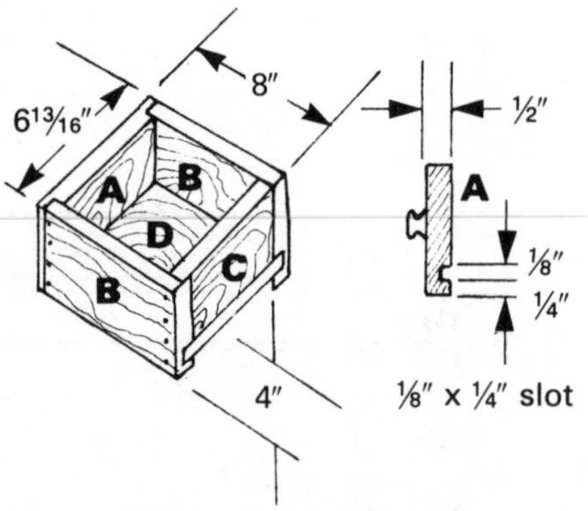

DETAIL — DESK DRAWERS

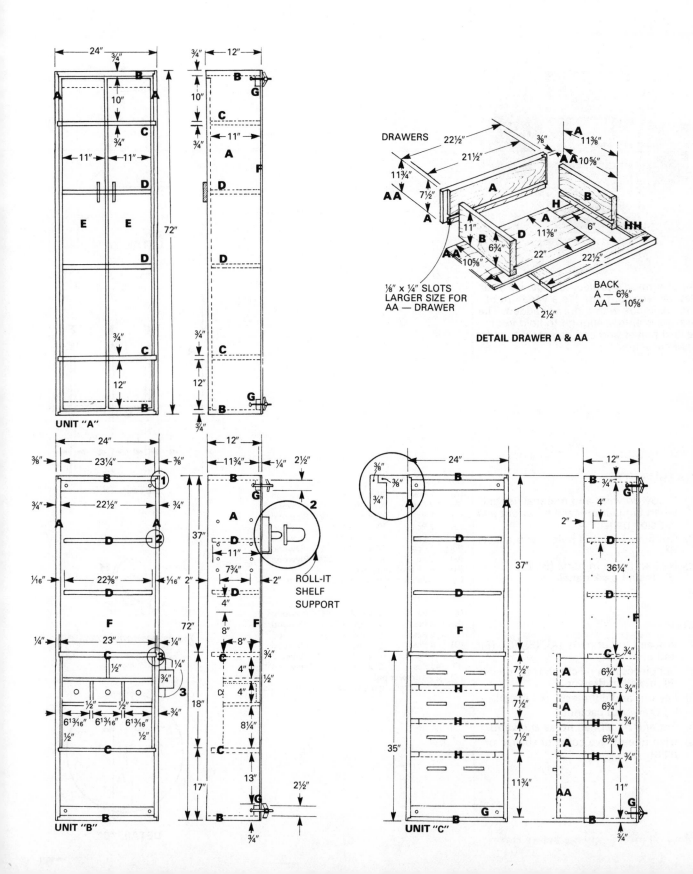

DRAWERS

¹⁄₈″ × ¹⁄₄″ SLOTS
LARGER SIZE FOR
AA — DRAWER

BACK
A — 6⅜″
AA — 10⅝″

DETAIL DRAWER A & AA

UNIT "A"

UNIT "B"

ROLL-IT
SHELF
SUPPORT

UNIT "C"

44
stereo wall unit

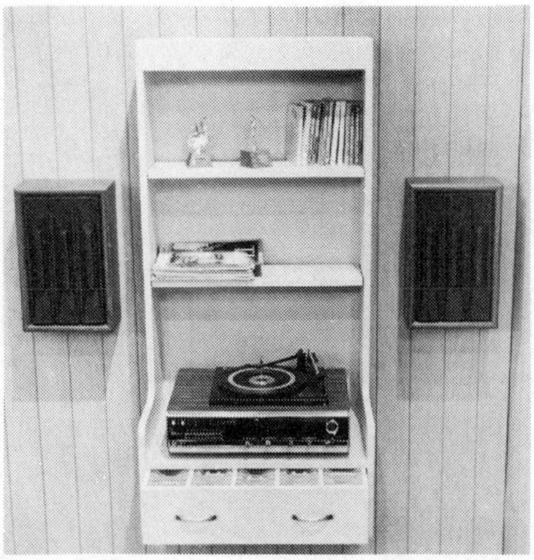

An afternoon's project to organize your den or rec-room fun. It's a variation of the basic box with a drawer added. The drawer is sturdy enough to hold your record player and can be set up to store tape cassettes.

INSTRUCTIONS:

(1) Study drawing and material list and when familiar proceed to lay out and cut side panels (A).
(2) Cut slots and drill holes for brackets (H).
(3) Nail and glue in parts (B), (C), (D), (E). Install back panel.
(4) Glue on edge trim and cut to size and sand.

DRAWER:

(1) Proceed to cut parts (A), (B), (C), (E), and assemble.
(2) Cut pieces (D) and cut slots for pieces (F). Install in drawer.
(3) Lay out and cut pieces (F). Install.
(4) Fit drawer to cabinet.
(5) Set and fill all nail holes and sand.
(6) Give one or two coats of shellac or paint.

Verify all measurements before cutting

MATERIAL LIST:

(A)	2 Pcs.	¾" x 18" x 54⅜"	Plywood
(B)	2 Pcs.	¾" x 18" x 24¼"	Plywood
(C)	1 Pc.	¾" x 6½" x 23¾"	Plywood
(D)	2 Pcs.	¾" x 3" x 23¾"	Plywood
(E)	1 Pc.	¾" x 4" x 23¾"	Plywood
(F)	2 Pcs.	¾" x 7¾" x 23½"	Plywood
(G)	1 Pc.	⅛" x 25¼" x 54⅜"	Plywood
(H)	8 — shelf brackets		
(J)	24 lineal ft. flexible wood edge trim		

DRAWER:

(A)	1 Pc.	¾" x 6⅛" x 23⅝"	Plywood
(B)	2 Pcs.	½" x 5⅜" x 22⅝"	Plywood
(C)	2 Pcs.	½" x 6⅛" x 17¼"	Plywood
(D)	4 Pcs.	½" x 5⅜" x 13⅞"	Plywood
(E)	1 Pc.	¼" x 17½" x 24⅛"	Plywood
(F)	45 Pcs.	⅛" x 4⅜" x 5⅜"	Plywood
(G)	2 — drawer pulls		

Misc.: Nails, glue, wood filler, shellac, paint.

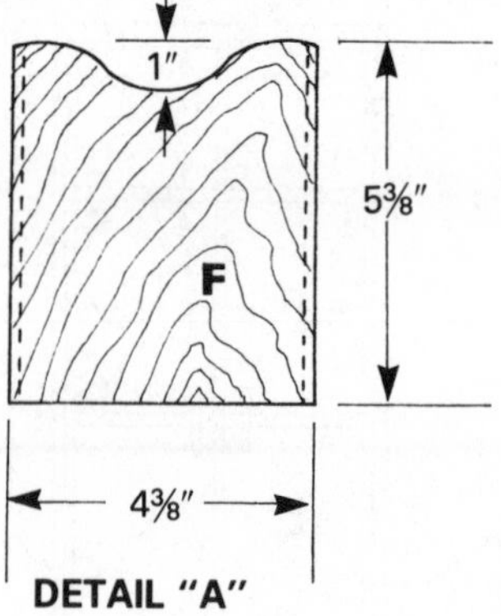
1"
5⅜"
F
4⅜"

DETAIL "A"

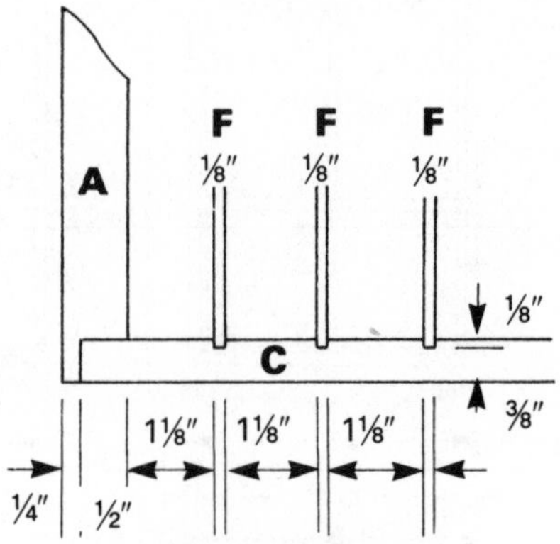
A
F F F
⅛" ⅛" ⅛"
⅛"
C
⅜"
1⅛" 1⅛" 1⅛"
¼" ½"

DETAIL "B"

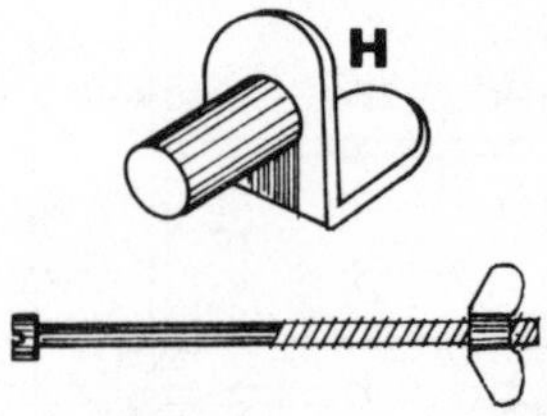
H

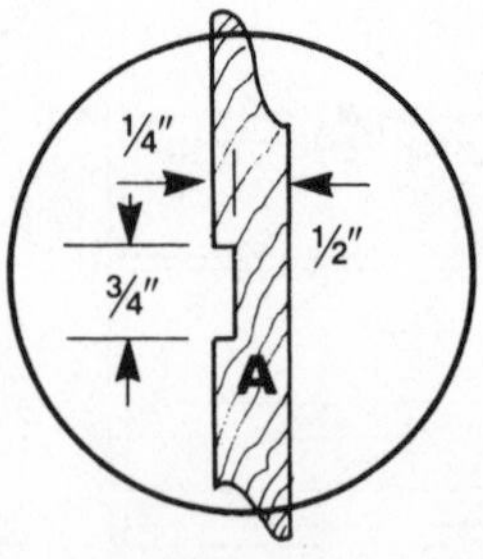
¼"
½"
¾"
A

DETAIL "C"

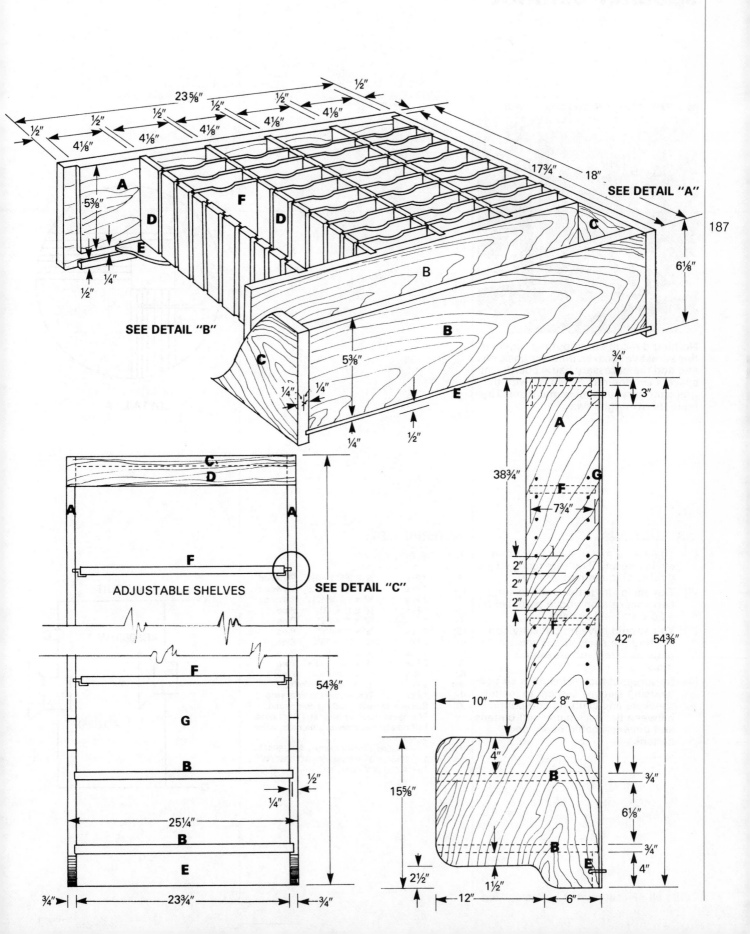

23⅝″
½″
½″
½″
½″
½″
4⅛″
4⅛″
4⅛″
4⅛″
4⅛″
4⅛″
½″
A
5⅜″
D
F
D
C
B
B
187
17¾″
18″
SEE DETAIL "A"
6⅛″
E
¼″
½″
SEE DETAIL "B"
C
5⅜″
E
¼″
¼″
¼″
½″

C
D
A
A
F
ADJUSTABLE SHELVES
SEE DETAIL "C"

F
G
B
½″
¼″
25¼″
B
E
¾″
23¾″
¾″
54⅜″

C
¾″
3″
A
38¾″
F
G
7¾″
2″
2″
2″
F
42″
54⅜″
10″
8″
4″
B
¾″
15⅝″
6⅛″
B
¾″
E
2½″
1½″
4″
12″
6″

45
speaker cabinet

Nothing difficult about putting together this attractive speaker. Build the basic box and add the necessary baffle boards and spacers as required. Finish off with the grill cloth of your choice and stain. Then build its twin right away.

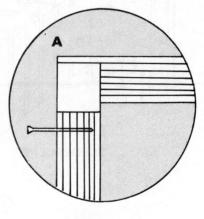

DETAIL "A"

INSTRUCTIONS:

(1) The above material list is for one enclosure and if two are required just double all quantities.

(2) The enclosure is designed to suit the two speakers on above parts list for a 20 watt Hi-Fi system.

(3) You should have no difficulty constructing the enclosure if you cut all parts as listed and shown on drawing.

(4) Be sure that the enclosure is air tight by using silicone cement to install speakers and caulking compound between the back panel and battens and between baffle board and battens.

MATERIAL LIST:
(for one enclosure)

(A)	2 Pcs.	¾" x 9⅞" x 10¾"	Plywood
(B)	2 Pcs.	¾" x 9⅞" x 14½"	Plywood
(C) + (D)	2 Pcs.	¾" x 9¼" x 13¼"	Plywood
(E)	4 Pcs.	¾" x 1" x 13¼"	Pine
(F)	4 Pcs.	¾" x 1" x 7¼"	Pine
(G)	4 Pcs.	¾" x 1" x 4¾"	Pine
(H)	2 Pcs.	⅝" x ⅝" x 13¼"	Pine
(J)	2 Pcs.	⅝" x ⅝" x 8"	Pine
(K)	2 Pcs.	¾" x 1¼" x 13⅛"	Pine
(L)	2 Pcs.	¾" x 1¼" x 9⅛"	Pine
(M)	1 Pc.	12" x 16" Grill cloth	
(N)	1 Pc.	Two screw terminal strip	
(O)		Silicone cement, caulking compound, fiber glass wool, or polyester fiber quilt, batting staples, screws, glue, nails, paint or stain.	
(P)		1 — Phillips 2-inch tweeters AD 2090/T. 1 — Phillips 8-inch woofer AD 8060/W. 1 — 4.7 μf 50V capacitor.	

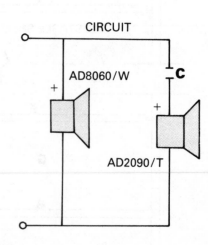

CIRCUIT

AD8060/W

C

AD2090/T

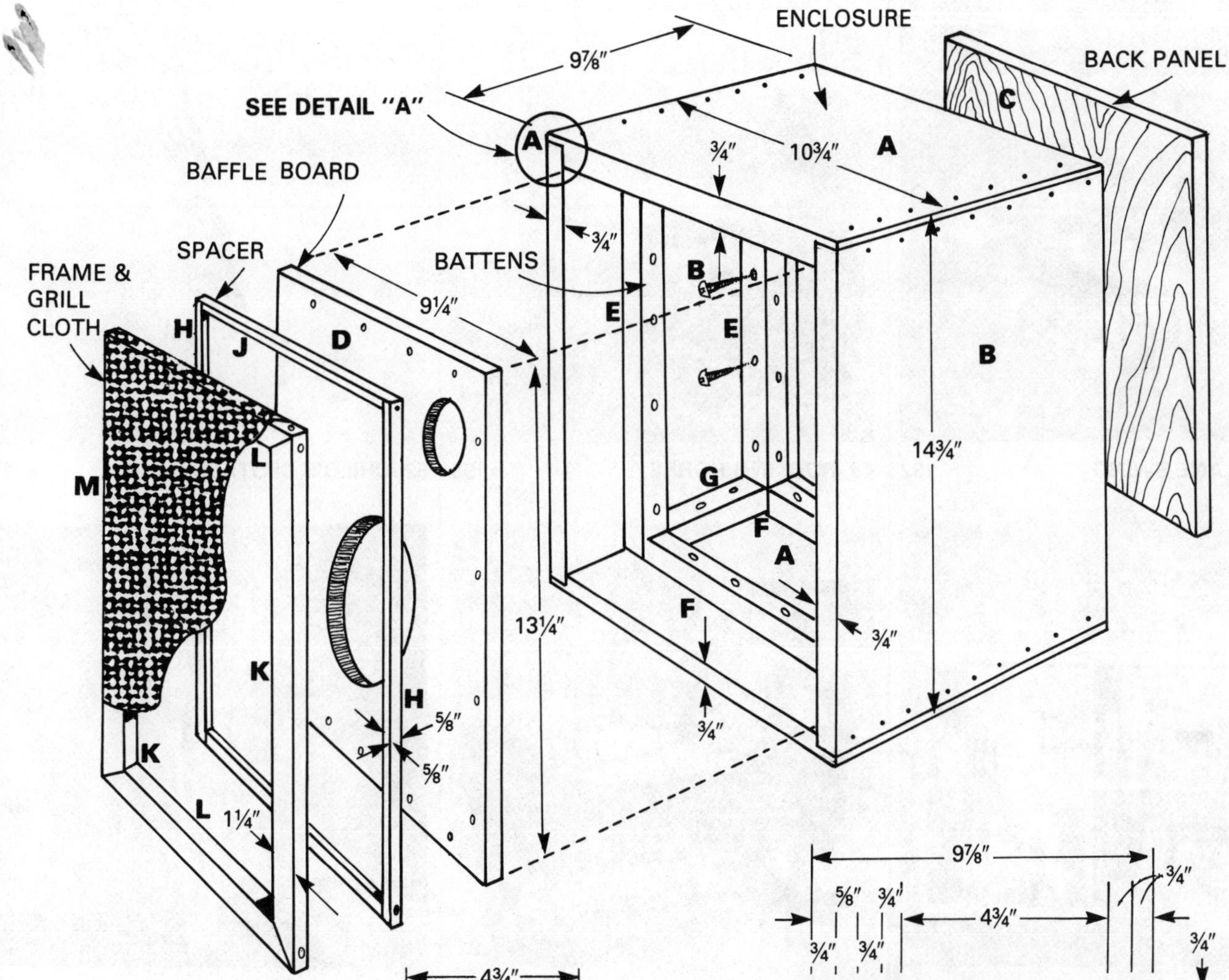
ENCLOSURE
BACK PANEL
9⅞″
SEE DETAIL "A"
A
BAFFLE BOARD
SPACER
FRAME &
GRILL
CLOTH
BATTENS
10¾″
¾″
¾″
9¼″
14¾″
13¼″
5⁄8″
5⁄8″
1¼″
¾″
¾″
¾″
A
B
C
D
E
E
F
F
G
H
H
J
K
K
L
L
M

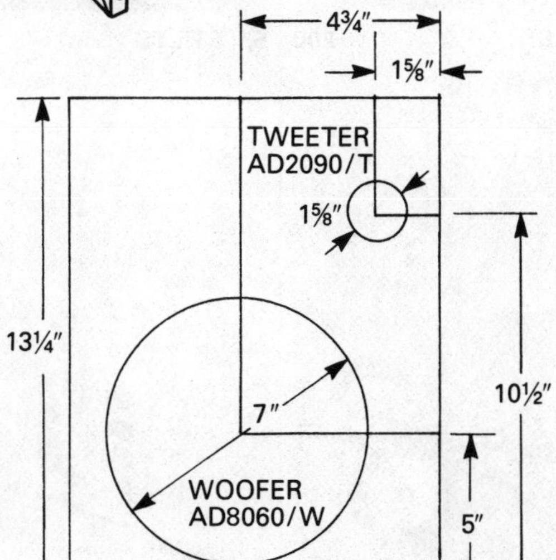
4¾″
1⅝″
TWEETER
AD2090/T
1⅝″
13¼″
10½″
7″
WOOFER
AD8060/W
5″
9¼″

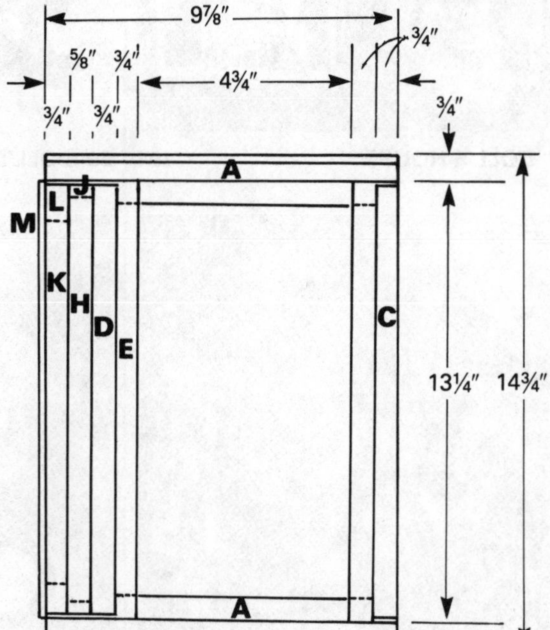
9⅞″
¾″
5⁄8″
¾″
4¾″
¾″
¾″
¾″
A
J
L
M
K
H
D
E
C
13¼″
14¾″
A
6¼″
¾″

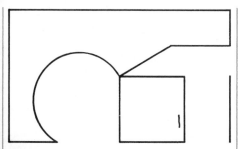

6
Child's corner

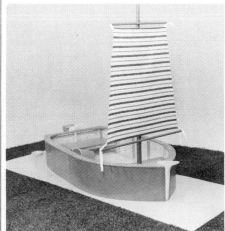

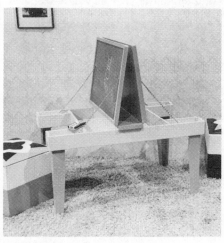

46
airplane swing

Little girls and little boys swing much better in airplane swings built by Dad. Let their spirits soar as you re-discover the fun of pushing swings when, with each huff'n puff, they shout: "Do it again, daddy".

DETAIL — WHEEL SUPPORT

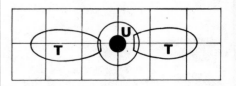

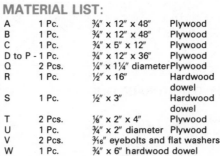

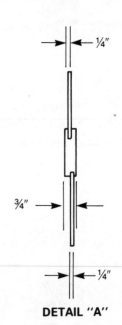

DETAIL "A"

INSTRUCTIONS:

1) From pieces of plywood as per above or a larger piece, proceed to mark off with a 2" grid. When completed, following drawing, layout all parts and proceed to cut.

2) Carefully locate slots in piece -A- for main wing and tail wing and cut out.

3) Cut wings and fit in place.

4) Cut all remaining parts and round off all sharp edges.

5) Assemble leg structure and screw and glue to wing B to A. Same for rear leg.

6) Attach seat and hand support to A.

7) Drill hole and install foot rest.

8) Paint with bright colours of your choice.

9) Drill and install eyebolts in wing B.

MATERIAL LIST:

A	1 Pc.	¾" x 12" x 48"	Plywood
B	1 Pc.	¾" x 12" x 48"	Plywood
C	1 Pc.	¾" x 5" x 12"	Plywood
D to P	1 Pc.	¾" x 12" x 36"	Plywood
Q	2 Pcs.	¼" x 1¼" diameter	Plywood
R	1 Pc.	½" x 16"	Hardwood dowel
S	1 Pc.	½" x 3"	Hardwood dowel
T	2 Pcs.	⅛" x 2" x 4"	Plywood
U	1 Pc.	¾" x 2" diameter	Plywood
V	2 Pcs.	³⁄₁₆" eyebolts and flat washers	
W	1 Pc.	¾" x 6" hardwood dowel	

¾" PLYWOOD BODY & REAR TAIL WING

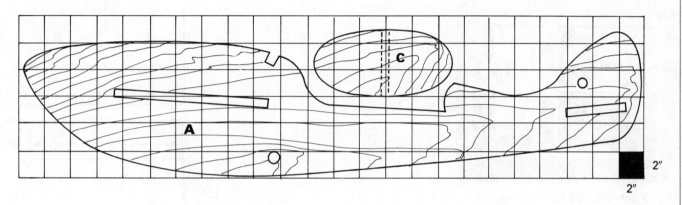

¾" PLYWOOD WING & PROPELLER CENTRE

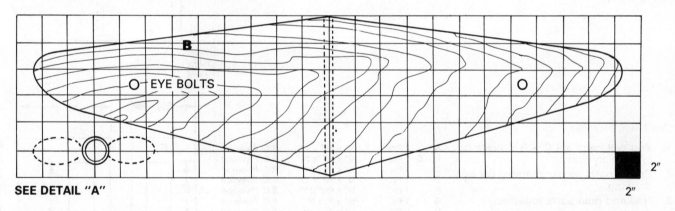

SEE DETAIL "A"

¾" PLYWOOD ALL PIECES

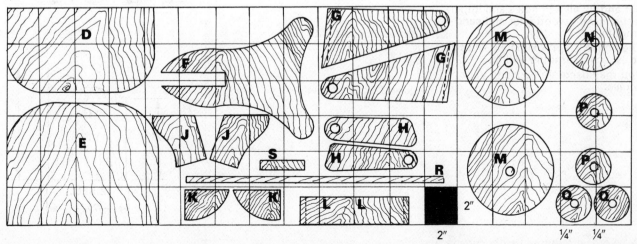

47
doll's house

Here's how big daddies become big heroes to their little girls. Fun-filled afternoons are just a little effort away. So, won't you put down your paper, roll-up your sleeves and make your little girl happy today?

INSTRUCTIONS:

1. You will need a 4'0" x 5'6" piece of ½" B.C. plywood.
2. Cut all parts as per material list and drawing.
3. Nail and glue parts together.
4. Determine bevel on roof panels and cut.
5. Nail and glue in place.
6. Set and fill all nail holes and imperfections with wood filler and sand smooth.
7. The house is approximately ½" scale so ½" scale furniture will fit.
8. You may decorate house to your choice.

MATERIAL LIST:

A.	2 Pcs.	½" x 16" x 18"	B.C. Plywood
B. + C.	2 Pcs.	½" x 16" x 21"	B.C. Plywood
D.	1 Pc.	½" x 7" x 21"	B.C. Plywood
E.	1 Pc.	½" x 10" x 21"	B.C. Plywood
F.	1 Pc.	½" x 6½" x 7"	B.C. Plywood
G.	1 Pc.	½" x 7" x 9"	B.C. Plywood
H.	2 Pcs.	½" x 7" x 10"	B.C. Plywood
J.	2 Pcs.	½" x 9¼" x 23¾"	B.C. Plywood

Wood filler, glue, nails, shellack, paint, sandpaper.

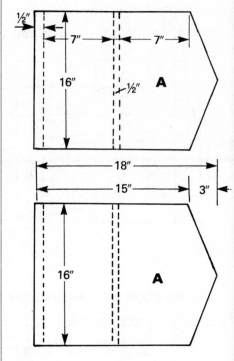

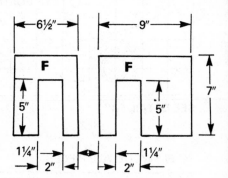

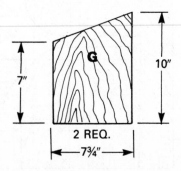

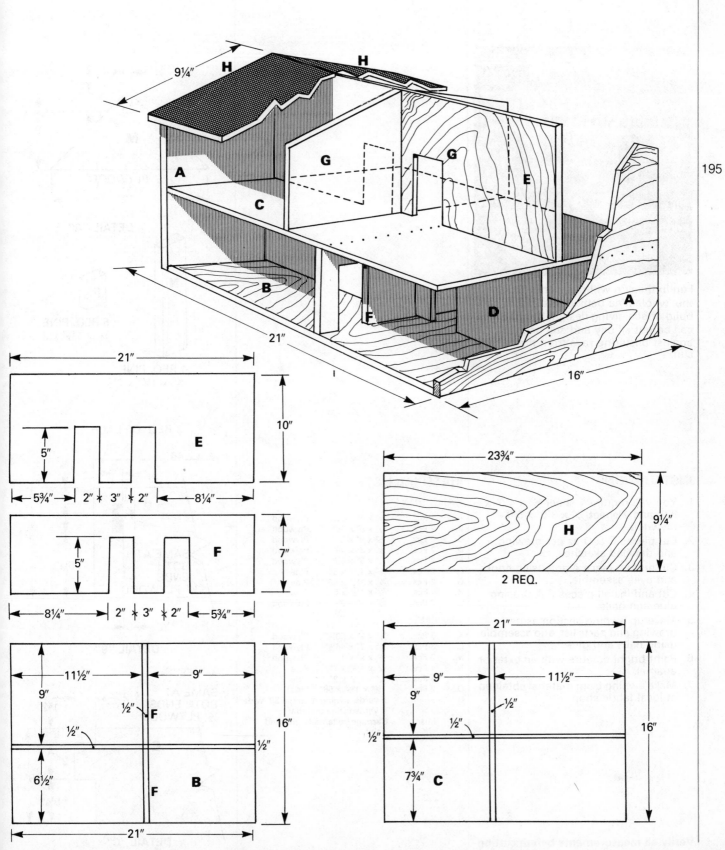

9¼"

H   H

A

C

G   G

E

B

F   D   A

21"   21"   16"

10"

5"

E

5¾"   2"   3"   2"   8¼"

7"

5"

F

8¼"   2"   3"   2"   5¾"

23¾"

9¼"

H

2 REQ.

11½"   9"

9"

½"   F

½"

16"

6½"   F   B

½"

21"

21"

9"   11½"

9"

½"

½"   ½"

16"

7¾"   C

48 covered sand box

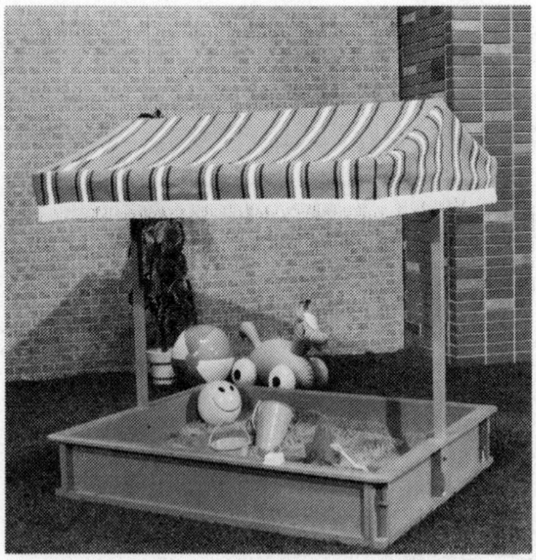

Fun in the sun without worry. That's the whole idea behind this easy to build shade giving design. Now the kids can be out all day and still be protected against blistering rays from the burning sun.

INSTRUCTIONS:

1. You will require 1 sheet ½" x 4'0" x 8'0" and 1 sheet ½" x 3'0" x 5'0" plywood.
2. Cut pieces C & D as per drawing, and detailed sketches.
3. Cut bottom piece A and using hooks and eyes assemble.
4. Cut and install pieces E & D using glue and nails.
5. Make up awning section as per drawing and parts list, and assemble, using nails and glue.
6. Paint bright colours with an exterior enamel.
7. Make awning from material obtained at local fabric shop.

MATERIAL LIST:

SAND BOX:

A.	1 Pc.	½" x 46" x 58"	Plywood
B.	2 Pcs.	½" x 9" x 46"	Plywood
C.	2 Pcs.	½" x 9" x 58"	Plywood
D.	2 Pcs.	½" x 3" x 48"	Plywood
E.	2 Pcs.	½" x 3" x 60"	Plywood
F.	2 Pcs.	¾" x 1½" x 54"	Pine
G.	2 Pcs.	¾" x 1½" x 46"	Pine
H.	14 Pcs.	¾" x 1½" x 8¼"	Pine
J.	2 Pcs.	½" x 3" x 3"	Plywood

AWNING:

K.	3 Pcs.	½" x 2" x 59½"	Plywood
L.	3 Pcs.	½" x 2" x 46½"	Plywood
M.	3 Pcs.	½" x 9" x 12"	Plywood
N.	4 Pcs.	¾" x 1½" x 7½"	Pine
P.	6 Pcs.	¾" x 1½" x 2"	Pine
Q.	2 Pcs.	1½" x 1½" x 58"	Pine
U.	—	5 yards awning material 30" wide 7 yards fringe material	
	Misc.:	Carriage bolts, nails, glue and paint.	

Verify all measurements before cutting

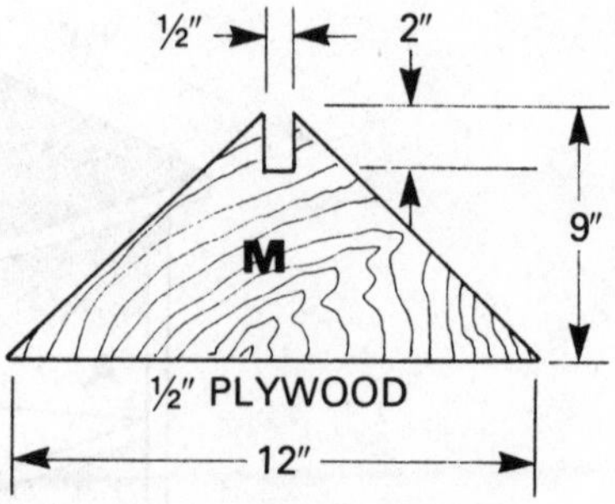
½"
2"
9"
M
½" PLYWOOD
12"

DETAIL "A"

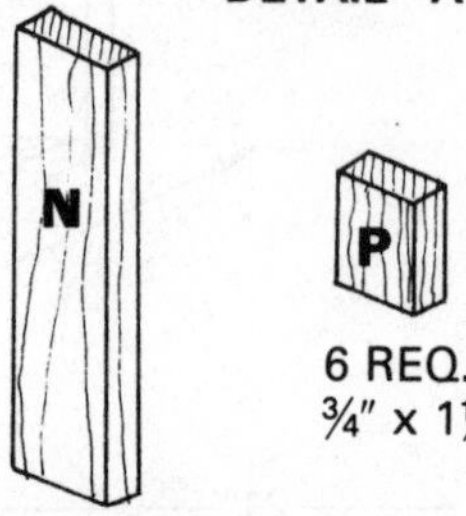
N
P

6 REQ. PINE
¾" x 1½" x 2"

4 REQ. PINE
¾" x 1½" x 7½"

2 REQ. OF EACH

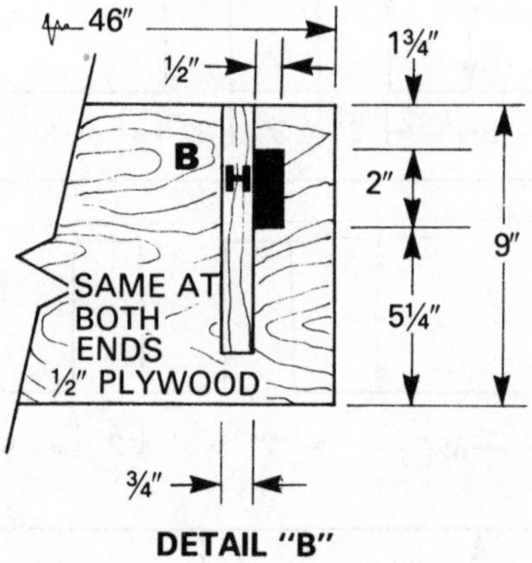
46"
½"
1¾"
B
H
2"
9"
SAME AT
BOTH
ENDS
½" PLYWOOD
5¼"
¾"

DETAIL "B"

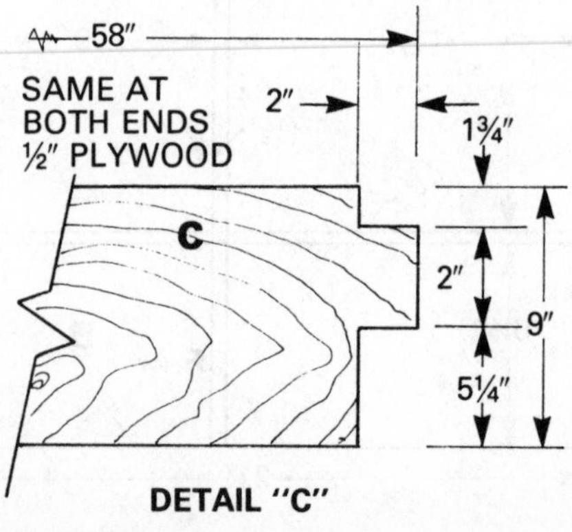
58"
SAME AT
BOTH ENDS
½" PLYWOOD
2"
1¾"
C
2"
9"
5¼"

DETAIL "C"

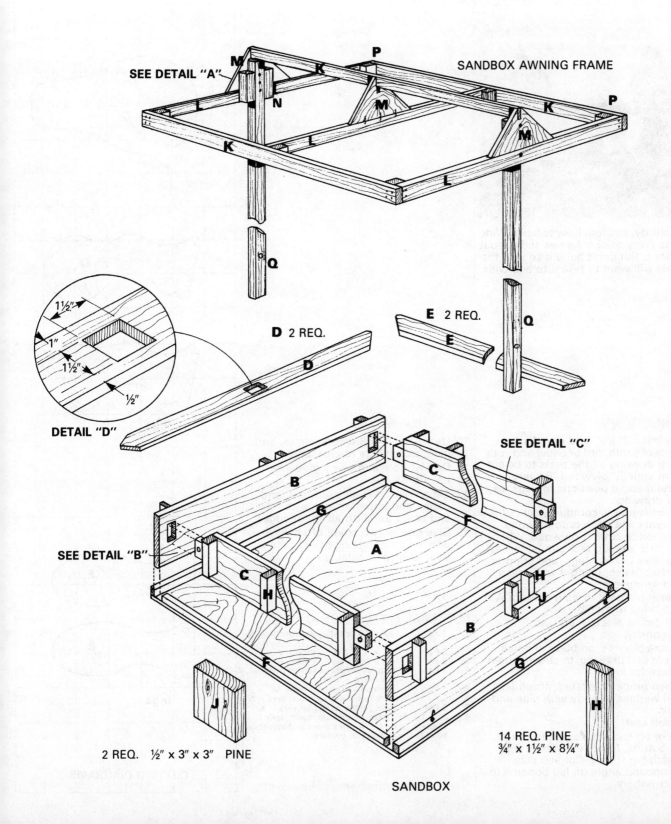

SANDBOX AWNING FRAME

SEE DETAIL "A"

M K P

N M K P

K L M

Q

1½"
1"
1½"
½"

DETAIL "D"

D 2 REQ.

D

E 2 REQ.

E

Q

SEE DETAIL "C"

C

F

SEE DETAIL "B"

B

G

A

C

H

H

J

F

B

G

J

2 REQ. ½" x 3" x 3" PINE

14 REQ. PINE
¾" x 1½" x 8¼"

H

SANDBOX

49
rocking horse

Safe, sturdy, and fun. Easy to build. Wide open to crazy color schemes and cut-out variations. But don't build it so wild that the kids will want to take it to bed with them.

INSTRUCTIONS:

1. Lay out a 2″ x 2″ grid on a large piece of cardboard or paper and copy from drawing all the parts to be cut from your ¾″ plywood. Be very careful about positions for legs, as per drawing.
2. When layout is complete, cut out patterns and trace onto plywood.
3. Proceed to cut out plywood. When all parts are cut, tack similar pieces together i.e. rear legs, and bring to perfect match, using a wood rasp and sandpaper.
4. Attach pieces B to both sides of A and bring to match.
5. Cut 2 pine blocks F and cut diagonally.
6. Locate pieces F on body of horse, as per grid drawing, to obtain proper stance for legs.
7. When properly located, attach legs and wedges to body with glue and nails.
8. Install seat.
9. Make up rockers, using pine strips on bottom, locate cross bars G to match leg stance. Cut and rasp compound angle on leg bottoms to fit crossbars.
10. Using 1½″ — #8 wood screws, and glue, attach legs to crossbars.
11. Drill ½″ hole and using glue insert tail. Comb out.
12. Set all nails. Fill all nail holes, end grains and imperfections with filler and sand. Sand off all sharp edges.
13. Give one or two coats of shellack and using non toxic paint, paint to your choice of colours.

MATERIAL LIST:

1.	1 Pc.	¾″ x 3′0″ x 4′0″	Plywood = A, B, C, D, E, G, H
2.	2 Pcs.	¼″ x ¾″ x 29⅜″	Pine = J
3.	2 Pcs.	¾″ x 3¾″ x 5½″	Pine = F
4.	1 Pc.	Shaggy carpet or similar material for mane = L	
5.	1 Pc.	½″ manilla rope for tail = M	
6.	2 —	Furniture nails, to attach ears = N	
7.	2 Pcs.	Firm rubber or felt for ears = K	
8.		1″ & 1½″ fin. nails, wood filler, sandpaper, shellack, glue, 1½″ — #8 screws and non-toxic paint to your choice of colours.	

Verify all measurements before cutting

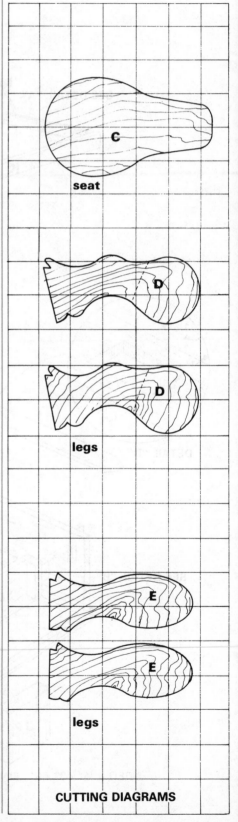

seat

legs

legs

CUTTING DIAGRAMS

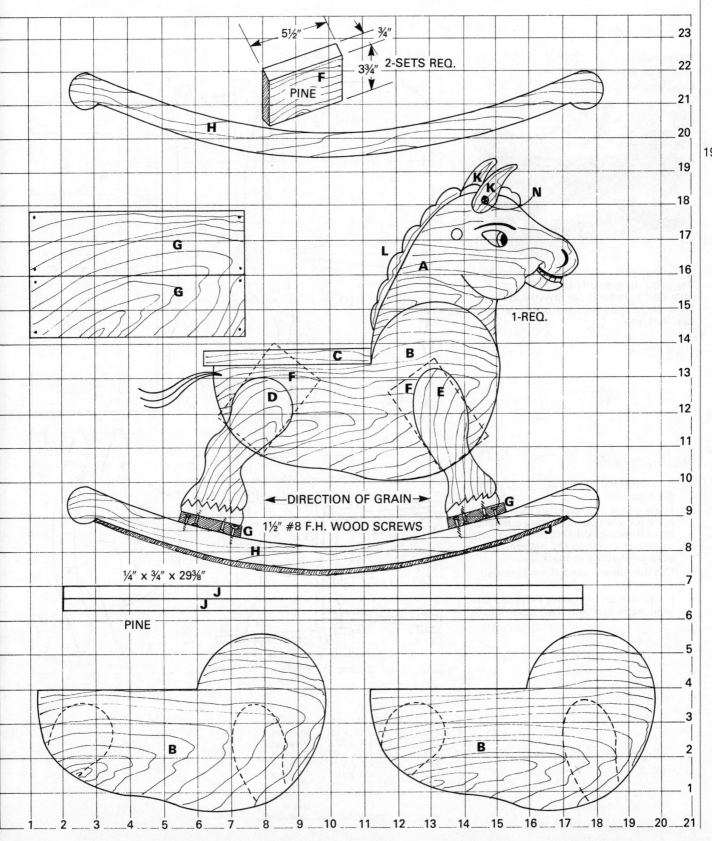

5½"

¾"

2-SETS REQ.

3¾"

F

PINE

H

G

G

K
K
N

L
A

1-REQ.

C
B

F
F
E

D

DIRECTION OF GRAIN

G

G
1½" #8 F.H. WOOD SCREWS

J

H

¼" × ¾" × 29⅜"

J
J

PINE

B

B

1   2   3   4   5   6   7   8   9   10   11   12   13   14   15   16   17   18   19   20   21

23
22
21
20
19
18
17
16
15
14
13
12
11
10
9
8
7
6
5
4
3
2
1

50
doll's cradle

Little mommies just love to rock their Raggedy Anns beddy-bye in this cute little doll's cradle made by you. Build it big enough and they may even want to nap in it, too.

INSTRUCTIONS:

1. You will need a piece of ½" x 30" x 48" plywood.
2. Draw a grid of 2" squares on a piece of heavy kraft paper and lay out parts from drawing. When completed cut them out and then lay patterns on your plywood and mark.
3. Cut the pieces, sand the edges and assemble.
4. If you use an antiquing finish do all your parts first and then assemble.

SCALE: 2″ TO THE SQUARE

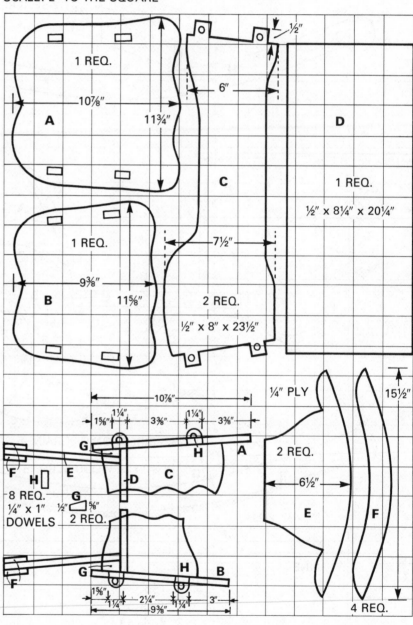

MATERIAL LIST:

A.	1 Pc.	½" x 11" x 12"	Plywood
B.	1 Pc.	½" x 10" x 12"	Plywood
C.	2 Pcs.	½" x 8" x 23½"	Plywood
D.	1 Pc.	½" x 8¼" x 20¼"	Plywood
E.	2 Pcs.	½" x 6½" x 15"	Plywood
F.	4 Pcs.	¼" x 3" x 15"	Plywood
G.	2 Pcs.	¾" x 1" x 8¼"	Pine
H.	8 Pcs.	¼" x 1"	Hardwood dowel
Misc.:		Nails, filler, glue, sandpaper, stain or paint.	

Verify all measurements before cutting

51
go-cart

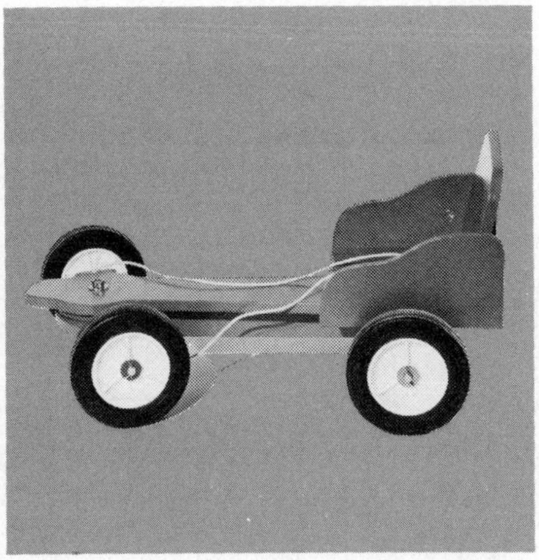

To every dad who's ever been a little boy himself — here's the go-cart dreams are made of. Help your little boy's dreams come true by surprising him with this sleek design built by you.

INSTRUCTIONS:

1. Carefully study drawing and material list, then proceed to cut parts as described and shown.
2. Round off all sharp edges and sandpaper.
3. Cut axles to length and drill holes for cotter pins and for holding screws.
4. Same procedure for swivel pin (J.)
5. Attach axles to cross bars (C) and (E) using clips and screws.
6. Using swivel pin (J), join A-B-C.
7. Attach rear axles to (E) and bolt this assembly to (A).
8. Nail and glue seat parts together and bolt to (A).
9. Using screws and glue attach part (D) to (A).
10. Fill all holes and imperfections and sand smooth.
11. Drill two small holes in cross bar for steering cord.
12. Give coat of shellack and paint to your choice of colours.

Verify all measurements before cutting

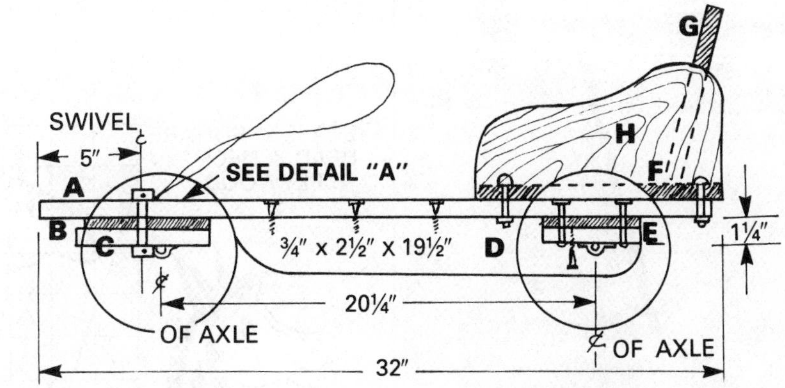

G
H
SWIVEL
5″
SEE DETAIL "A"
A
F
B
C
¾″ x 2½″ x 19½″
D
E
1¼″
20¼″
OF AXLE
OF AXLE
32″

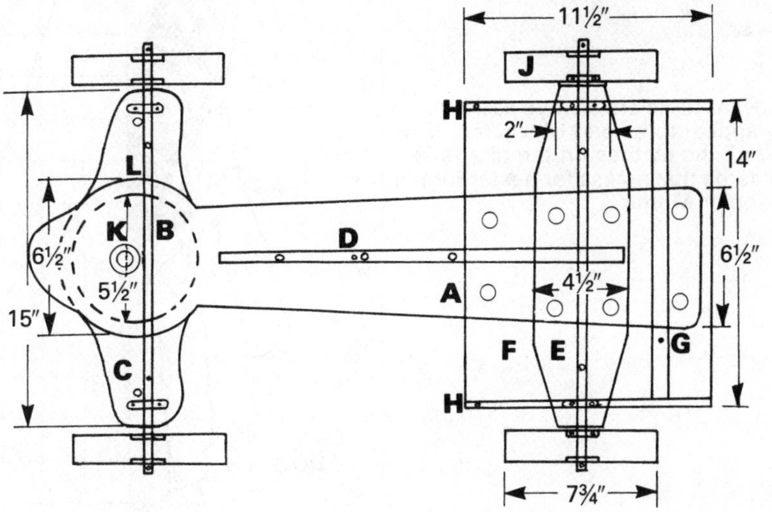

11½″
J
H
2″
14″
L
K
B
D
6½″
6½″
5½″
A
4½″
15″
C
F
E
G
H
7¾″

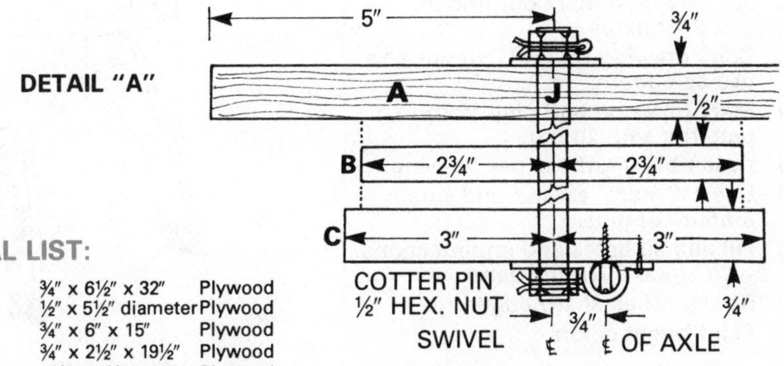

5″
¾″
DETAIL "A"
A
J
½″
B
2¾″
2¾″
C
3″
3″
COTTER PIN
½″ HEX. NUT
¾″
¾″
SWIVEL
OF AXLE

MATERIAL LIST:

A.	1 Pc.	¾″ x 6½″ x 32″	Plywood
B.	1 Pc.	½″ x 5½″ diameter	Plywood
C.	1 Pc.	¾″ x 6″ x 15″	Plywood
D.	1 Pc.	¾″ x 2½″ x 19½″	Plywood
E.	1 Pc.	1¼″ x 4½″ x 15″	Plywood
F.	1 Pc.	¾″ x 11½″ x 13″	Plywood
G.	1 Pc.	¾″ x 9″ x 13″	Plywood
H.	2 Pcs.	½″ x 6″ x 11½″	Plywood
J.	4 Pcs.	8″ dia. wheels	
K.	1 Pc.	½″ x 3¼″ threaded steel rod	
L.	2 Pcs.	½″ x 19″ steel axles	
M.	2 Pcs.	½″ Hex nuts, 10½″ plate washers, 6 cotter pins	
N.	8 Pcs.	¼″ x 1¾″ carriage bolts & nuts & washers	
O.	8 Pcs.	1¼″ — #8 F.H. steel wood screws, 4½″ clips	
	Misc.:	1½″ Finish nails, glue, paint & sashcord.	

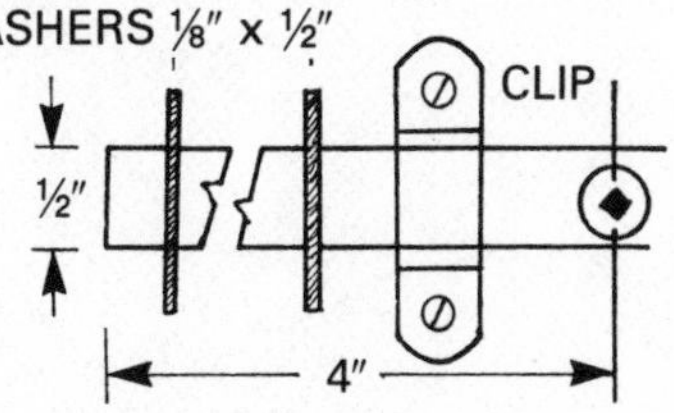

WASHERS ⅛″ x ½″
CLIP
½″
4″

COUNTER SUNK SCREW 1¼″ — #8

52
child's
clothes rack

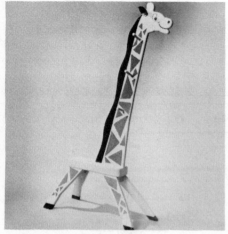

Unpleasant tasks are always easier to do
if they appear to be part of a game. Now
"pinning" the clothes on the giraffe is
a new game that makes for neater rooms
and happier Moms.

INSTRUCTIONS:

(1) Take piece of cardboard or paper
    30" x 42" and mark out grid in
    2" x 2" squares.

(2) Copy drawing on grid, cut out and
    use as pattern.

(3) Mark plywood and pine from
    patterns and cut out.

(4) Assemble giraffe as per drawing.

(5) Use 1½" nails, screws and small
    amount of glue.

(6) Fill all nail holes and imperfections
    with wood filler and sand.

(7) Round off all sharp edges.

(8) Paint bright colors.

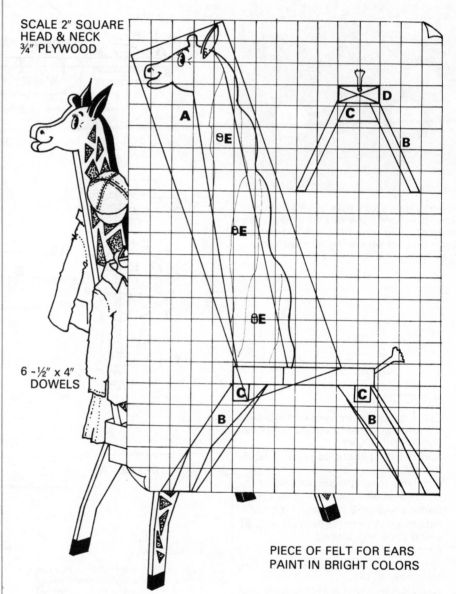

SCALE 2" SQUARE
HEAD & NECK
¾" PLYWOOD

6 - ½" x 4"
DOWELS

PIECE OF FELT FOR EARS
PAINT IN BRIGHT COLORS

MATERIAL LIST:

(A)	1 Pc.	¾" x 10" x 36"	Plywood
(B)	4 Pcs.	¾" x 2¾" x 16"	Pine
(C)	2 Pcs.	1½" x 1½" x 2"	Pine
(D)	1 Pc.	1¾" x 3¾" x 14"	Pine
(E)	6 Pcs.	½" x 4"	Hardwood dowels
(F)	4 Pcs.	2" #8 F.H. Steel wood screws	

1½" Finish nails, glue, paint, wood filler and
small piece of leather or felt for ears.
Rope for tail.

53
stilts

Not much to it. They are so easy and inexpensive to build you could almost make them wholesale. But what priceless fun and excellent exercise for the recipients. So, get started, and share in the fun.

INSTRUCTIONS:

1. When buying lumber for these stilts it is important that it be knot free and straight grained for safety reasons.
2. After cutting for length and width rout off all sharp edges.
3. Drill ¼" holes in lower section of stilts as per drawing to lower or raise foot pieces. Be sure all these holes match.
4. Cut foot pieces and drill ¼" holes to match stilts.
5. Sand and varnish or paint to your choice of colours.

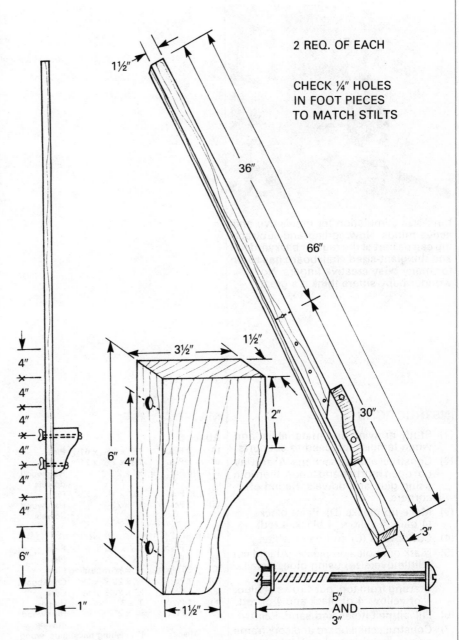

2 REQ. OF EACH

CHECK ¼" HOLES
IN FOOT PIECES
TO MATCH STILTS

1½"

36"

66"

1½"

4"
4"
4"
4"
4"
4"
4"
4"
6"

3½"

1½"

6"

4"

2"

30"

3"

1"

1½"

5"
AND
3"

MATERIAL LIST:

A.	2 Pcs.	1" x 3" x 66"	Pine or Birch.
B.	2 Pcs.	1½" x 3½" x 6"	Pine or Birch.
C.	2 Pcs.	¼" x 5"	Carriage bolts.
D.	2 Pcs.	¼" x 3"	Carriage bolts.
E.	8 Pcs.	⁵⁄₁₆" Flat steel washers.	
F.	8 Pcs.	¼" Steel wing nuts.	

Verify all measurements before cutting

54
abacus
and chalkboard

King-size stimulation for inquisitive and active minds. Now adding and subtracting can be part of the regular backyard fun and the giant-sized chalkboard has room for many busy creative fingers. No wonder baby-sitters think it's great.

INSTRUCTIONS:

(1) Study drawing and material list and when familiar, proceed to cut parts.

(2) Construct abacus sections (A) and lay out open mortise and tenon, then join using glue and dowels. Round off corners.

(3) Make up blocks (D). Paint blocks (4 blue, 4 yellow, 4 black, 4 red).

(4) Cut dowels (C) and paint white.

(5) Mark out holes on pieces (A) and cut a little oversize; using glue, install dowels with 5 blocks on each. Starting from top, put 4 rows of blue, 4 of yellow, 4 of black and 4 of red.

(6) Fill all nail holes and sand. Paint.

(7) Construct chalkboard and cork frame as per drawing and install boards.

(8) Fill, sand and paint.

(9) Join both sections with hinges (F).

MATERIAL LIST:

Abacus:

(A)	2 Pcs.	1½" x 2⅜" x 61½"	Pine
(B)	2 Pcs.	1½" x 2⅜" x 24"	Pine
(C)	16 Pcs.	⅜" x 20¼"	Hardwood dowels
(D)	80 Pcs.	1¼" x 1¾" x 2¾"	Pine
(E)	12 Pcs.	⅜" x 2"	Hardwood dowels

Cork and Chalkboard Section:

(A)	2 Pcs.	1½" x 1¾" x 61½"	Pine
(B)	2 Pcs.	1½" x 1¾" x 24"	Pine
(C)	30 Lin. ft.	⅜" x ⅝" moulding	Pine
(D)	1 Pc.	¼" x 20½" x 58"	Chalkboard
(E)	1 Pc.	½" x 20½" x 58"	Cork
(F)	1 Pr.	3" x 3"	Hinges
(G)	8 Pcs.	⅜" x 2"	Hardwood dowels
Misc.:		1" finishing nails, glue, wood filler, enamel.	

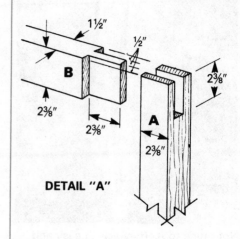

DETAIL "A"

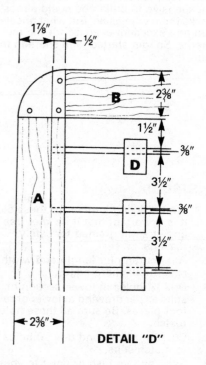

DETAIL "D"

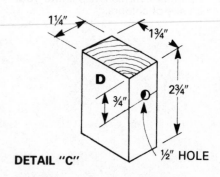

DETAIL "C"

½" HOLE

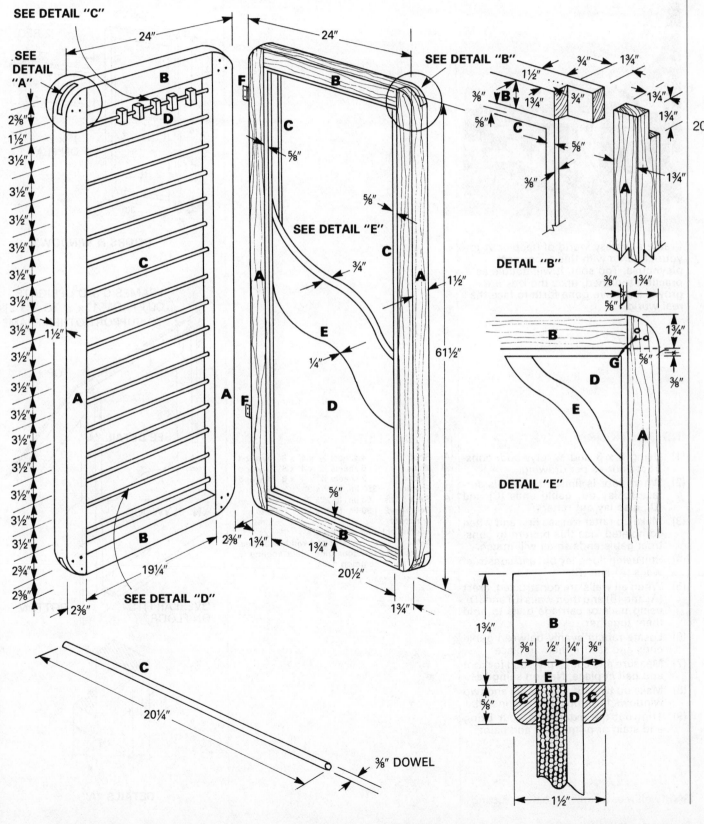

SEE DETAIL "C"

SEE DETAIL "A"

24"

24"

SEE DETAIL "B"

B

2⅜"
1½"
3½"
3½"
3½"
3½"
3½"
3½"
3½"
3½"
3½"
3½"
3½"
3½"
3½"
3½"
3½"
3½"
2¾"
2⅜"

1½"

C

A

B

C

A

F

B

A

SEE DETAIL "E"

⅝"

⅝"

¾"

E

¼"

D

C

E

A

1½"

61½"

⅝"

B

2⅜" 1¾"

1¾"

19¼"

20½"

1¾"

SEE DETAIL "D"

2⅜"

C

20¼"

⅜" DOWEL

205

1½" ¾" 1¾"

⅜" B ⅝" 1¾"
⅝" 1¾" ¾"

C ⅝" 1¾"

⅜" A

DETAIL "B"

⅜" 1¾"
⅝"

B 1¾"

G ⅝"

D ⅜"

E

A

DETAIL "E"

1¾"

B

⅜" ½" ¼" ⅜"

E

⅝" C D G

1½"

55
child's
playhouse

Create a fantasy world of happiness for your children with this super-neat playhouse. Too soon it will double as a practical toolshed, once the kids are grown and have gone forth to face the real world.

INSTRUCTIONS:

(1) Using 2 x 3 and ¾" plywood, construct floor as per drawing.

(2) When floor is finished, use this surface to lay out gable ends (C) and (D), also lay out rafters.

(3) Make up rafter trusses first and when completed, use this pattern to construct gable ends so all will match.

(4) Still using floor, lay out and construct walls (A) and (B).

(5) When all walls are constructed, erect (A) and (B) and then walls (C) and (D), using nails or carriage bolts to hold them together.

(6) Locate rafters evenly between gable ends and secure them in place.

(7) Measure and cut ½" plywood for roof and nail in place. Nail on shingles.

(8) Make up two 15" x 72" doors and two windows to fit opening and install.

(9) Trim out the exterior to your liking and stain or prime coat and paint.

MATERIAL LIST:

(A)	Roof	4 sheets ½" x 4' x 8'	Plywood
(B)	Walls	6 sheets ¼" x 4' x 8'	Plywood
(C)	Floor	2 sheets ¾" x 4' x 8'	Plywood
(D)	Framing	350 lin. ft. 1" x 3"	Pine
(E)	Floor joists	60 lin. ft. 2" x 3"	Pine
(F)	Doors and Windows	30 lin. ft. 1" x 2"	Pine
(G)	Roofing shingles — 1 square		

Misc. — Door and window hinges, hooks and eyes, door knob, glass, roofing nails, paint, common nails.

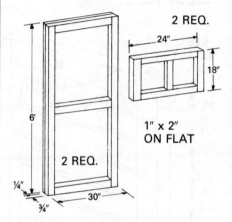

2 REQ.

24"

18"

6'

2 REQ.

1" x 2" ON FLAT

¼"

¾"

30"

DOORS & WINDOWS

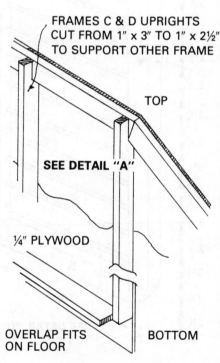

FRAMES C & D UPRIGHTS CUT FROM 1" x 3" TO 1" x 2½" TO SUPPORT OTHER FRAME

TOP

SEE DETAIL "A"

¼" PLYWOOD

OVERLAP FITS ON FLOOR

BOTTOM

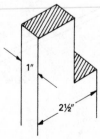

1"

2½"

DETAILS "A"

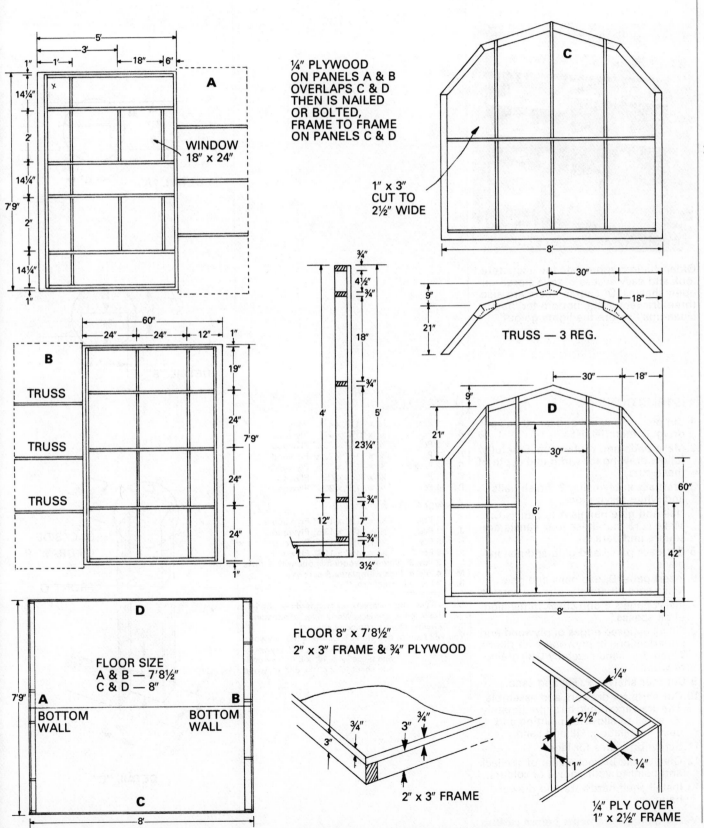

¼" PLYWOOD
ON PANELS A & B
OVERLAPS C & D
THEN IS NAILED
OR BOLTED,
FRAME TO FRAME
ON PANELS C & D

WINDOW
18" x 24"

A

B

TRUSS
TRUSS
TRUSS

C

1" x 3"
CUT TO
2½" WIDE

TRUSS — 3 REG.

D

D

FLOOR SIZE
A & B — 7'8½"
C & D — 8"

A   B
BOTTOM   BOTTOM
WALL   WALL

C

FLOOR 8" x 7'8½"
2" x 3" FRAME & ¾" PLYWOOD

2" x 3" FRAME

¼" PLY COVER
1" x 2½" FRAME

56
toy storage shelves

Older children appreciate the uncluttered look and easy access of toys stored on open shelves. Of course, there are also three drawers at the bottom for "fast clean-ups" before the lights go out.

INSTRUCTIONS:

1. Cut pieces to width and length, as per drwg. & material list.
2. Make dado and rabbet cuts. Carefully follow drawing for width and depth of these cuts.
3. Start assembly using 2" finish nails and white resyn glue.
4. Nail and glue panels A to panels C. Make sure that these four panels are square and parallel.
5. Cut back panel and glue and nail in place.
6. Insert panel D, use nails and glue. Make sure all dimensions are correct.
7. Insert panels E and check dimension of all spaces.
8. Fill all exposed edges of plywood and imperfections in plywood with filler When dry, sand carefully with grain of wood.
9. Cut four shelves P. Fill and sand.
10. Cut parts for drawers and assemble. The drawers should be approximately ⅛" small to allow for painting and easy installation. Fill and sand.
11. Screw on plates for legs.
12. Give whole project a coat of shellack and paint to your choice of colours.
13. Install shelf hardware and drawer handles.

Verify all measurements before cutting

MATERIALS:

A.	2 Pcs.	¾" x 11¾" x 47¾" Plywood
B.	1 Pc.	¾" x 11¾" x 47" Plywood
C.	2 Pcs.	¾" x 11¾" x 35¼" Plywood
D.	1 Pc.	¾" x 11¾" x 22½" Plywood
E.	2 Pcs.	¾" x 11¾" x 12¾" Plywood
F.	1 Pc.	⅛" x 36" x 47¾" Plywood
P.	4 Pcs.	¾" x 11¾" x 22¼" Plywood

Drawer Parts for Three

G.	3 Pcs.	¾" x 11⅞" x 14¾" Plywood
J.	3 Pcs.	¾" x 11⅜" x 13¾" Plywood
H.	6 Pcs.	½" x 11⅞" x 11⅜" Plywood
K.	3 Pcs.	⅛" x 14¼" x 11⅜" Plywood
L.	3 Pcs. 3" diameter wooden knobs with screws
M.	4 Pcs. 4" legs with plates & screws
R.	8 Pcs. adjustable shelf standards 21¾" long — "Roll-it"
S.	16 Pcs. shelf brackets for standards — "Roll-it"

Nails, glue, shellack, Wood filler, sandpaper, enamel to your choice of colours.
You will require one sheet ¾" x 4'0" x 8'0" plywood
one piece ¾" x 12" x 5'0" plywood
one piece ½" x 12" x 6'0" plywood
one sheet ⅛" x 4'0" x 8'0" plywood

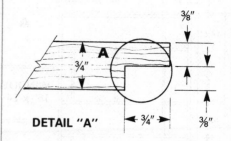

DETAIL "A"

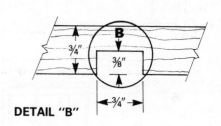

DETAIL "B"

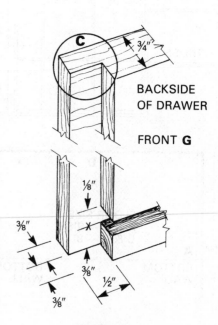

BACKSIDE OF DRAWER

FRONT **G**

DETAIL "C"

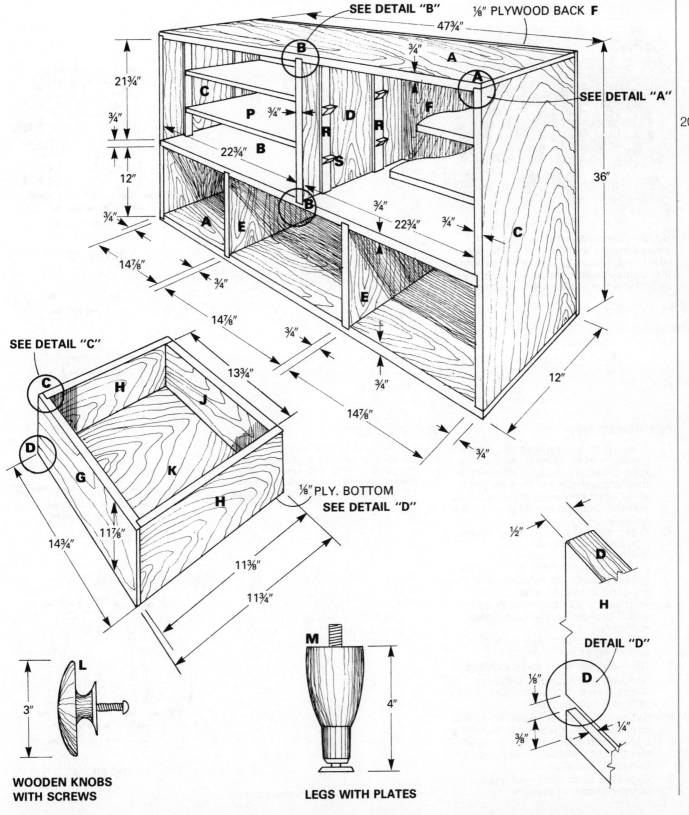

SEE DETAIL "B"

⅛" PLYWOOD BACK F

47¾"

B

¾"

A

21¾"

C

¾"

P   ¾"

D   R   F

R

R

12"

22¾"   B

S

B

¾"

A   E

22¾"   ¾"

¾"

14⅞"

¾"

E

C

36"

14⅞"

¾"

13¾"

¾"

SEE DETAIL "C"

C   H   J

14⅞"

¾"

SEE DETAIL "A"

209

12"

D   G   K

H

⅛" PLY. BOTTOM
SEE DETAIL "D"

11⅞"

14¾"

11⅜"

11¾"

½"

D

H

DETAIL "D"

L

3"

M

4"

⅛"

D

¼"

⅜"

**WOODEN KNOBS
WITH SCREWS**

LEGS WITH PLATES

57
table and chairs

Building fantasy-world furniture for playful minds is great practice for the real thing. Makes your kids happy while it enables you to hone your carpentry skills for more ambitious tasks later on.

INSTRUCTIONS:

1. It would be ideal if first you made a pattern of all parts on some heavy kraft paper or similar material and then place these patterns on your sheet of ½" plywood, which will give you the most economic use of your material.
2. When you have your layout made, proceed to cut parts.
3. Start assembly by nailing and gluing parts B & D together, remembering to keep the better side of the plywood to the outside.
4. Join legs to each other with parts A & C using glue and corrugated fasteners.
5. Attach pieces of pine E with glue and nails, as per drawing.
6. Glue and nail table top L in place.
7. Nail and glue together parts for chairs, being careful to give support to legs when nailing.
8. Set all nails and fill all nail holes and imperfections in plywood, including edges, with a wood filler. Sand all sharp edges so that there is no danger of splinters.
9. Give coat of shellack and paint to your choice of colours.

MATERIAL LIST:
(For one table and four chairs)
1. One sheet ½" x 4'0" x 8'0" plywood
2. Two pieces ¾" x 2¾" x 13" pine
3. Shellack, paint, glue, woodfiller, sandpaper, 1½" + 1" finish nails, ¼" corrugated fasteners.

Verify all measurements before cutting

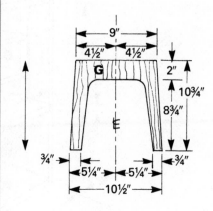

DETAIL "G"

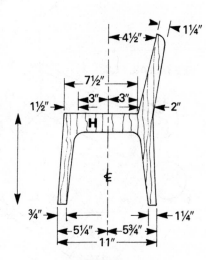

DETAIL "H"

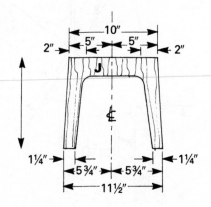

DETAIL "J"

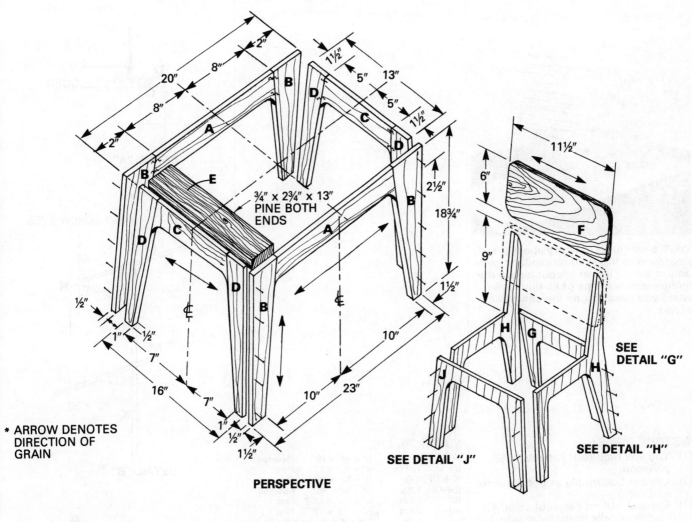

20″
8″
2″
8″
2″
A
B
B
A
E
¾″ × 2¾″ × 13″
PINE BOTH
ENDS
C
D
D
C
D
B
1½″
5″
13″
5″
1½″
C
D
D
B
A
2½″
18¾″
1½″
½″
1″
½″
7″
16″
7″
1″
½″
1½″
10″
10″
23″

* ARROW DENOTES
DIRECTION OF
GRAIN

PERSPECTIVE

11½″
6″
9″
F
H
G
H
J
SEE
DETAIL "G"
SEE DETAIL "J"
SEE DETAIL "H"

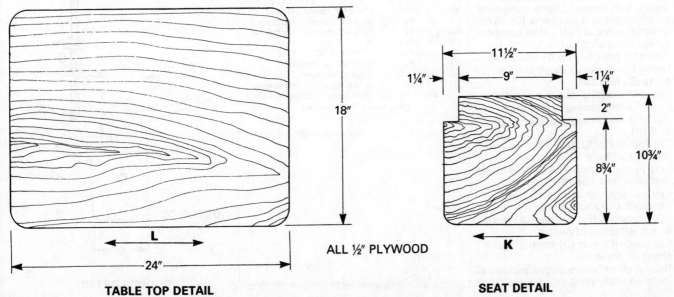

18″

L

24″

TABLE TOP DETAIL

ALL ½″ PLYWOOD

1¼″
9″
1¼″
2″
10¾″
8¾″

K

SEAT DETAIL

58
sailboat sandbox

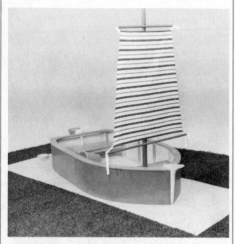

You'll never need to worry about stormy weather with this sailboat sandbox as the only storms it'll ever encounter are the enthusiastic screams of its tiny crew when you pass around the candy life-savers.

INSTRUCTIONS:

(1) You will require 1½ sheets of ½" plywood.
(2) Lay out bottom (A) as per drawing and cut.
(3) Cut and nail on parts (B) using 1½" common nails from under side.
(4) Using boat bottom, trace curvature on plywood and cut parts (C). When outside curve is cut, using compass, scribe the inside curve 1½" wide. Nail and glue on top of uprights (B).
(5) Using the guide as illustrated, scribe parts (D) and cut.
(6) Cut and install sides of boat (O). Use 1" common nails and glue.
(7) Cut and install seat supports (G) and (H).
(8) Cut the seats (E) and (F) to fit and install. Cut hole for mast.
(9) Line up mast socket (J) to hole in seat and glue, and nail in place.
(10) Lay out and cut rudder (Q) and bowsprit (N) and install.
(11) Cut parts (E), (F), (Q) and (A) from 4' x 8' sheet of plywood.
(12) Cut parts (C) and (D) from 2' x 8' sheet of plywood.
(13) Round off all sharp edges and set all nails and fill; sand all imperfections.

MATERIAL LIST:

(A)	1 Pc.	½" x 36" x 72"	Plywood
(B)	17 Pcs.	¾" x 1½" x 1"	Pine
(C & D)	1 Pc.	½" x 24" x 96"	Plywood
(E-F-Q)	1 Pc.	½" x 12" x 96"	Plywood
(G)	2 Pcs.	¾" x 1½" x 12½"	Pine
(H)	2 Pcs.	¾" x 1½" x 13"	Pine
(J)	1 Pc.	1½" x 4" x 4" with 1¾" hole Pine
(K)	1 Pc.	1¾" x 60" dowel	Pine
(L)	1 Pc.	¾" x 24" dowel	Hardwood
(M)	1 Pc.	¾" x 36" dowel	Hardwood
(N)	2 Pcs.	¾" x 1½" x 8"	Pine
(O)	5 Pcs.	¼" x 11" x 48"	Pine
(P)	1 Pc.	36" x 36" sail material	
(R)	12 Pcs.	#B-8 screw eyes	
(S)	1 Pc.	¼" x 8" dowel	Hardwood

Misc.: 1½" common nails, 1" common nails, glue, wood filler, shellac.

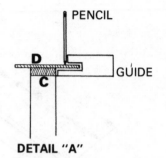

PENCIL

D

GUIDE

C

DETAIL "A"

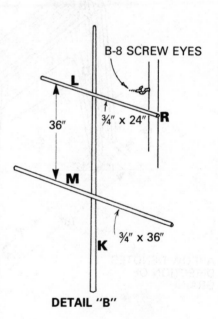

B-8 SCREW EYES

L

36"

¾" x 24"

R

M

¾" x 36"

K

DETAIL "B"

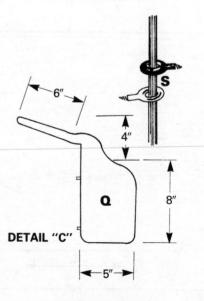

S

6"

4"

Q

8"

DETAIL "C"

5"

RUDDER DETAIL

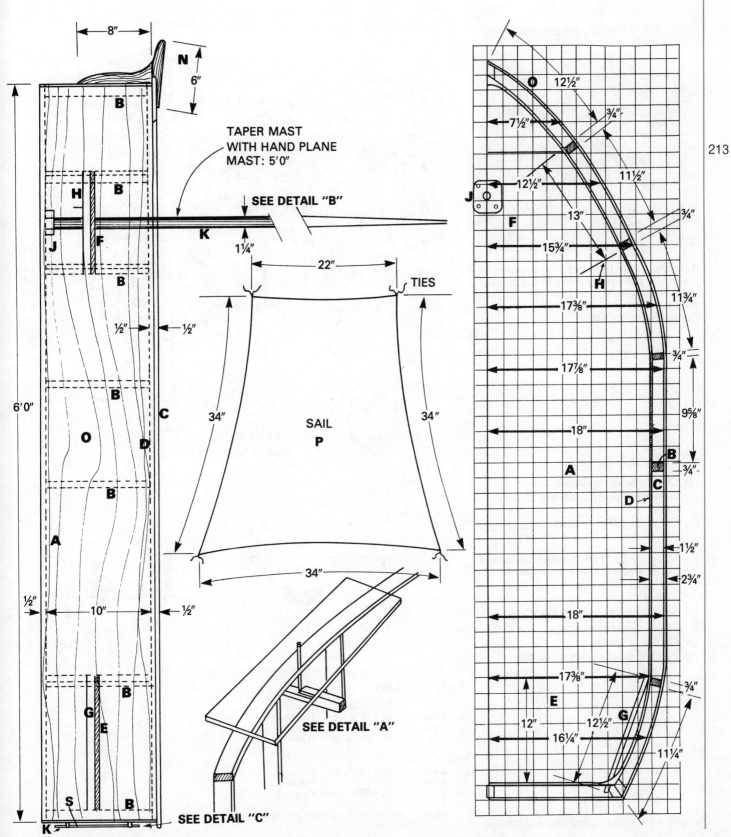

8"

N

6"

TAPER MAST
WITH HAND PLANE
MAST: 5'0"

SEE DETAIL "B"

B

B

H

B

K

J

F

1¼"

22"

TIES

½" ½"

34"

34"

C

O

D

SAIL

P

A

½"

10"

½"

34"

B

SEE DETAIL "A"

G

E

B

SEE DETAIL "C"

S

K

6'0"

12½"

O

¾"

7½"

12½"

11½"

J

¾"

F

13"

H

15¾"

11¾"

17⅜"

17⅞"

¾"

9⅝"

18"

B

A

¾"

C

D

1½"

2¾"

18"

17⅜"

E

G

¾"

12"

12½"

16¼"

11¼"

59
toy storage bins

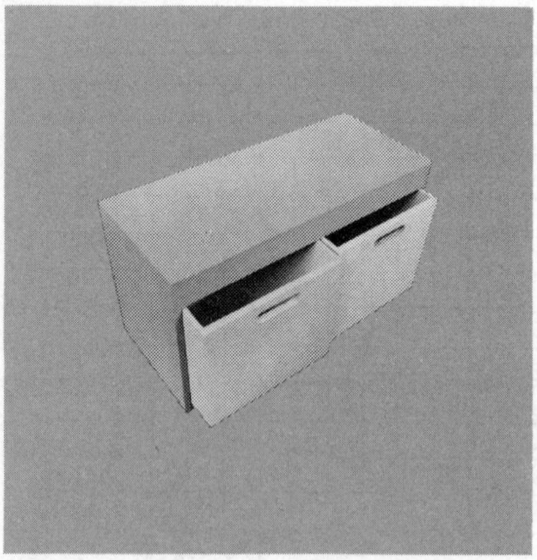

Build the basic box with two drawers in it and you have two attractive toy storage bins. Mount the box on casters, and it can be pushed to where the action is by even the tiniest youngster.

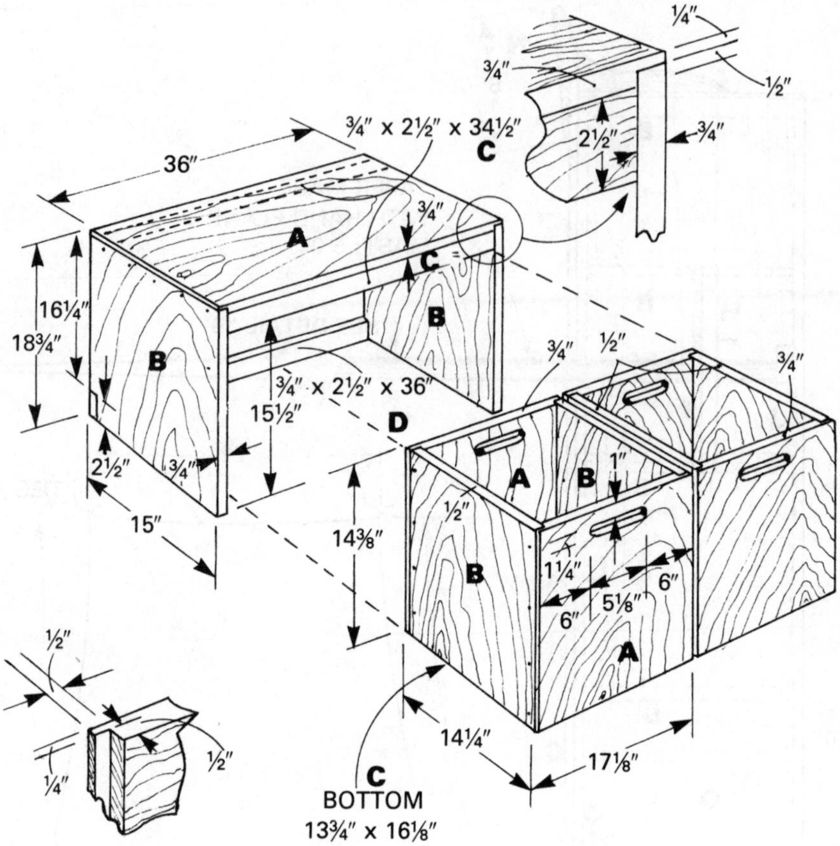

¼″
¾″
½″
¾″ x 2½″ x 34½″
C
2½″
¾″
36″
A
¾″
C
16¼″
18¾″
B
B
¾″ x 2½″ x 36″
15½″
D
2½″
¾″
15″
¾″
½″
¾″
A
B
1″
½″
14⅜″
B
1¼″
6″
5⅛″
6″
A
½″
½″
¼″
14¼″
17⅛″
C
BOTTOM
13¾″ x 16⅛″

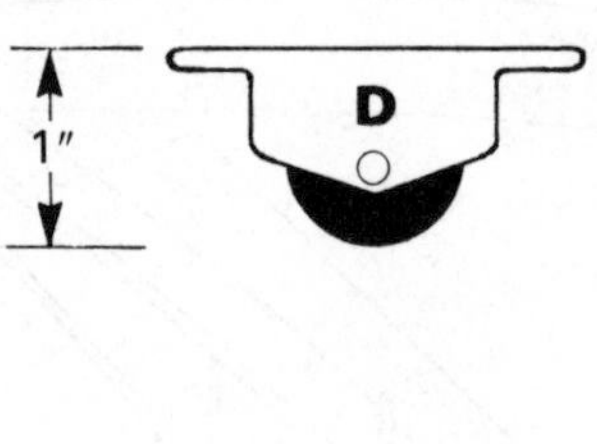

1″
D

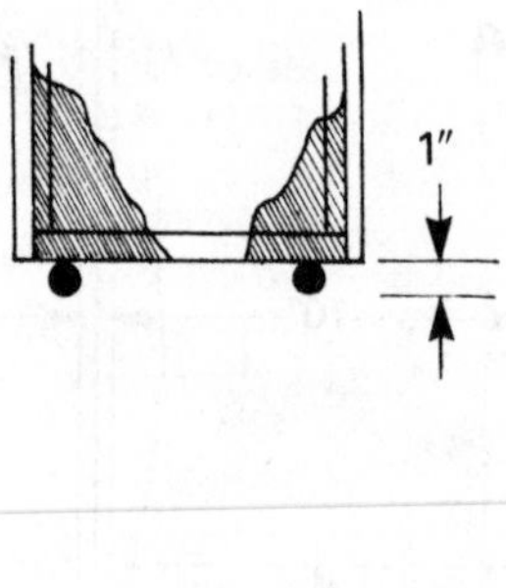

1″

INSTRUCTIONS:

(1) Cut parts for cabinets.
(2) Assemble using glue and 2″ finish nails.
(3) Set nails, fill and sand.

Bins:

(1) Make up parts for drawer fronts and backs and cut check on bottoms.
(2) Cut sides, assemble using 1½″ finish nails and glue.
(3) Set and fill nail holes. Sand.
(4) Install casters.
(5) Cut hand holes.
(6) Paint to your choice of colors.

MATERIAL LIST:

(A)	1 Pc.	¾″ x 15″ x 36″	Plywood
(B)	2 Pcs.	¾″ x 15″ x 18½″	Plywood
(C)	2 Pcs.	¾″ x 2½″ x 34½″	Plywood
(D)	1 Pc.	¾″ x 2½″ x 36″	Plywood

Bins:

(A)	4 Pcs.	¾″ x 14⅜″ x 17⅛″	Plywood
(B)	4 Pcs.	½″ x 14¼″ x 14⅜″	Plywood
(C)	2 Pcs.	½″ x 13¾″ x 14⅜″	Plywood
(D)	8	1″ high casters	

Misc.: 2″ and 1½″ finishing nails, glue, wood filler, paint.

Verify all measurements before cutting

60
rocking chicken

If your child is afraid of rocking horses — how about letting him have fun with this rocking chicken? If you follow the plan carefully, you can put it together quickly some rain-soaked Sunday afternoon.

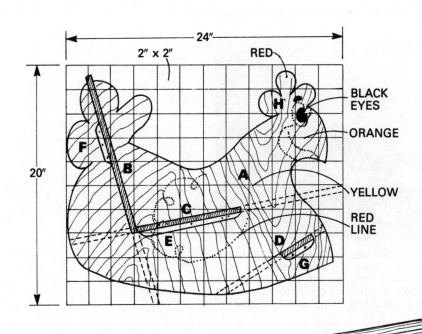

INSTRUCTIONS:

(1) You will require one piece of ½" plywood 39" x 42".

(2) I suggest that you use a piece of cardboard or heavy paper to make a pattern.

(3) Draw a series of two-inch squares and number them and copy drawing.

(4) When completed, cut out pattern and trace onto plywood, then cut.

(5) Slightly round off all plywood edges, then assemble, using nails or screws.

(6) Fill all edges of plywood with wood filler. Sand.

(7) Set and fill all nail holes, then sand.

(8) Give a primer coat of paint and when dry, sand lightly.

(9) Finish off by painting with a non-toxic paint.

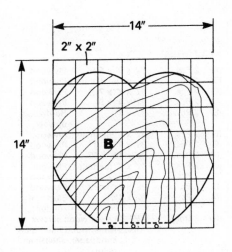

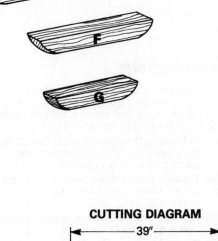

MATERIAL LIST:

(A)	2 Pcs.	½" x 20" x 24"	Plywood
(B)	1 Pc.	½" x 14" x 14"	Plywood
(C)	1 Pc.	½" x 9" x 14"	Plywood
(D)	1 Pc.	½" x 3" x 14"	Plywood
(E)	2 Pcs.	¾" x ¾" x 9"	Pine
(F)	2 Pcs.	¾" x ¾" x 4"	Pine
(G)	2 Pcs.	¾" x ¾" x 3"	Pine
(H)	1 Pc.	¾" dia. x 15"	Hardwood dowel

Misc.: (¾" No. 6 flat head wood screws, optional), nails, glue, wood filler, sandpaper and paint.

CUTTING DIAGRAM

61
see-saw

If you don't like rusty, store-bought see-saws, then you'll want to build this extra solid kid's delight. It is safe, stable and lots of fun. But be sure to super-sand it to protect tiny hands and bottoms.

INSTRUCTIONS:

(1) You will require one full sheet of ¾" plywood and about a square foot of ¼" plywood and some odds and ends as indicated in the material list.

(2) Following the drawing and list, carefully lay out on your plywood the parts to be cut and proceed.

(3) When all parts have been cut, round off all sharp edges with router or plane and sandpaper.

(4) Assemble the See-Saw structure first using glue, nails and screws.

(5) Assemble base structure in the same fashion.

(6) Fill all nail holes and imperfections and sand smooth.

(7) Give a coat of shellac to seal project and paint with a good exterior enamel.

(8) When all is dry, insert See-Saw assembly between H uprights and insert aluminum pipe M. Nail or screw on ¼" retainers J.

MATERIAL LIST:

(A)	2 Pcs.	¾" x 9" x 5'8"	Plywood
(B)	1 Pc.	¾" x 7½" diameter	Plywood
(C)	2 Pcs.	¾" x 2" x 7½"	Plywood
(D)	2 Pcs.	¾" x 4" x 9"	Plywood
(E)	2 Pcs.	¾" x 7"	Hardwood dowels
(F)	2 Pcs.	¼" x 6" diameter	Plywood
(G)	2 Pcs.	¾" x 8" x 10"	Plywood
(H)	2 Pcs.	¾" x 18" x 20"	Plywood
(J)	2 Pcs.	¼" x 2" diameter	Plywood
(K)	2 Pcs.	¾" x 6" x 20"	Plywood
(L)	1 Pc.	¾" x 22" x 22"	Plywood
(M)	1 Pc.	¾" x 4¼"	Electrical conduit
(N)	3 Doz.	1½" #8 steel wood screws	

Misc.: Nails, wood filler, glue, sandpaper, shellac and paint.

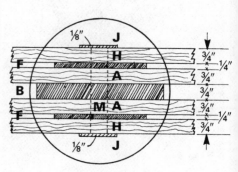

DETAIL "A"

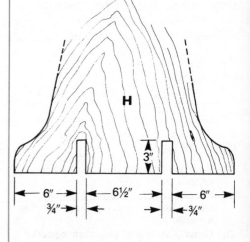

DETAIL "H"

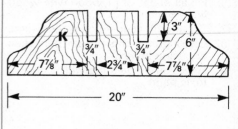

DETAIL "K"

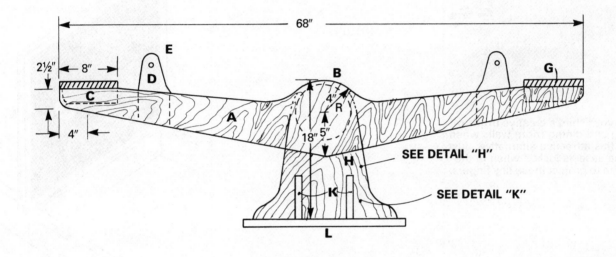

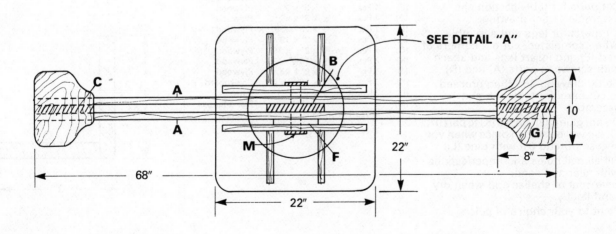

62
child's table
and easel

You'll get your child's creative urges off your living and dining room walls when you build this attractive alternative. Just be sure the easel is locked when in the 'up' position to protect those tiny fingers.

¼" x 15½" x 25"
CHALKBOARD

K   L

CHALK BOARD

INSTRUCTIONS:

(1) Study drawing and material list.
(2) Cut parts for table section and assemble as per drawing.
(3) Cut parts for legs and assemble. When completed, cut out corners of part (E) and insert legs and attach with screws to parts (A) and (D).
(4) Study drawing and then proceed to cut parts for table top and assemble.
(5) Do not glue chalkboard (K) to part (H). These will be held in place when you encase (K) and (H) with pine (L).
(6) Fill all nail holes and imperfections with filler and sand.
(7) Give coat of shellac and when dry sand lightly.
(8) Paint to your choice of colors.

MATERIAL LIST:

(A)	2 Pcs.	½" x 3" x 39"	Plywood
(B)	3 Pcs.	½" x 3" x 24"	Plywood
(C)	4 Pcs.	½" x 3" x 9"	Plywood
(D)	4 Pcs.	½" x 3" x 4"	Plywood
(E)	1 Pc.	¼" x 25" x 39"	Plywood
(F)	4 Pcs.	½" x 3" x 19"	Plywood
(G)	4 Pcs.	½" x 2½" x 19"	Plywood
(H)	2 Pcs.	½" x 15½" x 25"	Plywood
(J)	1 Pc.	½" x 6" x 25"	Plywood
(K)	2 Pcs.	¼" x 15½" x 25"	Chalkboard
(L)	12 Lin. ft.	¾" x 1"	Pine
(M)	2	1½" x 25"	Piano hinges

Misc.: Finish nails, screws, woodfiller, sandpaper, shellac, paint.

3"   F

G

3"

DETAIL "A"

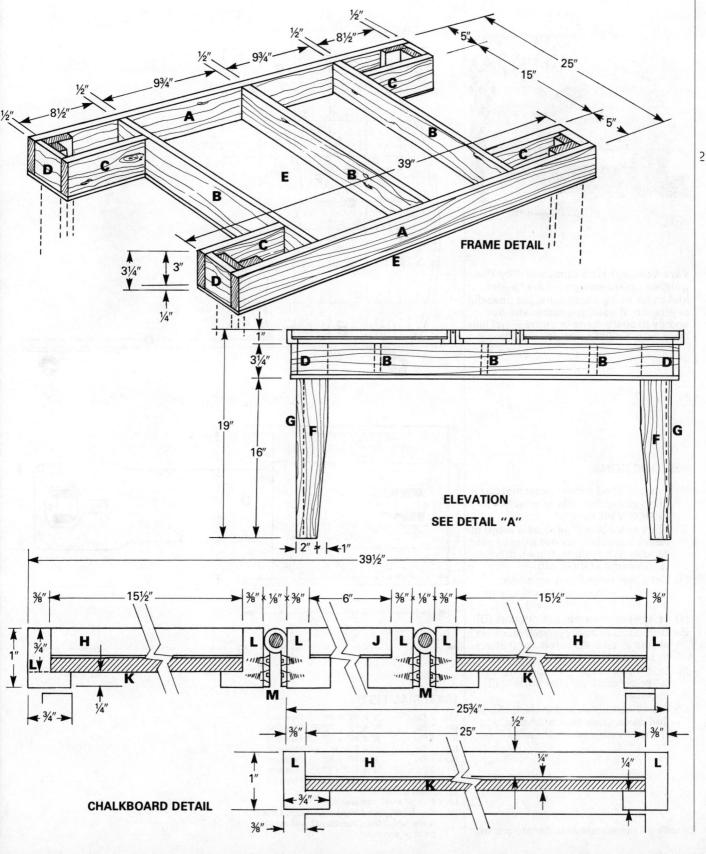

FRAME DETAIL

ELEVATION

SEE DETAIL "A"

CHALKBOARD DETAIL

63
child's scooter

Vava-Vrooom! Here comes the toy that gobbles up kid-energy by the tankful. Makes for noisy afternoons, but peaceful nights. So, if your youngster still has energy to spare come bedtime — get him busy with a child's scooter right away.

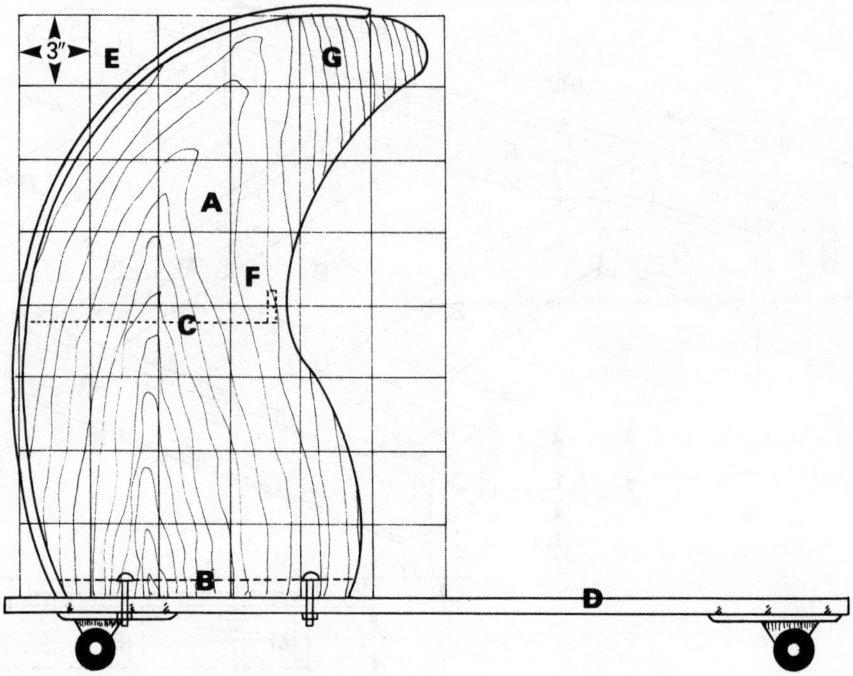

INSTRUCTIONS:

(1) You will need a roller skate that has a pivot above the axle to enable you to steer your scooter.

(2) Mark out a 3″ x 3″ grid on a piece of heavy paper and lay out sides of your scooter. When done, trace pattern on ½″ plywood and cut out.

(3) Cut other pieces and assemble. Apply ⅛″ plywood last, using white glue and 1″ common nails.

(4) Following drawing, cut out part (D).

(5) Drill holes in appropriate places on skates to take #8 screws and attach to board (D).

(6) Drill holes in (D) + (B) and, using ¼″ bolts, securely attach (D) + (B) together.

(7) Fill all nail holes and imperfections and sand. Give coat of shellac and paint to your choice of colors.

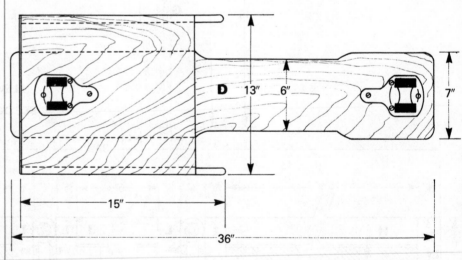

MATERIAL LIST:

(A)	2 Pcs.	½″ x 18″ x 24″	Plywood
(B)	1 Pc.	¾″ x 13″ x 13½″	Plywood
(C)	1 Pc.	¾″ x 13″ x 13″	Plywood
(D)	1 Pc.	¾″ x 7″ x 36″	Plywood
(E)	1 Pc.	⅛″ x 14″ x 36″	Plywood
(F)	1 Pc.	¼″ x 1¼″ x 13″	Plywood
(G)	1 Pc.	¾″ x 2¾″ x 13″	Plywood
(H)	Roller skate		
(J)	4 — ¼″ x 1¾″ carriage bolts.		

8 — ¾″ #8 round head steel wood screws
Nails, wood filler, sandpaper and exterior paint or enamel.

Verify all measurements before cutting

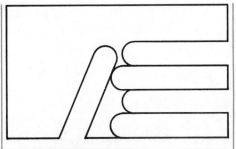

7
Bookcases
storages
dividers

64
child's wardrobe

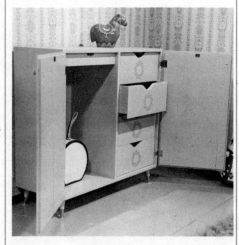

Kids always seem to have more toys and clothes than space to store them. If you have this familiar problem, then invest a few Saturday afternoons to correct the situation with this handsome child's wardrobe. Mom will love you for it.

INSTRUCTIONS:

(1) You will require one piece ¾" x 4' x 8', one (1) piece ½" x 36" x 40", one (1) piece ¼" x 30" x 36" and one (1) piece ⅛" x 30" x 36" plywood.

(2) Study drawing and material list and then proceed to cut parts for wardrobe.

(3) Assemble wardrobe as per drawing.

(4) Install pieces (G) and (F) to support drawers.

(5) Cut and install facings (E). Sand flush.

(6) Make doors and hang. Install hardware.

(7) Make up parts for drawers. Assemble and fit for easy sliding.

(8) Set and fill all nail holes and sand.

(9) Install legs.

(10) Give prime coat and two (2) coats finish paint. Add decals.

MATERIAL LIST:

(A)	1 Pc.	¾" x 14" x 36"	Plywood
(B)	1 Pc.	¾" x 14" x 34½"	Plywood
(C)	2 Pcs.	¾" x 14" x 29¾"	Plywood
(D)	1 Pc.	¾" x 14" x 28¾"	Plywood
(E)	12 Lin. ft.	¾" x ¾"	Pine
(F)	8 Pcs.	¾" x ¾" x 12½"	Pine
(G)	4 Pcs.	¾" x ¾" x 16⅞"	Pine
(H)	2 Pcs.	¾" x 2½" x 16⅞"	Pine
(J)	1 Pc.	½" dia. x 12½"	Hardwood dowel
(K)	1 Pc.	¼" x 30" x 36"	Plywood
(L)	2 Pcs.	¾" x 17½" x 29⅛"	Plywood
(M)	Misc.:	4" legs, 2 pairs Amerock No. t-1700 hinges, 2 magnetic catches, 2 door pulls, decals, wood filler, sandpaper and paint.	

Drawer:

(A)	4 Pcs.	¾" x 7⅛" x 16¾"	Plywood
(B)	8 Pcs.	½" x 6⅜" x 13¼"	Plywood
(C)	4 Pcs.	½" x 6⅜" x 15¾"	Plywood
(D)	4 Pcs.	⅛" x 13¼" x 16¼"	Plywood

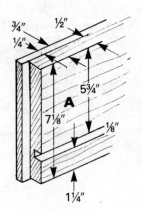

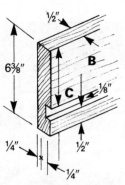

DRAWER DETAIL

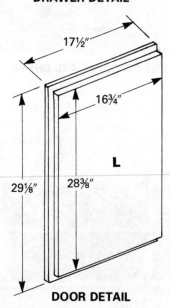

DOOR DETAIL

Verify all measurements before cutting

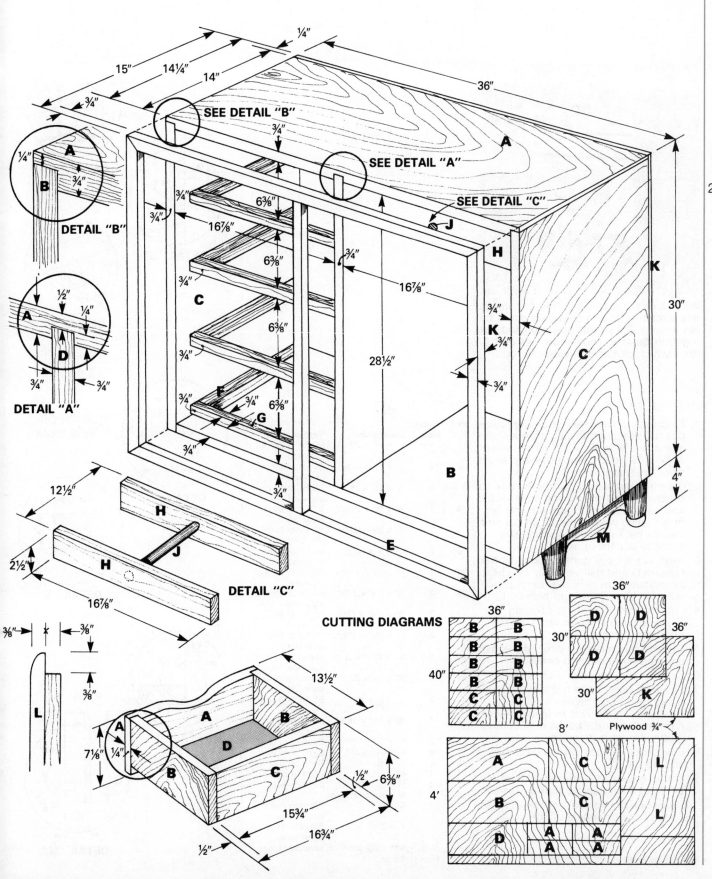

DETAIL "B"

DETAIL "A"

SEE DETAIL "B"

SEE DETAIL "A"

SEE DETAIL "C"

DETAIL "C"

CUTTING DIAGRAMS

65
child's cupboard chest

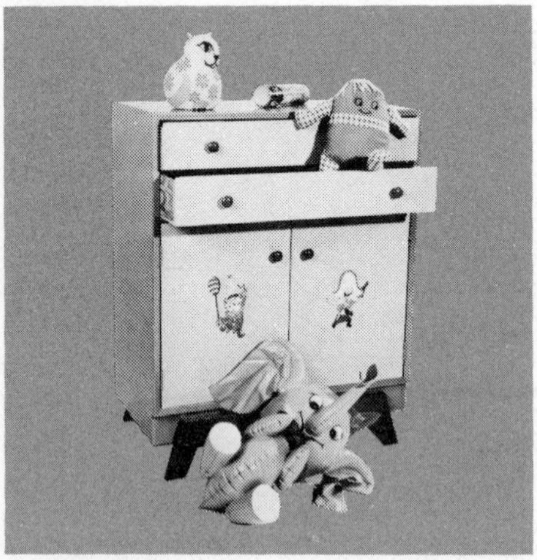

When kids are messy and hate to pick up, this attractive child's cupboard could be the answer. It's simple in design and put together quickly. Thrives on toys and dolls which clutter up living rooms.

INSTRUCTIONS

1. To construct this chest you will require one full sheet of half inch plywood and one piece ½" x 30" x 36" plus a piece of ¾" x 15" x 36", plus other materials as per material list.
2. Carefully cut pieces numbered one to seven as per drawing and material list and nail and glue together using ½" finish nails, when assembled,cut and nail on back panel #14, using this panel to square up work.
3. Next, cut ¾" x ¾" pine or birch as per blowup D and nail and glue on chest as indicated on drawing, same procedure for ½" x ½" strip in blowup C.
4. Cut and install doors to fit using 1" x 2" brass hinges; when fitted, install magnetic catches.
5. Cut and assemble leg structure as per drawing and attach to chest.
6. Cut parts for drawers and assemble.
7. When all parts have been assembled make sure that drawers and doors move easily. Be sure to install pieces numbered 8 and 9 as these will act as guides for your drawers.
8. Buy knobs of your choice for drawers and doors.
9. Set all nails and using wood filler, fill all holes and imperfections and sand.
10. Give one or two coats of shellack and paint to your choice of colours.

Verify all measurements before cutting

MATERIAL LIST:

Part No.	Pieces Req.	Dimensions	Type of Wood
1	1	½" x 15" x 30"	BC Fir or Birch plywood
2	2	½" x 15" x 32⅞"	BC Fir or Birch plywood
3 & 4	3	½" x 15" x 29"	BC Fir or Birch plywood
5	1	½" x 15" x 22¼"	BC Fir or Birch plywood
6	1	½" x 3½" x 29"	BC Fir or Birch plywood
7	2	½" x 9" x 14¼"	BC Fir or Birch plywood
21	2	½" x 14¼" x 18¾"	BC Fir or Birch plywood
16	2	½" x 4½" x 28⅜"	BC Fir or Birch plywood
17	2	½ x 3⅝" x 27⅜"	BC Fir or Birch plywood
18	4	½" x 3⅝" x 15⅜"	BC Fir or Birch plywood
19	2	⅛" x 15¼" x 28⅜"	Masonite or plywood
14	1	⅛" x 30" x 33"	Masonite or plywood
12	2	¾" x 5" x 28"	BC Fir or Birch plywood
13	2	¾" x 1¾" x 15⅛"	BC Fir or Birch plywood
8	2	¾" x ¾" x 15"	Birch or pine
9	4	5⁄16" x ¾" x 15"	Birch or pine
10	4	¾" x ¾" x 48"	Birch or pine
11	1	½" x ½" x 48"	Birch or pine
20	4	¼" x ¾" x 15⅜"	Birch or pine
15	2	Magnetic catches	
22	4	Knobs	Wood or metal of your choice
23	4	1" x 2"	Brass butts + ¾" screws

Nails, white glue, shellack, sandpaper, wood filler and paint

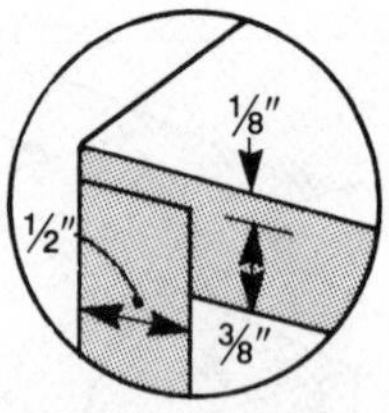
⅛"
½"
⅜"

DETAIL "A"

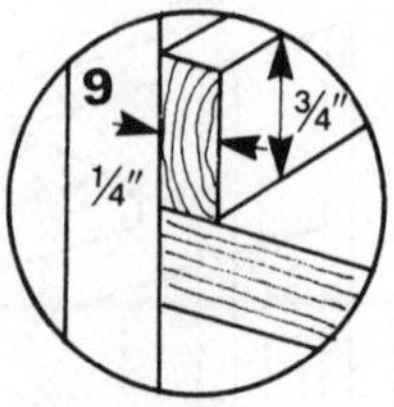
9
¾"
¼"

DETAIL "B"

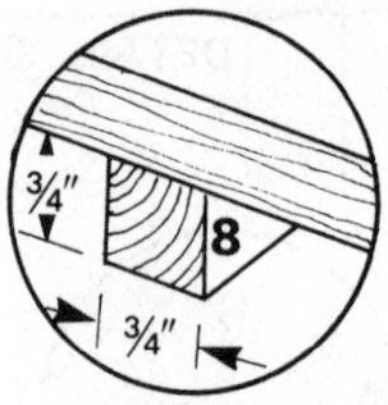
¾"
8
¾"

DETAIL "C"

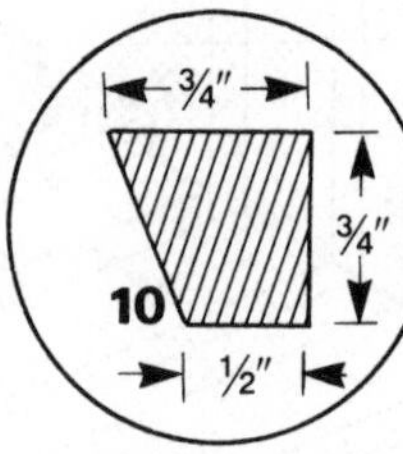
¾"
¾"
10
½"

DETAIL "D"

BIRCH OR PINE TRIM

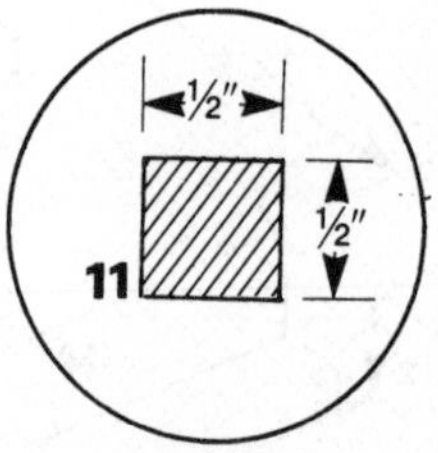
½"
½"
11

DETAIL "E"

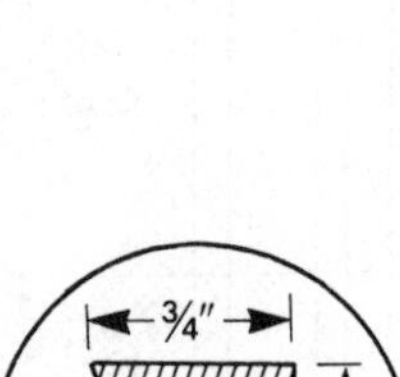
18
½"
F
⅜"
16
⅛"

DETAIL "F"

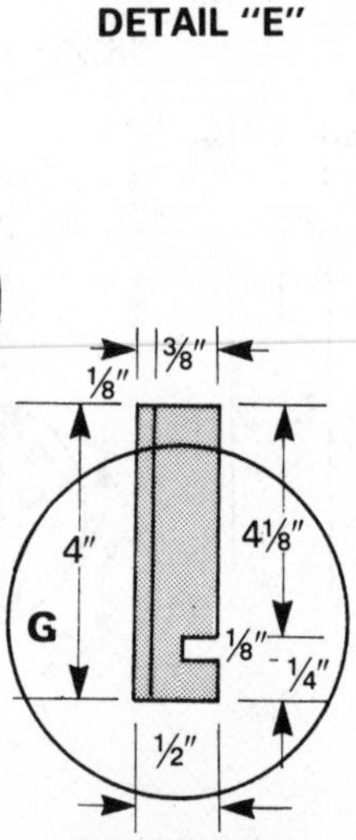
⅜"
⅛"
4"
4⅛"
G
⅛"
¼"
½"

DETAIL "G"

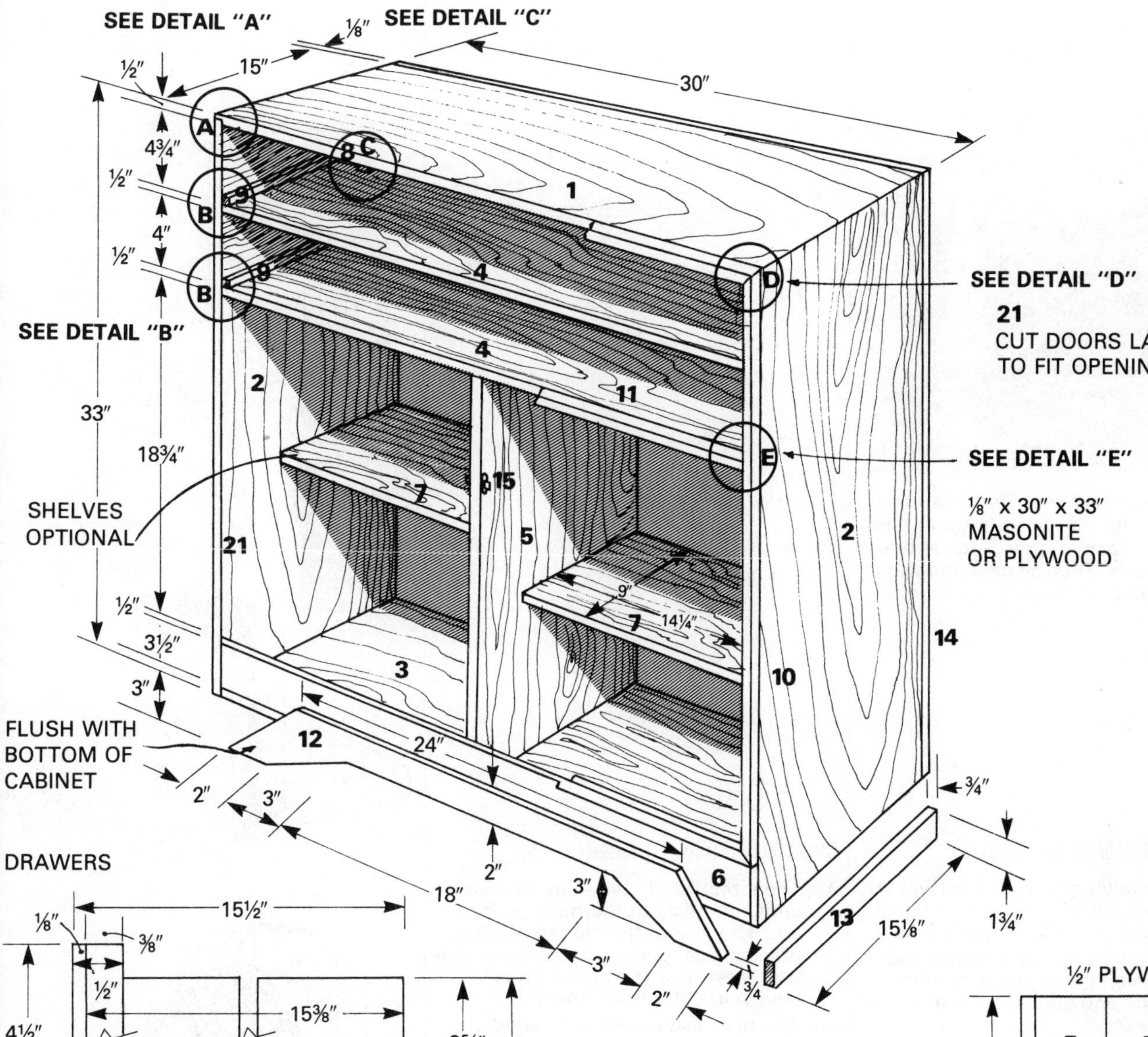
SEE DETAIL "A"
1/8"
SEE DETAIL "C"
1/2"
15"
30"
A
4 3/4"
C
8
1/2"
9
B
1
4"
1/2"
9
B
4
SEE DETAIL "D"
21
CUT DOORS LAST
TO FIT OPENING
SEE DETAIL "B"
4
2
11
33"
18 3/4"
SEE DETAIL "E"
E
SHELVES
OPTIONAL
7
15
1/8" x 30" x 33"
MASONITE
OR PLYWOOD
21
5
2
9"
1/2"
7
14 1/4"
14
3 1/2"
3
10
3"
FLUSH WITH
BOTTOM OF
CABINET
12
24"
3/4"
2"
3"
2"
18"
6
3"
13
1 3/4"
15 1/8"
3"
2"
3/4"

DRAWERS

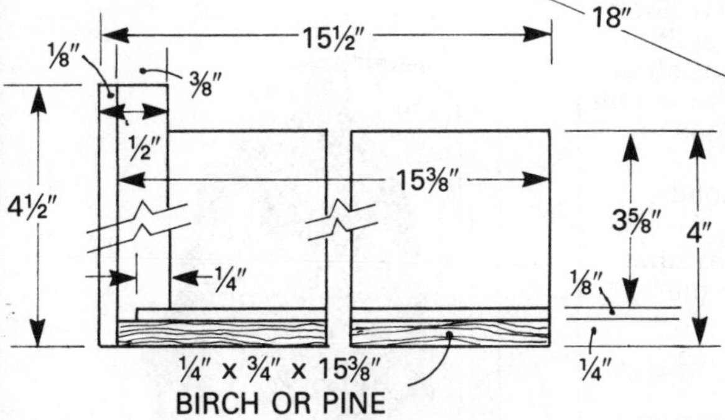
15 1/2"
1/8"
3/8"
1/2"
4 1/2"
15 3/8"
3 5/8"
4"
1/4"
1/8"
1/4" x 3/4" x 15 3/8"
BIRCH OR PINE
1/4"

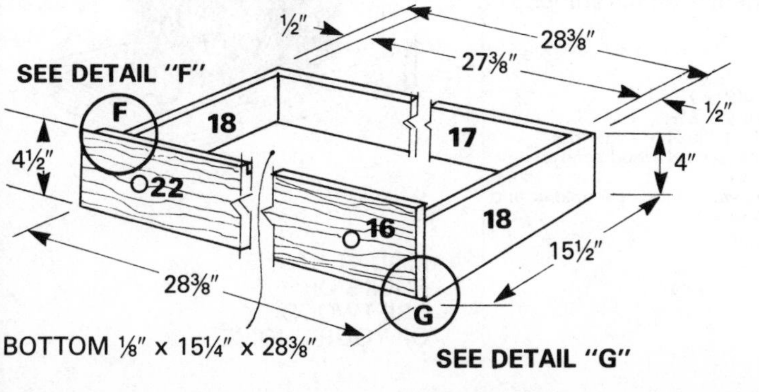
1/2"
28 3/8"
27 3/8"
SEE DETAIL "F"
F
18
17
1/2"
4 1/2"
4"
22
18
16
15 1/2"
28 3/8"
G
BOTTOM 1/8" x 15 1/4" x 28 3/8"
SEE DETAIL "G"

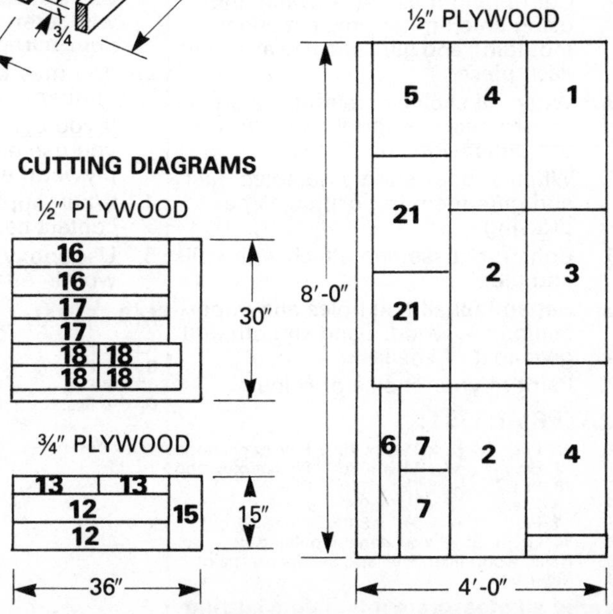
CUTTING DIAGRAMS
1/2" PLYWOOD
16
16
17
17
18
18
18
18
30"
3/4" PLYWOOD
13
13
12
12
15
15"
36"
1/2" PLYWOOD
5
4
1
21
21
2
3
8'-0"
6
7
7
2
4
4'-0"

66
book shelf
and book ends

The finish is everything. The construction is easy. All you need is some lumber, some attractive mouldings and a few basic tools. Then sit back and watch your friends admire your handywork.

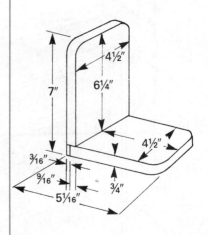

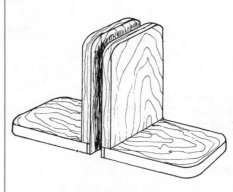

MOUNT STONES
ROCKS OR
DRIFTWOOD
OF YOUR CHOICE

INSTRUCTIONS: book shelf

1. If pine shelving is used, it will be 11¾" wide instead of 11½" and will give you a chance to true up the edges.
2. Cut to length as per drawing and using small miter box, cut panel moulding and glue and nail all round each piece.
3. When all shelves are made, start construction of upright supports as per dimensions on drawing.
4. When supports are assembled, nail and glue them in position as per drawing.
5. Construct base and attach with nails and glue.
6. Set and fill all nail holes and imperfections in wood. Sand smooth and give coat of shellack.
7. Paint to your choice of colours.

MATERIAL LIST:

A.	2 Pcs.	¾" x 11½" x 46"	Pine or plywood
B.	1 Pc.	¾" x 11½" x 36"	Pine or plywood
C.	28 Pcs.	⅜" x 1¼" x 11¼"	Pine
D.	8 Pcs.	¾" x 1¼" x 9⅜"	Pine
E.	1 Pc.	¾" x 2½" x 8'0"	Pine
F.	44 Lin. ft. of ½" x ⅞" panel moulding.		
G.	Nails, wood filler, shellack, sandpaper, paint.		
H.	Miter box.		

Verify all measurements before cutting

INSTRUCTIONS: book ends

1. The sizes listed above are for book ends, identical to the ones built by me. The size of the stones or other objects that you may wish to mount will determine the dimensions of your particular book ends.
2. You may use plywood or solid lumber.
3. If you use plywood, I suggest that you use edge trim to cover the plywood edges.
4. When applying edge trim, use contact cement.
5. Use epoxy cement to attach stones to wood.

MATERIAL LIST:

A.	2 Pcs.	¾" x 4½" x 7"
B.	2 Pcs.	¾" x 4½" x 5¹⁄₁₆"
C.	8 Pcs.	Lin. ft. 1" flexible edge trim
D.	6 Pcs.	Flat head steel wood screws 1½" - #6
Misc.:		Glue - wood filler - sandpaper and paint or stain.

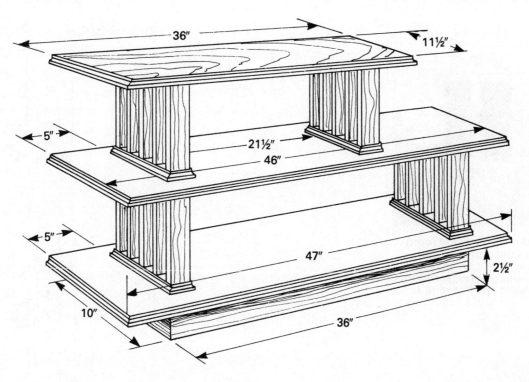

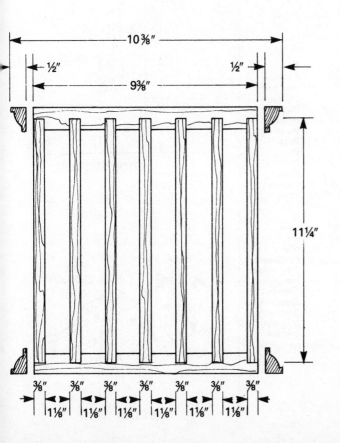

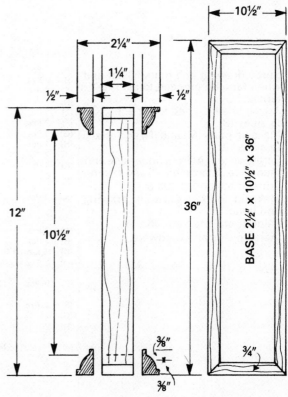

67
bookcase

A bookcase in the den or living room should not only hold books but be attractive as well. Here's an unusual design incorporating stained glass doors. A challenge to build and beautiful to look at.

INSTRUCTIONS:

(1) Study drawing and material list and when familiar proceed to cut materials.
(2) Attach shelf (D) and lower shelf (C) to sides (B).
(3) Make up parts (M) and (N) and attach to sides (B).
(4) Screw on top (A) from under side and then slide in top shelf (C) and secure.
(5) Cut and attach facings (K) and (L).
(6) Make up doors as shown on drawing and hang.
(7) Paint or stain to your choice.
(8) Install plexis and hardware.

MATERIAL LIST:

(A)	1 Pc.	¾" x 10" x 33"	Plywood
(B)	2 Pcs.	¾" x 9" x 33½"	Plywood
(C)	2 Pcs.	¾" x 9" x 32"	Plywood
(D)	1 Pc.	¾" x 9" x 31½"	Plywood
(E)	1 Pc.	¼" x 33" x 33½"	Plywood
(F)	2 Pcs.	¾" x 2½" x 29"	Plywood
(G)	2 Pcs.	¾" x 2½" x 7¾"	Plywood
(H)	1 Pc.	¾" x 1" x 35"	Pine
(J)	2 Pcs.	¾" x 1" x 11"	Pine
(K)	1 Pc.	¾" x 1½" x 33"	Pine
(L)	2 Pcs.	¾" x 1¼" x 33½"	Pine
(M)	2 Pcs.	¾" x 1¼" x 31½"	Pine
(N)	3 Pcs.	¾" x 1¼" x 6½"	Pine

Doors:

(A)	2 Pcs.	¾" x 1½" x 32"	Pine
(B)	4 Pcs.	¾" x 1½" x 13"	Pine
(C)	15 Linear ft.	¼" x ⅜"	Pine
(D)	2 Pcs.	13¼" x 30"	Decorative plexis glass
(E)	16 Pcs.	¼" x 2½"	Hardwood dowels
(F)	2 Prs.	1½" x 2½"	Brass hinges
(G)	2		Door pulls
(H)	2		Magnetic catches

Misc.: Nails, screws, glue, wood filler, sandpaper.

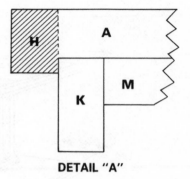

DETAIL "A"

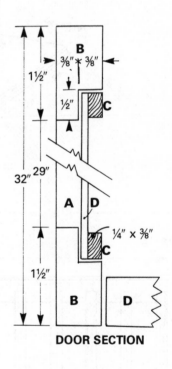

DOOR SECTION

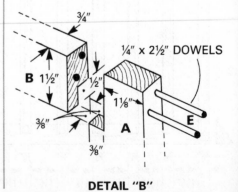

DETAIL "B"

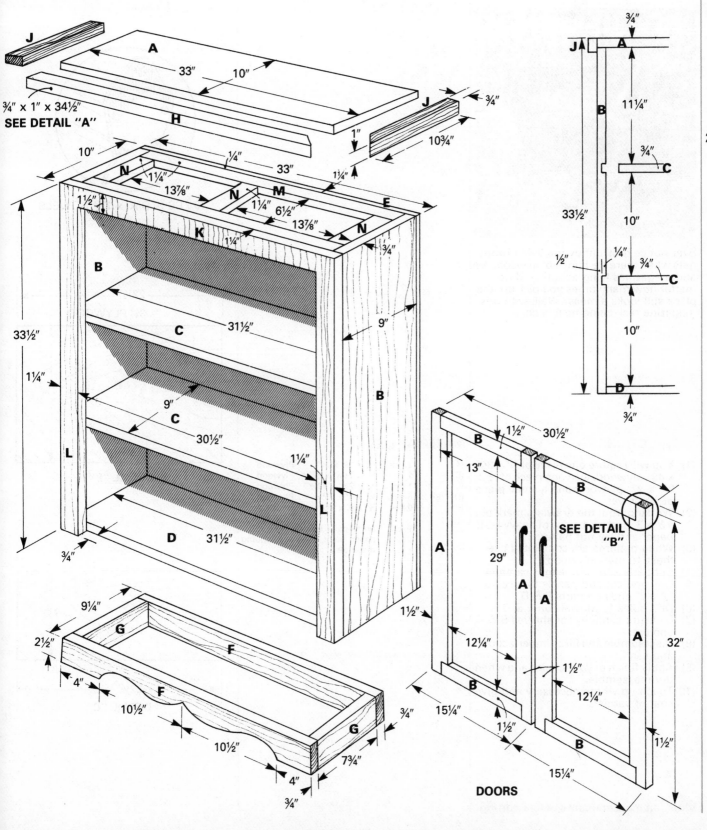

J

A

33"   10"

¾" x 1" x 34½"
SEE DETAIL "A"

H   J   ¾"

10¾"   1"

10"   ¼"   33"   1¼"

N   1¼"

13⅞"   N   M   E

1½"   6½"

K   13⅞"   N

¼"   ¾"

B

C   31½"   9"

9"   B

C

30½"

1¼"

L   L

D   31½"

¾"

9¼"

G

2½"   F

4"

F

10½"

10½"   G   ¾"

4"   7¾"

¾"

J   ¾"   A

B   11¼"

¾"   C

33½"   10"

½"   ¼"   ¾"

C

10"

D

¾"

1½"   30½"

B

13"

SEE DETAIL
"B"

B

29"

A   A

A

1½"

A   A

12¼"

B   1½"   32"

1½"   12¼"

15¼"

1½"

B   1½"

15¼"

DOORS

68
magazine rack

Ever notice how untidy the living room gets when there's a bunch of newspapers and magazines lying about? And no matter how many times you pick up, the place still looks a mess? Well, with this magazine rack being neat is easy.

INSTRUCTIONS:

(1) You will require one piece of ¾" x 30" x 48" plywood, also one piece of ½" x 27" x 27" plywood and a small piece of ⅜" dowel.

(2) Working from the drawing, mark out a 3" x 3" grid on a piece of heavy kraft paper and lay out patterns.

(3) When patterns are completed use these to mark plywood.

(4) Cut parts and sand edges carefully.

(5) Drill and cut end panels to receive ½" x 2" ends on parts E & D.

(6) Drill holes for dowels on E & D.

(7) Measure carefully for shelves B & C and cut.

(8) Disassemble and fill all imperfections and sand.

(9) Apply finish of your choice and when dry reassemble.

(10) Touch up where necessary and give coat of varnish.

MATERIAL LIST:

(A)	2 Pcs.	¾" x 18" x 24"	Plywood
(B)	1 Pc.	¾" x 11¼" x 22½"	Plywood
(C)	1 Pc.	¾" x 7½" x 22½"	Plywood
(D)+(E)	5 Pcs.	½" x 3" x 25½"	Plywood
(F)	10 Pcs.	⅜" dia. x 1½"	Hardwood dowels
Misc.:		Small nails, wood filler, sand-paper, paint, satin or antiquing materials	

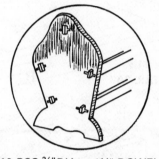

10 PCS ⅜"DIA. x 1½" DOWELS

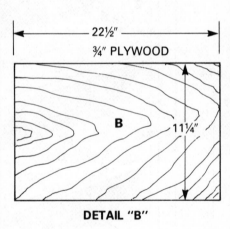

22½"

¾" PLYWOOD

B

11¼"

DETAIL "B"

C

7½"

22½"

DETAIL "C"

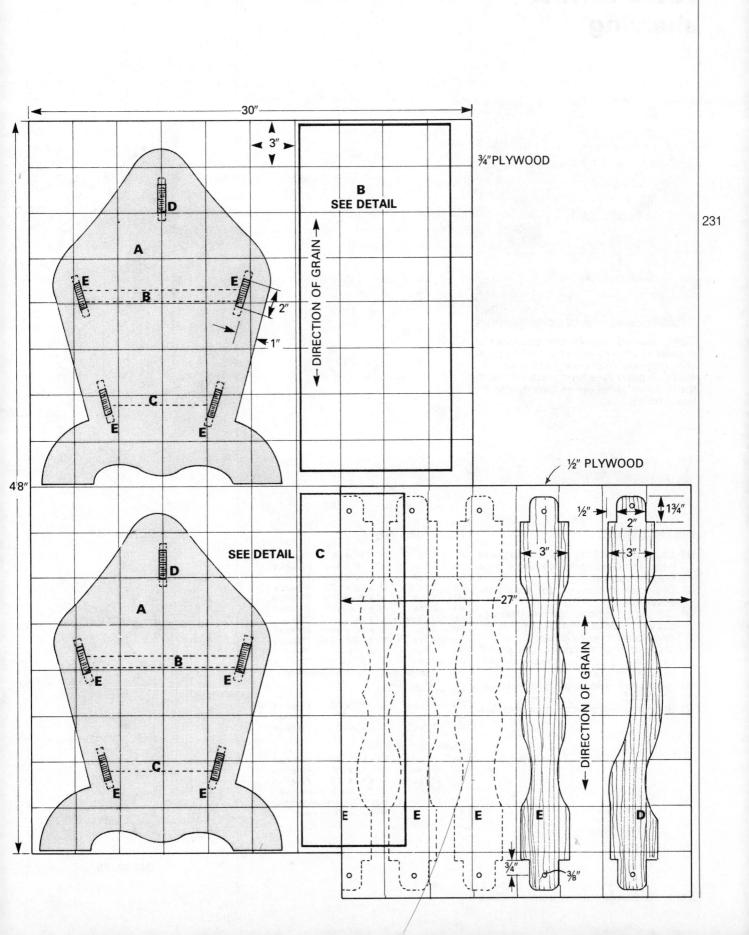

69
room divider
shelving

Build a room divider for that extra special illusion of privacy and cosiness. In addition, gain lots of shelving and drawer space. A good idea for homes where the main entrance opens directly into the living room.

INSTRUCTIONS:

(1) Study material list and drawing and when familiar proceed to cut parts for bottom section.
(2) Cut holes in piece (A) for post, then assemble.
(3) Cut parts for post, nail and glue as shown in illustration. When glue is dry, rip off 2" wide posts.
(4) Make up shelves and fit over posts.
(5) Lay out and cut shelf brackets and fit to holes in posts.
(6) Fill all nail holes and imperfections and sand.
(7) Stain or paint to your choice of colors.

MATERIAL LIST:

(A)	1 Pc.	¾" x 14" x 66"	Plywood
(B)	2 Pcs.	¾" x 14" x 64½"	Plywood
(C)	2 Pcs.	¾" x 14" x 25¾"	Plywood
(D)	1 Pc.	¾" x 10" x 12½"	Plywood
(E)	2 Pcs.	¾" x 2" x 60"	Plywood
(F)	2 Pcs.	¾" x 2" x 13"	Plywood
(G)	30 Linear ft.	¼" x 1¼"	Pine
(H)	1 Pc.	¼" x 14" x 66"	Plywood
(J)	2 Pcs.	¼" x 12⅛" x 32½"	Plywood
(K)	2 Pcs.	¼" x ½" x 64½"	Pine
(L)	2 Pcs.	¼" x ¼" x 64½"	Pine
(M)	5 Linear ft.	½" x ¾" Panel Moulding	

Posts:

(A)	2 Pcs.	½" x 13" x 70"	Plywood
(B)	18 Pcs.	½" x 2" x 13"	Plywood
(C)	12 Pcs.	½" x 2" x 9½"	Plywood

Shelves:

(A)	6 Pcs.	¾" x 8" x 33"	Plywood
(B)	12 Pcs.	¾" x ¾" x 33"	Pine
(C)	12 Pcs.	¾" x ¾" x 9½"	Pine
	Misc.:	1", 1½" and 2" finish nails, woodfiller, sandpaper, glue, shellac, stain or paint.	

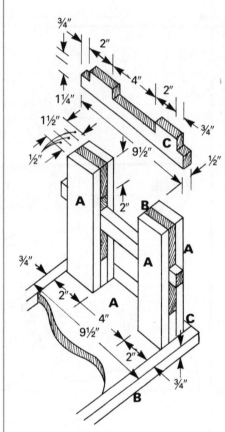

DETAIL "A"

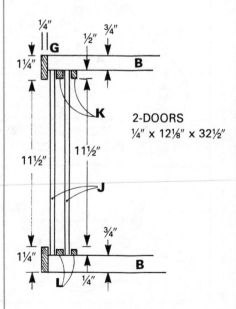

2-DOORS
¼" x 12⅛" x 32½"

DETAIL "B"

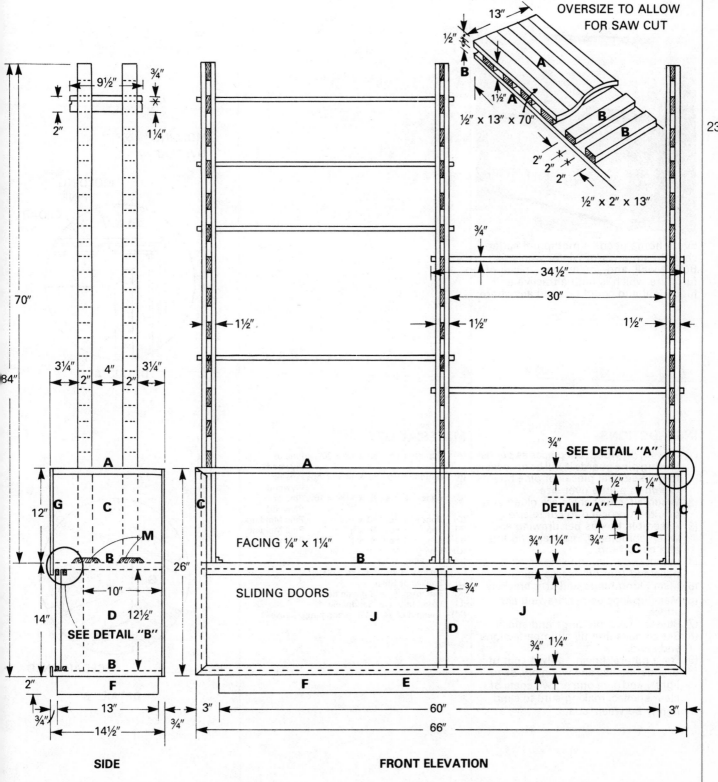

OVERSIZE TO ALLOW FOR SAW CUT

13"

½" x 13" x 70"

½" x 2" x 13"

¾"

34½"

30"

1½"

¾" SEE DETAIL "A"

DETAIL "A"

FACING ¼" x 1¼"

SLIDING DOORS

9½"

¾"

2"

1¼"

70"

84"

3¼" 4" 3¼"

2" 2"

12"

14"

10"

D 12½"

SEE DETAIL "B"

2"

13"

¾"

14½"

¾"

26"

3"

60"

3"

66"

SIDE

FRONT ELEVATION

70
cedar
storage chest

Every home needs a mothproof cedar chest to store warm winter woollens. Built it well, and you'll have a piece of furniture which is both attractive and functional and could be used anywhere.

INSTRUCTIONS:

(1) If using plywood, cut pieces as per list. If using pine boards it will be necessary to glue several pieces of pine boards together, a little over size.

(2) When all your panels are glued and dry, then proceed to cut to size.

(3) Assemble box as per drawing and when completed, mark around top and cut off top.

(4) Install cedar lining using small ⅝" nails and trim off excess lining.

(5) Install long hinge and arm brackets.

(6) Make up legs as per drawing and attach.

(7) Buy or make moldings and attach.

(8) Set all nails and fill all imperfections and sand.

(9) For a natural finish, apply 1 coat of orange shellac and when dry, sand lightly and give one or two coats of clear shellac, making sure to sand lightly between coats.

MATERIAL LIST:

(A)	Top	1 Pc.	¾" x 16" x 30"	Pine or Plywood
(B)	Bottom	1 Pc.	¾" x 14½" x 28½"	Pine or Plywood
(C)	Ends	2 Pcs.	¾" x 14½" x 16⅝"	Pine or Plywood
(D)	Bottom	1 Pc.	¾" x 1⅜"	Pine Molding
(E)	Top	1 Pc.	¾" x ⅝"	Pine Molding
(F)	Legs	1 Pc.	¾" x 1½" x 36"	Pine
(G)	Lining — 24 sq. ft. Aromatic cedar.			
(H)	2 Folding arms			
(I)	Approx. 3 lbs. 2" finish nails			
(J)	Shellac or Stain			
(K)	1 lb. pkg. ⅝" #19 gauge nails			
(L)	Wood filler and Sandpaper			
(M)	1 length of 24" x 1½" piano hinge (brass)			

MOLDING ⅝" x ¾"
OVERLAP ⅛"

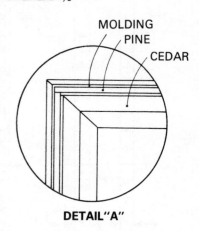

MOLDING
PINE
CEDAR

DETAIL "A"

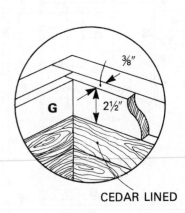

⅜"

G

2½"

CEDAR LINED

DETAIL "B"

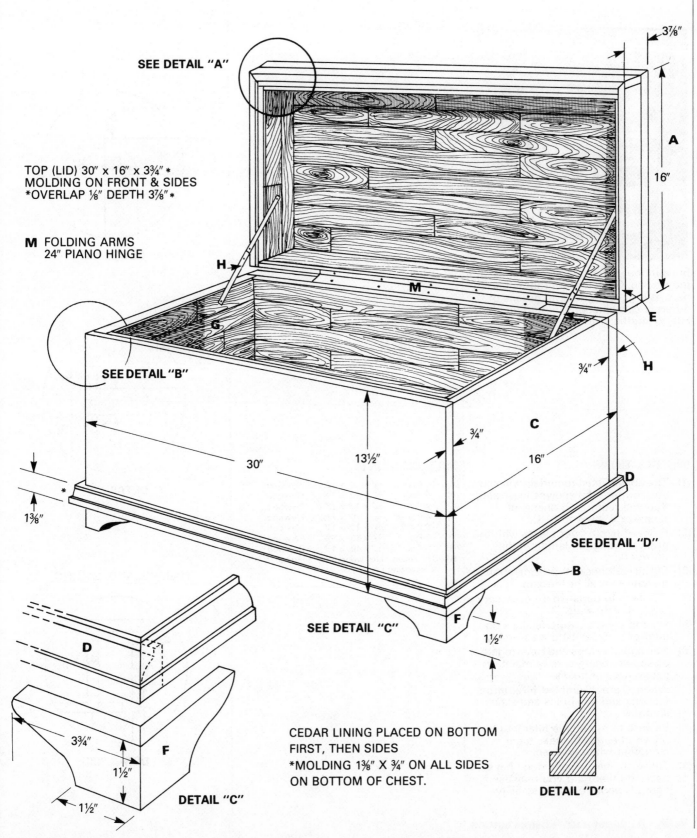

SEE DETAIL "A"

TOP (LID) 30" x 16" x 3¾" *
MOLDING ON FRONT & SIDES
*OVERLAP ⅛" DEPTH 3⅞" *

M FOLDING ARMS
24" PIANO HINGE

SEE DETAIL "B"

3⅞"

A

16"

E

H

¾"

C

30"

13½"

¾"

16"

D

SEE DETAIL "D"

B

1⅜"

SEE DETAIL "C"

F

1½"

D

F

3¾"

1½"

1½"

DETAIL "C"

CEDAR LINING PLACED ON BOTTOM
FIRST, THEN SIDES
*MOLDING 1⅜" X ¾" ON ALL SIDES
ON BOTTOM OF CHEST.

DETAIL "D"

71
modular
bookcase

Build it one unit at a time, or as the spirit moves you. Great idea for room re-arrangers as it goes together in dozens of different combinations. Fun to build. Fun to shuffle around.

INSTRUCTIONS:

(1) The above listed materials will allow you to make the shelves illustrated. You will require 1½ sheets of ¾" x 4' x 8' plywood.

(2) Proceed to cut your pieces with the grain running the length of the plywood.

(3) Cut all end checks in one operation so that they will all be the same ⅜" x ⅜".

(4) Cut dado in parts where necessary ¼" deep x ¾" wide.

(5) Fill and sand all imperfections on interior surfaces before assembly.

(6) Nail and glue tops and sides together as shown, being sure to maintain squareness of boxes.

(7) When all are assembled, fill all imperfections and nail holes and sand smooth.

(8) Be sure to rub a little filler into the plywood edges to make them smoother when finished.

(9) These shelves usually don't have backs on them but you may use a light plywood for more stability.

Verify all measurements before cutting

MATERIAL LIST:

(A)	14 Pcs.	¾" x 10" x 12"	Plywood
(B)	6 Pcs.	¾" x 10" x 29¼"	Plywood
(C)	4 Pcs.	¾" x 10" x 23¼"	Plywood
(D)	4 Pcs.	¾" x 10" x 11¼"	Plywood
(E)	6 Pcs.	¾" x 10" x 11"	Plywood
(F)	2 Pcs.	¾" x 10" x 9½"	Plywood
(G)	3 Pcs.	¾" x 10" x 15"	Plywood
(H)	1½" Finish nails, wood filler, sandpaper, shellac and paint.		

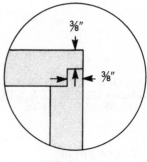

DETAIL "A"

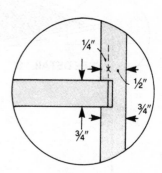

DETAIL "B"

NAILING AND GLUING

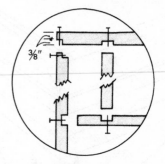

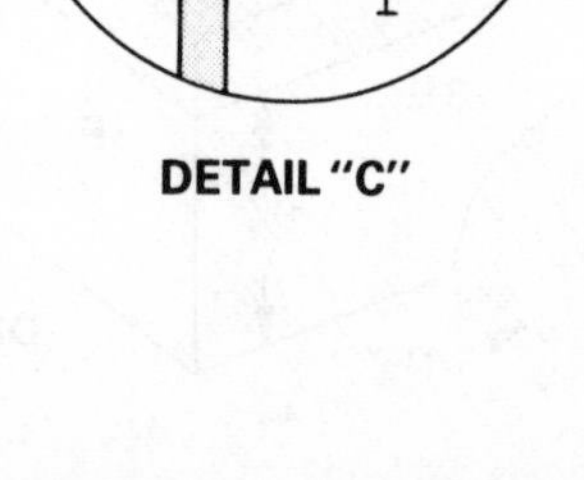

DETAIL "C"

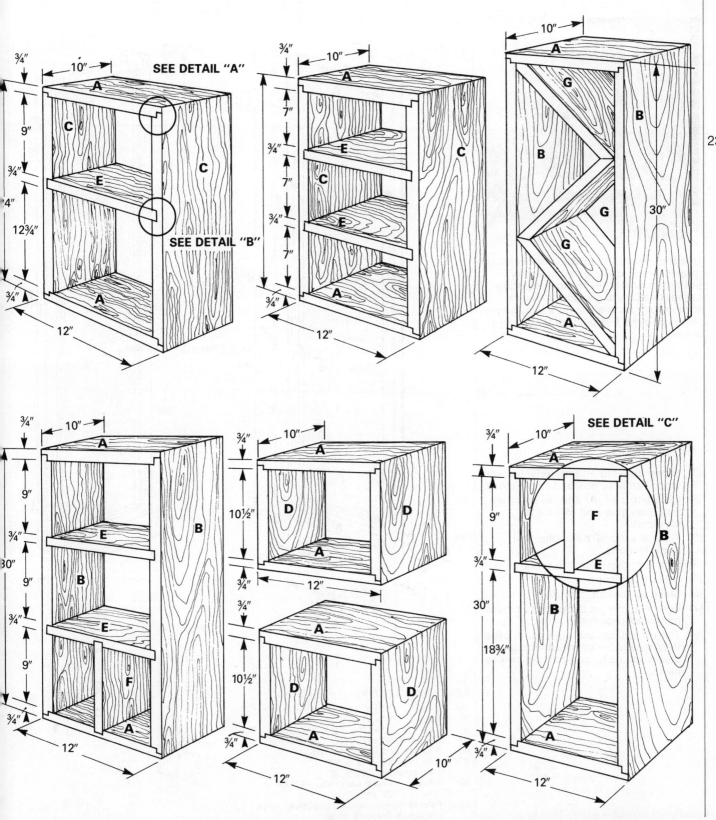

72
divider screen

Use it to gain extra privacy for overnight guests, when unexpected sickness strikes, or any other reason requiring some measure of privacy. A divider screen such as this can go a long way in increasing the flexibility of your living area.

INSTRUCTIONS:

(1) Study drawing and material list and when familiar, proceed to cut stock.
(2) Glue and nail (A) and (B) together and then glue and nail on ¼" plywood.
(3) Fill and sand all nail holes and imperfections.
(4) Paint or stain to match fabric colors.
(5) Nail on rod supports.
(6) Make up curtain material.
(7) Repeat above procedure for as many panels as required.
(8) The mouldings are optional. If used, they should be attached with glue and small nails, and painted beforehand.

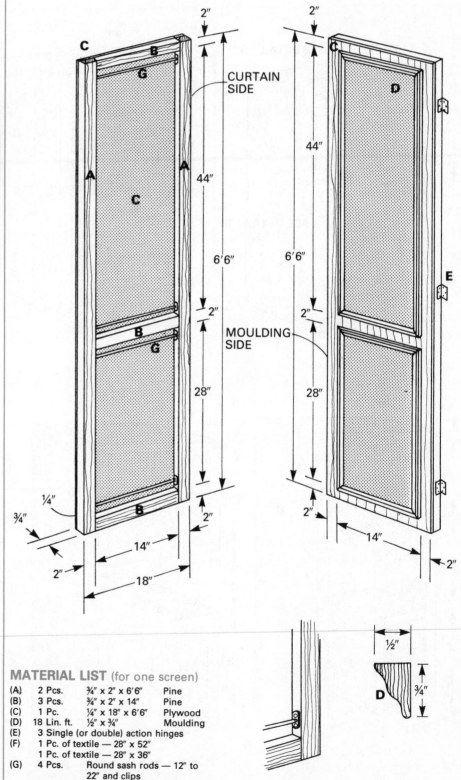

MATERIAL LIST (for one screen)

(A)	2 Pcs.	¾" x 2" x 6'6"	Pine
(B)	3 Pcs.	¾" x 2" x 14"	Pine
(C)	1 Pc.	¼" x 18" x 6'6"	Plywood
(D)	18 Lin. ft.	½" x ¾"	Moulding
(E)	3 Single (or double) action hinges		
(F)	1 Pc. of textile — 28" x 52"		
	1 Pc. of textile — 28" x 36"		
(G)	4 Pcs.	Round sash rods — 12" to 22" and clips	

Misc.: Paint or stain, woodfiller, sandpaper, nails, corrugated fasteners, glue.

Verify all measurements before cutting

8
Home decor

73 MIRROR AND CONSOLE   240

76 DOUGH BOX   245

79 STANDUP MIRROR   248

74 WOOD BOX   242

77 PINE HUTCH   246

80 WALL LAMPS   250

75 WINE RACK   244

78 FIREPLACE LOG RACK   247

81 CASTILIAN CABINET   252

73
mirror
and console

Brighten up your hallway with this mirror and console combination. Great for last minute hairdo and wardrobe checks before venturing forth into the daily grind, or getting ready for an exciting evening out on the town.

INSTRUCTIONS:

(1) You will need approximately 16 linear feet of molding for the frame and console. You may wish to use a molding of another sort but this should not make much difference.

(2) For the console supports, you may use two pieces of ¾" thick stock glued together if 1½" material is not available.

(3) Using a miter box for your molding cuts, proceed to construct your mirror frame and when completed, then cut the mirror to fit; same for back.

(4) Cut parts for console and assemble, using ¾" plywood for console surface.

(5) Fill all nail holes and sand. Stain or paint to your choice.

MATERIAL LIST:

Mirror Frame

(1)	2 Pcs.	⅞" x 1½" x 36"	#95 Ornamental Moldings
(2)	2 Pcs.	⅞" x ½" x 24"	#95 Ornamental Moldings
(3)	1 Pc.	¼" x 21½" m 27⅞"	Plywood
(4)	1 Pc.	⅛" x 21½" x 27⅞"	Mirror

Console

(1)	2 Pcs.	⅞" x 1½" x 36"	#95 Ornamental Moldings
(2)	2 Pcs.	⅞" x 1½" x 24"	#95 Ornamental Moldings
(3)	1 Pc.	¼" x 21½" x 27⅞"	Plywood
(4)	1 Pc.	⅛" x 21½" x 27⅞"	Mirror
(5)	2 Pcs.	¾" x 2¼" x 21"	Pine
(6)	1 Pc.	½" x 1" x 10'	Pine
(7)	12 Pcs.	1¼" #6 F. H. steel wood screws	
	Misc.:	1"-1½" finish nails, glue, wood filler, sandpaper, shellac and paint.	

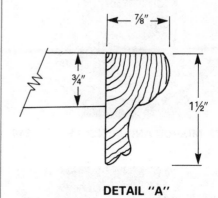

DETAIL "A"

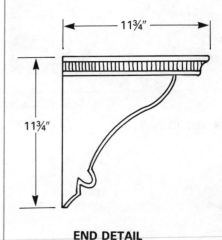

END DETAIL

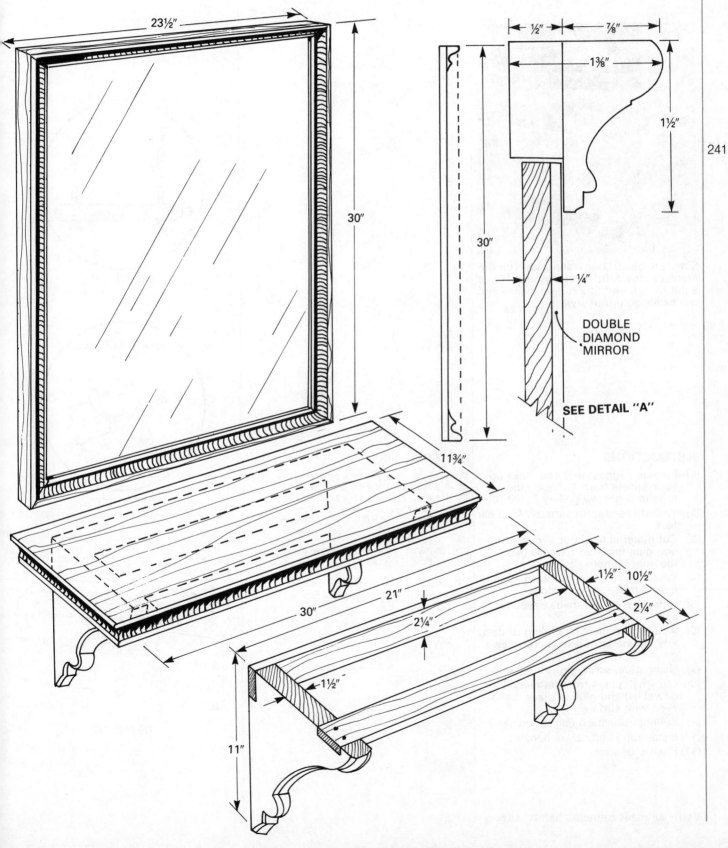

23½"

30"

½"   7⅞"

1⅜"

1½"

30"

11¾"

¼"

30"

DOUBLE
DIAMOND
MIRROR

SEE DETAIL "A"

241

1½" 10½"

2¼"

21"

30"

2¼"

11"

1½"

74
wood box

Simple to build. Long lasting. Ideal for the fireplace crowd. Build it for yourself or as a gift for a friend. It's sure to please and will never go out of style.

INSTRUCTIONS:

(1) I would suggest that you make up your panels from 1¼″ x 4″ pine tongue & groove gallery flooring.

(2) You will need approximately 40 linear feet.

(3) Cut material to about 1″ oversize and glue together to make panels the approximate size.

(4) When glue sets, sand down to an even surface on both sides.

(5) When panels are made, layout and cut.

(6) Assemble project by drilling ¼″ deep x ½″ diameter holes, where screws go.

(7) Using glue, screw project together.

(8) Cut small plugs from hardwood dowel (H) and glue in place. Sand even with surface.

(9) Bullnose all sharp edges and sand.

(10) Install rope and dowel handles.

(11) Shellac or stain.

MATERIAL LIST:

(A)	2 Pcs.	1¼″ x 11″ x 26″	Pine
(B)	2 Pcs.	1¼″ x 9¾″ x 15″	Pine
(C)	1 Pc.	1¼″ x 12″ x 23½″	Pine
(D)	2 Pcs.	1¼″ x 2¼″ x 16″	Pine
(E)	2 Pcs.	¾″ x 6″	Hardwood dowels
(F)	4 Pcs.	½″ x 6″	Sash Cord
(G)	38 Pcs.	2½″ #10 Steel F. H. Wood Screws	
(H)	1 Pc.	½″ x 12″	Hardwood dowel
(J)	Misc.:	Glue, sandpaper, shellac or stain.	

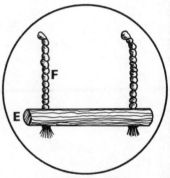

DETAIL "A"

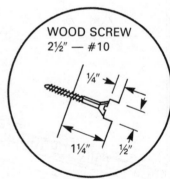

WOOD SCREW
2½″ — #10

¼″

1¼″   ½″

DETAIL "B"

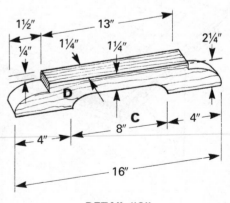

1½″   13″   2¼″

¼″   1¼″   1¼″

D   C   4″

4″   8″

16″

DETAIL "C"

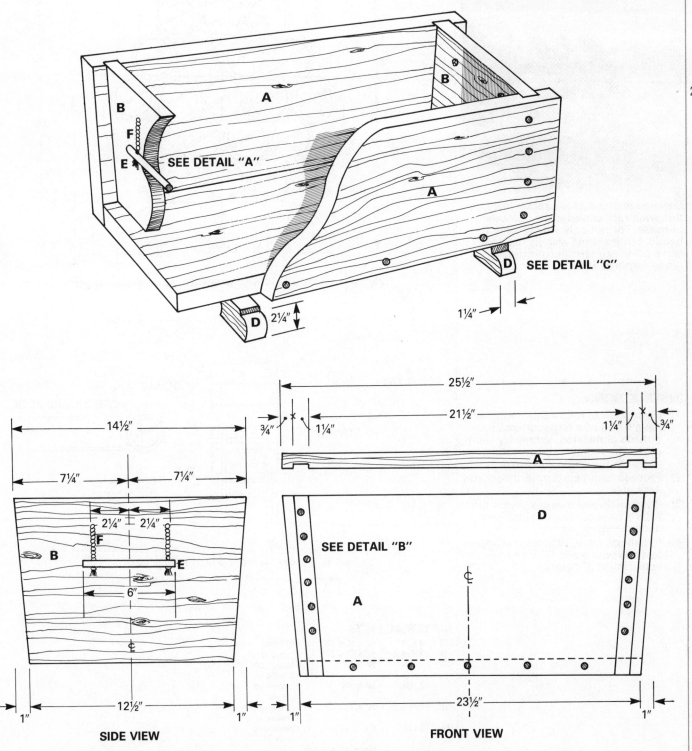

B

A

B

F

E

SEE DETAIL "A"

A

D   SEE DETAIL "C"

2¼"

1¼"

25½"

21½"

¾"   1¼"

1¼"   ¾"

A

14½"

7¼"   7¼"

2¼"   2¼"

F

B

E

6"

¢

D

SEE DETAIL "B"

A

¢

1"   12½"   1"

1"   23½"   1"

SIDE VIEW

FRONT VIEW

75
wine rack

Lest you mistake it for a rocket launcher, this wine rack serves a very serious purpose. For not only should wine be handy, but it should also lie flat until served. A very interesting piece of decorative furniture indeed.

INSTRUCTIONS:

(1) If you wish to follow this design and have tubes of a larger or smaller outside dimension, simply lay them out in the manner shown and cut (A+B) to the angle you arrive at.

(2) Proceed to cut parts accordingly and assemble.

(3) If you wish, you may cover your tube with a vinyl contact or simply wallpaper them.

(4) Set all nails and fill holes and imperfections with wood filler and paint to your choice of colors.

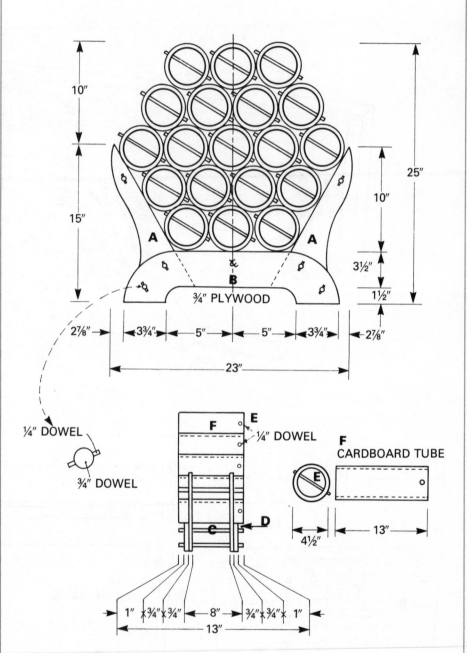

MATERIAL LIST:

(A)	4 Pcs.	¾" x 6" x 18"	Plywood
(B)	2 Pcs.	¾" x 6" x 24"	Plywood
(C)	6 Pcs.	¾" x 13"	Hardwood dowels
(D)	12 Pcs.	¼" x 1¼"	Hardwood dowels
(E)	19 Pcs.	¼" x 5"	Hardwood dowels
(F)	19 Pcs.	4½" x 13"	Cardboard tubes
	Misc.:	Nails, glue, paint, wallpaper	

76
dough box

A practical and decorative piece of furniture. Ideal for having coffee when perusing magazines or the daily paper. Keeps the papers neat and handy, and out of harm's way. Build one for yourself today.

INSTRUCTIONS:

(1) Study drawing and material list and when familiar, proceed with the layout of parts (A), (B), (C) and (D).

(2) Cut and assemble these parts using glue and screws.

(3) Cut the bottom panel to fit and install.

(4) Cut parts for top and assemble, nailing on parts (H) and (J) to part (F) from underside.

(5) Make up legs, two left and two right.

(6) Attach legs, using screws as indicated on drawing.

(7) Insert ⅜" plugs using glue.

(8) When glue is dry, sand all plugs even with surface. Note: All exposed edges should be rounded off where required before assembly.

(9) You will most likely need a clamping up panel as shown, in order to make up the wide panels you require.

(10) Fill all imperfections and sand. Finish with a stain of your choice.

Verify all measurements before cutting

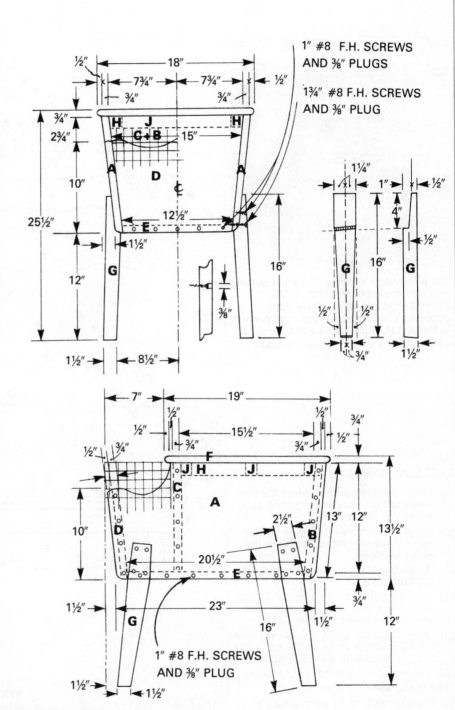

1" #8 F.H. SCREWS AND ⅜" PLUGS

1¾" #8 F.H. SCREWS AND ⅜" PLUG

1" #8 F.H. SCREWS AND ⅜" PLUG

MATERIAL LIST:

(A)	2 Pcs.	¾" x 13" x 26"	Pine
(B)	1 Pc.	¾" x 13" x 15½"	Pine
(C)	1 Pc.	¾" x 12" x 15½"	Pine
(D)	1 Pc.	¾" x 10" x 15"	Pine
(E)	1 Pc.	¾" x 12½" x 20½"	Pine or Plywood
(F)	1 Pc.	¾" x 18" x 19"	Pine
(G)	4 Pcs.	1½" x 2½" x 16"	Pine
(H)	2 Pcs.	¾" x 1½" x 15½"	Pine
(J)	3 Pcs.	¾" x 1½" x 14¼"	Pine
	Misc.:	Screws, ⅜" dowel, nails, glue, wood filler, sandpaper and stain.	

77
pine hutch

The pine hutch is a labor of love, requiring much attention to the final finish. Careful sanding and buffing, plus accurate staining to just the right pattern, will make the pine hutch a unique piece of furniture you'll be proud to own.

INSTRUCTIONS:

(1) Study drawing and material list and when familiar begin by cutting pine boards of (A) and (B).

(2) It may be necessary to glue two or more pieces together to obtain the wider sections.

(3) When boards are ready, lay out and cut both sides.

(4) Start assembly by nailing and gluing parts (A) and (B) together and then nail this section to pieces (M).

(5) Layout and cut parts (H), (J), (K) and (L). Nail and glue these pieces to (A) and (B) as shown on drawing.

(6) Make up door and hang in position.

(7) Fill and sand all imperfections.

(8) Stain or varnish to your choice of finish.

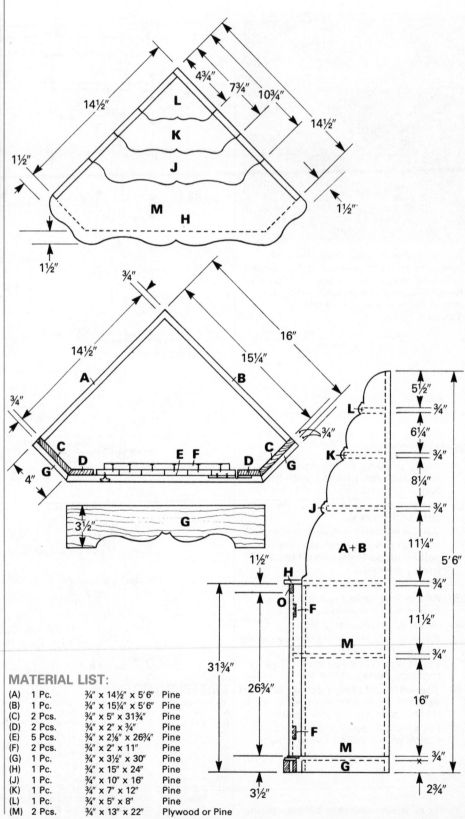

MATERIAL LIST:

(A)	1 Pc.	¾" x 14½" x 5'6"	Pine
(B)	1 Pc.	¾" x 15¼" x 5'6"	Pine
(C)	2 Pcs.	¾" x 5" x 31¾"	Pine
(D)	2 Pcs.	¾" x 2" x ¾"	Pine
(E)	5 Pcs.	¾" x 2⅛" x 26¾"	Pine
(F)	2 Pcs.	¾" x 2" x 11"	Pine
(G)	1 Pc.	¾" x 3½" x 30"	Pine
(H)	1 Pc.	¾" x 15" x 24"	Pine
(J)	1 Pc.	¾" x 10" x 16"	Pine
(K)	1 Pc.	¾" x 7" x 12"	Pine
(L)	1 Pc.	¾" x 5" x 8"	Pine
(M)	2 Pcs.	¾" x 13" x 22"	Plywood or Pine

Verify all measurements before cutting

78
fireplace
log rack

If your friends have a fireplace and you don't — well, here's a handsome gift to warm up the relationship. Build a few of them, and become the most popular guy of the fireplace crowd.

INSTRUCTIONS:

(1) Using a piece of heavy kraft paper about 24″ x 24″, proceed to lay out a grid of 2″ x 2″ squares.

(2) When grid is completed, mark out the arms, then cut them out and use as patterns to mark your plywood.

(3) When arms are cut and holes drilled, sand edges carefully and rout edges.

(4) Using glue and screws, attach arms together.

(5) Install dowels using small amount of glue.

(6) After cutting slats, rout top edges and, using 1½″ finish nails and a little glue, attach to arms.

(7) Fill and sand all nail holes and imperfections.

(8) Stain or paint to your choice of colors.

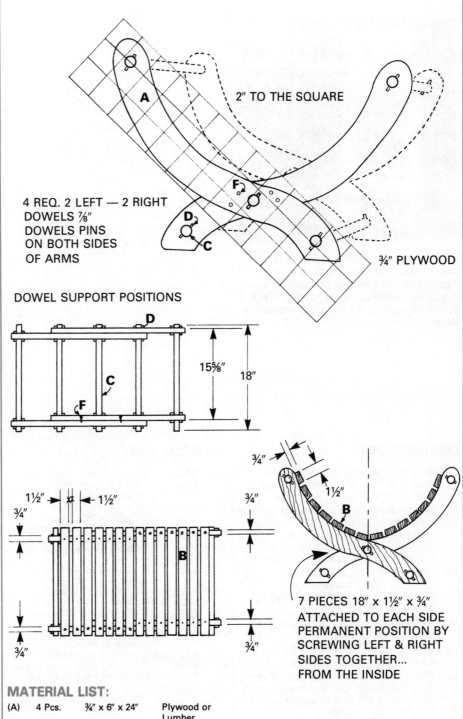

2″ TO THE SQUARE

4 REQ. 2 LEFT — 2 RIGHT
DOWELS ⅞″
DOWELS PINS
ON BOTH SIDES
OF ARMS

¾″ PLYWOOD

DOWEL SUPPORT POSITIONS

15⅝″   18″

7 PIECES 18″ x 1½″ x ¾″
ATTACHED TO EACH SIDE
PERMANENT POSITION BY
SCREWING LEFT & RIGHT
SIDES TOGETHER...
FROM THE INSIDE

MATERIAL LIST:

(A)	4 Pcs.	¾″ x 6″ x 24″	Plywood or Lumber
(B)	14 Pcs.	¾″ x 1½″ x 18″	Pine
(C)	5 Pcs.	⅞″ x 18″	Hardwood dowels
(D)	20 Pcs.	¼″ x 1¾″	Hardwood dowels
(E)	1 Lb.	1½″ finish nails	
(F)	8	1¼″ #8 F.H. steel wood screws	
	Misc.:	White glue, stain or paint, wood filler and sandpaper.	

247

79
standup mirror

If Mom does a lot of sewing — she'll appreciate this fine, standup mirror. You build her one like this, and it's a cinch she won't complain about all the sawdust coming up from the workshop down below.

INSTRUCTIONS:

(1) You will require about 12 linear feet of 2″ x 8″ pine and 12 linear feet of 2″ x 3″ pine.

(2) Study drawing and material list and when familiar proceed to cut out parts (A), (B), and (C). Use 2″ grid or make your own curve on (A). Locate and cut mortise on (A).

(3) When these pieces have been cut, sand and rout bullnose on all exposed edges, assemble (A), (B), and (C).

(4) Cut and make up frame, using ⅜″ dowels for joining.

(5) Drill holes in (A) and (D) for connectors.

(6) Place frame in position, insert connector through (A) and washer (G), using glue on end of connector that touches (D) and (G).

(7) Screw on round knobs.

(8) Install mirror and back panel, using 1″ finish nails on sharp angle to avoid hitting mirror.

(9) Finish as you wish.

Verify all measurements before cutting

MATERIAL LIST:

(A)	2 Pcs.	1½″ x 7½″ x 50″	Pine
(B)	2 Pcs.	1½″ x 5½″ x 20″	Pine
(C)	1 Pc.	1½″ x 5½″ x 26¾″	Pine
(D)	2 Pcs.	1½″ x 1⅞″ x 43¾″	Pine
(E)	2 Pcs.	1½″ x 1⅞″ x 18″	Pine
(F)	1 Pc.	¼″ x 18″ x 41″	Plywood
(G)	2 Pcs.	½″ x 2″ diameter	Pine
(H)	2 Pcs.	½″ Rigid Connectors (spindle— Flex. R.C.)	
(J)	2 Pcs.	2″ diameter Round Knobs (spindle—Flex. K.F. 121)	
(K)	4 Pcs.	¼″ x 1″ x 2½″ Pine Wedges	
(L)	8 Pcs.	⅜″ diameter x 4″ Hardwood Dowels	
(M)	8 Pcs.	⅜″ diameter Cabinet Maker's Screw Hole Plugs	
(N)	1 Pc.	⅛″ x 17¾″ x 40¾″ Mirror	
(O)	8 Pcs.	1¼″ #8 F.H. Steel Wood Screws	
Misc.:		Wood filler, sandpaper, glue.	

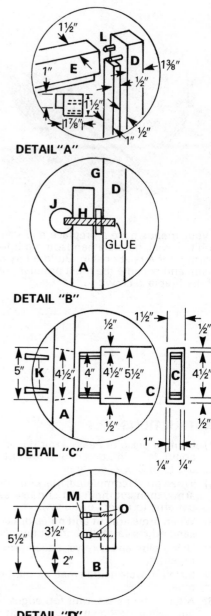

DETAIL "A"

DETAIL "B"

DETAIL "C"

DETAIL "D"

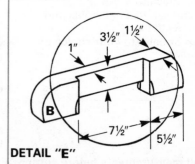

DETAIL "E"

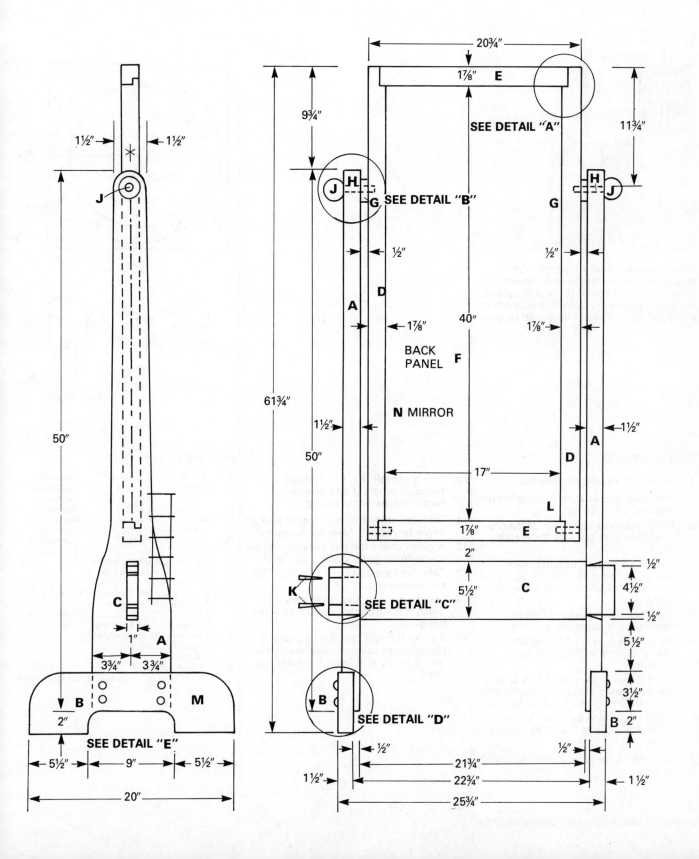

80
wall lamps

One has to be a bit of an electrician, carpenter and wrought-iron worker all rolled into one to get this one all together, but you'll also wind up with a very attractive light fixture you'll be proud to own.

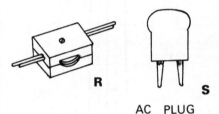

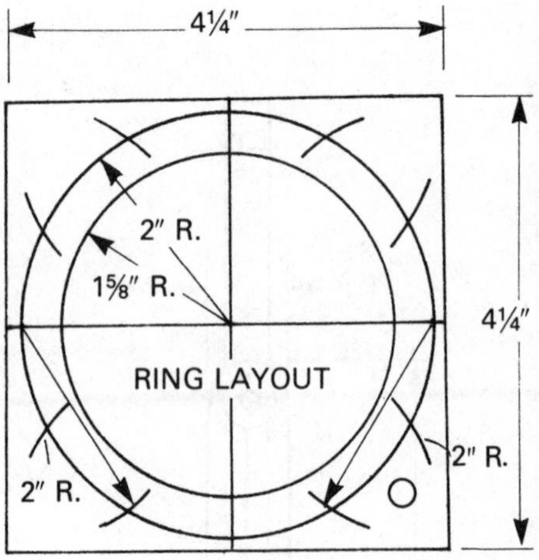

R   S

AC   PLUG

RING LAYOUT

4¼"

4¼"

2" R.

1⅝" R.

2" R.

2" R.

INSTRUCTIONS:

1. Cut all pieces as per drawing.
2. Assemble pieces B to A using white glue and allow to set.
3. Using masking tape, join 24 pieces E together and cut slot to receive ring F.
4. Glue two pieces F together with grains opposing each other. Do same for other three rings and allow glue to dry.
5. When set, lay out according to drawing with compass and cut.
6. Join pieces E to F using white glue only, and install fibreglass lampshade mat.
7. Cut and assemble pieces C & D and install between pieces B according to drawing. Drill holes for wire ⁵⁄₁₆".
8. Drill ⅜" hole in A between pieces C and drill hole at C & D to receive nipple.
9. Also drill ⅜" hole in A from bottom for wire.
10. Using rat-tail file, file halfway through nipple J and assemble hardware as per drawing.
11. Drill two small holes on top of A at an angle to receive nails for hanging.
12. A good chain for this project can be made from girl's waist chain belt.
13. Take out material G and stain project, then reassemble.
14. Locate on wall and drive two 2½" finish nails in holes on top of A for hanging.
15. A nicer job will result if you can wire these lamps to an unused wall switch and thereby eliminate the hanging cord.

MATERIAL LIST:

A.	2 Pcs.	¾" x 4½" x 7"	Hardwood
B.	14 Pcs.	¼" x ¾" x 7"	Hardwood
C.	4 Pcs.	¼" 1¾" x 9"	Hardwood
D.	2 Pcs.	¼" x ½" x ½"	Hardwood
E.	24 Pcs.	¼" x ¾" x 7"	Hardwood
F.	8 Pcs.	⅛" x 4¼" x 4¼"	Hardwood
G.	2 Pcs.	7" x 10¾"	Lampshade fibre-glass

H.	2 Brass caps with ⅜" thread
J.	2 — 1" x ⅜" threaded nipples
K.	4 Brass loops
L.	2 — 6" lengths of lightweight chain
M.	2 — ⅜" threaded nipples
N.	2 Pcs. ⅛" x ¾" x 3⅝" brass cross bars plus 8 Brass ⅜" — #4 R.H. wood screws
P.	2 Short length brass sockets
R.	2 Feed-thru cord switches
S.	2 A.C. plugs
T.	16 Feet lamp cord
	White resyn glue, sandpaper. Stain, if desired.

Verify all measurements before cutting

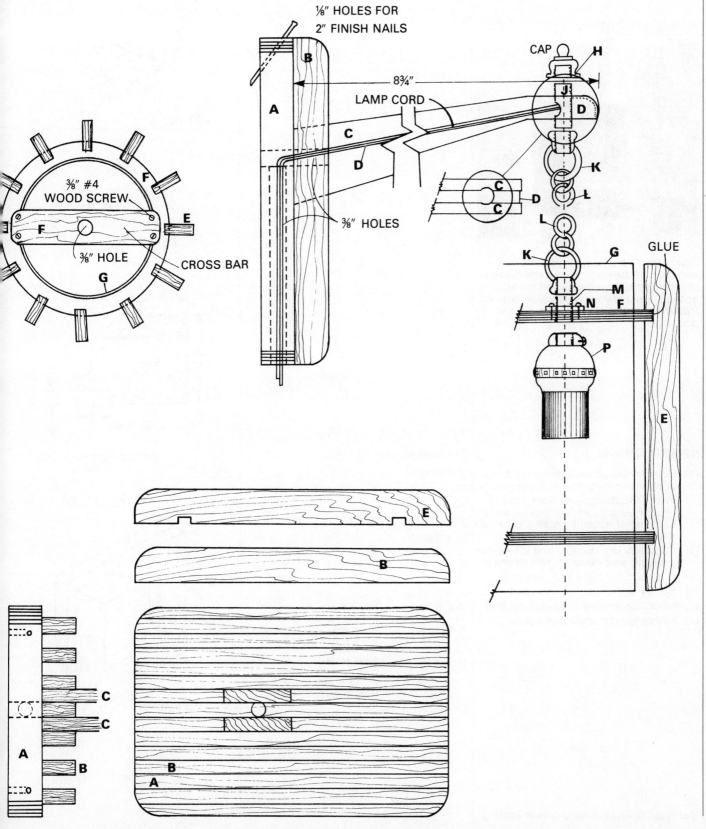

⅛" HOLES FOR
2" FINISH NAILS

B

A

8¾"

LAMP CORD

C

D

⅜" HOLES

⅜" #4
WOOD SCREW

F

E

F

⅜" HOLE

CROSS BAR

G

CAP   H

J

D

C

C

D

K

L

L

K   G   GLUE

M

N   F

E

P

E

B

A

C

C

A

B

B

A

81
castilian cabinet

This attractive cabinet is really just a variation of the basic box. As the assembly consists of two boxes and the bottom section, most of your work will be concentrated on the finishing of the cabinet doors.

INSTRUCTIONS:

(1) Buy or make up mouldings as close as possible to dimensions on drawing.
(2) When mouldings are ready, cut to proper lengths and assemble. Install back panel (C) and install (E), (D), (F) and (G).
(3) Cut parts (A), (B), (C), and (D) as per drawing and make up two cabinets.
(4) Cut parts for base and assemble.
(5) Set all nail holes, fill and sand.
(6) Install doors and magnetic catches.
(7) Finish to your choice of colors.

MATERIAL LISTS:

(2 cabinets)

(A)	4 Pcs.	¾" x 11⅞" x 28"	Plywood
(B)	4 Pcs.	¾" x 11⅞" x 14½"	Plywood
(C)	2 Pcs.	¾" x 11⅞" x 14"	Plywood
(D)	2 Pcs.	⅛" x 15" x 28"	Plywood

(1 base)

(E)	2 Pcs.	¾" x 4" x 25½"	Plywood
(F)	2 Pcs.	¾" x 4" x 10"	Plywood
(G)	1 Pc.	¾" x 4" x 9"	Plywood

(4 doors)

(A & B)	24	Linear ft. Pine moulding	
(C)	4 Pcs.	⅛" x 12¼" x 13¼" Plywood	
(D & E)	12	Linear ft. ½" x 2" Plywood	
(F)	4	Ornamental mouldings No. 3341	
(G)	4	Small knobs	
(H)	8	Small hinges and screws	
	Misc.:	1½" finish nails, wood filler, glue, sandpaper, magnetic catches.	

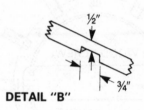

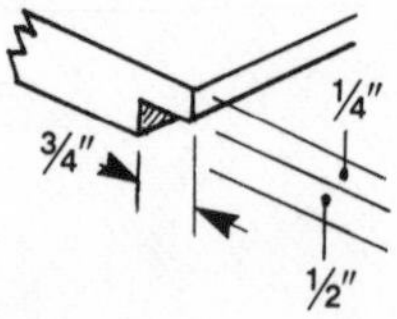

DETAIL "A"

DETAIL "B"

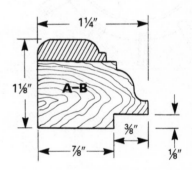

A–B

DETAIL "C"

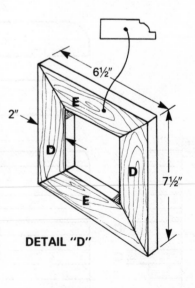

DETAIL "D"

G

252

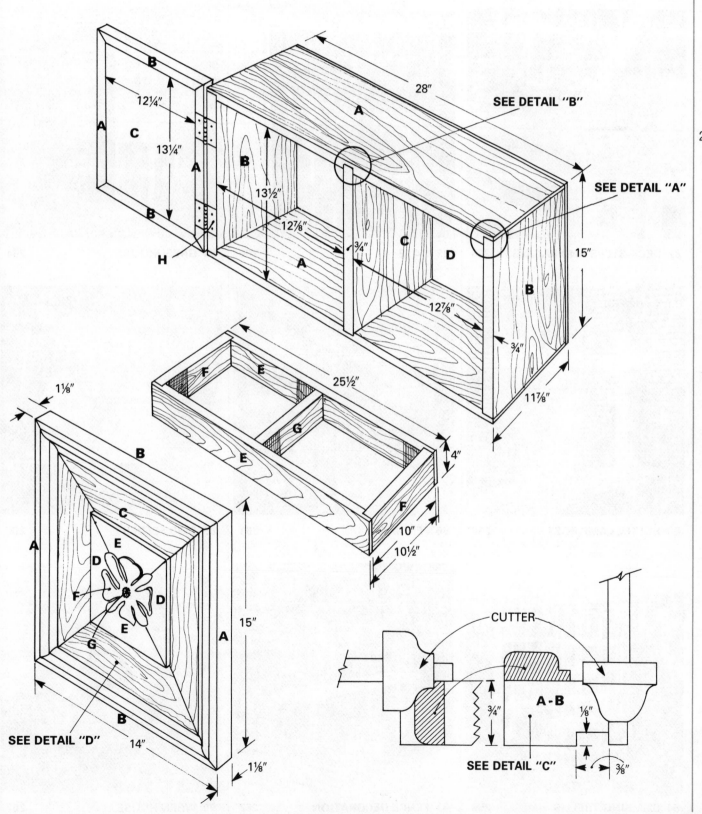

B

12¼"

A

C

13¼"

A

B

H

28"

SEE DETAIL "B"

A

B

13½"

12⅞"

A

¾"

C

D

SEE DETAIL "A"

15"

B

12⅞"

¾"

11⅞"

F

E

25½"

E

G

E

4"

F

10"

10½"

1⅛"

B

C

E

D

D

F

E

D

G

A

A

15"

SEE DETAIL "D"

B

14"

1⅛"

CUTTER

A - B

¾"

⅛"

SEE DETAIL "C"

⅜"

254

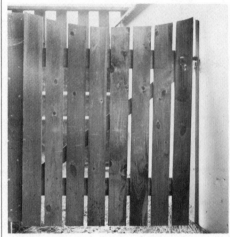

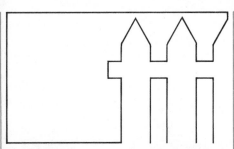

9
Patio and garden projects

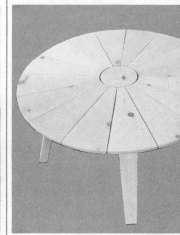

82
deck
steps and railings

Sooner or later any wooden back-entrance gives way to old age. When that time comes, you'll be well prepared to tackle a project like this with the design shown here.

INSTRUCTIONS:

(1) The drawing of a deck is intended to show some of the basic steps in building a structure of this kind. Dimensions are not shown, as the overall size is left to suit your requirements.

(2) First of all you should make a layout of your job in order to locate the position of the posts and the height of the ledger on the concrete wall.

(3) When post holes are located, dig down below frost level and install form for concrete part of post. Pour concrete and set steel pin for post.

(4) Drill holes in wall to secure ledger support and proceed to construct deck, using joist hangers and nails.

(5) When your structure is finished, give it a coat of wood preservative.

STEP STRINGERS:

(1) Measure height from ground to top of deck to establish the rise. To find the rise of each step you must divide the height by 7" or 8" rises or a figure as close as possible so that all your risers are equal.

(2) The tread is usually 10", therefore the cut on the stringer is 9", allowing for a 1" overhang.

(3) If for example, the total height is 28", then the risers will be 7" each and with a run of 27" having three treads of 9" each.

(4) Using a carpenter's framing square, use the numbers 7 & 9, proceed to mark out stringer.

(5) When all is laid out, cut 1¾" off bottom of stringer to allow for tread thickness so that all rises are equal when all the treads are on.

(6) If you are in doubt about the layout, practice on some scrap plywood before cutting actual stringers.

RAILINGS:

(1) Attach wall piece to concrete or brick with ¼" lag screws and shields and proceed as illustrated on drawing.

(2) Be sure to attach corner posts to deck securely, using screws or nails.

(3) Finish off railings by setting all nails, fitting and sanding a little.

(4) Paint or use wood preservative to your choice of colors.

Verify all measurements before cutting

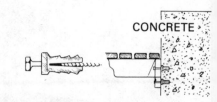

ATTACHING 2" x 6" AND 2" x 4"
LEDGER TO CONCRETE WALL

LAG SCREWS and SHIELDS ⅜"

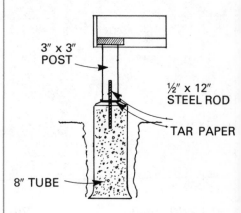

3" x 3" POST

½" x 12" STEEL ROD

TAR PAPER

8" TUBE

FRONT DECK SUPPORTS

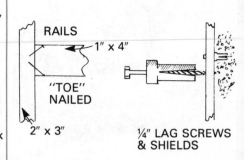

RAILS

1" x 4"

"TOE" NAILED

2" x 3"

¼" LAG SCREWS & SHIELDS

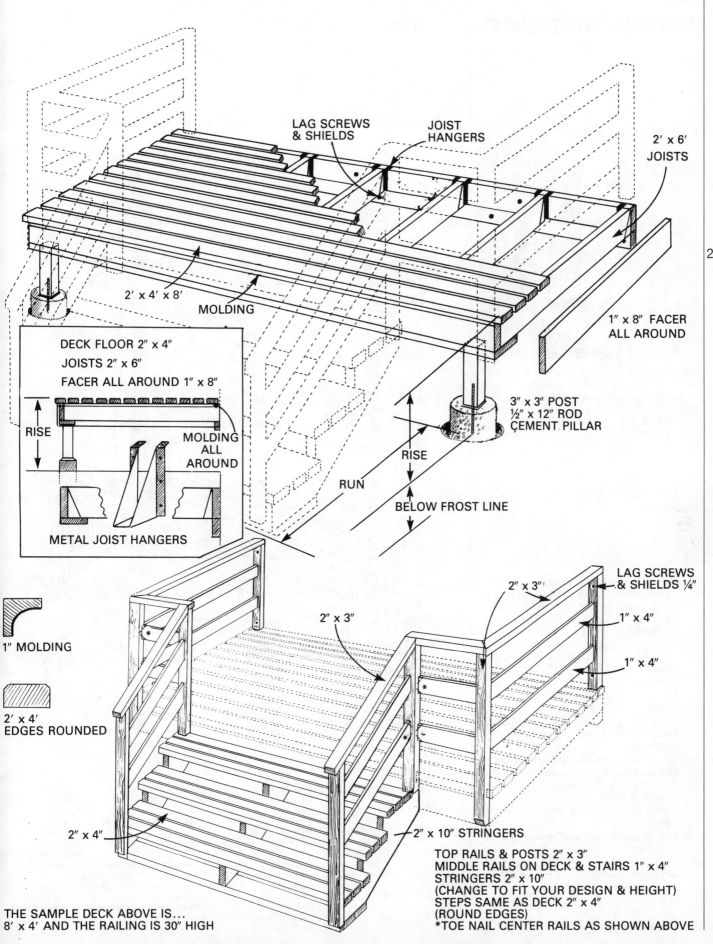

LAG SCREWS
& SHIELDS

JOIST
HANGERS

2' x 6'
JOISTS

2' x 4' x 8'

MOLDING

1" x 8" FACER
ALL AROUND

DECK FLOOR 2" x 4"
JOISTS 2" x 6"
FACER ALL AROUND 1" x 8"

RISE

MOLDING
ALL
AROUND

METAL JOIST HANGERS

3" x 3" POST
½" x 12" ROD
CEMENT PILLAR

RISE

RUN

BELOW FROST LINE

1" MOLDING

2' x 4'
EDGES ROUNDED

2" x 3"

2" x 3"

LAG SCREWS
& SHIELDS ¼"

1" x 4"

1" x 4"

2" x 4"

2" x 10" STRINGERS

TOP RAILS & POSTS 2" x 3"
MIDDLE RAILS ON DECK & STAIRS 1" x 4"
STRINGERS 2" x 10"
(CHANGE TO FIT YOUR DESIGN & HEIGHT)
STEPS SAME AS DECK 2" x 4"
(ROUND EDGES)
*TOE NAIL CENTER RAILS AS SHOWN ABOVE

THE SAMPLE DECK ABOVE IS...
8' x 4' AND THE RAILING IS 30" HIGH

83
settee lamp-post

Add an elegant touch of class to the outward appearance of your home with this easy to build settee lamp-post. No great effort or skills required. But its distinctive look will make passersby take a second glance.

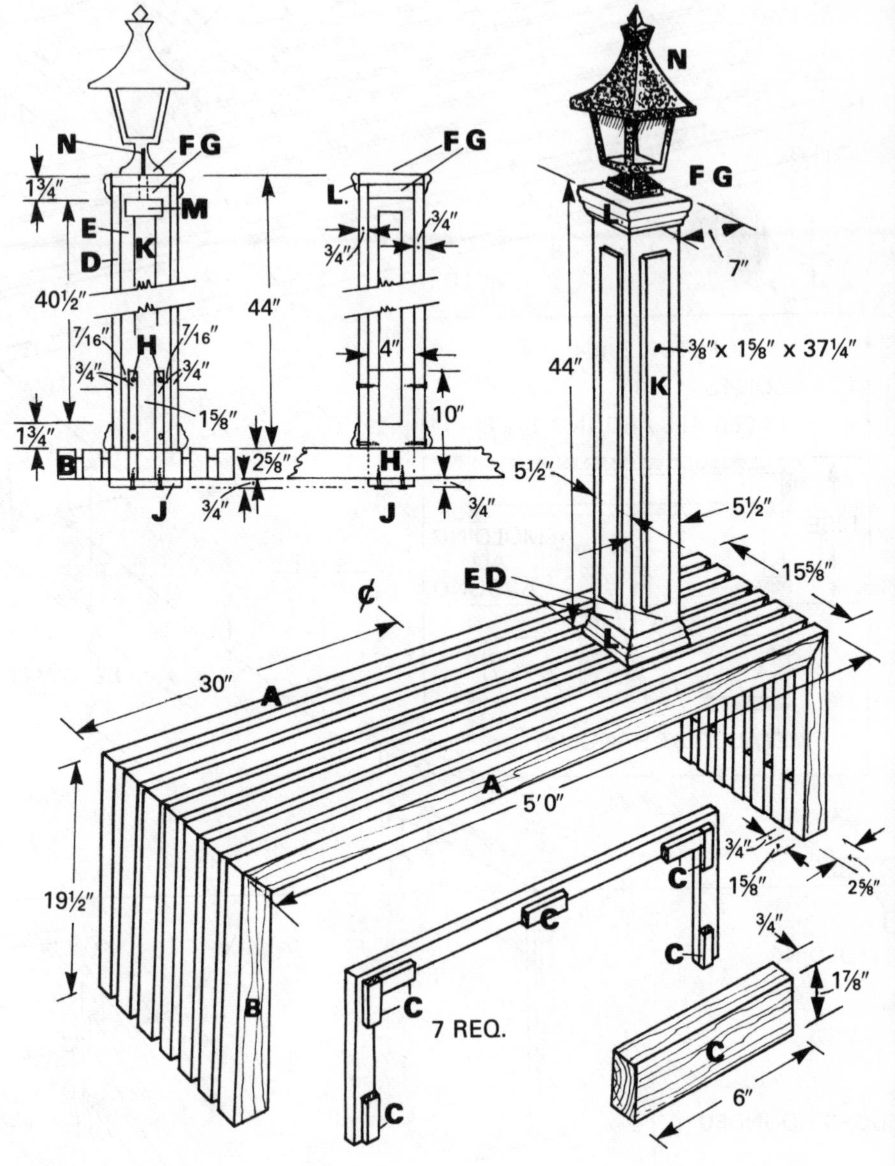

INSTRUCTIONS:

(1) You will require approximately 72 linear feet of 2 x 3, 16 linear feet of 1 x 6, 8 linear feet of moulding and 14 linear feet of ⅜ x 1⅝. All pine or redwood.

(2) Following material list and drawing, cut all parts for bench section, then glue and nail (A) and (B) sections together.

(3) Cut pieces (C), glue and nail them in place as per drawing.

(4) When bench is completed, cut parts for post and assemble as per drawing.

(5) Construct parts (G), (F) and (L) as a cap and install electrical fittings (M), (N), and (O). Then install and secure to top of post.

(6) Install post in bench and secure with part (J).

(7) Fill all nail holes and imperfections and sand.

(8) If you use pine give coat of exterior wood preservative stain or paint to your choice of color.

Verify all measurements before cutting

MATERIAL LIST:

(A)	7 Pcs.	1⅝″ x 2⅝″ x 60″	Pine or Redwood
(B)	14 Pcs.	1⅝″ x 2⅝″ x 19½″	Pine or Redwood
(C)	42 Pcs.	¾″ x 1⅞″ x 6″	Pine or Redwood
(D)	2 Pcs.	¾″ x 5½″ x 43¼″	Pine or Redwood
(E)	2 Pcs.	¾″ x 4″ x 43¼″	Pine or Redwood
(F)	1 Pc.	¾″ x 5½″ x 5½″	Pine or Redwood
(G)	1 Pc.	¾″ x 4″ x 4″	Pine or Redwood
(H)	2 Pcs.	¾″ x 4″ x 10″	Plywood
(J)	1 Pc.	¾″ x 4″ x 5½″	Pine or Redwood
(K)	4 Pcs.	⅜″ x 1⅝″ x 37¼″	Pine or Redwood
(L)	8 Linear ft. moulding		Pine or Redwood
(M)	1 Electrical junction box and connector		
(N)	1 Light fixture of your choice		
Misc.:	Sufficient length of plastic or aluminum covered underground wire Screws, nails, glue, stain or paint, wood filler, sandpaper.		

84
climbing trellis

Here's an afternoon of rewarding work all laid out for you. A climbing trellis to add shade and interest to your backyard. Follow the plan carefully and you'll wind up with a handsome piece of workmanship everyone will appreciate.

INSTRUCTIONS:

(1) Proceed by cutting parts for upright sections according to drawing and material list.
(2) Following drawing, nail and glue together parts for bench sections.
(3) Make up overhead section and attach to bench sections.
(4) When project is completed, locate position and true up, then drive stakes (O) into ground and using nails or bolts, secure (A) and (B) to them.
(5) Paint or stain as desired.

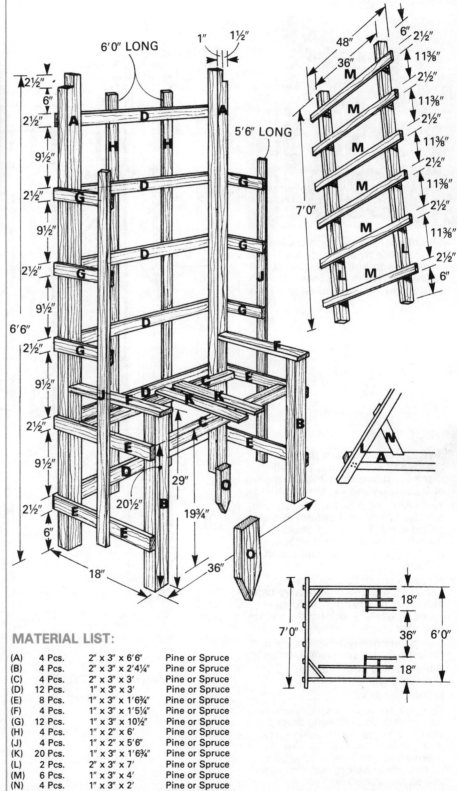

MATERIAL LIST:

(A)	4 Pcs.	2″ x 3″ x 6′6″	Pine or Spruce
(B)	4 Pcs.	2″ x 3″ x 2′4¼″	Pine or Spruce
(C)	4 Pcs.	2″ x 3″ x 3′	Pine or Spruce
(D)	12 Pcs.	1″ x 3″ x 3′	Pine or Spruce
(E)	8 Pcs.	1″ x 3″ x 1′6¾″	Pine or Spruce
(F)	4 Pcs.	1″ x 3″ x 1′5¼″	Pine or Spruce
(G)	12 Pcs.	1″ x 3″ x 10½″	Pine or Spruce
(H)	4 Pcs.	1″ x 2″ x 6′	Pine or Spruce
(J)	4 Pcs.	1″ x 2″ x 5′6″	Pine or Spruce
(K)	20 Pcs.	1″ x 3″ x 1′6¾″	Pine or Spruce
(L)	2 Pcs.	2″ x 3″ x 7′	Pine or Spruce
(M)	6 Pcs.	1″ x 3″ x 4′	Pine or Spruce
(N)	4 Pcs.	1″ x 3″ x 2′	Pine or Spruce
(O)	8 Pcs.	2″ x 3″ x 1′	Pine or Spruce

Verify all measurements before cutting

85 gate

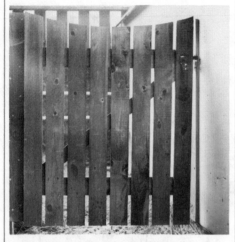

A well built gate keeps toddlers in — and unwelcome trouble out. You'll see how easy it is to build a functional, yet attractive gate when you follow the detailed instructions given on this plan.

INSTRUCTIONS:

(1) If you intend to attach the gate to the side of your house, you will first have to anchor a 2 x 4 by means of lag screws and expansion shields.

(2) You will need a carbide tipped drill, the size of which is determined by shield used. The shield usually has the size of the hole required stamped on it. ie: ⅜" lag screw and shield, ¾" hole.

(3) Measure space between face of 2 x 4 and post, and proceed to build gate as shown on drawing. Make gate approximately ½" smaller than space available.

(4) Using T-hinges or strap hinges and the proper size screws, mount gate.

(5) When gate is fitted, nail on a 1 x 2 stop on post.

(6) Install thumb latch.

(7) To mark and cut a slight downward curve to top of gate, hang a wet piece of string to top corners and mark along string. Cut with jig saw. To make an upward curve turn gate upside down before installing and use same procedure.

Verify all measurements before cutting

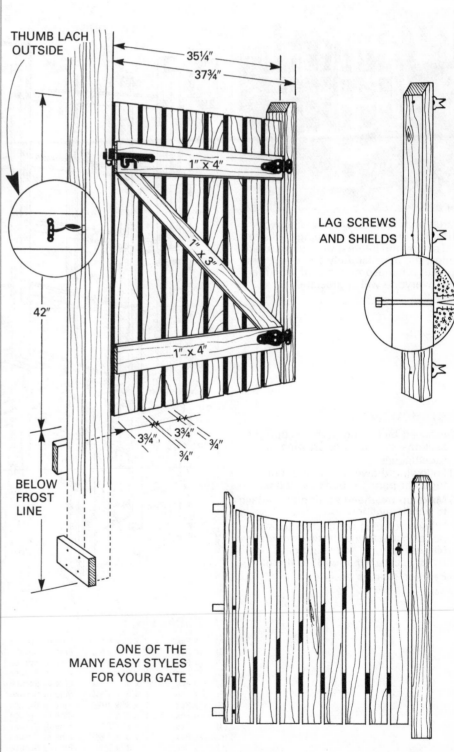

THUMB LACH OUTSIDE

35¼"

37¾"

1" X 4"

1" X 3"

42"

1" X 4"

3¾"   3¾"   ¾"

¾"

BELOW FROST LINE

LAG SCREWS AND SHIELDS

ONE OF THE MANY EASY STYLES FOR YOUR GATE

86
fencing

"Good fences make good neighbours"
goes the saying. But attractive fences
make for even better neighbours because
it shows that you care about the appearance of your home and thereby about
the appearance of the whole neighbour-
hood.

INSTRUCTIONS:

If you should decide to build a fence
of the type shown, the following
information will be of help to you:

(1) Dig corner hole approximately 30"
deep or at least below the frost line in
your area.

(2) Install post, using pickets and braces
to keep plumb, and fill with concrete
or well compacted fill.

(3) Using the 8' rails as spacers, locate
and dig hole for next post, etc.

(4) If using ¼" x 4' x 8' panels, nail on
1 x 2 frames to one side of posts and
rails and insert panel and nail on
other 1 x 2 frame. Then nail on intermediate uprights on both sides of
panel.

(5) Using a line to establish uniform
height, mark posts and cut off excess
and bevel top.

(6) Give one or two coats of exterior
wood preservative.

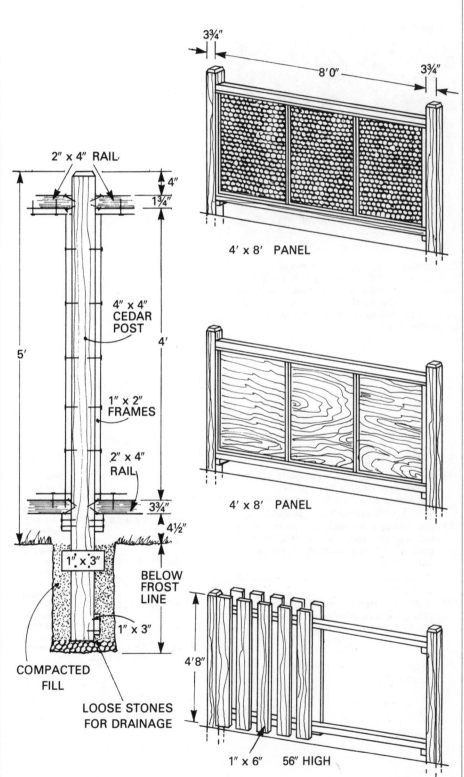

87
fence decoration

Customize your fence with these great cut-out ideas. While you're at it, build the attractive bench as well. Create your own "corner of the yard", or use this design as an interesting backdrop for your swimming pool.

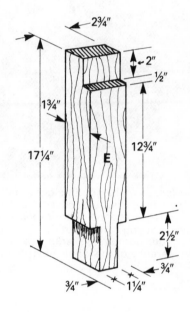

DETAIL "A"

INSTRUCTIONS:

(1) You will need approximately 40 linear feet of 2" x 3" pine or redwood and also 50 linear feet of 1" x 3" to construct this project.

(2) Following the drawing and material list, cut all pieces listed and, using glue and finish nails, proceed to assemble.

(3) When completed, set all nails and fill and then sand.

(4) If you are using pine, I suggest that you give a coat of exterior stain to your choice of colors.

MATERIAL LIST:

(A)	1 Pc.	1¾" x 2¾" x 8'	Pine or Redwood
(B)	1 Pc.	1¾" x 2¾" x 7'9½"	Pine or Redwood
(C)	2 Pcs.	1¾" x 2¾" x 1'10¼"	Pine or Redwood
(D)	4 Pcs.	1¾" x 2¾" x 1'5"	Pine or Redwood
(E)	6 Pcs.	1¾" x 2¾" x 1'5¼"	Pine or Redwood
(F)	6 Pcs.	¾" x 2½" x 1'6"	Pine or Redwood
(G)	5 Pcs.	¾" x 2½" x 7'7"	Pine or Redwood
(H)	24 Pcs.	¾" x ¾" x 4"	Pine or Redwood
	Misc.:	Nails, woodfiller, sandpaper, stain or paint.	

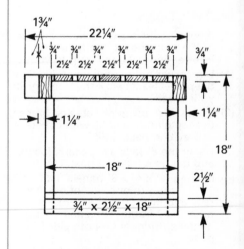

END ELEVATION

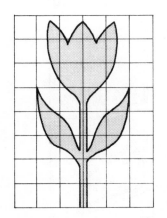
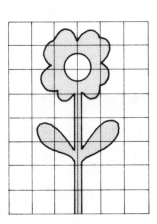
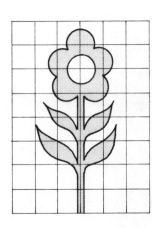
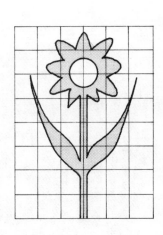

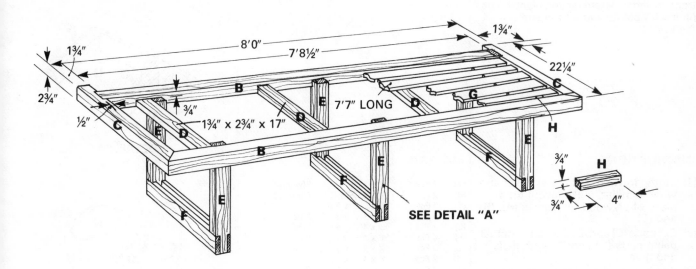

SEE DETAIL "A"

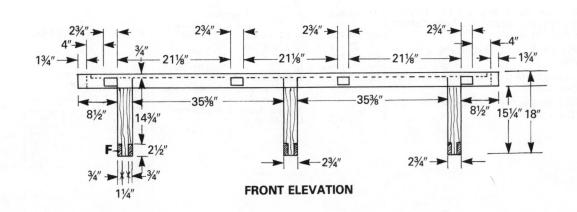

FRONT ELEVATION

88
greenhouse

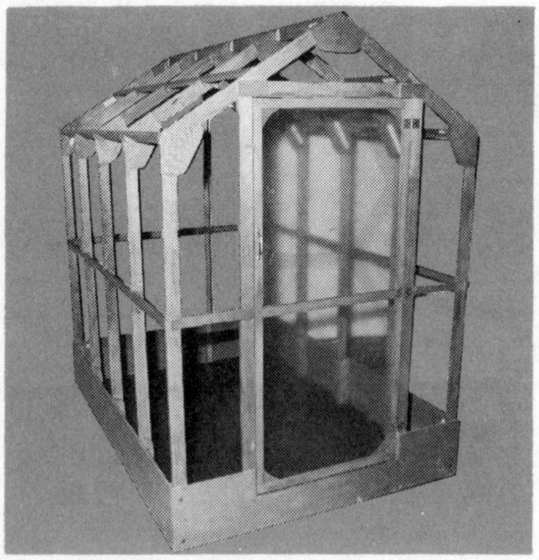

Give your plants a head start on summer with this attractive design. It's put together quickly and light enough to be transported to wherever you want it. Then fill it with plants and let the sun do the rest.

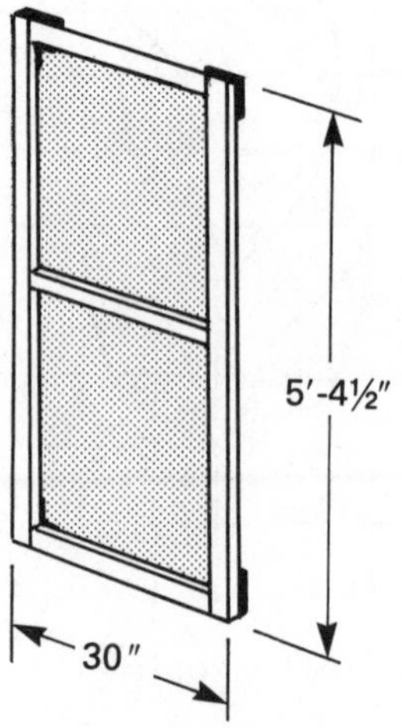

DOOR DETAIL

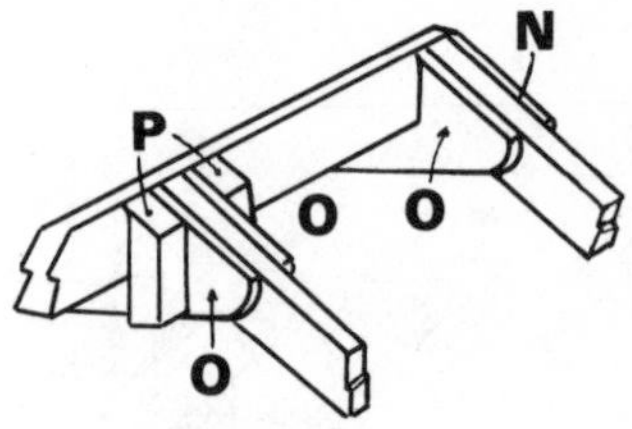

DETAIL "A"

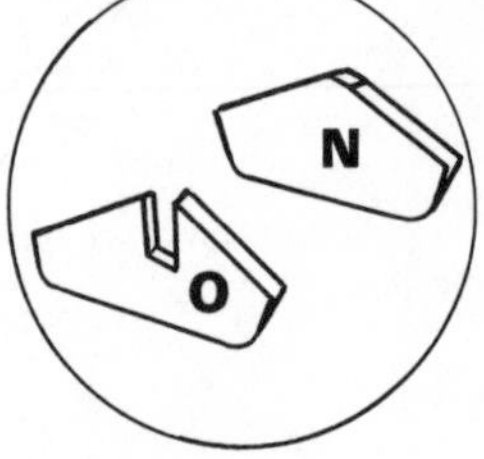

DETAIL "B"

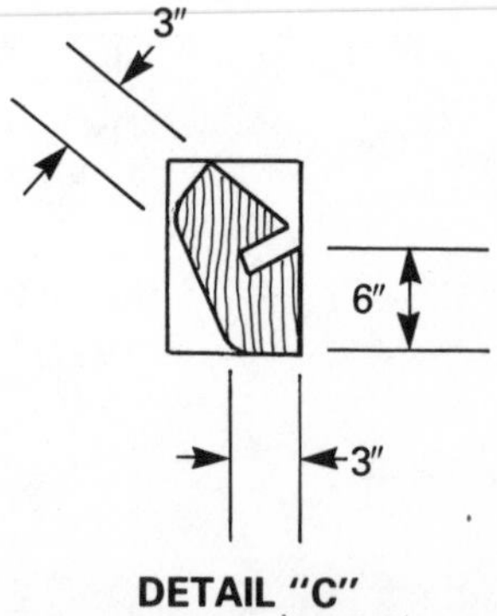

DETAIL "C"

INSTRUCTIONS:

(1) Study drawing and material list and when familiar, make layout on a piece of plywood for frames (A), (B) and (C).

(2) Cut parts (C) and (D) and join together using parts (O) and (N) with nails and glue.

(3) When frames are constructed attach to pieces (A) and (B).

(4) Install pieces (J) and (F). Use hooks and eyes on pieces (J) to hold frames (A) and (B).

(5) Make up door to fit opening and install.

(6) Give structure a coat of wood preservative stain.

(7) Using ¼″ staples, cover greenhouse with polythene.

MATERIAL LIST:

(A)	2 Pcs.	½″ x 11½″ x 7′	Plywood
(B)	2 Pcs.	½″ x 11½″ x 5′1″	Plywood
(C)	10 Pcs.	¾″ x 2½″ x 5′6″	Pine
(D)	10 Pcs.	¾″ x 1½″ x 3′	Pine
(E)	2 Pcs.	¾″ x 1½″ x 6′5″	Pine
(F)	4 Pcs.	¾″ x 1½″ x 7′	Pine
(G)	3 Pcs.	¾″ x 1½″ x 17 5/16″	Pine
(H)	2 Pcs.	¾″ x 1½″ x 10″	Pine
(J)	3 Pcs.	¾″ x 2½″ x 7′	Pine
(K)	2 Pcs.	¾″ x 2½″ x 74″	Pine
(L)	1 Pc.	¾″ x 2½″ x 30″	Pine
(M)	10 Pcs.	1¼″ x 2½″ x 11½″	Pine
(N)	24 Pcs.	¼″ x 7″ x 9″ (with slot)	Plywood
(O)	6 Pcs.	¼″ x 7″ x 9″ (no slot)	Plywood
(P)	24 Pcs.	¾″ x ¾″ x 2½″	Pine
(Q)	16 Pcs.	¾″ x ¾″ x 1½″	Pine
(R)	20 Lineal ft.	¾″ x 1½″	Pine for door
(S)	1 Pc.	Polythene 8′ x 30′	
	Misc.:	Hinges, screws, nails, glue, stain, staples, hooks and eyes, turn buttons, door pull and carriage bolts.	

Verify all measurements before cutting

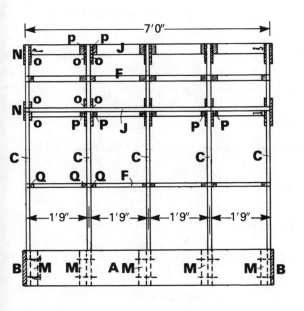

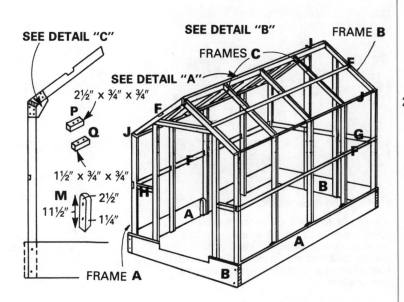

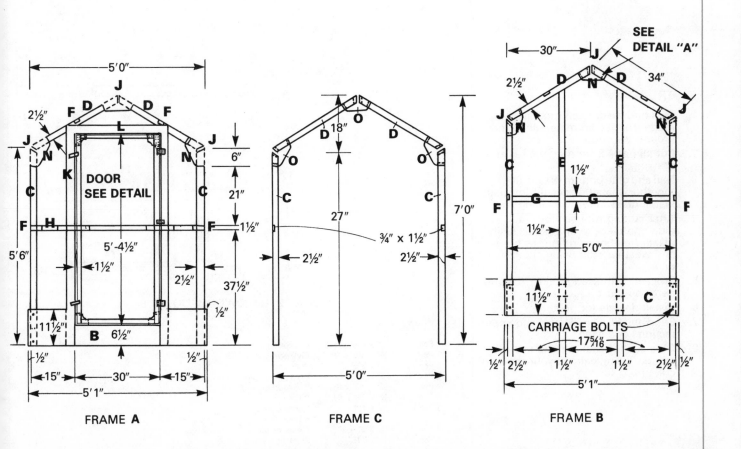

FRAME **A**

FRAME **C**

FRAME **B**

89
bird feeder

If you like to wake up to the happy chirping of feathered friends — here's your chance to build an inexpensive feeder that will attract all kinds of birds. Great idea for birdwatchers or camera enthusiasts.

INSTRUCTIONS:

1. This bird feeder can most likely be made from scrap materials found around the shop.
2. Cut all parts from material list and drawing.
3. Nail and glue bottom (B) and ends (A) together. Install pieces (F) for glass. Install glass before installing roof.
4. After cutting roof sections, nail and glue one piece to end panel. Using plastic/leather or rubber as hinge and weather stop using staples and glue.
5. Proceed with seed retainer (D) and perch support (E).
6. Install dowels for perch.
7. Sand and fill all nail holes and imperfections and sand.
8. Give coat of shellack and using exterior paint, paint to your choice of colours.

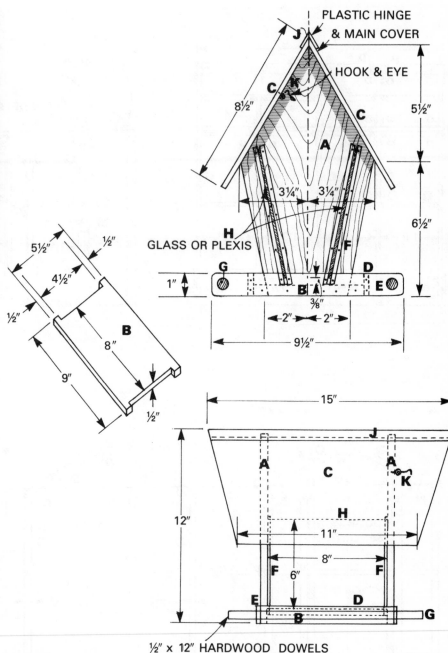

½" x 12" HARDWOOD DOWELS

MATERIAL LIST:

A.	2 Pcs.	½" x 6½" x 12"	Plywood
B.	1 Pc.	½" x 5½" x 9"	Plywood
C.	2 Pcs.	¼" x 8½" x 15"	Plywood
D.	2 Pcs.	¼" x 1" x 9"	Plywood or pine
E.	2 Pcs.	¼" x 12" x 9½"	Plywood or pine
F.	8 Pcs.	¼" x ¼" x 6¾"	Pine
G.	2 Pcs.	½" x 12"	Hardwood dowel
H.	2 Pcs.	⅛" x 6" x 8"	Plexis or glass
J.	1 Pc.	1½" x 15"	Plastic or rubber
	Misc.:	1 Pc. small hood & eye, nails, staples, glue, shellack and paint	

Verify all measurements before cutting

90
wren house

Here's a "let's do-it-together" project for father and son teams. Inexpensive fun, plus a good lesson in patience. Helps develop your children's interest in nature while caring for our feathered friends.

INSTRUCTIONS:

1. To construct both bird houses, you will require a piece of ¼" and a piece of ½" plywood approx. 2'0" x 3'0".
2. Cut the parts as per drawing, and assemble, using small nails and glue.
3. When installing the bottom, use ¾" — # 6 wood screws only, no glue. This will permit removal of bottom for yearly cleaning.
4. Paint exterior to your choice of colours using exterior type paint.

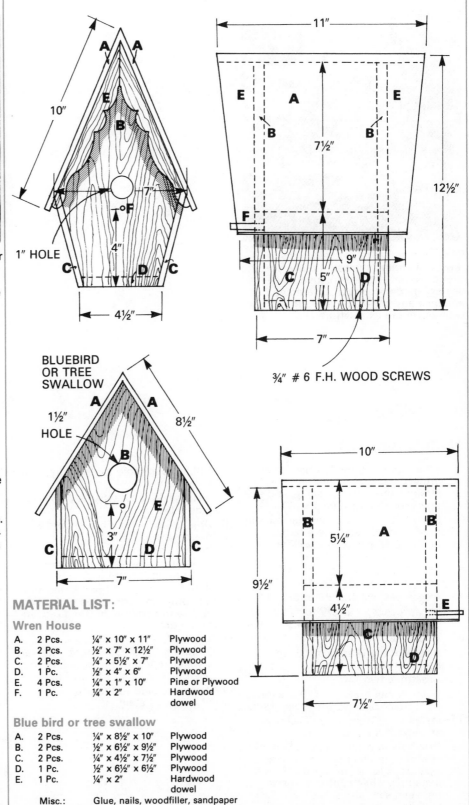

1" HOLE

4½"

BLUEBIRD OR TREE SWALLOW

1½" HOLE

8½"

7"

11"

7½"

12½"

9"

5"

7"

¾" # 6 F.H. WOOD SCREWS

10"

5¼"

9½"

4½"

7½"

MATERIAL LIST:

Wren House

A.	2 Pcs.	¼" x 10" x 11"	Plywood
B.	2 Pcs.	½" x 7" x 12½"	Plywood
C.	2 Pcs.	¼" x 5½" x 7"	Plywood
D.	1 Pc.	½" x 4" x 6"	Plywood
E.	4 Pcs.	¼" x 1" x 10"	Pine or Plywood
F.	1 Pc.	¼" x 2"	Hardwood dowel

Blue bird or tree swallow

A.	2 Pcs.	¼" x 8½" x 10"	Plywood
B.	2 Pcs.	½" x 6½" x 9½"	Plywood
C.	2 Pcs.	¼" x 4½" x 7½"	Plywood
D.	1 Pc.	½" x 6½" x 6½"	Plywood
E.	1 Pc.	¼" x 2"	Hardwood dowel
	Misc.:	Glue, nails, woodfiller, sandpaper screws, and paint.	

Verify all measurements before cutting

91
two seat
lounger

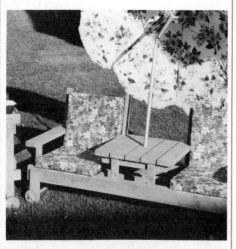

Careful attention to detailed plans, plus a few, free afternoons could make you the proud owner of this attractive "two-seater" garden lounger. Guaranteed to enhance any patio. A major project but well worth the extra effort.

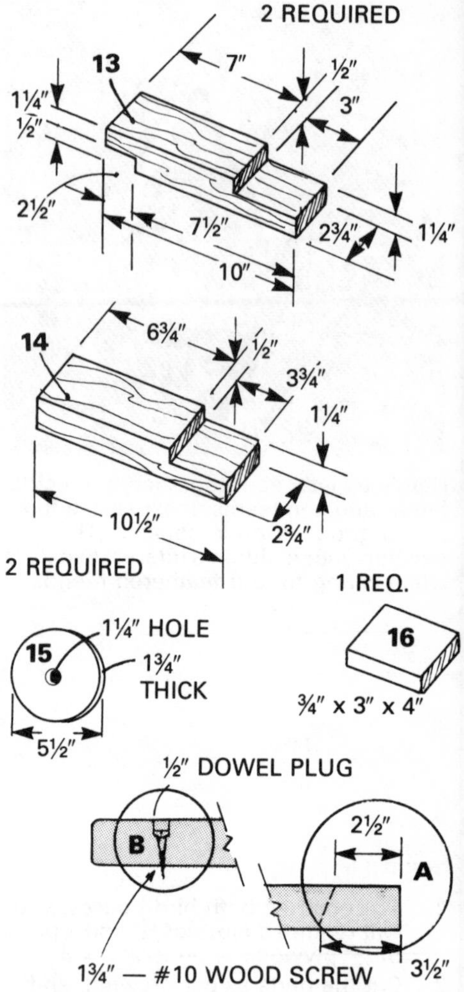

INSTRUCTIONS:

1. When ordering the lumber for this project, ask that all pieces be as straight and dry as possible and that any knots be firm ones.
2. Cut all parts as per material list and drwg., and if you have a router, bullnose all edges that will be exposed when assembled.
3. Start assembly by gluing and nailing pcs. #1 to pcs. #6.
4. Attach pcs. #7 and #8 to pcs. #1.
5. Locate pcs. #13 at 5½" each side of centre on front pc. #1, nail and glue.
6. Attach pc. #11 to #13.
7. Attach pcs. #14 to pcs. #6.
8. Nail and glue pc. #9 to pcs. #10. Assemble two.
9. Using metal brackets #19 & screws #21, attach backrests to lower frame.
10. Install pc. #12 between backrests at same level as pc. #11.
11. Drill hole in centre of pc. #5 to suit size of umbrella pole and nail and glue pc. #16 on underside of hole. Install pc. #5 in centre of space between seat areas.
12. Install arms, pcs. #2 & #3 & #4.

13. Drill hole in table top directly above hole in pc. #5.
14. Install axle, #17, wheels #15 and pins #18.
15. Drill ¼" holes for #5 sashcord as per drawing.
16. Weave cord as per drwg. and secure ends firmly by driving a nail down through ends from top.
17. Set all nails and fill nail holes and any other imperfections with filler and sand carefully in the direction of the grain.
18. The cushions for this lounger are 3" thick x 23" x 23" square. They are a water repellant material and are filled with a slab of foam rubber.
19. If you use pine you may give it a coat of redwood stain.

2 REQUIRED

13 · 7" · ½" · 3" · 1¼" · ½" · 2½" · 7½" · 2¾" · 1¼" · 10"

14 · 6¾" · ½" · 3¾" · 1¼" · 10½" · 2¾"

2 REQUIRED

15 · 1¼" HOLE · 1¾" THICK · 5½"

1 REQ.

16 · ¾" x 3" x 4"

½" DOWEL PLUG

B · 2½" · A · 3½"

1¾" — #10 WOOD SCREW

MATERIALS:

No.	Qty	Dimensions	Material
1.	2 Pcs.	1¾" x 5½" x 81"	Pine
2.	2 Pcs.	1¾" x 5" x 30"	Pine
3.	2 Pcs.	1¾" x 5½" x 28½"	Pine
4.	3 Pcs.	1¾" x 5½" x 28½"	Pine
5.	1 Pc.	1¾" x 5" x 24"	Pine
6.	4 Pcs.	1¾" x 3¾" x 25"	Pine
7.	2 Pcs.	1¾" x 3¾" x 12"	Pine
8.	2 Pcs.	1¾" x 3¾" x 10⅞"	Pine
9.	1 Pc.	1¾" x 2¾" x 27"	Pine
10.	4 Pcs.	1¾" x 2¾" x 24"	Pine
11.	1 Pc.	1¾" x 2¾" x 24"	Pine
12.	1 Pc.	1¾" x 2¾" x 24"	Pine
13.	2 Pcs.	1¾" x 2¾" x 24"	Pine
14.	2 Pcs.	1¾" x 2¾" x 10½"	Pine
15.	2 Pcs.	1¾" x 5½"	Diameter pine
16.	1 Pc.	¾" x 3" x 4"	Pine
17.	1 Pc.	1" x 35"	Hardwood dowel
18.	2 Pcs.	¼" x 3"	Hardwood dowel
19.	4 Pcs.	⅛" x 1" x 6"	Strap Iron
20.	100 Feet #5 sash cord		
21.	16 — 1" — #10 Bindhead Sheet Metal Screws		
22.	1 Quart Redwood Stain		
23.	Wood filler, Sandpaper		
24.	Material of your choice for four cushions		

Verify all measurements before cutting

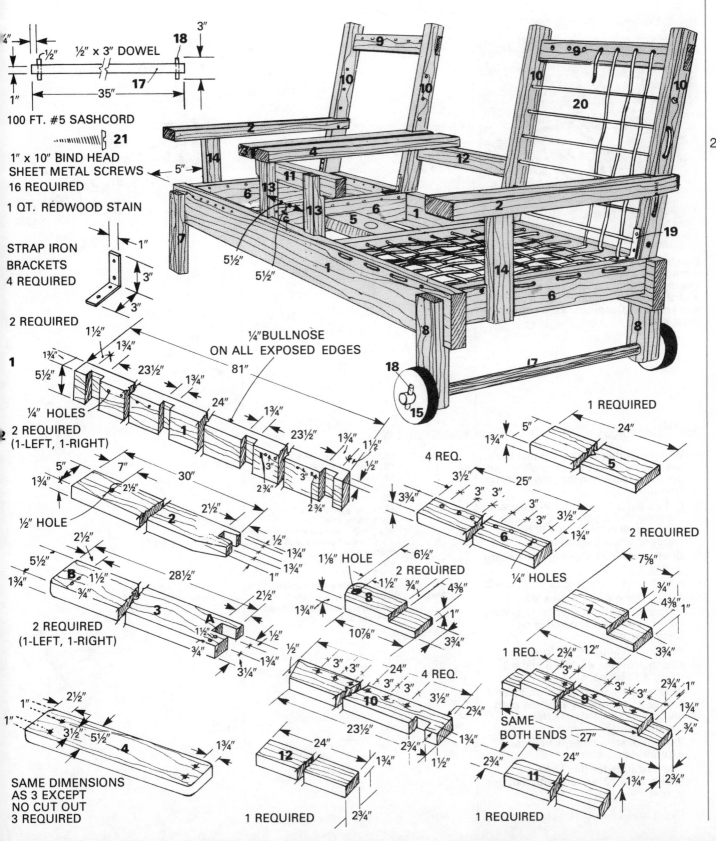

½" × 3" DOWEL **18** 3"

4" ½" **17** 35"

100 FT. #5 SASHCORD

21

1" × 10" BIND HEAD
SHEET METAL SCREWS
16 REQUIRED

1 QT. REDWOOD STAIN

STRAP IRON
BRACKETS
4 REQUIRED

2 REQUIRED

1" 3" 3"

1

1½" 1¾"

1¾" 23½" 1¾"

5½"

¼" HOLES

2 REQUIRED
(1-LEFT, 1-RIGHT)

¼" BULLNOSE
ON ALL EXPOSED EDGES

81"

24" 1¾"

23½" 1¾" 1½"

3" ½"

3"

2¾"

2¾"

5" 7" 30"

1¾" 2½" **2** 2½" ½"

1¾"

½" HOLE 1¾" 1"

2½" 28½" 2½"

5½" **B** 1½" ½"

1¾" ¾" **3** **A** 1¾" 1¾"

1½" ½"

¾" 1¾"

3¼"

2 REQUIRED
(1-LEFT, 1-RIGHT)

1" 2½"

1" 3½" 5½" **4** 1¾"

SAME DIMENSIONS
AS 3 EXCEPT
NO CUT OUT
3 REQUIRED

9

10 **10** **10**

20

2

14 **4** **12**

11

13 **6** **13** **5** **6** **1** **2** **19**

5½"

5½" **1** **14**

7 **6**

8 **8**

17

18 **15**

1 REQUIRED

5" 24"

1¾" **5**

4 REQ.

3½" 25"

3¾" 3" 3" 3" 3½"

6 1¾"

¼" HOLES

2 REQUIRED

1⅛" HOLE 6½"

2 REQUIRED

8 1½" ¾" 4⅜"

1¾" 1"

10⅞" 3¾"

½" 3" 3" 24" 4 REQ.

3" 3"

10 3½"

23½" 2¾"

24" 2¾" 1¾"

12 1¾" 1½"

1 REQUIRED 2¾"

7⅝"

¾"

4⅜" 1"

7

1 REQ. 2¾" 12" 3¾"

3"

9 3" 2¾" 1"

1¾"

SAME ¾"
BOTH ENDS 27"

11 24" 1¾"

2¾" 2¾"

1 REQUIRED

269

92
lawn chair

Here's a "his'n hers" project to take up a fun filled afternoon. He does all the sawing, cutting, nailing and gluing — and she does all the intricate weaving and knotting. Cushions can be bought in most stores.

INSTRUCTIONS:

1. When ordering lumber for this chair, ask that all pieces be as straight and dry as possible and that any knots be firm ones.
2. Cut all parts as per material list and drawing and if you have a router, bullnose all edges that will be exposed when assembled.
3. Start assembly by gluing and nailing pieces #1 to #2.
4. Attach legs #7 to pieces #1 and #2.
5. Attach piece #4 to pieces #3.
6. Glue and nail back support to pieces #2 as illustrated and screw on metal bar #8.
7. Attach arm support #6 to #2.
8. Attach arm rest #5 to #6 and #3 using 3" finish nails.
9. Weave sash cord as per drawing and secure end firmly by knotting cord and driving a finish nail down through cord.
10. If desired, stain chair with a good exterior wood stain.
11. The cushions for this chair are 3" thick x 23" x 23" square with a zipper in rear.

Verify all measurements before cutting

MATERIAL LIST:

1	2	1¾" x 3¾" x 29½" Pine
2	2	1¾" x 3¾" x 25" Pine
3	2	1¾" x 2¾" x 24" Pine
4	1	1¾" x 2¾" x 27" Pine
5	2	1¾" x 5" x 28" Pine
6	2	1¾" x 3¾" x 10½" Pine
7	4	1¾" x 3¾" x 11½" Pine
8	2	⅛" x 1" x 6" — steel or aluminum bar
9	8	1" - #10 steel sheet metal fine head screws
10	75 Ft.	#5 sash cord or ¼" nylon rope
11	2	3" x 23" x 23" — foam rubber
12	4	Square yards water repellant material, Glue, wood filler, sandpaper, woodstain, 2" finish nails and 3" finish nails.
	Misc.:	

1 2 REQ.

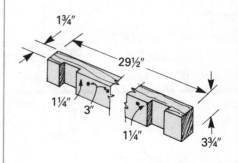

2 2 REQ.

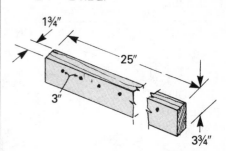

3 2 REQ.

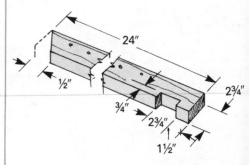

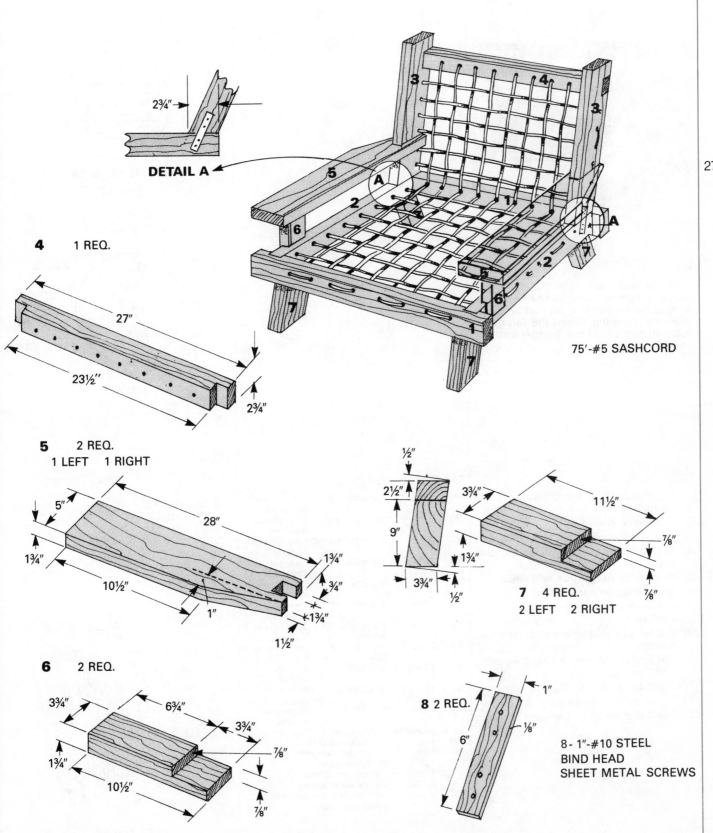

$2\frac{3}{4}''$

DETAIL A

3   4
3
5
A
2
1
6
2
1
7
A
2
5
6
1
7
7
1

75'-#5 SASHCORD

271

4   1 REQ.

27"

23½"

$2\frac{3}{4}''$

5   2 REQ.
1 LEFT   1 RIGHT

5"

28"

$1\frac{3}{4}''$

$1\frac{3}{4}''$

$\frac{3}{4}''$

$10\frac{1}{2}''$ 1"

$1\frac{3}{4}''$

$1\frac{1}{2}''$

½"

$2\frac{1}{2}''$

$3\frac{3}{4}''$

$11\frac{1}{2}''$

9"

$1\frac{3}{4}''$

$3\frac{3}{4}''$

½"

$\frac{7}{8}''$

$\frac{7}{8}''$

7   4 REQ.
2 LEFT   2 RIGHT

6   2 REQ.

$3\frac{3}{4}''$ $6\frac{3}{4}''$ $3\frac{3}{4}''$

$\frac{7}{8}''$

$1\frac{3}{4}''$

$10\frac{1}{2}''$

$\frac{7}{8}''$

1"

8 2 REQ.

6" $\frac{1}{8}''$

8- 1"-#10 STEEL
BIND HEAD
SHEET METAL SCREWS

93
garden lounger

Join the "patio set" with this dual-purpose garden lounger. The back is adjustable for either sitting up or just plain sun-napping. When the sun gets too hot, just wheel the lounger into a shadier spot.

INSTRUCTIONS:

(1) Cut materials as per drawing for lounge section.
(2) Cut check in side rails.
(3) Assemble, using glue and nails.
(4) Cut materials as per drawing for back rest.
(5) Assemble, using glue and nails.
(6) Bore holes as per drawing.
(7) Cut aluminum conduit and install back rest.
(8) Cut wheels and attach with clips to lounge.
(9) Cut and install legs, using glue and nails.
(10) Sand off all sharp edges.
(11) Set and fill nail holes.
(12) Sand and finish as per your choice.

MATERIAL LIST:

(A)	2 Pcs.	1¾" x 10" x 7"	Clear pine or Redwood
(B)	3 Pcs.	1¾" x 2¾" x 21½"	Clear pine or Redwood
(C)	2 Pcs.	1¾" x 2¾" x 17¼"	Clear pine or Redwood
(D)	2 Pcs.	1¾" x 5½" x 30"	Clear pine or Redwood
(E)	2 Pcs.	1" x 3" x 18"	Clear pine or Redwood
(F)	2 Pcs.	1" x 1¾" x 17"	Clear pine or Redwood
(G)	2 Pcs.	1¾" x 10" x 10" wheels	Clear pine or Redwood
(H)	2 Pcs.	1¾" x 6" x 16" legs	Clear pine or Redwood
(I)	2 Lengths	¾" x 24⅜"	Aluminum conduit
(J)	1 Length	½" x 24⅜"	Aluminum conduit
(K)	1 Length	½" x 20¾"	Aluminum conduit
(L)	2 Lengths	1" Pipe clips	
(M)	4	2½" masonite washers	
(N)	75 Ft.	#9 Braided sash cord	
(O)	1 Lb.	2½" finish nails	
	1 Doz.	2½" #10 wood screws	
	½ Doz.	1½" #8 wood screws	
	Misc.:	Paint, stain and wood filler, sandpaper, glue.	

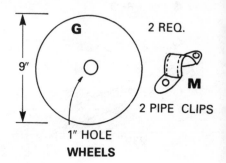

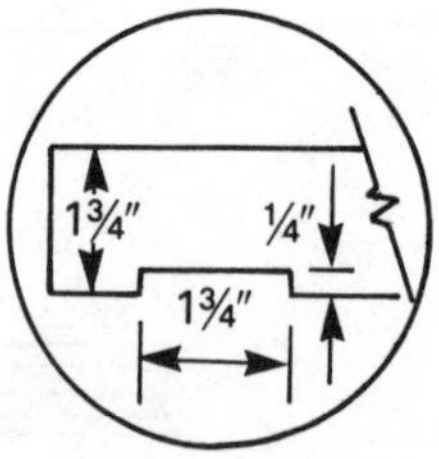

DETAIL "A" & "B"

G   2 REQ.

9"

M

2 PIPE CLIPS

1" HOLE
WHEELS

4 MASONITE WASHERS   N   2½"

1" HOLE
WASHERS

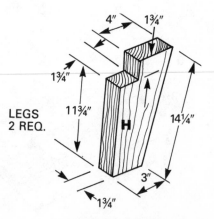

4"   1¾"

1¾"

LEGS 2 REQ.   11¾"   H   14¼"

3"

1¾"

LEG DETAIL

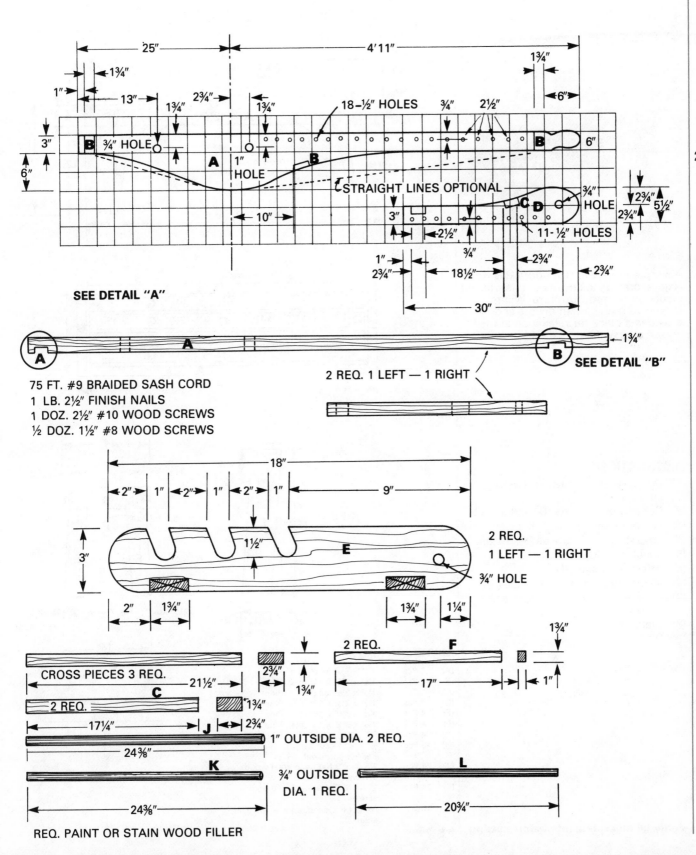

25"

4'11"

1¾"

1¾"

1"

13"

2¾"

1¾"

1¾"

18–½" HOLES

¾"

2½"

6"

3"

B

¾" HOLE

A

1"
HOLE

B

STRAIGHT LINES OPTIONAL

B

6"

6"

¾"
HOLE

2¾"

2¾"

5½"

10"

3"

C **D**

11–½" HOLES

1"

¾"

2¾"

2¾"

2¾"

18½"

2½"

30"

SEE DETAIL "A"

A

A

1¾"

B

SEE DETAIL "B"

2 REQ. 1 LEFT — 1 RIGHT

75 FT. #9 BRAIDED SASH CORD
1 LB. 2½" FINISH NAILS
1 DOZ. 2½" #10 WOOD SCREWS
½ DOZ. 1½" #8 WOOD SCREWS

18"

2"

1"

2"

1"

2"

1"

9"

3"

1½"

E

2 REQ.
1 LEFT — 1 RIGHT

¾" HOLE

2"

1¾"

1¾"

1¼"

1¾"

2 REQ.

F

1¾"

CROSS PIECES 3 REQ.

21½"

2¾"

1¾"

17"

1"

C

2 REQ.

1¾"

17¼"

J

2¾"

1" OUTSIDE DIA. 2 REQ.

24⅜"

K

¾" OUTSIDE
DIA. 1 REQ.

L

20¾"

REQ. PAINT OR STAIN WOOD FILLER

274

A simple project to test your skills on.
A good prelude to any major undertaking
involving outdoor furniture. Will fit
in well with all garden decors and
provides a place for relaxation at the
end of a busy day.

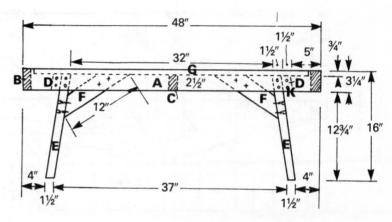

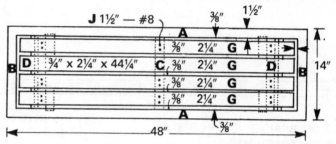

INSTRUCTIONS:

(1) Cut parts (A) and (B) and mitre
    corners.
(2) Cut and bevel parts (D) and install.
(3) Lay out legs (E) and cut. Install.
(4) Lay out and cut braces (F). Install.
(5) Install part (C).
(6) Attach seat slats (G).
(7) Insert plugs in all screw holes.
(8) Bullnose all exposed edges and
    sand.
(9) Stain or paint.

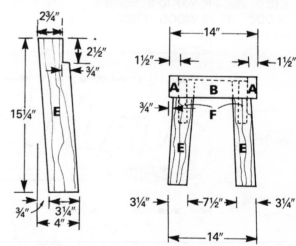

MATERIAL LIST:

(A)	2 Pcs.	1½" x 3¼" x 50" (o-s)	Pine
(B)	2 Pcs.	1½" x 3¼" x 15" (o-s)	Pine
(C)	1 Pc.	1½" x 2½" x 11"	Pine
(D)	2 Pcs.	1½" x 2½" x 11"	Pine
(E)	4 Pcs.	1½" x 3¼" x 16" (o-s)	Pine
(F)	4 Pcs.	1½" x 3¼" x 13" (o-s)	Pine
(G)	4 Pcs.	¾" x 2¼" x 44⅛"	Pine
(H)	48 Pcs.	⅜" x ⅜" — cut from ⅜" dia. hardwood dowel.	
(J)	24 Pcs.	1½" No. 8 flat head steel wood screws.	
(K)	24 Pcs.	2" No. 8 flat head steel wood screws.	
	Misc.:	Nails, glue, sandpaper, wood filler, stain.	

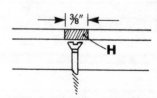

Verify all measurements before cutting | (o-s) = oversize

95
lawn table

Add to your summer enjoyment with this sturdy lawn table. Properly built and properly stained, it will give a lifetime of service to hold drinks and food steady. Great for outdoor chess, too.

INSTRUCTIONS:

1. If possible obtain lumber that is straight and dry and the knots are firm.
2. Put lumber to rough lengths and when you have cut one angle this will serve as a pattern for all other angles.
3. Using 2½" - #10 screws and white glue, assemble leg structure.
4. Place 2 x 6 on top of frame starting in the centre with a ¼" space between each other.
5. Drill ¼" deep x ¾" dia. holes for screws on surface pieces and drive in screws. When finished cut plugs from ¾" dowel and fill screw holes. Sand smooth.
6. Use a good wood preservative redwood stain or paint to your choice of colours.

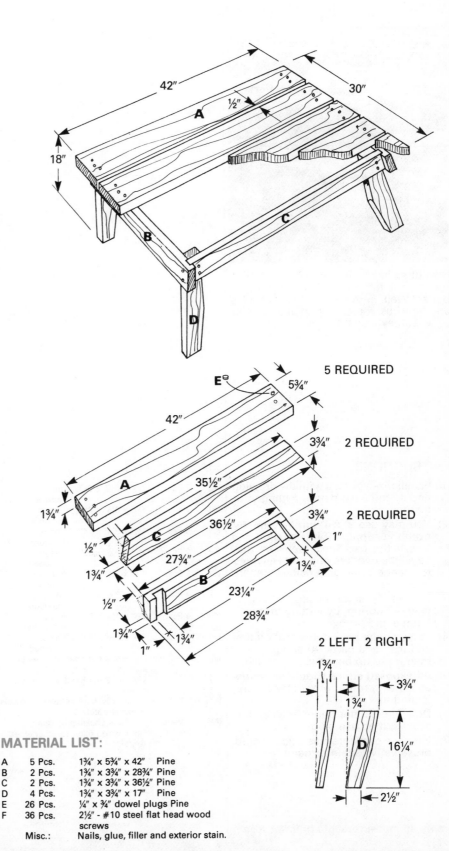

MATERIAL LIST:

A	5 Pcs.	1¾" x 5¾" x 42"	Pine
B	2 Pcs.	1¾" x 3¾" x 28¾"	Pine
C	2 Pcs.	1¾" x 3¾" x 36½"	Pine
D	4 Pcs.	1¾" x 3¾" x 17"	Pine
E	26 Pcs.	¼" x ¾" dowel plugs	Pine
F	36 Pcs.	2½" - #10 steel flat head wood screws	
Misc.:		Nails, glue, filler and exterior stain.	

Verify all measurements before cutting

96
bench
and table unit

How often have you seen picnic tables for sale and felt you could build them better? Well, here's a sturdy set of table and benches you can build at a fraction of what they'd cost to buy.

INSTRUCTIONS:

(1) Familiarize yourself with the drawing and material list before cutting your lumber.

(2) You may use 2" x 4" lumber directly from the supplier if it is straight and true. In that case the dimensions may be a little oversize and you will have to change some dimensions that are indicated.

(3) For the 1⅛" stock, I used 1¼" x 4" gallery flooring, by cutting off the tongue and groove.

(4) Make up the basic table section first and then add parts (A) and (C); then make up benches and attach.

(5) All exposed edges should be rounded off with router preferably before joining up.

(6) Drill ⅜" diameter about ⅜" deep for screws, then use plugs.

(7) If for use outdoors, use a good wood preservative, stain or paint.

MATERIAL LIST:

(A)	2 Pcs.	1½" x 3½" x 64¾"	Pine or Redwood
(B)	4 Pcs.	1½" x 3½" x 28⅞"	Pine or Redwood
(C)	4 Pcs.	1½" x 3½" x 14"	Pine or Redwood
(D)	2 Pcs.	1⅛" x 3½" x 35"	Pine or Redwood
(E)	2 Pcs.	1⅛" x 3½" x 26¼"	Pine or Redwood
(F)	4 Pcs.	1½" x 3½" x 12"	Pine or Redwood
(G)	4 Pcs.	1⅛" x 1½" x 8½"	Pine or Redwood
(H)	19 Pcs.	1⅛" x 2½" x 30"	Pine or Redwood
(J)	64 —	2½" No. 8 flat head steel wood screws	
(K)	64 —	1¾" No. 8 flat head steel wood screws	
(L)	128 Pcs.	⅜" dia. x ⅜" long hardwood dowels (approximately 4').	
(M)	2 Pairs	1½" steel backflap hinges	
	Misc.:	Glue, wood filler, sandpaper, stain or paint.	

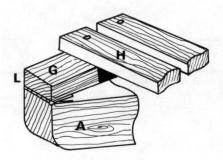

DETAIL "A"

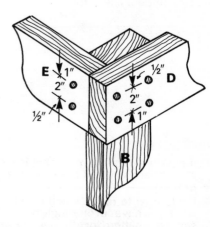

E ↕1"
2"
½"
½" ↕1"
2"
1"
D

B

DETAIL "B"

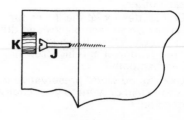

K
J

DETAIL "C"

Verify all measurements before cutting

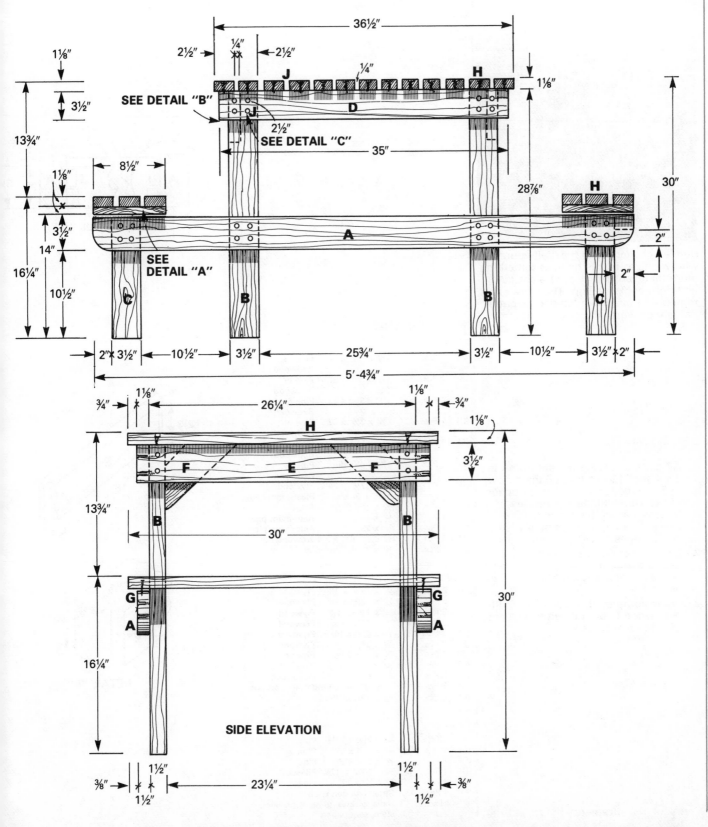

1⅛"

3½"

13¾"

2½"   ¼"   2½"

36½"

J   ¼"   H

SEE DETAIL "B"

J

SEE DETAIL "C"

2½"

D

1⅛"

8½"

1⅛"

3½"

14"

16¼"

10½"

SEE
DETAIL "A"

A

C   B   B   C

2"× 3½"   10½"   3½"   25¾"   3½"   10½"   3½"× 2"

5'-4¾"

35"

28⅞"

30"

2"

2"

H

¾"   1⅛"   26¼"   1⅛"   ¾"

1⅛"

3½"

H

F   E   F

B   B

30"

13¾"

G   G

A   A

16¼"

30"

SIDE ELEVATION

⅜"   1½"   23¼"   1½"   ⅜"

1½"   1½"

278

Here's a challenge for the do-it-yourselfer who wants to try his hand at something more involved than just straight cuts and right-angle nailing. The extra effort required to build this handsome patio bar is well worth it.

INSTRUCTIONS:

1 - All parts for frame are cut from pine 2 x 4 and I have trimmed them down to 3½" wide for trueing up purposes. I have also bullnosed all edges to soften sharp lines and help prevent damage to the otherwise sharp edges.

2 - If you carefully cut parts as per drawing and material list you should not encounter any problems in the assembly.

3 - When completed, set all nails and fill with wood filler and sand. Give coat of exterior wood stain.

MATERIAL LIST:

Frame:

(A)	2 Pcs.	1¾" x 3½" x 42"	Pine or Redwood
(B)	2 Pcs.	1¾" x 3½" x 37¾"	Pine or Redwood
(C)	2 Pcs.	1¾" x 3½" x 30½"	Pine or Redwood
(D)	2 Pcs.	1¾" x 3½" x 32"	Pine or Redwood
(E)	4 Pcs.	1¾" x 3½" x 16"	Pine or Redwood
(F)	2 Pcs.	1¾" x 5½" dia.	Pine or Redwood
(G)	1 Pc.	½" x 12½" x 34¼"	Plywood
(H)	1 Pc.	12½" x 34¼"	Plastic laminate
(J)	2 Pcs.	¾" x 1" x 33⅞"	Pine
(K)	1 Pc.	½" x 16"	Aluminum pipe
(L)	1 Pc.	½" x 23¼"	Aluminum pipe
(M)	2 Pcs.	¼" diameter x 2" hardwood dowel	
(N)	4 Pcs.	¼" x 2" dia. Plywood	

Cabinet:

(A)	2 Pcs.	½" x 13½" x 30⅞"	Plywood
(B)	3 Pcs.	½" x 13½" x 15"	Plywood
(C)	2 Pcs.	½" x 14" x 11½"	Plywood
(D)	3 Pcs.	½" x 12½" dia.	Plywood
(E)	3 Pcs.	½" x 6½" x 14¹¹⁄₁₆"	Plywood
(F)	2 Pcs.	½" x 3¾" x 16"	Plywood
(G)	2 Pcs.	½" x 1" x 23⅜"	Plywood
(H)	1 Pc.	¾" x ¾" x 13"	Pine
(J)	3 Pcs.	6" dia.	lazy susans
(K)	2 Pcs.	1" x 13" piano hinges, and screws	
(L)	2 Pcs.	Magnetic catches	

Drawer:

(A)	1 Pc.	¾" x 2½" x 12½"	Pine
(B)	2 Pcs.	¾" x 2½" x 17"	Pine
(C)	1 Pc.	¾" x 2" x 9½"	Pine
(D)	1 Pc.	⅛" x 10¼" x 17⅜"	Plywood
(E)	2 Pcs.	¾" x ¾" x 17"	Pine
(F)	1 Pc.	Small wooden knob	
Misc.:		Nails, screws, glue, wood filler, stain, sandpaper.	

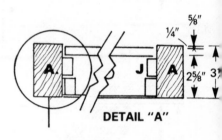

DETAIL "A"

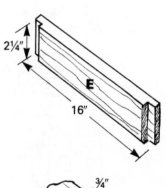

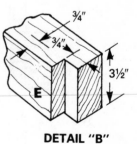

DETAIL "B"

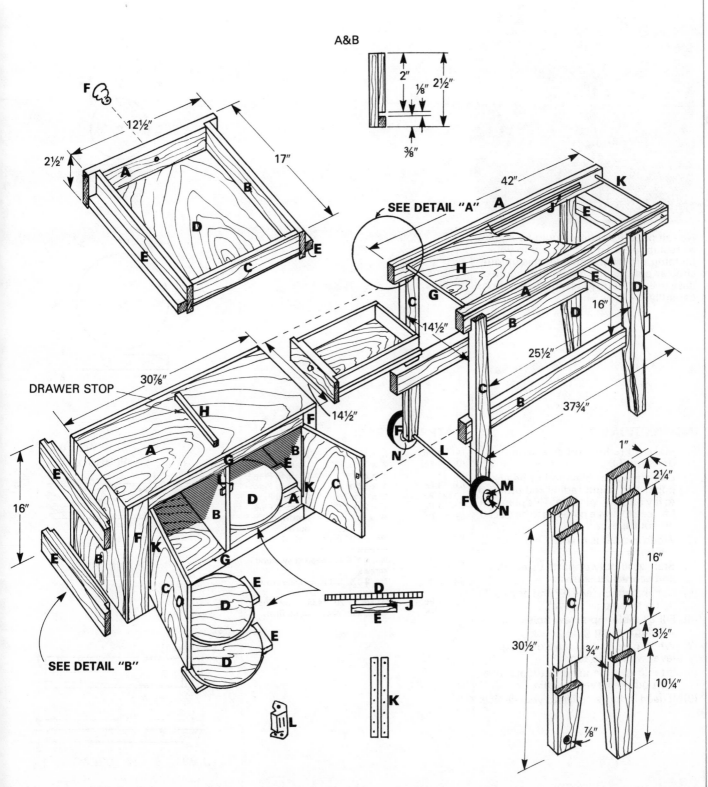

A&B

2"
⅛"
2½"
⅜"

F

12½"

2½"

A

B

D

E

C

17"

SEE DETAIL "A"

A

J

K

E

H

G

C

B

A

E

D

16"

D

B

25½"

C

37¾"

B

DRAWER STOP

30⅞"

H

A

G

E

B

E

F

14½"

14½"

F

N

L

F

N

M

16"

E

B

F

K

G

D

B

A

K

C

D

C

G

1"

2¼"

16"

C

D

3½"

¾"

E

D

E

D

SEE DETAIL "B"

D

J

E

30½"

7⁄8"

10¼"

K

L

C

98
circular
patio table

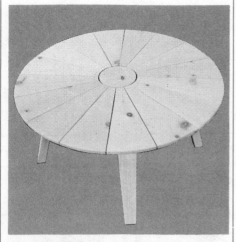

Not all patio furniture should be square or rectangular. To add variety to your building program, consider this unique circular patio table. It is actually quite easy to build if you follow the instructions carefully.

INSTRUCTIONS:

(1) Make up radius rod as shown on drawing (L).

(2) Use a piece of plywood or heavy paper and using radius rod proceed to lay out plan of table. This plan will be used to make patterns to be traced on your lumber.

(3) When lumber is marked, start cutting the parts.

(4) Start assembly of parts using glue and screws as shown.

(5) Cut and attach legs (E) and braces (F) using screws as shown.

(6) Fill all table top screw holes with ¼" plugs using glue.

(7) When glue is dry, sand off plugs level with table top.

(8) If table is to be used outdoors, use a wood preservative stain.

(9) If used indoors, finish to your choice.

MATERIAL LIST:

(A)	1 Pc.	2" x 12" x 6'	Dressed Pine
(B)	1 Pc.	2" x 12" x 12"	Dressed Pine
(C)	1 Pc.	1" x 8" x 8"	Dressed Pine
(D)	1 Pc.	1" x 12" x 12'	Dressed Pine
(E)	1 Pc.	2" x 4" x 7'	Dressed Pine
(F)	1 Pc.	2" x 2" x 2'6"	Dressed Pine
(G)	1 Pc.	¼" x 8'	Hardwood dowel
(H)	100 —	No. 6 1¼" flat head steel wood screws	
(J)	8 —	No. 8 1½" flat head steel wood screws	
(K)	8 —	No. 8 1¾" flat head steel wood screws	
(L)	1 Pc.	⅛" x ¾" x 20" Radius Rod Pine	
	Misc.:	Glue, sandpaper, wood filler.	

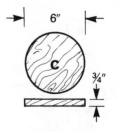

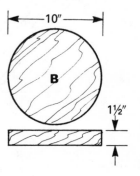

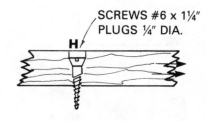

SCREWS #6 x 1¼"
PLUGS ¼" DIA.

H

DETAIL "B"

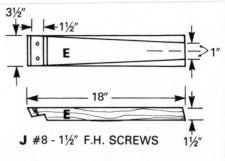

3½"

1½"

E

1"

18"

E

J #8 - 1½" F.H. SCREWS   1½"

DETAIL "C"

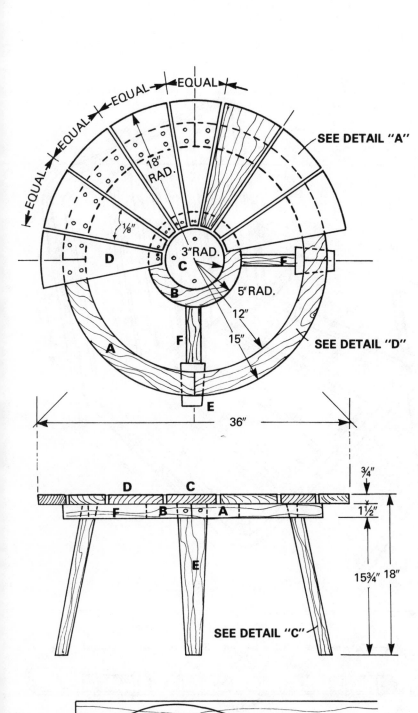

EQUAL — EQUAL
EQUAL
EQUAL
EQUAL
EQUAL

18" RAD.

⅛"

SEE DETAIL "A"

3"RAD.

C

D

B

5"RAD.

F

12"

F

A

15"

SEE DETAIL "D"

E

36"

D   C

F   B   A

¾"

1½"

15¾" 18"

E

SEE DETAIL "C"

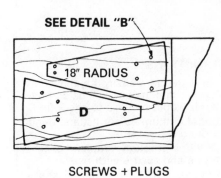

K #8 - 1¾" SCREWS

F   F

6"

1½" — — ← 1½"

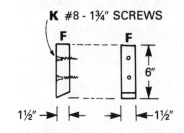

SEE DETAIL "B"

18" RADIUS

D

SCREWS + PLUGS

DETAIL "A"

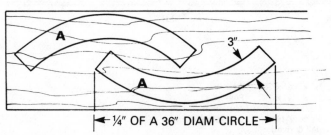

A

3"

A

← ¼" OF A 36" DIAM·CIRCLE →

DETAIL "D"

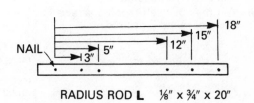

NAIL

3" 5" 12" 15" 18"

RADIUS ROD **L**   ⅛" x ¾" x 20"

99
renew lawn
chairs

Why throw away those old lawn chairs just because the webbing is torn or rotting away. Renew them with a bit of ingenuity, some stock lumber and a few helpful hints from our plan.

INSTRUCTIONS:

(1) For a standard chair, the above lumber dimensions will be correct, but it would be wise to check first.

(2) Cut aluminum as per list and bend around chair frame.

(3) Drill hole through strap and chair frame and secure with rivet.

(4) Cut seat slats to required thickness, width and length.

(5) Using router, round off all edges.

(6) Stain and varnish slats.

(7) Locate slats on straps and using proper size drill, make hole through slat and strap and rivet in place.

(8) Adjust slat again if necessary and drill and rivet balance.

(9) You may use self-tapping screws in place of rivets if desired.

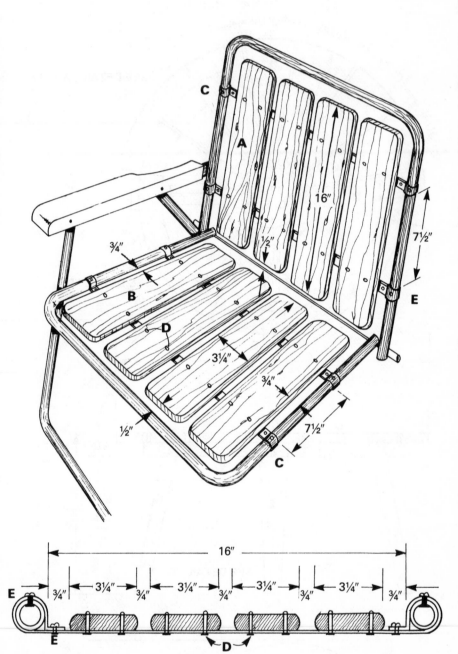

MATERIAL LIST:

(A)	4 Pcs.	⅝" x 3¼" x 16"	Pine	
(B)	4 Pcs.	⅝" x 3¼" x 14"	Pine	
(C)	4 Pcs.	¹⁄₁₆" x ¾" x 24"	Aluminum	
(D)	32 Pcs.	³⁄₁₆" x ⅞" blind rivets — (aluminum nail & rivet)		
(E)	8 Pcs.	⅛" x ⁵⁄₁₆" blind rivets (aluminum rivet & steel nail)		
	Misc.:	Stain and varnish, sandpaper and proper size drill to suit rivets.		

Verify all measurements before cutting

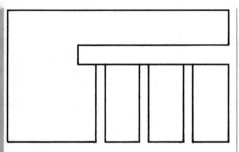

10
Work area

If this work table looks familiar to you — look again.

Yes, it's the one Mr. Chips uses every week on TV when he demonstrates and builds some of the projects you've seen in this book.

Besides being spacious and rock-steady, it is also designed in such a way that it goes together very easily, with a minimum of effort and waste

While you're at it, build the storage rack as well. Great for storing all that lumber you'll need when tackling your next project.

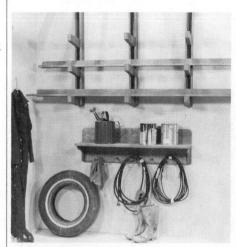

100 GARAGE STORAGE 284

101 WORK TABLE 286

100
garage storage

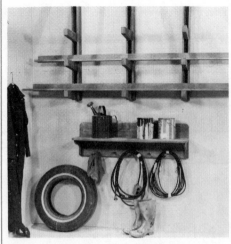

A "quickie" project that pays handsome dividends. It unclutters your garage, puts everything within handy reach and saves time and effort when looking for things. Nothing to it — but to do it.

INSTRUCTIONS:

(1) I have suggested ¾" plywood for the stiles (B) for greater strength. Spruce or pine will be fine for the ledgers (A). The spacing dimensions are optional to suit your particular requirements as well as the total length of (A).

(2) Use some glue when attaching (B)-(A) as well as the screws. Nails will be O.K. if desired; used 2½" common nails.

(3) Nail or screw to floor joists as indicated. If joists are running the wrong way for you, install a bridge between them as illustrated in circle (A). Every fourth joist should be sufficient to locate your hangers.

MATERIAL LIST:

(A)	2 Pcs.	¾" x 4" x length desired	Plywood
(B)	3 Pcs.	1¾" x 3¾" x 16" (2 x 4) Spruce	
(C)	2 Doz.	1¾" #10 Flat head steel wood screws	

Shelf Section:

(A)	1 Pc.	¾" x 14" x 4'	Plywood
(B)	1 Pc.	¾" x 8" x 4'	Plywood
(C)	2 Pcs.	¾" x 7¾" x 7¾"	Plywood
(D)	5 Pcs.	¾" x 6"	Hardwood dowel

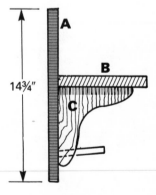

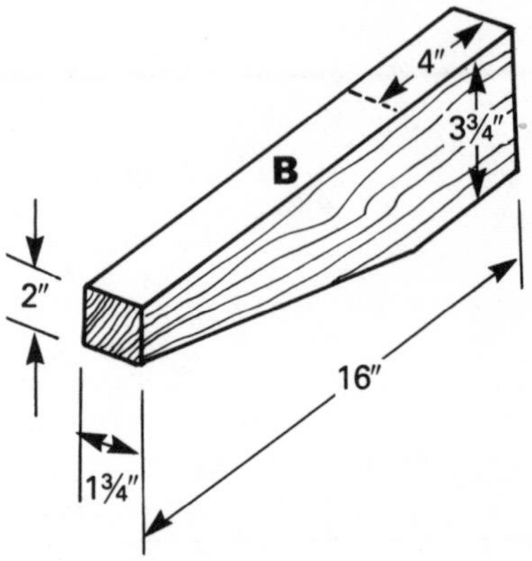

DETAIL "A"

DETAIL "B"

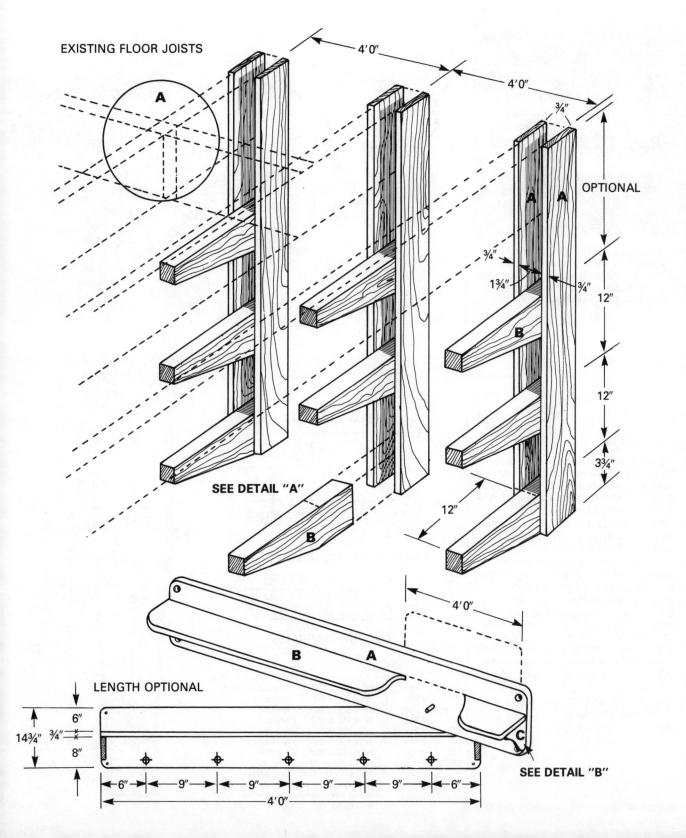

EXISTING FLOOR JOISTS

A

4' 0"

4' 0"

¾"

OPTIONAL

A   A

¾"

1¾"   ¾"

12"

B

12"

12"

3¾"

SEE DETAIL "A"

B

4' 0"

B   A

LENGTH OPTIONAL

6"

14¾"   ¾"

8"

6"   9"   9"   9"   9"   6"

4' 0"

C

SEE DETAIL "B"

101
work table

Here's a super solid work table to hold your work rock-steady when precise work is important. Designed to give you ample work space, you'll wonder how you ever got along without it.

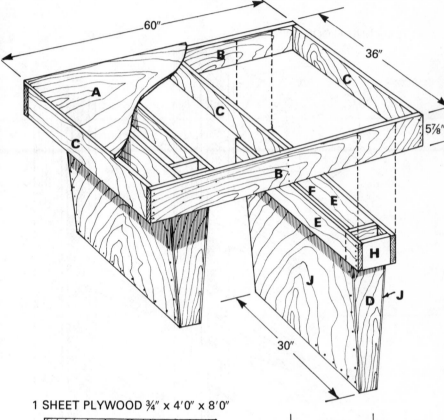

INSTRUCTIONS:

(1) To build this work table you will require one sheet of ¾" x 4' x 8', and one piece ¾" x 2' x 8' of plywood. You will also require a piece of ¼" x 4' x 5' plywood.

(2) This project is a very simple job and requires that you cut pieces to width and length only.

(3) Assemble the leg structures first, using nails and glue, making sure that all pieces are square and true.

(4) Next, assemble frame for table top, and before putting on top piece (A) attach legs using 1½" screws through piece (B) into piece (H). I suggest that you do not use glue, as you may wish to take legs out for storage, etc.

(5) When legs are attached, nail and glue on top (A).

(6) Set all nails and fill with wood filler if desired, and sand.

(7) Give coat of shellac and paint.

Verify all measurements before cutting

1 SHEET PLYWOOD ¾" x 4'0" x 8'0"

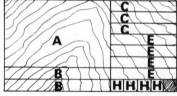

1 PIECE PLYWOOD ¾" x 2'0" x 8'0"

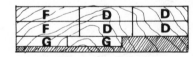

CUTTING DIAGRAMS

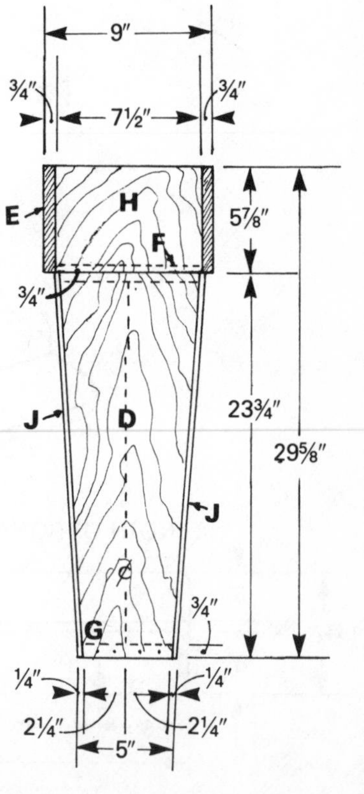

MATERIAL LIST:

(A)	1 Pc.	¾" x 36" x 60"	Plywood
(B)	2 Pcs.	¾" x 5⅞" x 60"	Plywood
(C + E)	7 Pcs.	¾" x 5⅞" x 34½"	Plywood
(D)	4 Pcs.	¾" x 7½" x 29⅝"	Plywood
(F)	2 Pcs.	¾" x 7½" x 34½"	Plywood
(G)	2 Pcs.	¾" x 4½" x 28½"	Plywood
(H)	4 Pcs.	¾" x 5⅞" x 7½"	Plywood
(J)	4 Pcs.	¼" x 23¾" x 30"	Plywood
(K)	2 Doz.	1½" #8 F.H. steel wood screws	
	Misc.:	2" finish nails, 1" finish nails, glue, wood filler, sandpaper, shellac and paint.	

Plan index

All projects redrawn
by Bernard Lamy

DECO-PLANS INC.

P.O. BOX 90, Boucherville, P.Q. J4B 5E6
P.O. Box 3000, Cornwall, Ont. K6H 5R8
P.O. Box 870, Plattsburgh, N.Y. 12901

Printed in Canada   **by**   Richardson, Bond & Wright, Limited.